DELETED
? d.

the claire michaan cattan edition

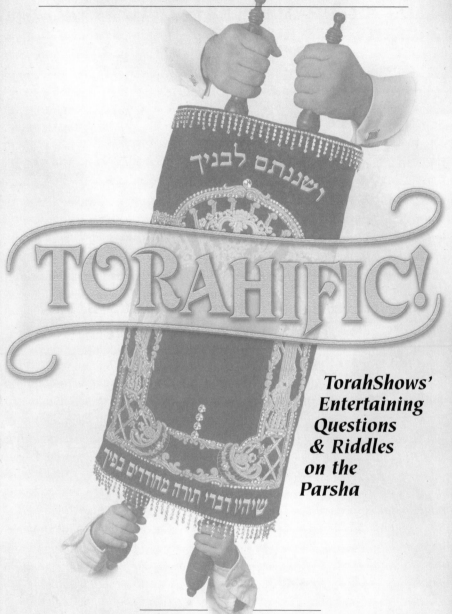

TORAHIFIC!

TorahShows'
Entertaining
Questions
& Riddles
on the
Parsha

BY RABBI MAIMON ELBAZ

DIRECTOR OF THE INSPIRING

TORAHSHOWS SERIES

the claire michaan cattan edition

**Entertaining & Informative
Questions & Riddles on the Parsha
for Young & Old Alike**

ISRAEL BOOK SHOP
Lakewood, NJ

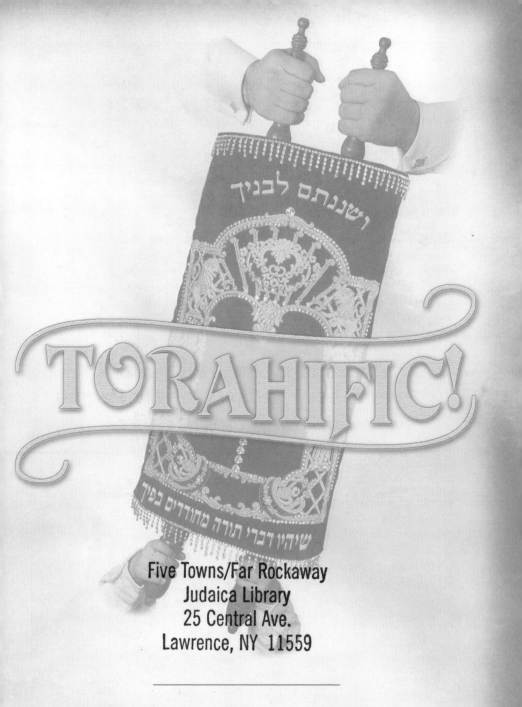

TORAHIFIC!

Five Towns/Far Rockaway
Judaica Library
25 Central Ave.
Lawrence, NY 11559

BY RABBI MAIMON ELBAZ

DIRECTOR OF THE INSPIRING

TORAHSHOWS SERIES

For more information regarding the TORAHSHOWS SERIES please contact:
Rabbi Maimon Elbaz
718.336.3369 / 718.382.0788 / Torahshows@yahoo.com

We invite you to visit our educational CHILDREN'S TORAH CENTER at:
Ahi Ezer Torah Center, 1950 East Seventh Street, Brooklyn, NY 11223

Cover Design: Calligraphix / 718.438.1334
Photography: Portrait Gallery / 718.438.5111
      Sefer Torah *mantle* courtesy of Best Embroidery / 718.633.8300

Book Design & Typography: DC Design / 732.901.4784

Distributed by:
ISRAEL BOOK SHOP
501 Prospect Street, Lakewood, NJ 08701
(732) 901-3009 | fax (732) 901.4012
info@israelbookshoppublications.com
www.israelbookshoppublications.com

Printing & Binding by:

אריאל
|| הוצאה לאור
62 Arosa Hill
Lakewood, NJ 08701
PHONE/FAX 732.905.0091

Owing to the large volume of material that is presented here, it is possible that some inadvertent errors may have remained in the text. The author would be most grateful if you would send any comments and questions so that the necessary corrections or clarifications can be made for future reprints.

DEDICATED TO
THE LOVING MEMORY
OF

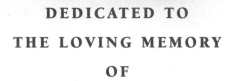

Claire
Michaan Cattan

BY HER LOVING DAUGHTER
SELMA (CATTAN) COHEN-SABAN & FAMILY

**DEDICATED IN MEMORY
OF OUR LOVING PARENTS**

*Rabbi & Mrs.
Avrohom and Esther
Elbaz*

ת.נ.צ.ב.ה.

תפארת בניס אבותם

AS THE TORAH GIVES
LIFE, HAPPINESS AND STRENGTH,
OUR INCREDIBLY WONDERFUL
PARENTS GAVE US
LIFE, HAPPINESS AND STRENGTH.

THEY TOUCHED SO MANY LIVES
WITH THEIR GRACIOUSNESS AND
LOVE FOR B'NEI TORAH

by their loving children
Mordechai & Dassie Smolarcik
Elie & Miriam Elbaz
Dov & Simy Szocheit
Shloimie Elbaz
Chaim Mordechai & Suzie Elbaz
Dr. Larry & Dora Kurz
Dovid Anton & Nechama Rothstein
Maimon & Malky Elbaz
& families

The following friends believed in TorahShows and stood nearby to establish this educational series!

1. ADJMI FAMILY

2. GAVRIEL AHDUT

3. EZRA ASHKENAZI

4. SAMMY AYAL

5. DAVID BALASIANO

6. DR. MAYER BALLAS

7. FRANK BEDA

8. BENNO, SHALAM & GROSS FAMILIES

9. VICTOR BIBI

10. ZEV BOHM

11. JOJO CHEHABER

12. MARK CHEMTOB

13. ALBERT COHEN

14. DR. JACK COHEN

15. SOLOMON DABAH

16. HAL DWEK

17. JO DWEK

18. SHELOMO DWEK

19. STEVEN BALASIANO & ALAN ESSES

20. DR. JACQUES DOUECK

21. RAYMOND FAYENA

22. DR. ELLIOT GHATAN

23. EZRA GRAZI

24. MARTIN HADDAD

25. DR. STEVEN HADDAD

26. BERT HIDARY

27. ISSAC JEMAL

28. DR. LARRY KURZ

29. MAYER LATI

30. EZRA & ELIE LEVY

31. ISAAC MALUL

32. NISSIM MEZRAHI

33. MAX MIZRAHI

34. MOSHE MOGRABI

35. RALPH MUHADEB

36. SHARON NAIM

37. RUDY BROTHERS

38. JOSEPH SAKA

39. RAYMOND SALEM

40. CHARLES SARWAY

41. JOEY SETTON

42. JOEY SHAMES & JOEY CHEHABER

43. DAVID SHWEKEY

44. BARUCH SINGER

45. ELLIOT SUTTON

46. CAREY SUTTON

47. VICTOR SUTTON

48. MORRIS SUTTON

49. SAM SUTTON

50. STEVEN SUTTON

51. JO WEISS

52. MICHAEL WAHBA

53. THE B'NEI AHI EZER MINYAN, MY TEENAGE TALMIDIM!

Thank you for your generous sponsorships!

מרדכי גיפטער
ישיבת טלז
Rabbi Mordecai Gifter
28570 Nutwood Lane
Wickliffe, Ohio 44092

בעז"ה

עש"ק לסדר ויחי י"ז טבת התשנ"ז

לכבוד יקירי וחביבי ר' מיימון שיחי' בן לידידי הרב ר' אברהם ז"ל

לשמחה היה לי לראות שאתה עומד להוציא מדי שבוע בשבוע ירחון

המכונה מסכת השבוע, אשר היא משמשת לדחף לקרב לב תשב"ר

ללימוד משניות וגמרא. וכבר אמרו חז"ל "אין העולם מתקיים אלא

בשביל הבל תינוקות של בית רבן".

יהא ד' בעזרך ותזכה לרוב ברכה והצלחה במפעלך

באהבה

ב"ה

Rabbi Y. Belsky
506 EAST 7th STREET
BROOKLYN, NEW YORK 11218

ישראל הלוי בעלסקי
941 - 0112

I would like to introduce you to a wonderful innovative program that has great promise for the enrichment of Torah youth in our community.

Rabbi Maimon Elbaz has opened a central Torah "Station" for Yeshiva youth with a host of enjoyable, exciting programs. These activities are all designed to inspire, to educate and to create a warm Torah environment wherein children can discover the many joys of Torah life during parts of the day which would ordinarily go to waste.

His activities include:
- personal introductions to leading Talmidei Chachomim
- the availability of a plethora of listener-friendly Torah Tapes
- Limud Hamishnayos in the most inviting way imaginable
- slide shows explaining numerous Torah topics in a lively appealing manner
- plus many others

Rabbi Maimon has plans for the construction of a central location which would provide a haven for positive reinforcement of Yeshiva values. All Mechanchim who have witnessed Rabbi Maimon's work have been deeply impressed by his exceptional ability, his vibrant and charismatic personality and his charming sincerity and energetic devotion. Many children have been "turned on" as a result of his programs and have subsequently sparkled in every facet of their Yeshiva performance.

It would be a remarkable service for the "Klal" to have this ambitious project successfully completed. I can foresee that this would be the address to which many Yeshivos would turn when problems arise with their students, and that the dropout rate would sharply diminish as a result.

I strongly encourage everyone to support these projects. Whoever joins with Rabbi Maimon Elbaz will be a partner in a great Torah endeavor and will merit the blessings of Hakadosh Boruch Hu.

הרב חיים בן עוליאל
Rabbi Haim Benoliel
1705 East Fifth Street
Brooklyn, N.Y. 11223
(718) 336-0079

בס״ד

Yeshivat Mikdash Melech
1326 Ocean Parkway
Brooklyn, N.Y. 11230
Tel: (718) 339-1090
Fax: (718) 998-9321

June 5 '01

Dear Friend —

Our community is fortunate to have Rabbi Maimon Elbaz ש׳ dedicated to the spiritual welfare and growth of our children.

He is a dynamic, caring and extremely capable young man and leader with a proven record of extraordinary success in motivating and inspiring the children to love Torah and Mitzvoth.

We a need a Center for these important activities and Rabbi Elbaz ש׳ is ready to throw himself into the task. This goal can only be reached with the generous support of community members who realize the priority of guarding our most important possession — our children.

בברכת ה׳ (הנודה),

Rabbi H Benoliel

ב״ה

OVADIA YOSSEF	עובדיה יוסף
RISHON LEZION	הראשון לציון
AND PRESIDENT OF TORAH SAGES COUNSIL	ונשיא מועצת חכמי התורה

JERUSALEM _ח׳ כסלו תשס״ב_ ירושלים

המלצה

הריני ממליץ בזה עבור הארגון החשוב " בית מדרש לתשב״ר " בעיר ניו
יורק בהנהלתו של הרב מימון אלבאז שליט״א, אשר ידיו רב לו בחינוך
ועושה רבות ונצורות למען ילדי ישראל שלא ילכו לרעות בשדות זרים
בשובם מבית הספר, ששם שומעים דברי תורה בשילוב עם משחקים
חינוכיים, וחידונים בהלכה ובאגדה בספר מיוחד ששמו "ושננתם לבניך"
שבו אלפי שאלות לשינון וחידוד התלמידים, וכמו כן משמיעים משניות
בעל פה, ועוד תוכניות לילדים ובני נוער , איישר חילם לאורייתא .
מצוה רבה לסייע בידם בעין יפה וברוח נדיבה, ומה׳ תשאו ברכה.
ויהי רצון שנזכה לראות בהרמת דגל התורה והיראה, מתוך שמחות וגיל.
ובזכות הבל פיהם של תינוקות של בית רבן, שעליהם עומד העולם, נזכה
להושע תשועת עולמים, בביאת גואל צדק במהרה בימינו. ומלאה הארץ
דעה את ה׳ כמים לים מכסים. אמן ואמן.

עובדיה יוסף

לשכה בבית המדרש יחוה דעה רח׳ הרב שמעון אגסי 1 הר נוף ירושלים
טל׳ 6525666 פקס׳ 6513655

ו׳ כסלו, תשס״ב

(718) 436-1133

RABBI YAAKOV PERLOW
1569 - 47TH STREET
BROOKLYN, N.Y. 11219

יעקב פרלוב
ביהמ"ד עדת יעקב נאוואמינסק
ברוקלין, נ.י.

בס"ד גב אב ייל א תשס"א

I am familiar with the work and success of
Rabbi Mairon Elbaz in behalf of Torah education.
His devotion to inculcate our true and sacred values
in Jewish children — in many extra-curricular ways —
is truly remarkable. He deserves every support in
all his endeavors. The publication of "Torahpic",
which Rabbi Elbaz has authored, will certainly enhance
the scope of Torah knowledge to young and old alike.
May Hashem bless his efforts with continued growth
and success.

יוד"ש אוהבו
Yaakov Perlow

Rabbi CHAIM P. SCHEINBERG	**הרב חיים פינחס שיינברג**
Rosh Hayeshiva "TORAH ORE"	ראש ישיבת "תורה אור"
and Morah Hora'ah of Kiryat Mattersdorf	ומורה הוראה דקרית מטרסדורף

בס"ד

מכתב ברכה

Erev Shabbos Hagadol
Nissan 5759

I am happy to hear of the wonderful work Rabbi Maimon Elbaz is doing in *chinuch* through extra curricular enrichment.

Rabbi Maimon, *shlita,* has opened a children's Torah station at Ahi Ezer Torah Center as Pirchei Agudas Yisroel's Central Sephardic Branch. The goal is a precious one; to afford all young yeshiva students a haven where they can enjoy growing in Torah and Mitzvos outside their yeshiva schedule. As our sages have written in the Talmud *(Berachos 62a),* "בשעת המכניסין פזר בשעת המפזרים כנם". It is delightful that boys from different yeshivos unite for *kevod shamayim* on a regular basis.

I wish Rabbi Maimon success in his many innovative Torah projects; the color coded tape series of *"Kol Haneshama,"* slide presentations of *mitzvos, mishnayos* and *Gedolei Yisroel* called *"Torahvisions,"* and the inspiring collection of questions and riddles for *"Mitzvanaire"* which sharpen the minds of the youth while awakening them to know more and more of our glorious Torah.

May *Hashem* continue to bless Pirchei Ahi Ezer and Rabbi Maimon Elbaz with success to continue these programs, publications, and productions for years to come. I pray that many students will utilize these opportunities which are greatly beneficial for them. May all those who help in supporting these extremely worthy efforts be blessed with long life and success in all their endeavors.

אשרי ילדותנו שלא ביישה את זקנותנו

[handwritten signature]

רחוב פנים מאירות 2, ירושלים, ת.ר. 6979, טל. 537-1513 (02), ישראל
2 Panim Meirot St., Jerusalem, P.O.B. 6979, Tel. (02) 537-1513, Israel

בס״ד

Phil and Mary Edlis Elementary School • Beatrice J. Stone Yavne High School • Jacob Sapirstein Campus

בית חנוך עברי דקליבלנד

Hebrew Academy of Cleveland
1860 SOUTH TAYLOR ROAD • CLEVELAND, OHIO 44118 • (216) 321-5838 • FAX (216) 932-4597

RABBI N. W. DESSLER
Dean

IRVING I. STONE ל״ז
Chairman (1976 - 2000)

May 1, 2002

RABBI SIMCHA DESSLER
Educational Director

RABBI ELI DESSLER
Financial Director

IVAN A. SOCLOF
President

MORRY WEISS
Immediate Past President

MELVIN WAXMAN
Vice-Chairman of the Board

Rabbi Maimon Elbaz
2124 East 9th Street
Brooklyn, New York 11223

Dear Reb Maimon,

On behalf of the administration of the Hebrew Academy of Cleveland, please accept our sincerest appreciation for your dedication, commitment, time and effort in bringing the Children's Torah Show to our student body.

The show was exciting! The audience was clearly intrigued and captivated! The question and answer period which culminated the program was spectacular!

At the Academy, we take special pride in the fact that you are an Academy alumnus. We thank you for sharing your talents with our students. Your efforts are most appreciated.

Sincerely,

Rabbi Simcha Dessler
Educational Director

AN AGENCY OF
THE JEWISH COMMUNITY FEDERATION
OF CLEVELAND

"A People Survives As Long As It Transmits Its Heritage From One Generation To The Next"

Table of Contents

Preface

Ithank Hashem with all my heart for giving me the *zechus* and privilege to be able to teach *Tinokos Shel Beis Rabban* during their extra-curricular hours. Most of my work in *Chinuch* takes place during those after-school hours. These are the hours where a child can reinforce everything he has learned, or *chas v'Shalom* destroy it. As founding director of the **Children's Torah Center at Ahi Ezer Synagogue** fifteen years ago in Brooklyn, it is my pleasure and joy to present this collection of favorite **Parsha Questions & Riddles** to the greater community.

People are usually amused by a good riddle or a clever question. When reading this *sefer*, be prepared to find thousands of challenging and eye-opening questions, riddles, answers and sources. Similar to an exciting story, the lessons are entertaining and will stimulate the imagination of the readers and listeners.

Since Torah is the life-blood of Am Yisroel, we are required to think and talk Torah at every available moment. When I was in charge of the candy store at the Telz Yeshiva in Cleveland, I often offered a riddle for a free pizza or popcorn in order to start a conversation in Torah and *Yiras Shamayim*. My customers enjoyed a chance to win a *treat* but were even more pleased when they realized that the *lesson* they learned would have a profound impact on their daily life.

I later shared these brain-teasers at our *Father & Son Shabbos*

Program. Using attractive prizes and nosh, we motivated the children (and the teens!) to run around asking parents, adults and *talmidei chachamim* for any clue to answer their puzzle. I loved seeing the interaction of *Yidden* working together to figure out the *Dvar Torah riddle.* Many friends said the riddles were *"terrific"* and suggested I write them down (in my Palm Pilot) so that they wouldn't be forgotten. We therefore started a weekly sheet which was distributed in many local Shuls under the name *"Torahific!"*

I believe that a Shabbos table filled with all kinds of delicious food, heartwarming songs, moving stories and intriguing questions and riddles work wonders for developing happy *neshamos* prepared for another energetic week of *Avodas Hashem.* If only a resource of short-and-sweet material would be available to families it would add much **geshmak** to the Jewish home. Many parents told me that when they use the weekly sheet, the entire meal becomes elevated and the *derech eretz* displayed is a true *Kiddush Hashem.* I joked, that, *"Im ein Torah ein derech eretz!" (Avos 3:17)*

Just as fresh fruit cut into bite-size pieces can be an irresistible nutritious treat, so too, may our readers find these selected morsels of Torah insights exciting and rewarding.

The Midrash in Shir Hashirim inspired me to compile this exciting collection of questions and riddles which I coined "Torahific." The Midrash states that when one lets nonsense enter his head out goes Torah and similarly Torah replaces nonsense. Since society is constantly bombarding our minds with nonsense how urgent it is to plant in our minds Torah!?

We all know that even one tiny match-stick can ignite a blazing fireplace that will give pleasure and warmth to everyone near it. Who doesn't love that cozy and comforting feeling? So too we must strive to ignite the souls of our fellow Yidden. It only takes one word of Torah (even a riddle) to spark up a soul! Fulfilling this duty has proven to be enormously rewarding and pleasurable.

Acknowledgements

I am hesitant to relate this tiny personal experience but I believe it is most important. When I was in the Hebrew Academy of Cleveland I was an average student with average grades. However among my scores was a *Gimel* (C) in *Chumash*. My loving **mother** *a"h* lovingly praised my other grades but asked me why it was that in *Chumash* I was weak? Her sweet words and twinkle in her eye encouraged me to try harder. It is in tribute to her that I organized this collection based on **over 10,000 sources on *Chumash*!** My dear mother came from Morocco to Cleveland, and was dedicated to the Roshei Yeshiva's every instruction which has instilled in our family faith in Hashem and His ambassadors. May this sefer serve as a source of *nachas* to my dear mother (*hareini kaparas mishkava.*)

One summer, my friend **David Massre** commented, "Rabbi, I really missed you - my kids were bored without your weekly thought-provoking and eye-opening questions. I have an idea. I will sponsor a hotline for men, women and children to be able to call every day and hear a lesson worth remembering." I was touched by his sincere friendship and generous offer. I tried to come up with fascinating *Midrashim* and *Chazal* to present in less than 60 seconds during the voice-mail recording. The challenge was big, but very rewarding. For several years many listeners pushed their speed-dial 1-917-TORAH-01 and were delightfully inspired. *Chazak u'baruch!*

Over ten years ago, I met a graphic designer **Yitzy Cohen**, who patiently designed the layout for the weekly circular that has graced many Shuls every Shabbos. He made the text appealing and easy to read. I am grateful for his hard work and good taste. I am fortunate to work with **Eli Blitman** of the Poster Printers as well. He enhanced the TorahShows image with the collage on page 399.

I am grateful to **Mrs. Deenee Cohen** and **Mrs. Henshy Barash**, professional graphic designers at **DC Design** located in Lakewood, New Jersey - the world renown city of Torah. With wisdom and much patience, they expertly designed this book with impressive creativity and meticulous attention to detail, which undoubtedly enhanced this book.

I am proud to be working hand in hand with **Israel Book Shop** to bring this long-awaited series to the public. I am impressed with the skill and sensitivity of the staff in making sure the *sefer* was produced expeditiously. May **Reb Moshe Kaufman** be blesssed with *nachas* from this publication, and with *gezunt* and *shtarkeit* to continue his wonderful service to the Am HaTorah.

I would like to extend my *birchas hedyot* to my friend **Reb Dovid Pancer** to continue bringing the sweet sound of Torah to the public. He graciously welcomed my Torah Tapes to be played on his **Kol Haloshon** network for many to enjoy. (Try us: 718-906-6400 EXT. 161)

This *sefer* would never have been completed and polished if not for my esteemed Rebbi and friend, a true *talmid chacham* in our midst, the *gaon*, **Rabbi Shmuel Yosef Lercher** *shlita*. In his humbleness, he constantly made me feel that every question was of utmost significance. His diligence and scope of knowledge in Torah are truly amazing. The reader will find his *bekius* (expertise) reflected throughout this book. I would like to thank him from the bottom of my heart for all his assistance.

I am indebted to **Rabbi Yitzchok Feldheim** for painstakingly reviewing many samples of this book and pointing out areas that needed to be corrected.

Every author needs an editor and I have been fortunate to have the compassionate and competent editors **Rabbi Hillel Yarmove** *shlita* and **Rabbi Moshe Rockove** *shlita* working tirelessly on this project. Their feedback was always valuable and I thank them for their patience in reviewing the manuscript. **Issac Malul**, a lawyer by profession, involved himself (5:15 am) to painstakingly edit volume two. I can't thank him enough! **Rabbi Zev Peretzky** *shlita*, an author of note, proofread this book and shared his skills with us as well. **Rabbi Nosson Scherman** is appreciated for encouraging the concept of this book.

As for my devoted *chavrusa*, sincere critic, and close friend **Reb Avrohom Leib Berger** *shlita*, I never saw someone *nosei b'ol im chaveiro* like you! Your keen perception for detail, your meticulousness and your drive for perfection can only be matched by your diligence. *Kol hakavod* to you!

All those guys that complimented the sheets in Shul saying "*Gevaldig!* I love it." Thanks for the camaraderie.

A good teacher doesn't merely lecture monotonously but rather engages the students in electrifying give-and-take. I hope this *sefer* provides many illuminating thoughts on the issues that matter most. I hope that before Pesach this *sefer* will have to be put away with the *chometz* due to its frequent use and accompanying food marks just as I have to put away *The Midrash Says*, the classic masterpiece by **Rabbi Moshe Weissman** *shlita*, who has inspired my mind and my pen countless times.

The great *tzadik* and *chossid, mori v'Rebbi* **Harav Getzel Fried** *shlita* showed me so much attention and love that I hope I can repay his kindness by him seeing *nachas* from my *talmidim*. He demonstrated how a *talmid* can be tremendously influenced after Yeshiva hours. It is for that reason that I focus on after Yeshiva programs such as the special **Pirchei Agudas Yisroel**, where some of my young fans nicknamed me the "Riddler Rebbe." I have personally witnessed countless times how a *shiur* (in Mishnayos etc.) can be revitalized when combined with a riddle.

Sponsors are the great people behind the scenes who take great satisfaction in strengthening Klal Yisroel. To mention a few of those indispensable friends who generously gave us so many prizes and gifts for our students to motivate them to participate in our programs: **Ellis Safdeye** - may he have *refuah sheleima*, **Robert Azar, Sammy Ayal, Allen Saka**, and **Shlomo Mizrahi**. **Shemuel Kairy**, thank you for taking me and buying me a top quality copier to print the sheets for the shuls. Your *zerizus* is truly a *yerusha* from your legendary father Mr. Yom Tov (Walter) Kairy *a"h*. After each *parsha* will also appear the names of those "friends of the children" who helped us immeasurably! *I bow to them in gratitude.*

I am grateful to **Meir Maslaton** for suggesting the ambitious undertaking of designing a card-collection series presenting our most fundamental TorahShows images and Torahific thoughts for youth to learn and grow from. *Chazak u'baruch.*

Although hundreds of wonderful Rebbeim and friends mold the character of a *talmid*, there is one person that stands out. In my life the people that influenced me the most were my mentor **Rabbi and Mrs. Pesach Siegel** *shlita*. I will never forget the attention and care that they gave me (not to mention the chocolate chip cookies). Their guidance and direction came from the soul and went into the soul!

I appreciate all the leadership that the exemplary Menahel **Rabbi Chaim Aharon Weinberg** *shlita* does for **Yeshivat Ateret Torah**, which our children are fortunate to attend. I would also like to thank the extraordinary director of the Yeshiva, **Rabbi David Ozerey** *shlita*, for all his heroic dedication to our community. I am indebted to the legendary and world-renown Rosh Yeshiva **Hacham Yosef Harari-Raful** *shlita* for his powerful influence and for suggesting that I print this sefer in Hebrew. *B'ezras Hashem* I hope to do that in the very near future.

I would like to thank all of my former Yeshivos, particularly **Telz Yeshiva** of Cleveland & Chicago, and **Mikdash Melech** of New York & Jerusalem, **Ner Yisroel** of Baltimore, and **Emek** of Mexico. My devoted Rebbeim, *chavrusos*, and *talmidim*, please cherish these words, and realize that you all have a portion in this *zechus* of spreading *yedios hachaim* to generations of *Ehrliche Yidden*.

There are special baalei batim that dedicated the funds for the full-size game shows that have graced the walls at the Children's Torah Center, and have helped me convey my lessons. Note: Heaven forbid to refer to Torah as a game. It was just my way of enticing the kids to run to learn. *Eis la'asos la'Hashem hafaru Torahsecha!* I sincerely thank **Abie Shalam**, **Leon Cohen**, and **Victor Bibi**.

I greatly appreciate **Rabbi and Mrs. Moshe Rosner** of **Camp Rayim** for graciously welcoming my family for beautiful summers filled with Torah and *Yiras Shamayim*. Their confidence and *varmkeit* helped bring out the best in me. My family was fortunate to be in such a pleasant *Makom Torah*. Camp Rayim provided an excellent environment allowing me to develop the new **TorahShows** series. The campers at Rayim showed great enthusiasm for my challenging questions before, during and after mealtimes.

It is with deep appreciation that I thank **Rabbi Meir Frischman** of **Camp Agudah** and his phenomenal staff for warmly welcoming my family to their Machene Kadosh. It's a dream come true! I enjoyed creating challenging riddles for our exceptional campers, and many boys appreciated their new Riddler Rebbi.

Thank you **Rabbi Shlomo Waddiche** and **Rabbi Louma Shalam** for being such role models for me at Camp Shivte Yisrael. You made me feel most welcome into the wonderful Sephardic community.

Amongst the master builders of Torah in the Sephardic community of New York are the towering giants Maran Harosh Yeshiva, **Harav Haim Benoliel** *shlita* and **Harav Dovid Lopian** *shlita*. Without their constant efforts on behalk of the Klal I don't know where we would be. I wish them continued growth *m'chayil el chayil*.

Noam Sayegh, your gift of the gold and velvety vest that I wear for my intriguing *Game Shows* really adds to the excitement. *Yasher koach!* I hope your talents are recognized in the Holy Land.

Reb Chaim Yosef Bernath of **Calligraphix** has done it again! His magical ability to turn concept into stunning reality is truly magnificent. The cover came out even more beautiful than imagined.

Thank you **Reb Elya Naimon** of **Best Embroidery** located in Boro Park for sharing with us your gorgeous Sefer Torah depicted on the cover of this book.

I thank the Staff of **Hamodia** for welcoming my material in their all-encompassing local and international newspaper. This is a privilege that I cherish.

I am indebted to Haim Cohen-Saban for having the title of this book dedicated in loving memory of Claire Michaan Cattan a"h. Your valuable input and comments enhanced the book's layout. May this book serve as an appropriate tribute to her unquenchable thirst for Torah! *Te'hei nishmatah tzerura b'tzeror hachaim.*

My dear wife **Malky** *shetichyeh* has successfully demonstrated what a modern day *Eishes Chayil* is. *Sheli shelah!* Thank you for your supernatural commitment, trust, and patience in *TorahShows*. Before we were married, she taught the **Ahi Ezer** girls program after school while I taught the boys. Both my wife and I are still involved in this endeavor. May we be *zoche* to continue teaching our wonderful children *sheyichyu* and the greater Jewish community with a joyous *ruach haTorah*. May our dear children, **Rochel, Leah, Avrohom, Naomi, Aharon and Esther** live up to her excellent example. It is the exceptional example of her parents, **Mr. & Mrs. Aharon Salem** that keeps us inspired. I greatly appreciate her brothers and sisters who continuously improved the quality of this product.

Our Sephardic community of Brooklyn has been blessed with the exemplary leadership of **Hacham Sion Maslaton** *z"tl*. He was a living Sefer Torah who deeply loved the *Am HaTorah*. Countless times at his Shabbos table he promised us gifts if we answered his Torah riddles. We will cherish his memory forever. *Tibadel l'chaim* Grandma **Mrs. Victoria Maslaton's** kindness and support over the years has exceeded beyond the call of duty. May Hashem continue to grant her strength and *nachas* from her distinguished family.

I dedicate this *sefer* in loving memory of my unforgettable father affectionately known as **Reb Avrohom,** *zt"l*. His love for Torah and Bnei Torah was tangible. His heart of gold was 24 karat! *Yehi zichro baruch!* Also my gracious mother **Esther,** *a"h*, a genuine *Eishes Chayil*, is my constant inspiration. May they be *meilitz yosher* for all their sons and daughters and grandchildren, *bli ayin hara*, and may we all see the prophecy fulfilled *v'heishiv lev avos al banim v'lev banim al avosam, Amen!*

Maimon Elbaz
Eved L'avdei Hashem
Rosh Chodesh Elul, 5766

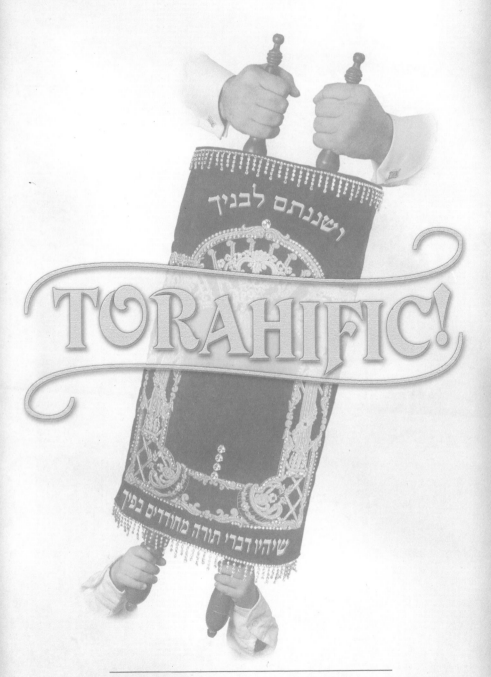

sefer bereishis

פרשת בראשית

?

1. Why did Hashem create for us two worlds: this world and the World to Come?

(*Rashi, Bereishis Rabbah 1:6, Vayikra Rabbah 36:4, Yeshayah 43:7, Avos 6:11, Yoma 38a, Shemos Rabbah 17:1, Mesilas Yesharim - mentioning Eiruvin 22a; see Uktzin 3:12*)

2. Why did the people before the Flood live a very long time, the average life span being 857 years?

(*Ramban, Seder Hadoros 130*)

FUndamental Answers!

"יגעתי ומצאתי!"

("*I worked on these questions, and I found these answers!*")

1. *Hashem*, the One and Only God, created everything in the universe for "*Kevod Shamayim*," which means for His honor. We mention this under the *Chupah* of a new couple when we say, "*Shehakol Bara Lechvodo*" (every single thing was created for Hashem's honor). Hashem, the Supreme King, made "*Olam Hazeh*" – planet Earth – for the people who would accept the Torah (that means us!). By learning Torah and keeping the *mitzvos,* we bring the greatest honor to Hashem! "*Olam Haba*" – the World to Come – was created to give immeasurable reward to those who love and fear Hashem, and inconceivable punishment to those who ignore Him. What is most amazing is that Hashem has given us free choice, and the more we follow His will, the more *we will enjoy this world as well!* Our job is to be constantly aware of Hashem's all-encompassing Presence, and not act as though we are oblivious to Him and His will. Hashem wants us to enjoy His Divine Being and to benefit to the utmost from the beauty of His Divine Presence. This is the greatest pleasure attainable in the entire galaxy!

2. Ramban says that the first generations (whose longevity was more than ten times that of generations today, their average life span being 857 years) lived longer

3. Hashem created the world in six days. Why didn't Hashem create the entire world in just one second?

(Rambam Avos 5:1, Rabbeinu Bachya on Parshas Tetzaveh, Toras Ha'olah)

4. Which book did Adam Harishon receive from an angel?

(Beis Hamidrash)

5. Why was Adam created with dust gathered from around the entire world — and especially from the spot where the *mizbeiach* would eventually be situated?

*(Sanhedrin 38b, Bereishis Rabbah 14:8,
Rambam Beis Habechirah 2:2, Maharal in Gur Aryeh)*

because Adam was created directly by Hashem. Other commentators say that they owed their longevity to eating a healthy diet of vegetables rather than one of meat and wine. The original vegetables were much more healthful than those of today, since the soil before the Flood was superior. In addition, these early generations did not act immorally, and immorality shortens one's life (see *Avos* 4:21). Others say that Hashem generously gave the early generations of human beings extra time to disseminate the recognition of His infinite power and of His unlimited wonders. They were also given time to develop the world for the betterment of later generations.

3. Hashem granted us a six-day workweek filled with accomplishment and purpose, followed by a period of Shabbos rest so that we would emulate Him and rest on Shabbos, thereby testifying to His creation of the world. Also, Hashem wanted us to appreciate all the different components that make up this amazing world. This Divinely ordained schedule can also teach us patience—that not everything has to be done in one day: Rather we can strive each day to reach our goals. As the saying goes, "Rome (or the world for that matter) was not built in one day!" Hashem taught us to have a system for achieving success.

4. An angel named *Raziel Hamalach* gave Adam Harishon a book as a gift. (Incidentally, a book makes a great gift!) This book is filled with the secrets and mysteries of *Kabbalah,* and forecasts future historic events. We have a tradition that keeping a copy of this book called *Raziel Hamalach* in our homes is a *segulah* for Heavenly protection, so that we be spared from fire and other harm.

5. Hashem gathered dust from the entire world to use in the creation of Adam. This way the ground would accept man after his demise. Adam's head was made from the dust of Eretz Yisroel—in particular from the dirt of the site of the future *Mizbeiach.* Hashem said, "I will make him from the place where he will receive forgiveness, and consequently he will survive." Mankind was created from the very spot reserved for the service of and sacrifice to Hashem in order to remind human beings always to serve Hashem through sacrifice!

6. Who was the first person to pray to Hashem?

(Rashi, Chullin 60b, Kaf Hachaim-R' Chaim Falagi z"tl)

7. Adam named all the creatures according to their unique nature. Why did he name the dog *"kelev"*?

(Erchei Hakodesh vol. 1- pg. 283)

8. Why did the *tzaddik* Chanoch go up to Heaven alive?

(Rashi, Seder Hadoros 930)

9. How often do we bless Hashem for the glorious sun that lights up our days?

(HaTorah V'haTefillah; see Berachos 59b)

10. Why is the sky blue?

(Chullin 89a; see Maayan Beis Hashoeivah-Rav Shimon Schwab zt"l)

---

6. Adam was the first person to pray. Hashem delayed the growth of the trees and vegetation until there was someone to pray for them. We see from this that Hashem wants us to pray for our growth and well-being as well.

7. Adam named each creature according to its essence. A dog is called *"kelev,"* which means *"kol lev"* (all heart). This name thus describes the loyalty and love that a dog possesses for its owner (and for no one else!). No wonder that it's been said "a dog is man's best friend." The name of this creature should inspire us also to be completely faithful and loving to our Master.

8. Chanoch was an outstanding *tzaddik* and Torah scholar. However, his generation was wicked and decadent. Hashem knew that if Chanoch remained alive, the evil people would influence him negatively. Therefore, Hashem removed Chanoch from this world alive and brought him directly into *Gan Eden*.

9. We thank Hashem for the sun every day in the longest *berachah* of all:*"Baruch Yotzer Hame'oros,"* (which begins right after *Borchu*.) If it were not for light, we could not fully enjoy anything in the world. That is why it deserves the longest *berachah* (almost 300 words!). Every 28 years we are required to say a unique *berachah* praising Hashem for creating the sun in its special place in the galaxy. The *berachah* is said at the time when the sun is at the same position it was in when Hashem created it.

10. One reason the sky is blue is because it reflects Hashem's Heavenly Throne of Glory, which is the color of sapphire.

Answers&Facts

---

11. Why did Hashem make Adam unconscious while He formed Chavah?

(Rashi, Love Your Neighbor-Rabbi Zelig Pliskin shlita)

12. Why is Kayin considered to be a mass murderer?

(Rashi)

13. Why did Hashem make the moon?

(Bereishis Rabbah 6:1, Eiruvin 65a)

14. Why did Hashem originally create Adam and Chavah attached to each other (somewhat like Siamese twins)?

(Berachos 61a, Raavad, Vilna Gaon, Shaarei Aharon)

15. Which species of fruit was the Eitz Hadaas (The Tree of Knowledge which was forbidden to eat)?

(Bereishis Rabbah 15:8, Berachos 40a)

---

11. Adam was put to sleep during Chavah's creation from his rib so that he would not see the "surgery" and despise her. From here we can learn a lesson in human relationships, one that is especially relevant to a spouse: Sometimes we need to "fall asleep" and not notice the other person's faults.

12. It was as if Kayin killed countless multitudes of people because, through the murder of his brother Hevel, he simultaneously destroyed all the potential children who would have descended from him. Who can know the ramifications of a sin? Why, it seems that Kayin killed 1/7 of the human population on that tragic day!

13. One opinion in the *Gemara* states that Hashem made the moon as a kind of night-light in order to enable us to learn Torah even in the dark of night. (Of course, the early generations actually used candlelight to learn during the night while today we use electricity, but Hashem wanted to demonstrate that even at night one must strive to learn Torah.) The moon also regulates our Jewish calendar by dictating the beginning of each new month.

14. Adam and Chavah had, at first, to be created attached to each other so that their mutual impulse would be to care for one another. Just as we care for ourselves, so too must we care for each other!

15. The Tree of Knowledge was either a grapevine, a fig tree, a wheat stalk, or an *esrog* tree – contrary to the belief of many people who think that the tree from which Adam and Eve ate was an apple tree.

---

16. What was Adam doing when Chavah had a conversation with the snake?
(Bereishis Rabbah 19:3 and 17:6; see Avos d'Rabi Nosson 1:6)

17. How do we know that bad *middos* (character traits) can cause the worst sins?
(Seichel Tov, Bereishis Rabbah 22:7)

18. What natural disaster happened in the year 266?
(Seder Hadoros, Bereishis Rabbah 27:7)

19. How many *mishnayos* did the righteous sage Mesushelach know?
(Seder Hadoros 687, Yalkut 44; see Gemara Avodah Zarah 14b)

20. Did Hashem plan to eventually let Adam eat from the Tree of Knowledge?
(Vayikra Rabbah 25:2, Am HaTorah, quoting Avos d'Rabi Nosson)

---

16. Adam was napping when Chavah was being tricked by the snake into eating the forbidden fruit. The *Midrash* says that many downfalls begin when people go to sleep. From here we can also learn that a teacher must keep a watchful eye on his students if he wants to educate them properly.

17. Kayin was jealous of his brother Hevel, who was more righteous than he, so he killed him. Indeed, the consequences of jealousy can be fatal!

18. Enosh was the *rasha* who introduced the foolish beliefs that we call *avodah zarah*. His generation sinned through *avodah zarah* and was punished by the *Okainus's* (Atlantic Ocean's) flooding and destroying 1/3 of their population. This was a warning to the world not to forget that Hashem is the first and only Power: He has complete control over everything!

19. Mesushelach was a great *talmid chacham* who knew *900* orders of *Mishnah!* (Perhaps there used to be many more *mesechtos* [tractates] of *Torah Shebaal Peh*. After all, we find that Avraham Avinu possessed 400 books dealing with *avodah zarah*.]

20. Hashem planned on letting Adam taste the *Eitz Hadaas* after Shabbos had begun. But Adam allowed himself to be persuaded by his wife, Chavah, to taste it before then. His lack of patience and self-control cost him and all his descendants their very lives. We must trust that Hashem has many pleasures in store for mankind; we do not need to enjoy them before their time!

Answers&Facts

21. Why is it dangerous for a pregnant woman to step on cut-off fingernails or toenails?

(See Niddah 17a, Moed Katan 17a, and Sh'lah)

22. Why did Hashem stop in the middle of creating the *sheidim* (demons) on Friday?

(Bereishis Rabbah 7:5)

23. How do we know that sinning causes a person to lose his or her beauty?

(Zohar vol. 3:83)

24. Hashem had warned Adam that he would die on the very same day he would eat from the Eitz Hadaas. Why didn't he die right away?

(Ibn Ezra, Riva)

---

21. Before Adam ate from the Tree of Knowledge, he was adorned with a fingernail-like covering for beauty and protection. However, when Chavah persuaded him to eat from the forbidden fruit, he lost this safeguard; just a little remained on his fingers and toes. Thus pregnant women should not step on a cut-off piece of nail, for by doing so they allude to the sin of their ancestress Chavah and possibly put themselves in grave danger.

22. Hashem stopped in the middle of making the demons even though He really could have finished their creation. He wanted to demonstrate to us that no matter what you are doing on *Erev Shabbos*, when it comes close to evening – stop, and don't finish your work! Just consider it done!

23. Before Chavah sinned by eating the forbidden fruit, she was so much more beautiful. We learn from here that when people sin, they lose much of their original beauty.

24. Adam greatly regretted his sin of not obeying Hashem. He became a *baal teshuvah* and cried and mourned. So Hashem extended his life. Also, when Hashem said, "On the *day* you eat from it you will surely die," He meant one thousand years because it says in *Tehillim* that Hashem's "day" is that long. Adam was therefore supposed to live 1,000 years, but he donated 70 years of his life to Dovid Hamelech.

---

25. The world cannot exist without constant Torah-learning. In that case, who sustained the world from Adam until Avraham?

(Tanna d'Bei Eliyahu, Nefesh Hachaim chapter 4, Pesachim 68b and 118b, Chagigah 14a, Avodah Zarah 9a)

26. Which *mitzvah* can atone for one's sins?

(See Sefer Chareidim, chapter 73)

27. In the future, who will shine like the sun and the stars?

(Shabbos 88b, Bava Basra 8b)

28. How much greater is learning Torah on Shabbos than learning on a weekday?

(Ben Ish Chai on Parshas Shemos- 2nd year)

---

25. Until the Torah was given the world was sustained by the kindness of Hashem! As the *pasuk* says, *"Olam chessed yibaneh"* ("the world is built on kindliness").

26. Many *mitzvos* can atone for sins. One of these special *mitzvos* is keeping Shabbos properly.

27. Daniel prophesied that in the future those who have brought merit to the community will shine like the very stars. This prophecy refers both to those who teach Torah to young children and those who speak out against wrongdoing. Also Devorah prophesied that people who are insulted but don't insult others, who hear their disgrace but don't answer back, and who serve Hashem with love and are joyous even when pained, will in the future shine like the sun!

28. Learning Torah on Shabbos is a thousand times more beneficial for your *neshamah* (soul) than learning during the week. We are commanded to learn as much Torah as we can at every available moment. If one must work during the week, at least he should learn as much as he can over Shabbos. (One minute of learning Torah on Shabbos is equivalent to approximately 17 hours of learning Torah during the week!)

Answers&Facts

29. Which seven things did Hashem create before He created the world?

(Pesachim 54a)

30. Why does Hashem want us to make a *berachah* (blessing) on the moon every month?

(Mechilta)

31. How was Chanoch taken up to Heaven?

(Seder Hadoros 930)

32. Why are the tongues of snakes split?

(Osiyos d'Rabi Akiva 3)

33. When was Parashas Bereishis read publicly every single day of the year?

(Taanis 27b)

---

29. The seven things that Hashem made *before* creating the world were: *Torah, Teshuvah, Gan Eden, Gehinnom*, the *Kisei Hakavod* (His Throne of Glory), the *Beis Hamikdash*, and the name of *Moshiach*.

30. Hashem wants us to make a blessing on the moon's renewal monthly in order that we look up to Heaven at least once a month!

31. Chanoch went up to Heaven on a fiery horse that descended from Heaven and was lifted back up by a strong wind.

32. The tongues of snakes are split at the tip because the original snake spoke falsely about Hashem. That snake, which represented the *Yetzer Hara*, tried to weaken Chavah's awe of Hashem by lying and saying that Hashem ate from this tree in order to create the world.

33. During the time of the *Beis Hamikdash*, different shifts of *Yisroelim*, called *Maamados*, fasted and prayed that Hashem would accept the *Korbanos* of *Am Yisroel* to atone for their sins. Every day they would read *Parshas Bereishis* in order to show that the world lasts only because Hashem forgives our sins.

---

34. How long did Chavah live? Who buried her in the Mearas Hamachpeilah?

(Seder Hadoros)

35. What is the reason that generally boys do not get married at the age of 13?

(Tur Even Ha'ezer Hilchos Piryah V'rivyah 1, Be'er Heitev 1:3, Baal Hatanya)

36. Who was the first person to bring a *korban* to Hashem?

(Bamidbar Rabbah 4:8)

37. Does the particular day of the week on which you were born have any influence on your future?

(See Shabbos 156a and Rashi there)

---

34. Chanoch buried Chavah. She was 987, and Adam lived to be 930. She thus outlived her husband by 57 years.

35. Although boys are obligated to pursue *mitzvos* from the age of *bar mitzvah*, the obligatory *mitzvah* of getting married is postponed a number of years for them because at the young age of thirteen, boys are often immature and not knowledgeable enough in Torah to become responsible fathers. By dedicating several years to Torah study however, they become more intellectually mature and will thus be able to guide their own children on the path of Torah.

36. Adam *Harishon* was the first *bechor*. He thus adorned himself with a sort of *bigdei kehunah* and offered the first *korban* to Hashem. *Korbanos* play a very important role in man's *Avodas Hashem*. In fact, the world stands in the merit of Torah learning, *korbanos* in the Beis Hamikdash (or our prayers, which substitute for the *korbanos*), and acts of kindness (*Avos* 1:2)!

37. Some Rabbis believe that the day of the week on which a person is born influences his personality. A person born on Sunday has the quality of leadership, as Sunday is the beginning of the week. A person born on Monday may have a tendency to be angry, since division took place on Monday with the separation of the waters above and the waters below. Someone born on Tuesday will probably be wealthy but not so modest, as food and plant life were created on that day and grew wildly. Someone born on Wednesday will

Answers&Facts

38. Why did Hashem ask Adam, *"Ayekah?"* ("Where are you?")? After all, Hashem knows everything!

(Rashi, Ben Ish Chai)

39. Who is considered a murderer even though he never killed anyone?

(Yevamos 63a; see Maseches Kallah 1)

40. In what manner does the Midrash compare *mishnayos* to a wife?

(Zohar vol. 1:27b)

41. After the Mabul what is the maximum age that a human being could live?

(See Bereishis 6:3)

---

probably be brilliant, for the sun, moon, and stars were created on that day. One born on Thursday will probably be kind, as fish and birds (all of which cause no trouble to people when they search for food) were created on that day. One born on Friday will probably run after *mitzvos*, since *Erev* Shabbos is when everyone rushes to prepare for Shabbos. A person born on Shabbos will probably be very holy, for Shabbos is the holiest day of the week. But after all is said and done, a person's attitude and deeds will determine his success or failure!

38. *"Ayekah"* is an abbreviation for *"Ani yode'a kol hanistaros!"* I know everything—even if it's hidden! Hashem was saying to Adam, "Do you think you can hide from Me?" Another explanation is: "Why did you stoop so low as to kill your own brother? How far have you strayed?!"

39. If someone refuses to get married and have children, it's as if he had murdered his potential descendants!

40. Just as a wife will honor and respect her husband when he keeps the Torah, and will oppose him when he does not, so too, one who studies *Mishnayos* well will merit much goodness and help from Heaven, while one who ignores his study of *Mishnayos*, will suffer!

41. Hashem said that after mankind sinned so greatly, their life spans would decrease drastically. Instead of living for close to one thousand years, people would live only to a maximum of 120 years. There were some exceptions whereby extremely righteous people were granted a longer life, such as Kaleiv ben Yefuneh or Rav Preida who lived over 400 years.

---

42. Why was there a custom to marry on Wednesday night?

(Kesuvos 5a)

43. Until when can a man delay getting married in order to focus on his Torah learning?

(Shulchan Aruch Even Ha'ezer 1, Kitzur Sefer Hamitzvos, Dibros Moshe- Siman 63, Chazon Ish- Kiddushin 29b, Chazon Ish Even Ha'ezer- Siman 148)

44. Why should one want to have many children?

(See Yevamos 62a and see Rambam Hilchos De'os 3:3)

45. Why should we all try to be *shadchanim* (matchmakers)?

(Maharsha on Shabbos 31a)

46. How far is *Gehinnom* from *Gan Eden*?

(Raziel Hamalach 42; see Sukkah 52a)

---

42. Hashem blessed the fish and birds on Thursday that they be fruitful and multiply. It thus became a popular custom to get married on Wednesday (night), so that the blessing of fruitfulness given on that day should affect the new couple as well.

43. The *Mishnah* says that the time to marry is at the age of eighteen. If a man wishes to postpone this *mitzvah* in order to concentrate on his Torah learning, he can delay getting married until he is twenty-four, or even later if necessary. However, it is better for one to get married earlier, since *"Lo tov heyos ha'adam levado"* ("it is not good for man to be alone") and *"Tovim hashenayim min ha'echad!"* ("two are better than one") (*Mishlei*).

44. Parents should want to have many children in order to fulfill the *mitzvah* of *Peru U'revu,* and in order that at least one of them will hopefully become a *talmid chacham* in whose merit the parents will enjoy *Gan Eden.*

45. The first *mitzvah* mentioned in the Torah is to have children. Our Rabbis encourage everyone to play the role of matchmaker and make *shidduchim* so that all Jews can build their own homes and fulfill this *mitzvah.* One needs a *zechus* (special merit) to receive *Siyata D'Shemaya* (Divine assistance) to unite single people in a happy marriage.

46. *Gan Eden* is right next door to *Gehinnom;* only a thin wall with a scale suspended above it separates them. I think that the significance of their closeness is to remind us of how careful we must be not to sin and lose our great reward. On the other hand, if we have sinned, we can then do *teshuvah* and still enter *Gan Eden.*

Answers&Facts

47. Why are many science books considered as containing *kefirah* (denial of Hashem)?

(Rabbi Avigdor Miller zt"l)

48. Which two angels insulted mankind by concentrating on their failings, only to fail themselves later on?

(Rashi to Parshas Shelach 13:33, Midrash Avkir; see Rosh in Haddar Zekeinim)

49. Yuval was a master musician. What was his big mistake?

(Rashi, Tochachos Mussar quoting Yeshayah 43:7)

50. Which future people did Hashem show to Adam Harishon?

(Sanhedrin 38b, Bereishis Rabbah 24:2)

51. Why did the wise and righteous Adam eat from the Eitz Hadaas?

(Kochav M'Yaakov-Rav Yaakov Abu Chatzeira z"tl)

---

47. Unfortunately, there are scientists who deny that Hashem created the world. They falsely claim that the world came into being billions of years ago as the result of a "big bang" in space. Many scientists assert that man descended from apes, and they deny the amazing deeds of the All-Powerful Creator and Sole Controller of the Universe – *Hashem Yisborach!* They should consider: Is it possible that the computer that printed these organized words could have materialized out of thin air? Heaven forbid! Logically, there is a Supreme Designer of this multifaceted world!

48. Shamchazai and Azael were angels who mocked man's frailty in sinning. Hashem then sent them both down to earth to face temptation, and they failed miserably.

49. Yuval was an evil musician because he played the harp and the flute for *avodah zarah*.

50. Hashem showed Adam all the Torah scholars and Jewish leaders of future generations who would eventually be born.

51. Perhaps Adam knew the decision of the *Gemara* (Berachos 34b) that a *baal teshuvah* is greater than a regular *tzaddik*. So he sinned by eating the Eitz Hadaas in order to do *teshuvah* and become even closer to Hashem. But his idea was wrong because the Sages warned that one must not say, "I will sin and I will repent!"

---

52. Why did Hashem fashion Chavah from Adam's rib and not from another part of his body — such as his ear, eye, or leg?

(Bereishis Rabbah 18:2)

53. When did a *tzaddik* create a man from the ground?

(Otzar Hamaasiyos; see Sanhedrin 65b)

54. In whose merit does the entire world exist?

(Zohar 1:1, Shabbos 119b, Chullin 89a, Sukkah 45b, Avos 1:2, Nedarim 31b)

55. Why did Hashem create the Eitz Hachaim (Tree of Life)?

(Pesikta Zutrasi)

56. Why is it preferable for a woman to light the Shabbos candles?

(Shulchan Aruch - Orach Chaim 263:2)

---

52. Hashem did not create Chavah from the mouth lest she talk too much, nor from the ear lest she eavesdrop, nor from the foot lest she always want to go out. Rather, Hashem created Chavah from a rib, which is covered, so that she should always be modest.

53. It is told that in 1580, the saintly Rabbi Betzalel Loewe *z"tl*, known as the *Maharal*, made a non-speaking 'man'. This occurred when persecution of Jews was rampant, and Rabbi Loewe felt that the Jews needed a robotic bodyguard. Rabbi Loewe was 67 years old when he made *Yossele the Golem*, who patrolled the Jewish city of Prague and safeguarded it for ten years.

54. The world exists in the merit of: (a) the breath of schoolchildren learning Torah and praying, (b) people who keep their mouths closed so as not to quarrel with those who have insulted them, (c) thirty-six *tzaddikim* in every generation, (d) humble people, and (e) Jews who study Torah, pray, and are kind.

55. The *Eitz Hachaim* was created so that *tzaddikim* would eat from it in *Gan Eden* and live forever.

56. The soul of man is likened to a flame. Chavah extinguished the flame of mankind (since the result of her sin was death to humanity); consequently, women are urged to relight the flame. Indeed, lighting Shabbos candles helps rectify the sin of Chavah, the first woman.

Answers&Facts

---

57. On which day of the calendar did Hashem start creating the world?

(Rashi, see Rosh Hashanah 10b)

58. Why did some sages say it would have been better if people had not been created?

(Eiruvin 13b)

59. Why did Hashem create a multitude of various creatures, yet He created man alone?

(Mishnah Sanhedrin 5:4)

60. How many years were there from the creation of the world until Moshe Rabbeinu instructed the Torah to Klal Yisroel?

(Seder Hadoros)

57. Hashem started creating this world on the 25th day of *Elul*. Man was created on the first of *Tishrei*, which is known as *Rosh Hashanah*. Just as Adam was judged on that first day for his error, so too is all mankind judged annually on *Rosh Hashanah*.

58. There was a great debate among the Rabbis whether or not it was good that man was created, since so many people sin. They decided that really most people would have been better off not being created, considering the damage they do by sinning. Now that they have been created, however, let them make the most of their lives by serving Hashem.

59. Man was created alone in order to remind us that if you save one person, it's as though you saved the whole world; similarly, if someone kills another person, it's as though he destroyed the whole world! Also, Hashem did not want people to claim, "My father was greater than your father because he was created first."

60. 2,448 years elapsed from the Creation of the world until the time at which the eighty-year-old Moshe Rabbeinu—during the twenty-sixth generation— delivered the Torah to the Jews. Interestingly enough, the Name of Hashem is *begamtria* twenty-six, thus alluding to the fact that Moshe was the greatest prophet ever to communicate with Hashem!

61. What does Adam reply to all the *tzaddikim* who condemn him for bringing death upon them?

(Bamidbar Rabbah 19:18)

62. How enjoyable is Gan Eden?

(Avos 4:17)

63. When did a reptile talk to a human being?

(Devarim Rabbah 5:10, Sotah 9b)

64. Who acts like our friend, but is in reality, our greatest enemy?

(Chovos Halevavos Shaar Yichud Hamaaseh chapter 5, Pele Yo'etz; see Baba Basra 16b)

---

61. All the *tzaddikim* criticize Adam for having brought death to the world. He answers, "I committed only <u>one</u> sin, while everyone else has committed at least four [or many more]!"

62. *Chazal* say that one moment in *Gan Eden* (the World of Reward) is more pleasurable than all the pleasures in this world combined. The rewards and punishments are so immense that Hashem actually had to create separate worlds in order to reward the righteous and punish the wicked.

63. The original snake (*Hanachash Hakadmoni*) was given the power of speech. He was also the king of the animal world. He walked upright on feet like humans, and he even ate the food of man. However, he lost these gifts and privileges when he sinned. Until today, the *Yetzer Hara* still talks to us, for he is our inner evil inclination that tries to persuade us to sin. We must learn from the punishment of Adam and Chavah not to listen to the snake inside us – the *Yetzer Hara* – because crime does not pay! The *Gemara* says that it's a pity Adam sinned, because Hashem would have provided each Jew with two handsome snakes as his assistants at his beck and call, to do his work for him.

64. The *Yetzer Hara* acts like a friend, offering us all types of pleasures, but more often than not, these pleasures are forbidden and harmful. The *Yetzer Hara* offered Chavah a "tasty and beautiful fruit," but he didn't tell her that eating it would cost her her very life! Life is a series of tests. Therefore, we must always be aware of this "secret" enemy that is within us!

Answers&Facts

65. Why did Akilas become a *ger* (convert to Judaism)?

(*Shemos Rabbah 30:12*)

65. Once upon a time, there was a gentile named Akilas who wanted to convert to Judaism. He told King Adriyonus that he wanted to become a Jew. The king thundered, "You want to attach yourself to this nation? How much did I disgrace them? How many of them did I kill? You desire to mix with the lowest nation, do you? What did you see about them that makes you want to join them?" Akilas answered, "Even the young among them know exactly what G-d's schedule was when He created the world: what was created on the first day, what was created on the second day, etc. They know how many years ago the world was created. They must be very close to G-d if He reveals to them what He did! They know on what merits the world exists, and their Torah is all truth." The king permitted him to learn Torah on condition that he study but not undergo a *Bris Milah*. He responded that even the wisest gentile cannot fathom the greatness of the Torah unless he first undergoes a *Bris Milah*. We learn from this story how much Hashem loves us in that He has confided to us His wondrous doings. Hashem has also informed us that the entire world was created for *Am* Yisroel to honor Him by being His devoted people.

Dedicated in honor of my wife
RUTHY
by Dr. Jacques Doueck

פרשת נח

?

1. How long did the *tzaddik* Noach live?

(Bereishis 9:29, Midrash Tanchuma 2:2)

2. Why did all the creatures inside the *Teivah* (Ark) start screaming?

(Seder Hadoros 1656)

3. What skill did both Noach and Shlomo Hamelech share?

(Zohar Chadash 22b)

fUNdamental Answers!

"יגעתי ומצאתי!"

(*"I worked on these questions, and I found these answers!"*)

1. Noach lived until the year 2006, a total of 950 years. He lived to see the whole world populated once again. He also witnessed the development of all seventy nations, which were composed of his descendants.

2. The *Teivah* was shaking in the raging waters and was ready to crack. The lions roared, the cows mooed, the wolves howled, and all the creatures screamed from pain. Their voices were heard from afar. Noach and his sons screamed and cried, too. They were very scared. Noach prayed to Hashem; the waters calmed, and the *Teivah* became more secure.

3. Noach and Shlomo *Hamelech* understood the languages of all the creatures and could communicate with them.

4. Why didn't Noach pray that his wicked generation be saved?

(Rabbeinu Bachya, Zohar 254b)

5. Why did Hashem let the lion hurt Noach just because he came late once with its food?

(Bereishis Rabbah 30:6, Rav Eliyahu Meir Bloch zt"l, Tanchuma 9, Rav Mordechai Gifter zt"l)

6. Which sins caused the devastating *Mabul* (World Flood) of 1656?

(Gemara Sanhedrin 108a, Bereishis Rabbah 31:1)

7. Which question should Noach not have asked Hashem?

(Pirkei d'Rabi Eliezer, chapter 23)

---

4. Noach knew that only a *"minyan"* of *tzaddikim* would be able to spare the world from punishment, and there were only eight in his family, plus Mesushelach. The same is true of Avraham Avinu (18:32); he prayed that if there were but ten *tzaddikim* in Sedom, the city should be saved in their merit. A *minyan* is so important for the well-being of a city!

5. Noach was busy around-the-clock feeding each animal its particular food. He could hardly sleep that entire year! Once, he delayed the lion's meal, and as he was about to leave the *Teivah* at the end of the year, the lion struck him. He went away limping and coughing blood. He was punished because not taking care of that lion's health could have weakened all future lions. One commentator points out how careful a *rebbi* must be to teach his *talmid* well, since not taking care of a *talmid* could, G-d forbid, weaken all his future generations as well. Others understand that Noach was able to step on snakes and scorpions and not get hurt, since he was involved in *chessed* (kindness), but once he was late for the lion, he lost this protection.

6. The generation of Noach did every sin possible. They were especially steeped in immorality and idolatry. But it was theft that "broke the camel's back" and caused their tragic fate to be sealed. Stealing is one of the worst sins. Therefore, that generation has no share in the World to Come and won't rise at the time of *Techiyas Hameisim* either.

7. When Hashem commanded Noach to gather at least two of each species of animals and birds, Noach was overwhelmed and asked, "How can I manage

---

8. **What was the weather like before the Flood?**
   (Malbim quoting Midrash, Seder Hadoros, Shaarei Aharon, The Midrash Says)

9. **Why didn't people eat meat before the Mabul?**
   (Bereishis Rabbah 34:13, Radak, The Beginning-Rav Avigdor Miller zt"l)

10. **What was the date of the *Mabul*?**
    (Rashi)

11. **With what did Noach wish to reward his sons for all their assistance in managing his "zoo"?**
    (Tanchuma 15)

---

to bring all the creatures to the ship?" He didn't realize that Hashem wanted him to have the *zechus* (special merit) of bringing the animals himself. However, once he questioned Hashem about his task, he lost his *zechus*, and the animals came by their own instinct. From here we learn to have confidence: We must never doubt our ability to do great work for Hashem; Hashem will help!! Indeed, we find that there are two types of people—those who think *"Ich ken nisht..."* (I can't do that) and those who think *"Ich ken yuh..."* (I can do it). We must not paralyze ourselves by telling ourselves that we can't accomplish our goal. If Hashem tells us to do it—then it *can* be done!

8. The weather was originally as pleasant as could be. But the people became spoiled, thereby denying their need for Hashem. Indeed, during the week before the Flood, the weather was like that of *Gan Eden* so that the people would see what they would be missing unless they repented. Finally, there were earthquakes, darkness, lightning, thunder, and trembling—all to move them to do *teshuvah*. But they *still* did not get Hashem's message.

9. At the beginning of Creation, mankind was not permitted to eat from the animal kingdom. Fruits and vegetables supplied all the required nutrients that the human body needed for survival! After the *Mabul*, however, the soil lost its previous strength, and Hashem permitted people to gain protein by consuming animals, birds, and fish.

10. The *Mabul* began on the *17th of Cheshvan*. (Americans rightfully mourn 9/11 as a day of national disaster, but when you think about it, an even bigger disaster occurred to mankind on the lunar date 2/17.)

11. Noach wanted to have more sons so that each new son would become an assistant to the older, already hard-working ones.

Answers&Facts

12. What deal did Noach make with the giant Og Melech HaBashan?

(Pirkei d'Rabi Eliezer, Yalkut Shimoni)

13. How did the residents of the Teivah breathe oxygen if the ark was sealed tight?

(Sifsei Chachamim)

14. What was the purpose of the tzohar (window/luminous gem)?

(Peninim Al HaTorah quoting Ateres Mordechai)

15. Where did Noach get the luminous gem(s) to light up the Ark?

(Targum Yonasan 6:15)

16. Why is stealing a small amount just as severe as stealing a large amount?

(Yesod V'Shoresh HoAvodah, Love Your Neighbor)

---

12. Noach agreed to drill a hole in the side of the *Teivah* in order to pass food to Og, on condition that he would swear to be the slave of Noach and his descendants forever. Og hung on for a long ride and survived.

13. There was a pipe that let air into the *Teivah* (just like on a submarine). This would explain how they were able to withstand the smell of the animals as well.

14. The *window* let in light. It also let Noach see the consequences both of that generation's corruption, and of his not praying for them.

15. Noach got luminous gems from *Gan Eden*.

16. Stealing a little is really like stealing a lot because all the future generations of the victim of the theft might possibly have gained from that money if they had been able to use it.

17. Our planet was not tilted at first. This resulted in consistently delightful weather. But the people grew arrogant and denied needing Hashem's supervision. By tilting the globe, Hashem produced a change in the world's climate, which brought about more sickness, and people thus became much more humble.

---

17. Why is the Earth's axis tilted 23.5 degrees?

(I heard in the name of the Malbim)

18. Who mourned for humanity for seven days before the Mabul?

(Bereishis Rabbah 32:7, The Midrash Says)

19. Why did the flood rains pour down for forty days?

(Rashi)

20. Why did Noach bless a certain creature that it should live forever?

(Sanhedrin 108b)

21. How did all the various species of small and large creatures fit into the *Teivah*?

(Ramban)

22. From where did Noach learn Torah?

(Rashi to Sanhedrin 56b; see Zohar Bamidbar 153, Zohar 21:58)

---

18. Hashem "sat *shivah*" (so to speak) for mankind *before* He destroyed the world. In addition, the *Gadol Hador*, Mesushelach, Noach's righteous grandfather, passed away a week before the *Mabul*. Hashem hoped that society would take his passing to heart and repent that week – but they didn't.

19. The violent rain lasted for forty days – which corresponds to the forty days necessary for an embryo to form, since that immoral generation troubled Hashem to create babies that should not have been born.

20. Noach saw one bird called *"Orshina"* (Phoenix) exhausted on a shelf. He asked it, "Don't you need food, too?" It replied, "I saw that you were busy, so I didn't want to bother you!" A grateful Noach blessed that creature that it would never die.

21. It was a miracle for so many creatures to be able to fit under one roof!

22. Noach learned a great deal of Torah. He learned from Adam's and Chanoch's *sefarim* about *Avodas Hashem*. For example, he learned how to bring a *korban* to Hashem. The *Midrash* (Bereishis Rabbah 34:12) says that Hashem blessed Noach to be fruitful and fill the world in the merit of his bringing *korbanos*.

23. What did Korach have in common with the Dor Hamabul (Generation of the Flood)?

(Baal HaTurim)

24. Where did Noach get the grapevine from which he produced the wine that made him drunk?

(Targum Yonasan 9:20, Taam V'daas, Maharzu 36:4, The Midrash Says)

25. Why didn't Noach have children until he was 500 years old?

(Rashi, Bereishis Rabbah 26:2)

26. Why didn't Noach's mussar (criticism) make the wicked people repent?

(Sanhedrin 108b)

27. Why did Noach hide for a while from the people of his generation?

(Zohar volume 1:58b, Seder Hadoros 1422)

---

23. Korach's enormous wealth led to his arrogance and downfall. Similarly, the Generation of the Flood lost out by being too comfortable! They became arrogant and denied that it was *Hashem* Who was sustaining them. (See *Devarim* 8:14)

24. Noach got the grapevine from *Gan Eden*. One can understand Noach's desire to drink wine after the destruction of the world—to cheer him up after seeing that utter disaster. It was like making a "*L'chaim*—to life!" He also hoped that the wine would give him the strength to be able to have more children.

25. Hashem did not want Noach to have children who would be killed in the Flood because of their sins. So Noach was childless until he was very old. In his old age, he fathered righteous children.

26. Noach scolded his generation too harshly. That's why they didn't listen to him! Criticism works only if it is given gently and sensitively, with love and caring.

27. Noach avoided interaction with the people of his generation so that he shouldn't follow in their wicked ways. He was also fearful that they would kill him on account of his constant preaching to them to do *teshuvah*.

28. How do we see that "jealousy," "lust," and "honor-seek-ing" are deadly sins?

(Torah Mi'Tzion)

29. Where are the remains of the Teivah located today?

(Seder Hadoros)

30. The rebellious people of the Dor Haflagah were punished with being scattered throughout the world. Why weren't they punished worse than the Dor HaMabul; after all, didn't they want to wage war against Hashem Himself?

(Rashi, Bereishis Rabbah 38:6)

31. Why didn't Noach stop the rebels from building the "Tower of Bavel" in their attempt to fight against Hashem?

(Mili d'Avos, Ralbag, Sichos Mussar)

32. How long did Avraham learn under the tutelage of Noach, Shem, and Eiver?

(Sefer Hayashar, Seder Hadoros 1958)

28. Kayin's jealousy of Hevel caused him to murder his brother. He was cursed that no offspring of his would endure. The people of the generation of the *Mabul* were filled with evil desires that brought about their annihilation. The people of the *Dor Haflagah* wanted honor, but they did not reach their goal; on the contrary, they failed miserably!

29. There are people today who believe that the remains of the *Teivah* are located in Turkey on Mount Ararat. (I have heard that it is submerged in ice and that the local residents are hostile and don't like visitors.)

30. The people of the *Dor Haflagah* sinned against Hashem, but peace and unity reigned among them, and they were good to one another. On the other hand, the people of the *Dor HaMabul* treated each other badly, as well as sinning against Hashem.

31. We have a concept called *"aveirah goreress aveirah"* ("one sin begets another"). Perhaps, since Noach did not save his generation, he lost the opportunity of saving the next generation as well.

32. From age ten to age forty-nine (until the year 1997 after Creation), Avraham learned *"Mussar Hashem"* from the *tzaddikim* of his time. Avraham was 58 when Noach died; interestingly enough, the *gematria* (numerical value) of Noach is 58!

Answers&Facts

33. What did the wicked kings Nimrod and Pharaoh have in common?

(Seder Hadoros 1948)

34. What trick did Avraham play in his father's idol shop?

(Bereishis Rabbah 38:13)

35. What did Avraham pray when Nimrod ordered him to bow down to the fire?

(Seder Hadoros)

36. Why was Sarah also called "Yiskah"?

(Rashi, Megillah 14a)

33. Nimrod and Pharaoh both tried killing the foremost leaders of our people after finding out about them through astrology. Nimrod tried to kill Avraham, and Pharaoh wanted to kill Moshe.

34. Avraham smashed all the idols in his father's *avodah zarah* shop. Then he put the sledgehammer into the biggest idol's hand and said to his father, Terach, "He did it!" His father replied, "That's ridiculous; they [the idols] have no power!" to which Avraham declared, "Listen to your own words! Why do you worship them if they have no power?"

35. Avraham was furious at seeing his own father, as well as his neighbors, involved in *avodah zarah*. His father was angry that Avraham had smashed his idols, so he brought him to Nimrod to be sentenced to death. Avraham lifted his eyes to Heaven and said, "Hashem, look at these wicked people and judge them!" Avraham was put into prison and sentenced to death in a fiery furnace. Hashem Himself came down to protect Avraham by burning off his handcuffs while allowing him to walk around safe and secure for three days inside the blazing furnace. Nimrod couldn't even take him out because eight men were burned up trying to do so. Because of this miracle, a tremendous number of people showered Avraham with gifts, and hundreds converted and became his followers!

36. "Yiskah" means "will see." In other words, Sarah, who was Avraham's niece and wife, would be able to see with the clarity of *Ruach Hakodesh*. In addition, she was so beautiful that everyone wanted to see her. "Yiskah" also means "princess."

37. Who was the first person to mint coins?

(Seder Hadoros 1878)

38. What happened to the Tower of Bavel?

(Sanhedrin 109a, The Midrash Says)

39. Why isn't Avraham's miraculous fireproof rescue from Ur Kasdim mentioned explicitly in the Chumash?

(Rabbi Avigdor Miller zt"l)

40. Why is a rainbow so pretty if in reality it is a sign that Hashem is angry?

(Hevel Tashbar)

41. What are the "Seven Mitzvos" that non-Jews (the descendants of Noach) must keep?

(Sanhedrin 56b; see Bereishis Rabbah 34:8, and see Iggeres HaTiyul, Ben Yehoyada)

---

37. Terach was the first one to mint coins. Interestingly enough, Avraham and Sarah were portrayed on the coins of their time!

38. *Chazal* tell us what happened to the Tower of Bavel. Its top third was burned, the bottom third sank into the ground, while the middle third remained. It was so high that if you stood on top of it, the palm trees below seemed like grasshoppers. Interestingly, at a museum in Baghdad depicting ancient Bavel from the times of Nevuchadnetzar, *Migdal Bavel* can be seen in a painting.

39. Avraham's life of *Kiddush Hashem* surpassed the merit he had earned for being ready to die for Hashem's sake. Therefore, only Avraham's greater merit is mentioned explicitly.

40. The reason that a rainbow is so beautiful is to remind us of the world's beauty, a gift from Hashem that we should not ruin with our sinful actions. If we do *teshuvah*, however, life will be beautiful once again.

41. Non-Jews have Seven *Mitzvos*: a) not to eat a living creature, b) not to curse Hashem, c) not to steal, d) to have a justice system maintained by courts, e) not to murder, f) not to commit adultery, and g) not to believe in any god other than Hashem. (The *Midrash* suggests a few more *mitzvos* that they have as well.)

Answers&Facts

42. How are non-Jews supposed to learn about their "Seven Mitzvos" in order to keep them?

(Ran's Introduction to Gemara; see Rambam Hilchos Melachim 8:10-11, and see Sanhedrin 59a)

43. How was the *tzaddik* Iyov related to Avraham Avinu?

(Seder Hadoros)

44. What does the Gemara mean when it states, "Let Nimrod testify for Avraham"?

(Gemara Avodah Zarah 3a, The Beginning, Bereishis Rabbah 37:2)

45. What should we do when we see a rainbow?

(Berachos 59a, Shulchan Aruch Orach Chaim 229:1, The Beginning)

46. After the Mabul, which generations never witnessed a rainbow?

(Bereishis Rabbah 35:2, Kesuvos 77b, Rashi)

42. The Seven *Mitzvos* of the non-Jews can all be derived through common sense. They thus are able to figure them out on their own. They are liable for punishment for not using their intellect to live up to the moral standards expected of them. When Jews are in authority, they should educate the non-Jews about their Seven *Mitzvos*. Any non-Jew who keeps the Seven *Mitzvos* out of respect for Hashem (Who has commanded them) is called a pious gentile and has a portion in the World to Come!

43. According to one opinion, Iyov was the grandson of Nachor (Avraham's brother). Thus, Avraham was Iyov's great-uncle. Iyov followed his great-uncle's example of kindliness, and his house was open on all four sides, just as Avraham's tent was.

44. Nimrod was able to capture people's hearts and minds. Nimrod saw that Avraham was too strong a *"maimin"* (believer) to fall prey to his missionary methods.

45. When we see a rainbow, we must be grateful for Hashem's promise not to destroy the world again. We thank Him with the *berachah*, "Blessed are You, Hashem …Who remembers to keep His promise and fulfill His word" (*Shulchan Aruch* 229). We must also reflect on Hashem's patience and improve our ways.

46. The following generations never saw a rainbow in their lives: the generation of Chizkiyah, who were so knowledgeable in Torah that even the young children were well-versed in *Shas*; the generation of Rabban Shimon bar Yochai; and – some say – the generation of the *Anshei K'nesses Hagedolah*!

47. Which strange creatures were made after the Dor Haflagah?

(Seder Hadoros 1973; Meleches Shlomo - Kelayim chapter 8; see Bereishis Rabbah 38:8)

48. When was there a flood before the occurrence of the Mabul?

(Seder Hadoros; see Bereishis 38:4)

49. How is it possible that a Jew and an idol-worshipper can commit the same *aveirah* (sin), yet the idol-worshipper is punished much more severely?

(Eiruvin 62b)

50. Why is a non-Jew liable to receive the death penalty if he keeps Shabbos?

(See Sanhedrin 58b, and see Rabbi Avigdor Miller Speaks, page 33-ArtScroll)

---

47. The *Seder Hadoros* describes nineteen weird figures that appeared in the *Dor Haflagah*. Some of the men involved in building the Tower were scattered, while others were transformed into monkeys, apes, and elephants as a punishment! That's one reason why the special *berachah* of *Mishaneh Haberi'os* is said the first time a person sees a monkey or an elephant. (We thus see the absurd *Theory of Evolution* turned on its ear: People did not come from monkeys; monkeys came from people!)

48. The first flood destroyed one third of mankind during Enosh's lifetime, in year 266 after Creation, when people started making up their own gods and calling themselves god. The second flood, the famous *Mabul* in the days of Noach, was in the year 1656, approximately three hundred years before Avraham was born. The Generation of the Flood should have learned its lesson from the Generation of Enosh, and the Generation of the Tower should have learned its lesson from the Generation of the Flood!

49. If a Jew steals money, he must return it (and he is sometimes required to pay twice or even four or five times the stolen amount). An idol-worshipper, however, is liable to the *death penalty* for stealing even an amount as small as a dime!

50. Shabbos is Hashem's exclusive gift to the Jews, and a *non-Jew* who keeps Shabbos is liable to the death penalty. Can a stranger take the queen's diamond engagement ring and "get away with" his theft?!

Answers&Facts

51. What serves as the "Teivah" nowadays to protect us from the "flood of corruption and decadence" raging in our own society?

(Sichos Mussar, 5733-Rav Chaim Shmulevitz zt"l)

52. How old were our ancestors Avraham and Sarah when they married each other?

(Seder Hadoros)

53. How hot was the water that destroyed the wicked Generation of the Flood?

(Bereishis Rabbah 28:9, The Midrash Says)

54. Were there dinosaurs early in history?

(Bereishis Rabbah 31:13, Rabbi Avigdor Miller z"tl; see Haamek Davar 7:2)

55. Why didn't Noach curse his immoral son Cham directly instead of cursing Canaan, who was Cham's son?

(Bereishis Rabbah 36:7, Parpera'os L'Torah, Radak)

---

51. The world today is *flooded* with violence, corruption, hatred, and mindless evil! The way to be saved from these negative influences is by running into the *yeshivos gedolos*, the *Teivahs* of our times!

52. Avrom was twenty-five when he married Sarai, who was fifteen at the time.

53. Each drop of water was first boiled in *Gehinnom* before it was sent to dissolve the wicked generation of the *Mabul*.

54. It is very likely that there were massive creatures such as dinosaurs; after all, even many humans were gigantic! Presumably these creatures perished in the *Mabul*.

55. Canaan was cursed because *he* was the one who spoke *lashon harah* about Noach by letting others know of his grandfather's immodesty during his drunkenness. Moreover, Cham was once blessed by Hashem, and a person who has been *blessed* by Hashem cannot be *cursed* by man.

---

56. Who wrote the Sefer Harefu'os (The Book of Cures and Remedies)?
(Tashbetz 445, Ramban's Introduction to Chumash, Beis Midrash)

57. Who cried when it was already too late to remedy the situation?
(Zohar volume 8:254b, Midrash Eichah on Yirmiyah 30:15)

58. Why was the raven sent out to discover whether there was dry land?
(Bereishis Rabbah 33:5)

59. Why is it meritorious, and indeed quite advantageous, to speak Lashon Hakodesh all the time?
(Pele Yo'etz, Sifri on Parshas Haazinu, Pesachim 113a)

---

56. After the *Mabul*, Noach (or his son Shem) recorded the *Book of Medicines* from Raphael Hamalach (the Angel). Others believe that it was Shlomo Hamelech who authored this book. The *Sefer Harefu'os* was later hidden away by King Chizkiyah. He wanted people to *pray and repent* when they were struck by illness, rather than just rely on this book.

57. Noach cried over the disappearance of mankind. Hashem said, "Now you cry for them! You should have cried out in prayer for them in the first place!"

58. Noach reasoned that a raven cannot be used as a *korban*, nor is it a kosher bird that in the future can be eaten by Jews—so why not risk sending it out? However, Hashem told Noach that every creature has a purpose and that one day, ravens would save Eliyahu *Hanavi* from hunger (*Melachim I* 17:6). Interestingly enough, although ravens are the cleverest of birds, they are mean and show no mercy to their offspring. Their young are hatched with white feathers so they don't recognize them as their own. Therefore, Noach used this cruel bird as a means of imploring Hashem to have mercy on mankind and not to overlook their needs. Hashem replied, "Now you are praying for them that I should have mercy, you should have prayed for them before."

59. *Lashon Hakodesh* was the original language spoken by mankind. The Hebrew language is the superior one used by Hashem, the angels, and the prophets. *Lashon Hakodesh purifies one's soul* even when one speaks about common, mundane matters! The most obvious advantage of knowing the Holy Tongue is that since you have become familiar with the language of the Torah, you will be better able to understand the Torah itself, more quickly and on a deeper level.

Answers&Facts

60. Why didn't Noach's generation repent when the rain poured torrentially?

(Eiruvin 19a, Yalkut Shimoni on Yeshayah 514)

61. How did the wolves and the sheep, the cats and the dogs, the spirits and the *sheidim* (demons), and the rattlesnakes and the bats all live in harmony with Noach's family?

(Rashi, Bereishis Rabbah 31:13)

62. Whose younger brother was also his father-in-law?

(Sanhedrin 69b)

63. Why didn't Shem and Eiver destroy idols as Avraham had done?

(Hasagos HaRaavad on the Rambam Hilchos Avodah Zarah 1:3, Rabbi Moshe Goldberger shlita)

---

60. The generation of the *Dor HaMabul* was so wicked that they did not repent even in the face of suffering. They chose to believe that every occurrence was a mere coincidence, not a consequence from the hand of G-d. Sometimes we find that even *reshaim* – such as Pharaoh, Bilam, and the people of Nineveh – did repent to avoid punishment, but they did so only temporarily.

61. Hashem made a special treaty that caused even natural enemies to live in peace in the *Teivah* during that long year. From this we learn that the animal kingdom, like everything else in Creation, is subject to Hashem's Divine plan.

62. Haran was two years younger than his brother Avraham. Sarah was born when her father Haran was eight. It was most appropriate that Haran should have Avraham as his son-in-law, since Haran also gave his life *"Al Kiddush Hashem."*

63. The generation of Shem and Eiver hid their idols when these elderly sages arrived. But young Avraham saw through the deceit of these wicked people. They couldn't outsmart him; consequently, he became the first person to oppose *avodah zarah* successfully. Indeed, today's young people can take a lesson from the youthful Avraham and become tomorrow's greatest teachers!

Dedicated in honor of
**MY PARENTS DAVID & SARAH
AND MY BROTHER URI**
by Mayer Lati

פרשת לך לך

1. Why did Hashem tell Avraham Avinu to leave his home and travel?

(Bereishis Rabbah 39:1, The Beginning; see Midrash Tanchuma 3; Doresh Tov, Eitz Yosef, The Midrash Says)

2. How old was Avraham Avinu when he recognized that Hashem created and continuously controls the universe?

(Nedarim 32a; Rambam Hilchos Avodas Kochavim 1:3, Raavad, Hagahos Maimonis; Pirkei d'Rabi Eliezer 26)

fUndamental Answers!

"יגעתי ומצאתי!"

("I worked on these questions, and I found these answers!")

1. Hashem told Avraham to travel so that all the other people in the world could learn from his wonderful personality traits. In the course of his travels, many people converted to Judaism through the inspiration of his superior example. In addition, Hashem wanted Avraham to separate himself from his original gentile family. Since Avraham was the holiest person in the world and the ancestor of the holy nation of Am Yisroel, Hashem wanted him to settle in the holiest place on earth—Eretz Yisroel.

2. Avraham realized that Hashem is G-d when he was just three years old! Surely, his belief and faith in Hashem increased immensely as he got older. There are other opinions that claim that Avraham was older when he realized that Hashem is G-d. According to these opinions, he was either 13, 40, 48, or 50. We can understand that as a person becomes older his perceptions deepen, too.

3. At what age did Avraham Avinu begin lecturing for Hashem's honor?

(Seder Hadoros)

4. How long was Avraham imprisoned for publicly opposing the worshipers of *avodah zarah*?

(Seder Hadoros)

5. When may a Jew reside outside of Eretz Yisroel?

(See Tosafos on Avodah Zarah 13a; Tosafos on Kesuvos 110b, Responsa of Maharit, Sifri, Terumas Hadeshen Kesavim 82)

6. What was the symbolism of Avraham's battle against the four kings?

(Bereishis Rabbah 42:2, Ramban)

7. Why did Avraham Avinu risk taking 318 Bnei Torah to war?

(Shaarei Aharon quoting Zohar and Yefas To'ar)

---

3. Avraham started preaching about Hashem's awesome, complete power at age 52 or 60. (Presumably, he started at a much younger age, but at this age he was much more experienced and effective.)

4. Avraham was imprisoned in Kuta and Kardo for ten years. In those days, the people were steeped in idolatry until Avraham debated with them and demolished all their theories. However, so foolish were they that they punished Avraham, the one who spoke the truth.

5. A Jew may leave Eretz Yisroel in order to learn Torah or to get married. Some Rabbis have said that it is easier to live a Jewish lifestyle *outside* of Eretz Yisroel (where one won't transgress the many obligations that exist in Eretz Yisroel, such as *Terumah* or *Shemitta*, etc.). Basically, one can live in America or anywhere else in the Diaspora if he honestly feels that he will gain more spirituality or economically by doing so! Nevertheless, let us yearn to move to Eretz Yisroel, for *Chazal* say, "Living in Eretz Yisroel is equivalent to fulfilling all the *Mitzvos!*"

6. Just as four kings tried ruling the world but they lost against Avraham, so too, four nations will try to rule the Jews in exile, but in the end the Jews will reign! Those four nations that exiled the Jews were Bavel, Madai, Yavan, and Edom.

7. Avraham did not want to cause a *Chillul Hashem* by people saying that he did not care to save his nephew. So he intended to ransom Lot with money.

8. When can giving someone honor make you rich?

(See Bava Metzia 59a, Kiddushin 31a, and Shabbos 119a)

9. What were the shepherds of Avraham and Lot arguing about?

(Bereishis Rabbah 41:5, Rashi)

10. Why did Avraham accept Pharaoh's presents? After all, don't we know that *"sonei matanos yichyeh"* (one will live longer if he doesn't accept gifts)?

(Bereishis Rabbah 41:6, Divrei Yoel quoting Ramban)

11. Why did Avraham not want to keep the money of Sedom?

(See Rashi; The Beginning)

However, when he saw angels coming to help him fight by miraculously turning the enemies' arrows into straw and their swords into dust while he himself could throw sand and it would turn into swords, he decided to use force.

8. There are numerous *mitzvos* that can cause one to become wealthy. One of these *mitzvos* is honoring one's wife. The *Gemara* attributes Avraham's extraordinary wealth to the great honor he accorded his wife Sarah.

9. Avraham's animals always went muzzled so as not to steal, but Lot's animals grazed on private property. Avraham's servants reprimanded Lot's servants for stealing. Lot's men rationalized, "G-d promised the Land of Canaan (Eretz Yisroel) to our master's uncle, Avraham, and our master, Lot, is one day going to be his heir, so we can graze on these properties, which are virtually ours." Avraham's men replied, "These are not Avraham's yet, and in any event *his own son* will inherit them." In fact, Avraham's nephew, Lot, looked like him, and Avraham was worried that people might suspect *him* of being the thief, so he really had to stop Lot's shepherds.

10. Avraham accepted Pharaoh's presents as an omen that someday his descendants would receive gifts from Pharaoh when they left Mitzrayim.

11. Avraham didn't want the King of Sedom to claim that *he* had made Avraham rich. Furthermore, Avraham did not want to touch his *"treife"* (spiritually unclean) money, which had been acquired through crooked and wicked ways. Another problem with taking such money is that by doing so, it would have made it harder for him to criticize the king and his subjects.

Answers&Facts

12. Why did Hashem save the wicked King of Sedom?

(Bereishis Rabbah 42:7, Ramban)

13. Why was it necessary for Sarah to be captured by Pharaoh?

(The Beginning, Rabbi Avigdor Miller zt"l)

14. When did the stars shine visibly during the day?

(Bechor Shor, Shaarei Aharon)

15. What ever became of all those people whom Avraham and Sarah had converted?

(Pri Tzaddik, Pirkei d'Rabi Eliezer 29, Rav Eliyahu Meir Bloch zt"l)

16. Why did the Bnei Yisroel have to become slaves in the land of Egypt?

(See Nedarim 32a and Tosafos on Shabbos 10b)

---

12. The King of Sedom was spared from death in the tar pit in order to be able to testify to Avraham's miraculous victory in battle. In addition, those people who were skeptical about how Avraham was rescued from Nimrod's furnace now believed in that miracle, too.

13. We can all learn a lesson from Pharaoh's kidnapping of Sarah: Even when a situation appears dismal and hopeless, it may eventually bring success and good fortune. Indeed, Avraham's fame and wealth increased from this "misfortune."

14. During the *Bris Bein Habesarim*, when Hashem promised Avraham that his sons would be like the stars, Hashem made the stars themselves twinkle in broad daylight.

15. It seems that the converts of Avraham and Sarah did not remain steadfast, because these converts' children were not as trained as well as their parents had been.

16. Avraham should not have challenged Hashem's word by saying, "How can I know that I will have a son?" By questioning Hashem, he caused his progeny to become slaves. Moreover, as a result of Yosef being sold as a slave in Mitzrayim, Avraham's descendants also had to suffer in Mitzrayim.

---

17. What happens when you wish one another, "Good morning," "Good night," "Have a nice day," "Mazel Tov," "*Gezuntheit*," or "*Shabat Shalom*", etc.?

(*Tosafos on Chullin 49a, Love Your Neighbor*)

18. Why is it most praiseworthy to begin each day with the song of praise "Adon Olam"?

(*Parpera'os L'Torah, Minhag Yisroel Torah*)

19. How is the human body prepared to heal the Bris Milah quickly?

(*Pathways to the Torah-Aish Hatorah*)

20. Why does reciting the Parshios of Korbanos protect us?

(*See Gemara Taanis 27b; Bereishis Rabbah 44:14*)

21. Who was the first person to give *Maaser* (tithe) to a Kohen?

(*Bereishis Rabbah 43:6, Bamidbar Rabbah 12:13*)

---

17. When you bless a Jew, Hashem blesses you, too! So be careful to wish your family and your fellow Jew, "Have a nice day," "Good luck," or "Be well!" Even saying, "G-d bless you!" after someone sneezes will bring you better health, as well. On the other hand, be careful never to curse another Jew, lest you suffer the consequences.

18. According to some, Avraham Avinu authored the inspiring poem and song *Adon Olam*. Saying it, evokes his merits. There is a *halacha* that every time we mention the Name of Hashem, we must have in mind that He is the Master of All, always! The recitation of *Adon Olam* in the morning with *kavanah* (concentration) can help a person fulfill this obligation all day long.

19. The body has a certain clotting agent that is found in an infant's blood on the eighth day than any other day.

20. Avraham asked Hashem, "How do I know that my descendants will survive if they sin?" Hashem replied, "They will bring Korbanos, and I will forgive them." Avraham then asked, "What about the generations after the Beis Hamikdash is destroyed?" Hashem answered, "If they say Korbanos, I will forgive and protect them as well."

21. Avraham gave ten percent of his riches as *ma'aser* to Shem, his *Rebbi* (also known as Malki Tzedek). Shem then taught Avraham the laws relating to the *Kohein Gadol*.

Answers&Facts

22. What did Avraham do with the money and gifts that Pharaoh gave him?

(Rashi to Parshas Chayei Sarah 25:6)

23. Why was the father of the Arabs called "Yishmael"?

(Pirkei d'Rabi Eliezer)

24. What is an example of a Jewish city that was so holy that it was even compared to Eretz Yisroel?

(Chazon Ish)

25. Why did the kings Pharaoh and Avimelech give away their daughters as maids to Sarah?

(Bereishis Rabbah 45:1, Rashi, Seder Hadoros, Pirkei d'Rabi Eliezer 26)

26. Why is the *berachah* of *"Refa'enu"* the eighth *berachah* of Shemoneh Esrei?

(Megillah 17b)

22. Avraham gave Pharaoh's gifts as an inheritance to Hagar's sons (who were, after all, technically Pharaoh's grandchildren). He himself did not want to benefit from such impure presents.

23. The name Yishmael was very appropriate for the ancestor of the Arabs. *"Yishmael"* means *"G-d will hear,"* meaning that in the end of the days, the Jews will call out to Hashem because of Arab persecution, and Hashem will hear their prayers and cries! Then He will take revenge upon the enemies of the Jews and save the Jewish nation from any further danger and harm.

24. Radin, the city of the great spiritual leader, the *Chofetz Chaim*, was considered to be a "Torah center for world Jewry." This could also be said of many other great cities, such as Vilna in the days of the *Vilna Gaon*. There's no doubt that the holiness of the great leaders of a city has a very positive effect on their place of residence.

25. Pharaoh saw that Hashem miraculously protected Avraham's family. Pharaoh told his daughter, Hagar, "You're better off being a maid in Sarah's home than being a princess in my palace." Avimelech felt that way, too.

26. The *Anshei K'nesses Hagedolah* instituted *"Refa'einu"* as the eighth blessing of *Shemoneh Esrei,* for it is a plea to heal those Jewish boys getting a *Bris Milah* on the eighth day of their lives.

27. Why did Sarah give her maid Hagar to Avraham as a wife?
(Yevamos 64a, Bereishis Rabbah 45:3)

28. What was the greatest *chessed* that Avraham performed?
(Olam Chessed Yibaneh 256, Love Your Neighbor)

29. For which *mitzvah* in particular did Hashem create the world?
(See Yirmiyah 33:25 and Nedarim 31b)

30. What did Hashem tell Avraham Avinu when he was bleeding from the Bris Milah?
(Tanchuma Parshas Vayeira)

31. Which *berachah* should one give his son on the day of his Bris Milah?
(Targum Yonasan Parshas Vayechi)

---

27. After Sarah was childless (though she had lived in Eretz Yisroel) for ten years, she gave Hagar to Avraham to marry, so he could have children. She knew that the pain she endured in having to share Avraham would serve as a *zechus* for her to have her own children.

28. Avraham's greatest *kindness* was not merely his physical hospitality and generosity, but rather his spiritual generosity (i.e., teaching *Avodas Hashem* to mankind). There is no greater act of kindness than to patiently guide your fellow Jew to believe in Hashem and fulfill His Torah.

29. The existence of the universe depends on certain *mitzvos*—particularly the *mitzvah* of Bris Milah.

30. When Avraham was bleeding from his *Bris Milah*, Hashem comforted him by saying that in the future when his descendants sin and deserve punishment, the blood of his *Bris Milah* would serve as a protector and guardian.

31. You should bless your son on the day of his *Bris Milah* that he become a *tzaddik* like Ephraim and Menashe, the first Jews born in *galus*, who remained steadfast in their observance of Torah morals—so much so that they were counted among the *tzaddikim* of the preceding generation!

Answers&Facts

32. Why should a father choose a great *tzaddik* to be his son's Mohel?

(Tochachos Chaim 55-Rav Chaim Falag'hi)

33. Which Jews will Avraham Avinu rescue from Gehinnom?

(Eiruvin 19a, Bereishis Rabbah 48:8)

34. Why does Hashem want us to cut off the Orlah (foreskin)?

(Bereishis Rabbah 46:4, Rambam, Abarbanel)

35. Why is it beneficial to have someone learn Torah next to the baby boy's crib the entire week before, or at least the night before, his Bris?

(Kav Hayashar chapter 73, Pele Yoetz)

32. The *Mohel* has a lifetime influence on the baby whom he has initiated into Judaism, so the *greater* the *tzaddik* that he himself is, the better start in life such a child acquires.

33. Avraham saves all descendants who kept the *mitzvah* of Bris Milah, by sparing them from *Gehinnom*. However, anyone who has defiled his *Milah* and has not kept it holy is given a new foreskin: Avraham takes the *Orlah* of newborn boys who have died without a *Bris* and puts it on them; afterwards, they fall into *Gehinnom*.

34. The foreskin is a useless piece of skin. (Many doctors and scientists agree that people are healthier without it!) By removing it, the Jew demonstrates that we don't need the extras in life: we need only what will help us fulfill G-d Almighty's bidding. Also, removing the *orlah* reduces one's physical and animalistic drives. Moreover, when one observes this command and cuts his very skin for Hashem, he thereby testifies to his faith in and love for Him.

35. If men study Torah near the newborn's crib during his first week in *Olam Hazeh*, the child will be endowed with great holiness that will help him to master Torah, guard his *Bris Milah*, and produce a cord of kindness that will enable him to assist many others in the world!

36.
Why must Eliyahu Hanavi attend every Bris Milah?

(Pirkei d'Rabi Eliezer, Avudraham, Zohar; see Pri Tzaddik)

37.
Why was it better that Yitzchak was born at Avraham's old age of 100?

(Zohar quoted in Sefer Habris, Bereishis Rabbah 46:2, Kol Yehudah, Rav Yitzchak Hutner zt"l)

38.
How is it possible that triplets are born and yet their Bris Milah must occur on three different days?

(Mishnah Shabbos 19:5)

39.
What great benefit does one gain from attending a Bris?

(Pirkei d'Rabi Eliezer, Kav Hayashar chapter 73)

40.
Can the Mohel carry the Milah knife on Shabbos to the place of the Bris?

(See Shabbos 130a)

---

36. Eliyahu criticized the Bnei Yisroel for not being faithful to Hashem. He said that the Jews are not careful with the *mitzvah* of *Bris Milah*. Because of this *Lashon Hara*, Hashem told him, "You must now travel throughout the world and see how My people perform *Bris Milah!*"

37. It was better that Yitzchak was born in Avraham's old age, because by that time, Avraham already had a *Bris Milah* and did not have a *Yetzer Hara*.

38. If triplets are born Friday evening at twilight time, the baby born right before sunset has his *Bris Milah* on the following Friday, the one born after dark has his *Bris Milah* on Shabbos, and the middle one born during *Bein Hashemashos* must wait until Sunday to have his *Bris Milah*.

39. One of the great rewards of attending a *Bris Milah* is *Mechilas Avonos*: one's sins are pardoned! This is because Eliyahu Hanavi refuses to be in the company of "sinners."

40. Rabbi Akiva does not allow the *Mohel* to carry his scalpel in a public domain on Shabbos to perform a *Bris Milah*. However, Rabbi Eliezer permitted it because he felt that carrying it publicly shows that *Bris Milah* is even greater than Shabbos! *Halachically* the *mohel* may not carry it on Shabbos.

Answers&Facts

41. What beautiful Minhag do some fathers have after the Bris Milah of their sons?

(Machzor Vitri, HaTorah V'haMitzvah)

42. Which *tzaddik* had his Bris Milah performed in secret?

(Tosafos on Avodah Zarah 10b, Toras Ha'olah)

43. Why weren't we just born without foreskins?

(Bereishis Rabbah 11:6, Sefer HaChinuch)

44. In what merit do the descendants of Yishmael reside in our homeland?

(Zohar; see Bach on Yoreh De'ah 260, Sh'lah)

45. Why do some fathers say Birchas Shehechiyanu at their son's Bris Milah?

(Vilna Gaon; see Bach on Yoreh De'ah 260)

---

41. Some have an amazing *minhag* to take ten men some time following the *Bris Milah* and dress the boy up in beautiful clothes. They then put a *sefer* (Torah book) on the baby and say, "This (boy) *shall fulfill what's written in this* (the Torah)." Then they put a quill into his hand and pray that the boy grow up to be a skilled writer of *Toras Hashem!*

42. At the time that Rabbi Yehuda the Prince, the editor of the *Mishnah*, was born, the Romans considered it a crime to perform Bris Milah, so his parents circumcised him in secret. It is well-known that one who is careful to keep his *Bris Milah* holy will receive much Torah as a reward. Rabbi Yehuda's parents risked their very lives in order to keep this wonderful *mitzvah!* Is it any wonder that he merited so much Torah?!

43. Man is not born perfect! He must strive to better his character. By perfecting his body through the act of *Bris Milah*, he demonstrates his desire to perfect himself.

44. One who is very careful with *Bris Milah* will merit living in Eretz Yisroel. Arabs that are the descendants of Yishmael have been doing circumcision for thousands of years, thus granting them some sort of merit to live there.

45. *Ashkenazim* have the custom not to say *shehechiyanu* at a *Bris Milah*, since the baby is in pain. Others do not recite this *berachah* because the

---

46. Which Mitzvah did Yehoshua Bin Nun's generation need to perform before entering Eretz Yisroel?

(Sefer Yehoshua 5:2; see Yevamos 75a)

47. When doesn't Eliyahu Hanavi stay for a Bris Milah?

(Zohar quoted in Sefer Habris)

48. Who was the Mohel for Avraham Avinu?

(Midrash Tanchuma 19, Bereishis Rabbah 49:2, The Midrash Says)

49. Why are even non-religious Jews careful in the performance of the *mitzvah* of Bris Milah?

(See Shabbos 130a)

50. What will happen to one who never had a Bris Milah?

(See Rambam and Raavad in Hilchos Milah 1:1)

---

mitzvah is not yet "completed" until the newly circumcised child successfully guards his *Milah* throughout his lifetime. Nonetheless, many *Sephardim* do make the *berachah* of *shehechiyanu* at the *Bris Milah* of their son (and likewise it is the general *minhag* of Eretz Yisroel). Incidentally there is a special prayer parents can say that the newborn baby keep his *Bris Milah* holy.

46. Yehoshua Bin Nun needed to circumcise the Bnei Yisroel before they could enter Eretz Yisroel.

47. If a chair is not designated, *"Zeh hakisei shel Eliyahu Hanavi, zachur latov"*, the prophet doesn't stay at the *Bris Milah*.

48. It was very hard for Avraham to do his own *Milah*. In fact, his hand was shaking! So Hashem Himself assisted him!

49. Any *mitzvah* that our ancestors did with joy, the Jews the world over still do with joy. Indeed, at the performance of a *Bris Milah* they celebrated - and so do we!

50. One who intentionally never underwent a *Bris Milah* will die younger than he might have died otherwise. Some say he will die before sixty and be cut off from *Olam Haba*, Heaven forbid!

Answers&Facts

Questions & Riddles

51. Why do Ashkenazim make a Shalom Zachor the first Friday night after the birth of a baby boy?
(Shach)

52. Why is the Orlah (foreskin) placed in a bowl of dirt after the Bris Milah?
(Zohar quoted in Sefer Habris)

53. Is it proper to dance at a Bris Milah?
(Pirkei d'Rabi Eliezer)

54. Why is the *mitzvah* of Milah even greater than the *mitzvos* of Shabbos and Tefillin?
(Nedarim 31b, Seichel Tov)

55. What skills should a true Talmid Chachom possess?
(See Chullin 9a)

56. Which famous people were born circumcised?
(Sotah 12a, Avos d'Rabi Nossan 2)

51. *Ashkenazim* make a *Shalom Zachor* to comfort the newborn boy for forgetting all the Torah he has learned in his mother's womb. However, they are happy that he can now labor and toil to regain the Torah that he has lost.

52. The foreskin is placed in dirt to recall that the Jewish people will increase like the dust.

53. It *is* proper to dance at the occasion of a *Bris Milah!*

54. Shabbos and *tefillin* are great signs of our connection to Hashem. However, *Bris Milah* is even greater, because it is fulfilled day and night whereas Shabbos is once a week and *tefillin* once a day.

55. A *talmid chachom* should know *Safrus, Shechita,* and *Milah*. Most importantly, he should have the skill to communicate to other people his fear of Hashem and his knowledge of the Torah.

56. Moshe Rabbeinu, Noach, Dovid Hamelech, Iyov, Adam Harishon, Yosef Hatzaddik, Yaakov Avinu, Shem, Yirmiyahu Hanavi and other *tzaddikim* were born "*Orlah*-less."

57. What happens to one who attends a Bris Milah and does not partake of the Seudah (feast) afterward?

(Tosafos on Pesachim 114a, Rema on Yoreh De'ah 265:12)

58. Why will many circumcised males be ineligible to partake of the Korbon Pesach when Moshiach comes?

(Chochmas Adam 149:17)

59. Avraham Avinu was scrupulous in keeping all the *mitzvos* that would later be given to his descendants on Har Sinai. So why didn't Avraham Avinu undergo Bris Milah before he was 99 years old?

(Midrash Tanchuma 17, Bereishis Rabbah 46:2, Vilna Gaon)

60. Why did Hashem compare us to the stars and the sand?

(Gemara Megillah 16a)

61. Why didn't Avraham return the youths of Sedom to their king?

(Eitz Yosef, Bereishis Rabbah 43:4)

---

57. One who doesn't partake of the *Seudas Mitzvah* is, G-d forbid, put in *cherem* (excommunication) by Heaven. It is as if he is not appreciative of the *mitzvah*.

58. When Moshiach comes, many people will be shocked to find out that their *Milah* was not done properly and that they can't fulfill and partake of the *Korban Pesach*, until their *Milah* is done properly.

59. Avraham wanted all future converts to feel comfortable, no matter how late in life they undergo their *Bris Milah*.

60. Hashem compared us to stars and to grains of sand, both of which are so numerous. This is also an allusion to the potential in every Jew to reach up to the heavens or to sink to the ground. It's all up to you!

61. Amazingly, Avraham returned all the Sedomites to the king of Sedom, except for the children. Avraham detained these youngsters in order to teach them the correct way to live and to save them from the bad influence of their elders. Avraham felt that he could work with the youth but not with the adults, since the adults were already set in their wicked ways.

Answers&Facts

62. Why did Avraham not want to leave his hometown?

(Bereishis Rabbah 37:7, see The Midrash Says)

63. What was Avraham's reaction when they wanted to crown him king for winning the war?

(Bereishis Rabbah 42:5)

64. Why did Hagar have a baby immediately, while Sarah had to wait 75 years until she had one?

(Bereishis Rabbah 45:4, Atarah L'melech)

65. How were Avraham and Sarah a great team?

(Bereishis Rabbah 39:14)

66. What type of behavior do many Arabs, the descendants of Yishmael, possess?

(Bereishis 16:12, Bereishis Rabbah 45:9; see Ramban 16:6)

---

62. Avraham didn't want to leave his home town so that people shouldn't suspect him of neglecting to do *Kibud Av* by not taking care of his father. So Hashem told him, "Don't worry: you are now exempt from this commandment, although no one else is."

63. After the battle of the kings, people wanted to crown Avraham the new king. They lifted him onto a large platform and said, "You are our king, you are our prince, you are our god." Avraham declined the honor and said, "The world is not lacking its King, and the world is not lacking its G-d." Avraham accepted only the honorary title "Prince of G-d Among Us."

64. The *Midrash* says, "Weeds grow rapidly, but wheat takes much toil to make it grow." Similarly, people need to do much more work to produce *tzaddikim,* and sometimes that work is in the form of *tefillah.* Rav Pam *zt"l* in *Atarah L'melech* writes that Sarah couldn't bear the pain of seeing other women without babies when she had a baby, so Hashem first gave all the other ladies a baby and only then He gave Sarah a baby.

65. Avraham converted the men, while Sarah converted the women.

66. Although many people are peaceful, others are violent, *Rachmana litzlan!* The Torah even predicts of Yishmael that "he will be a wild man; his hand will be against everyone."

67. Which world-famous Mohel performed over 100,000 Bris Milahs with legendary devotion and self-sacrifice?

(Otzar Habris)

68. What should be expected to happen when the kingdoms of the world fight with one another?

(Bereishis Rabbah 42:4)

67. The legendary Rabbi Yosseleh Weisberg, *zt"l*, who served as Chief Mohel in Yerushalayim for many decades, performed close to 100,000 Bris Milahs! *(I thank Hashem for the privilege of having been trained and certified as a Mohel by his son Rabbi Moshe Weisberg, shlita, who is the national supervisor of Mohelim in Eretz Yisroel.)*

68. Just as Avraham was elevated to great fame and fortune after the war against the kings, so too will the Jewish nation receive fame and fortune at the advent of Moshiach when the kingdoms of the world are fighting among themselves!

Dedicated in loving memory of
HACHAM BINYAMIN BEN SARAH SERUYA ZT"L
by an anonymous sponsor

Answers&Facts

פרשת וירא

1. Why were the three angels who visited Avraham Avinu – Michoel, Gavriel and Refael – disguised as a sailor, a baker, and an Arab?

   (Bereishis Rabbah 48:9, Maayanah Shel Torah)

2. Why did all the sick people throughout the world become healed at the time of Yitzchak's birth?

   (Bereishis Rabbah 53:8, Atarah L'melech-Rav Avraham Pam zt"l)

fUNdamental Answers!

"יגעתי ומצאתי!"

("I worked on these questions, and I found these answers!")

1. Planet Earth is comprised of three parts: water, desert, and inhabited land *(Talmud)*. Hashem sent Avraham angels in disguise, representing each area of the world, to visit him after his *Bris Milah*. This implied that the whole world was made for Avraham and his descendants!

2. When Sarah prayed for her needs, she always prayed for others who were in need as well. She prayed for the childless, the blind, the lame, the mentally deficient, etc. Thus, when her prayers were answered, so too were those many others healed as well!

3. Why did Avraham ask his friends, Aner, Eshkol, and Mamrei, for their opinions about Bris Milah if Hashem had already ordered him to perform the Bris Milah?

(Rambam Hilchos Eivel 14:6)

4. Which *mitzvah* mentioned in Parshas Vayeira is a *segulah* for having children?

(Rabbeinu Bachya in Kad Hakemach)

5. How can a penniless person still do the great *mitzvah* of *tzedakah* (charity)?

(Rambam Hilchos Matnos Aniyim 10:7)

6. Which Mitzvah earns a greater reward: a) giving visitors food, b) giving guests drinks, or c) escorting one's company as they leave?

(Rambam Hilchos Eivel 14:2)

7. How is it possible to visit the sick, yet not fulfill the *mitzvah* of Bikur Cholim?

(Rambam Hilchos Eivel 14:6)

3. Avraham wasn't asking his friends if he should undergo *Bris Milah*. He was simply asking if he should do it privately or publicly. One reason he thought not to publicize it was so no enemy should attack him during his recuperating time.

4. Inviting (poor) guests is a great *segulah* for having children. Right after Avraham welcomed the wayfarers, he fathered a son. Similarly, the Shunamite woman bore a righteous son named Chavakuk after she had been Elisha's hostess.

5. If you get a poor person a job, it's considered like giving *tzedakah*, in the greatest way possible, since you put him "back on his feet" in a dignified way!

6. Escorting guests out, after their stay in your house, is even greater than welcoming them and serving them nourishment! People feel very important when you take your time to escort them (even if you live on an upper floor).

7. Besides tending to the needs of the ill and cheering them up, part of the *mitzvah* of *Bikur Cholim* is to pray for the ill person to recover.

8. Why was Sarah punished for laughing when the guests blessed her to have a son?
(Ramban)

9. Why aren't women accepted as witnesses in a Jewish court?
(Chizkuni)

10. Why was "Yitzchak" called that name?
(Bereishis Rabbah 53:7, The Beginning)

11. Why did Avraham call himself "dust and ashes"?
(Rashi to Chullin 89a, Bereishis Rabbah 49:11)

12. What constitutes the greatest service to Hashem?
(Beis Yosef Hilchos Taanis Siman 571)

---

8. Sarah was punished for laughing when she was blessed to bear a son. She should have said, "Amein, kein yehi ratzon!" as a sign of Bitachon (faith in Hashem) and hope. Sarah was therefore punished by not seeing her son married during her lifetime.

9. Sarah denied laughing when Hashem confronted her. Women are very emotional and are therefore not allowed to testify in a Jewish court, lest they follow their emotions instead of their intellect.

10. Not only was 'Yitzchak' (literally: he will laugh) called that name because people laughed in joy and surprise over his supernatural birth, but his name also implied that at the end of Galus it will be our nation who will laugh! The name also alludes to Yitzchak's parents, to Mattan Torah, and to Bris Milah: י is begematria 10, alluding to their desire that the Bnei Yisroel accept the Ten Commandments on Har Sinai; צ is 90, which refers to Sarah who gave birth to him at 90 years of age; ח is 8, which refers to his being the first person to have a Bris Milah on the eighth day; ק is 100, which alludes to Avraham's age at his son's birth.

11. Avraham referred to himself as dust and ashes because if Nimrod's attempt at burning him would have succeeded, he would have become ashes, and had he lost the war against the kings, he would have become dust. Great people don't forget the kindnesses which Hashem has done with them.

12. THE GREATEST SERVICE TO HASHEM IS TO EDUCATE OUR YOUTH IN THE WAYS OF THE TORAH! (Maran Beis Yosef) That is the main reason why Hashem loved Avraham so much. Avraham commanded his children to live in righteousness and justice. A proof of this principle may be found in Pirkei Avos where the Tannaim mention their greatest principles in life. Indeed, this principle is mentioned in the very first Mishnah, "The Anshei Ke'nesses Hagedolah said, '...and establish many students!' "

Answers&Facts

---

13. Under what circumstances would Avraham charge a lot of money for his hospitality?
(Pesikta, Bereishis Rabbah 49:4)

14. How do we see that we must always run to do *mitzvos*?
(Seichel Tov, Haamek Davar, Berachos 6b; see Bava Metzia 33a)

15. Which *mitzvah* should we be most careful to do?
(Tur Yoreh De'ah 247, Rambam Hilchos Matnos Aniyim 10:1; see Peah 1:1)

16. Which of Sedom's sins really brought about their doom?
(Yechezkel 16:49, Pirkei d'Rabi Eliezer 25)

17. Which *mitzvah* do many Gedolim do before praying?
(Tur Yoreh De'ah 249:19)

---

13. If Avraham's guests refused to thank Hashem for the food that he served them, he would charge them the cost of these expensive meals served in the desert.

14. Even when Avraham was recovering from his painful *Bris Milah*, he hastened to welcome the strangers. Avraham told Sarah to rush and prepare fresh food for his guests. Then he *ran* to the guests to greet them and feed them. As we clearly see, all the actions of *tzaddikim* are done quickly. *Zerizus* is indeed a *tzaddik's* hallmark.

15. The *mitzvas asei* (positive commandment) that is most important to fulfill is giving *tzedakah* all the time! A dime or a quarter might seem insignificant, but that's not really so. A Jew should not let a day go by without doing the *mitzvah* of *tzedakah*. If he doesn't have resources, he should try to fundraise for the needy by soliciting from the wealthy.

16. In the wicked city of Sedom, *one* kind girl gave a poor man a loaf of bread, and she was tortured to death for this "crime". Lot's daughter, Plotis, too, was taken out to be burned for having given a poor man some bread. It's quite obvious that Sedom did not want to support the poor lest they take away their money. Hashem, Who is the Ultimate Benefactor, had to eradicate Sedom, the City of Selfishness!

17. Many *Gedolim* give *tzedakah* before every *tefillah*. When Hashem sees that you have pity on others, He has more pity on you.

---

18. Why did Lot's wife turn into a pillar of salt?

(Bereishis Rabbah 51:5, Yalkut Reuveini)

19. What did Avraham pray for as he was running to greet the passersby?

(Bechor Shor)

20. Why didn't Hashem want Lot and his wife to look back at Sedom's destruction?

(The Beginning)

21. What were the ten biggest tests that Hashem gave Avraham Avinu?

(Pirkei Avos 5:3, Avos d'Rabi Nosson 33, Rabbeinu Yonah, Rashi, Rambam on Pirkei Avos)

---

18. Ivris, Lot's wife, was so miserly and stingy that she wouldn't even give the guests salt for their food. Furthermore, she tried to have her angelic guests killed by loudly informing the inhabitants of Sedom that she needed salt for her "GUESTS".

19. Avraham prayed that the guests would not leave until he had successfully fulfilled the *mitzvah* of *Hachnosas Orchim!*

20. Lot's wife also deserved to be punished along with Sedom. She should not have looked at them suffer, because she was no better than they were. Also Hashem did not want Lot's family to "look back" and regret having to leave that sinful place.

21. Avraham's 10 most famous tests and challenges were (according to one opinion):
1. He chose death by fire to defend Hashem's honor, thereby defying *avodah zarah*
2. He left his homeland and family to go to an unknown destination—*Eretz Cana'an*
3. He arove there at a time of famine
4. Sarah was kidnapped by Pharaoh and Avimelech
5. Avraham had to rescue Lot, his nephew, through waging war;
6. Sarah was childless, and Avraham thus had to marry Hagar;
7. Avraham had to send Yishmael away for being wicked;
8. Avraham had to have his *Bris Milah* surgery at age 99;
9. *Akeidas Yitzchak:* Avraham had to be willing to sacrifice his greatest love, his son, to Hashem;
10. Sarah passed away before Avraham had acquired a burial place for her. (Some commentaries include the *Bris Bein Habesarim*, in which Avraham envisioned his descendants suffering in Galus, as one of the ten most challenging tests.) The tests were to see if he had faith in Hashem or if he would doubt Him. The tests also proved why Hashem chose Avraham as His favorite, to make him the patriarch of His Chosen People.

Answers&Facts

22. Which *mitzvah* can save a person from Gehinnom?

(Zohar, Nedarim 40a)

23. Why did Hashem let King Avimelech take Sarah?

(The Beginning)

24. How did Hashem show the world that the elderly couple Avraham and Sarah really had their own baby in their senior years?

(Bava Metzia 87a, Bereishis Rabbah 53:9, Eitz Yosef)

25. Are the remains of Lot's wife visible nowadays?

(Gemara Berachos 54b, Seder Hadoros 2047, Shulchan Aruch Orach Chaim 8)

26. How do we know that *tzaddikim* talk a little and do a lot?

(Bava Metzia 87a)

---

22. Many *mitzvos* can save a person from *Gehinnom*. For example, the *mitzvah* of having a properly done *Bris Milah* will save one from *Gehinnom*! Also visiting the sick will spare one from *Gehinnom*! Most important, the diligent learning of *Mishnayos* can spare one from *Gehinnom*!

23. Sarah's capture by Avimelech, and her subsequent riches, both serve as a reminder to us that the Jews will outlast all their enemies and that Hashem will richly reward His people.

24. Lest cynical people suspect that Yitzchak was an adopted baby, Hashem made him appear as if he were Avraham's identical twin. Then the aristocratic and noble women who had joined the feast became unable to nurse their own babies because their milk had suddenly dried up, so they desperately asked Sarah to nurse their babies for them. Miraculously, she was able to nurture all of them.

25. According to many authorities, Lot's wife is still visible today in Sedom. (Why, we believe we even have a picture of her salt-stone pillar in our slide show, "TorahShows," Vol. I!)

26. Avraham originally offered *matzah* but ended up serving a meat meal even more exquisite than one that King Solomon might offer. On the other hand, many other people "offer the world" but don't do a thing!

27. Why did the Chofetz Chaim often sing Shalom Aleichem *during* the Friday-night Shabbos Seudah rather than *before* the meal, as is commonly done?

(Torah L'daas)

28. How did Avraham find the special Me'aras Hamachpeilah?

(Pirkei d'Rabi Eliezer 36, The Midrash Says)

29. Who was one of the world's first terrorists?

(Bereishis Rabbah 53:11; see Maayan Hayeshuah)

30. Which city in Israel had volcanic eruptions and earthquakes for 25 years in order to shake the people into doing Teshuvah?

(Bereishis Rabbah 49:6, Tanchuma 10)

31. Who are the three people who were considered outcasts from Judaism and whose descendants still despise the Jews today?

(Chesronei HaShas – Sanhedrin)

---

27. Sometimes the *Chofetz Chaim* sang *"Shalom Aleichem"* during the meal so that his hungry guests got to eat sooner.

28. When a calf ran away, Avraham followed it into the *Me'aras Hamachpeilah*, where Adam and Chava were buried. This cave was chosen as the burial site for the *Avos*, since it is appropriate that Adam and Chava be buried along with their greatest descendants.

29. Like a typical Arab terrorist *yemach shemo*, Yishmael tried to kill Yitzchak.

30. Sedom had volcanic eruptions and earthquakes for many years in order to shake them up to do *teshuvah*. Guess what? They didn't get the message.

31. Timnah, Yishmael, and Yeshu were all rejected from joining our people. Their spiritual descendants antagonize us even today: Amalek, and some of the Arab world, and some of the followers of Yeshu.

Answers&Facts

32. How do we know that it is important to welcome guests even if your house is a mess?
(Radak, see Peah 7:4)

33. Which person mentioned in Parshas Vayeira suffered from an Ayin Hara?
(Rashi to 16:5 and 21:14)

34. How did Avraham test the character of Yishmael's wives, Meriva and Fatima?
(Seder Hadoros)

35. Why did Hashem let the wicked Yishmael survive severe thirst if his descendants would later kill Jews by thirst?
(Rashi, Bereishis Rabbah 53:19, Tosafos on Rosh Hashanah 16b)

32. Many people refuse to welcome guests if their house is messy. They're being foolish, because Hashem gave us the *mitzvah* of *Hachnosas Orchim*, and the poor guests just want shelter. They don't care how fancy the house looks. The *Torah* even tells us to give incomplete grape clusters (known as *Olelef*) to the poor to remind us that they need food and that they don't care how perfect it looks.

33. Hagar miscarried her first baby because of *Ayin Hara*, since she bragged that she was more special than Sarah.

34. Many years after Yishmael was sent away, Avraham went to visit him, but he wasn't there. So Avraham tested his daughter-in-law by asking for some hospitality, while concealing his identity. When she angrily refused, Avraham left a hint for Yishmael to exchange her for a more compassionate wife, which is what he did. The next time he visited, Avraham was pleased at the peace and tranquillity in Yishmael's home, and he prayed to Hashem to fill Yishmael's house with everything good.

35. At the age of 13, Yishmael did not commit the serious sins that his descendants would later perform, and therefore his prayer for survival was answered: they found water and he lived. [Interestingly, Arabs still "pray" today, so our *tefillah* must overpower theirs.]

36. In whose merit did the Bnei Yisroel get the *Mann*, the *Be'er*, and the *Ananei Hakavod* during their forty-year journey through the desert?

(Maharsha on Bava Metzia 86a, Bereishis Rabbah 48:12)

37. Why did Avraham not want to discuss with Sarah his future plans for the *Akeidah*?

(Tanchuma)

38. Whose home was similar to Avraham's in that it had doors on all four sides?

(Avos d'Rabi Nosson)

39. Why are the Jews referred to as "A totally righteous nation" (Yeshayah 60:21)?

(Zohar 2:23)

---

36. The delicious *Mann*, miraculous Be'er, and the *Ananei hakovod* super-miraculous protection that the Bnei Yisroel received in the desert came about in great part because of the merit of Avraham Avinu's hospitality and generosity. (These miracles also occurred in the respective merits of Moshe, Aharon, and Miriam.)

37. Avraham didn't tell Sarah of his plans for sacrificing Yitzchak at the *Akeidah*, lest she object and convince him to change his mind. So he left early, while she was yet sleeping. She woke up and assumed that Avraham had taken Yitzchak to *yeshivah*. But the Satan scared her to death by dramatizing the actual sacrificing of Yitzchak.

38. The house of the famous Iyov had entrances on all four sides so that he could welcome guests. (After all, according to many opinions, the righteous Iyov was Avraham's great-nephew!)

39. Yeshaya Hanavi called the Jews "the all-righteous nation," since they virtually all undergo *Bris Milah*. (Unfortunately, there are still many Jews from the former Soviet Union who still don't comprehend the significance of this major *mitzvah*.) Lehavdil, the Arabs perform *Kerisas Haorlah* that has no *Kedushas Bris Milah*.

Answers&Facts

40. What did Avraham tell the angel at the *Akeidah*?

(Yalkut Shimoni, Tanchuma, Pesikta)

41. Why did the ram keep getting stuck in the thicket?

(Yerushalmi Taanis 2:4)

42. How did the Satan try to prevent Akeidas Yitzchak?

(Seder Hadoros 2084)

43. Why do we ask Hashem (during the conclusion of the Amidah) to "make us like the dust"?

(Tosafos on Berachos 17a)

40. Avraham insisted to the angel who told him not to sacrifice Yitzchak that he wanted only Hashem to inform him. Then Hashem opened the skies and said, "I insist." Then Avraham declared, "I want this always to be a defense for my descendants so that they may endure." Hashem retorted, "On *Rosh Hashanah,* let them blow the *shofar* made from a ram to recall this unparalleled merit so that it may atone for their sins and save them."

41. The ram (which by the way was destined for this purpose from the creation of the world) kept getting its horns stuck in a thicket; finally Avraham freed it. So too, the Jews have gotten stuck time after time in their different sins and their various exiles, but eventually Hashem will free them!

42. The Satan disguised himself as a humble, wise man. Indeed, he criticized Avraham for such an act of bloodshed. Avraham shouted at him! Then the Satan disguised himself as a handsome young man, and went over to Yitzchak, saying, "Your father is insane to attempt to kill you." Avraham told Yitzchak, "Ignore him; he is the Satan, and he is trying to make you disobey the orders of Hashem." Avraham screamed at that "man". The Satan then changed himself into a raging river and threatened to drown them both. Avraham was shocked because he knew that there was never a river there. He told Yitzchak, "It's the Satan again." Avraham screamed at the Satan and cried out to Hashem, "May Hashem shout at you, Satan; we are going to do Hashem's *mitzvos!*" The Satan became scared of Avraham's warning, and he stopped bothering them. The river dried up instantly. Avraham then hid Yitzchak as he was setting up the altar so that the Satan shouldn't throw a rock at him and cause him a *mum* (disqualifying defect). We see from here that the Satan invents ploys and illusions to try to make people sin. Avraham's greatness lay in his ability to go against the fiber of his being in order to fulfill the will of Hashem. He defied his nature of loving kindness in order to be "cruel" by attempting to kill his beloved and precious son.

43. We ask Hashem to make us as numerous as the dust of the earth. Also we are reminded that we shouldn't care about receiving honor from people.

44. Why did Avraham not want Eliezer or Yishmael to be present at the Akeidah?

(Rabbeinu Bachya, Malbim)

45. Why did the angel call Avraham's name twice: "Avraham, Avraham..."?

(Rashi, Bereishis Rabbah 56:7, Kli Yakar)

46. How do we see that we must chase out negative influences from our homes?

(Shemos Rabbah 1:1)

47. How did Lot's wife's name, "Ivris," fit her character?

(Seder Hadoros)

48. Why was Lot considered a *rasha* for moving to Sedom, thereby endangering himself?

(Yoma 38b, Bereishis Rabbah 50:11, The Midrash Says)

---

44. Avraham did not want Yishmael or Eliezer present at the actual *Akeidah* lest they stop him or give the *mitzvah* an "*Ayin Hara*."

45. The angel called Avraham's name twice. Repeating one's name shows endearment. Also, Avraham was concentrating so hard on the *mitzvah* that he didn't hear the angel call him the first time.

46. Hashem told Avraham to follow Sarah's command "*Gareish es ha'amah hazos,*" to banish Hagar, because her son was a bad influence on Yitzchak! Similarly, we must remove any *treife* media from the home.

47. Some say that Lot's wife's name was Ivris, meaning "blind," because she was blind to the suffering of others. Her stone heart eventually became a stone body! Actually, the attackers in Sedom were also blinded as a clear indication of their blindness to the pain of others. Regarding Moshe, the Torah states, "he saw the suffering of the Jews." It takes a great person to sympathize with others and take action to help the unfortunate.

48. Lot wanted to live in Sedom so that he could imitate their bad behavior. For moving into an evil neighborhood, one is called a *rasha*! A person is influenced by his surrounding society and culture! Eventually, Lot became perverted just like the people of Sedom, for he committed incest with his daughters. Lot also wanted to avoid Avraham's company, because compared to this saint he appeared wicked, whereas compared to the people of Sedom, he appeared righteous. Our Rabbis advise us that it's better to be the tail of a lion than the head of a fox (*Pirkei Avos* 4:15).

Answers&Facts

---

49. Where did Avraham tell Sarah he wished to take Yitzchak, although he was really heading for the site of the *Akeidah*?

(Midrash Tanchuma 22)

50. Where did the *millions of Jewish martyrs* of the Crusades, Spanish Inquisition, and the Holocaust obtain the courage to die "*Al Kiddush Hashem*"?

(Rav Chaim Volozhiner in Ruach Chaim 5:3, Tosafos Yom-Tov, Apiryon, Sfas Emes)

51. How old was Yishmael when he was banished from Avraham's home?

(Bereishis Rabbah 48:9)

52. Why did the generous Avraham give Yishmael only bread and a jug of water when he sent him away?

(Bereishis Rabbah 53:3, Eitz Yosef)

---

49. Avraham told Sarah that he had recognized Hashem at the age of three. But he felt that Yitzchak still had not received enough *Chinuch* even at 37. Therefore, he wanted to send him to a great *yeshivah*. Sarah agreed and said, "Go in peace!"

50. Our ancestors Avraham and Yitzchak showed total devotion to Hashem by their willingness to sacrifice everything they had to Hashem. Obviously, that same faith and dedication exist as part of the chemistry of the Jewish people as well.

51. Yishmael was 37 when he was expelled from Avraham's home. Now let's contrast our forefather with that of the Yishmaelites (Arabs). Yitzchak at 37 was being prepared to die for Hashem's honor; Yishmael at 37 was trying to kill Yitzchak!

52. Although Avraham was always generous to all wayfarers, when he banished his wayward son Yishmael from his home, he gave him only a jug of water as an indication that not only was he not destined to be his heir, but he also was not even worthy of much care.

---

53. Why did Hashem make the weather abnormally hot while Avraham was recuperating from his *Bris Milah?*

(Rashi, Bereishis Rabbah 48:8)

54. How do we know that when you mention a *tzaddik's* name, you should also bless him?

(Bereishis Rabbah 49:1)

55. Why were ashes placed on the foreheads of leading Rabbis when they were fasting for rain during a time of drought?

(Taanis 16a, Bereishis Rabbah 49:11)

56. From where do we see the importance of a *Minyan?*

(Bereishis Rabbah 49:13)

57. Why did Lot's daughters sin by committing incest?

(Bereishis Rabbah 51:8,10)

---

53. Heat has a healing quality. In addition, Hashem did not want the whole world to enjoy themselves when such a *tzaddik* was in pain. Also Hashem didn't want Avraham to trouble himself to invite guests when his body needed rest.

54. When Hashem mentioned Avraham's name, to tell him what was about to happen to Sedom, He said, "I have shown Avraham both *Mattan Torah*, and Gehinnom; should I not reveal to my friend Avraham what will happen to Sedom? *And* Avraham will become a great nation!" We see from here that when you mention the name of a *tzaddik* you should give him a *berachah* at the same time. (Some have the custom to say, "...*zul zein gezunt un shtark.*")

55. In order to evoke mercy on behalf of the endangered Jews, suffering from a drought, ashes were placed on the leaders' heads to recall the merit that Avraham was willing to be burned to ashes for Hashem's honor.

56. Even the wicked city of Sedom would have been spared much destruction had there been ten *tzaddikim* there.

57. Lot's daughters honestly thought that the world was destroyed again. They figured that the *Mabul* destroyed the world through water, and now the destruction was coming through fire. They thought that it was up to them to ensure that humanity would survive. Lot's oldest daughter's **intention was for Heaven**, and therefore Moshiach will come from her. Moshiach will also save the world from destruction and bring the world to perfection.

Answers&Facts

58. What happened to the gentile infants whom Sarah Imeinu nursed?

(Bereishis Rabbah 53:9)

59. Why was Avraham originally going to let Yitzchak marry a daughter of Aner, Eshkol, or Mamrei?

(Bereishis Rabbah 57:3)

60. Which "saying" helps you find something that you are missing?

(Bereishis Rabbah 53:19)

61. What did Avraham ask Hashem after the *Akeidah?*

(Bereishis Rabbah 57:4, Eitz Yosef, Bereishis Rabbah 56:11)

62. Why did Avraham move southward in Cana'an after the destruction of Sedom?

(Bereishis Rabbah 52:3,4)

58. All the infants who nursed from the *tzaddeikes* Sarah merited greatness. Many later converted to Judaism. (Antoninus, a Roman emperor, also converted as a result of being nursed by Rabbi Yehuda HaNasi's mother.)

59. Many of Avraham's friends had righteous daughters, but right after the *Akeidah*, Avraham was informed through *Ruach Hakodesh* that Yitzchak's destined wife had just been born.

60. There is a tradition that if you recite the following quotation, you will find what you are missing: *"Rabbi Binyamin said: 'Everyone is blind until Hashem opens their eyes!'"* One may learn this lesson from the desperate Hagar's search for water to save her dying son in the desert; after she prayed, she realized that the water was right there in front of her eyes!

61. After the extremely intense test of the *Akeida*, Avraham asked that he not be given the test of suffering. Instead, it was given to Iyov, his great nephew.

62. Avraham had to move so that people would not confuse him with his nephew, Lot, who was guilty of immorality. The Torah says, "And you should be clean before Hashem and the Jews."

63.
Hashem loves the *mitzvah* of *Bikur Cholim*. Why isn't it an explicit *mitzvah* in the Torah?

(Tochachos Mussar; see Igros Moshe Yoreh De'ah 1:223)

64.
What did Hashem tie in heaven while Avraham tied Yitzchak on earth?

(Bereishis Rabbah 56:5)

---

63. An ill person once complained that he was receiving almost no visitors. He claimed that it caused him much resentment and hatred toward his neighbors. Perhaps, the reason that *Bikur Cholim* is not an explicit commandment in the *Torah Shebiksav* is because had it been so, the punishment would have been very great for those who don't make it their business to visit the sick.

64. When Avraham bound Yitzchak on the altar, Hashem simultaneously bound the angels of the nations above that they not harm the Jews. Once the Jews sinned in the days of Yirmiyahu, however, those angels were untied. May the enemies of Am Yisroel be tied up again, and may Moshiach come and save the Jews from harmful enemies soon! *Amein.*

Dedicated Le'ilui Nishmat
OUR GREAT UNCLE, MOSHE BEN YOSEF & FARHAH BIBI A"H
AND OUR AUNT REBECCA (MASLATON) BIBI A"H
by Victor Bibi

פרשת חיי שרה

1. How do we see that we should greet each other happily even if we are not really in the mood to do so?

(Midrash Hagadol 28:18)

2. How do we see that before one righteous person passes away, another one is born?

(Seforno, Yoma 38b, Bereishis Rabbah 58:2, Koheles Rabbah 1:10, Rabbeinu Bachya)

fUndamental Answers!

"יגעתי ומצאתי!"

("I worked on these questions, and I found these answers!")

1. The *Gemara* (*Berachos* 17a) tells us that Rabban Yochanan Ben Zakai was always the first one to greet everyone. Greeting others sincerely is a wonderful social gesture, and a good habit to develop. Even when Avraham's beloved wife passed away, he made sure to be sensitive to the feelings of others, and he politely bowed in respect to the people of Cheis! Imagine how much pain Avraham was in, but he nevertheless thought of others. Some people blame their inappropriate behavior on their having "a bad day", but not Avraham Avinu.

2. When the sun sets in one part of the world, it actually rises in a different part. Similarly, the same day the righteous Sarah departed from the world, the righteous Rivkah entered the world! Did you know that Rabbi Yehuda Hanasi, was born the very day on which Rabbi Akiva passed away?! When Rebbi passed away, Rav Ada

Questions & Riddles

3. Why did Esther Hamalka rule over "127" countries?
(Bereishis Rabbah 58:3, Esther Rabbasi 1:8, S'fas Emes)

4. Why didn't Chava want Sarah Imeinu buried next to her in the Me'aras Hamachpelah?
(Zohar quoted in Shaarei Aharon 128)

5. Why did the Satan want Sarah Imeinu to die right after Akeidas Yitzchak?
(Rabbeinu Yonah in Pirkei Avos, Kehilas Yitzchak)

6. How did the *mitzvah* of *netilas yadayim* (washing the hands) save Eliezer's life?
(Baal HaTurim 54:33; see Yalkut Shimoni 109)

bar Ahava was born. The Midrash enumerates other such incidents, as well. After the many losses of *Gedolei Yisroel* in our times, who knows which children will grow to fill their places?

3. Esther's rulership over 127 lands was directly connected to Sarah Imeinu's 127 years of life. You see, every second of Sarah's life earned her a family of Jewish descendants, and each hour, day, month, and year earned her more and more cities, states, and countries of Jewish descendants! Everything people do today directly affects their future offspring.

4. Chavah felt ashamed of herself for having brought death to mankind. When Avraham came to bury Sarah, Adam and Chava rose up to leave. They said, "We are eternally ashamed before Hashem because of our sin. Now you want to add to our pain by having our actions compared to your great deeds." Avraham promised to pray to Hashem that Adam not be shamed. Only then did Adam and Chava agree to be put to rest again.

5. The Satan tried so very hard to prevent the monumental *Akeida*. When he saw that there was no stopping Avraham and Yitzchak, he tried to kill Sarah and cause Avraham to regret having done such an act. But Avraham would not let himself be depressed. He was proud of and happy about his monumental accomplishment. Thus he didn't cry too much when Sarah died so that no one should say he was sad that he performed the *Akeida*!

6. Besuel and Lavan tried poisoning Eliezer's food, so that they could rob all the riches. But when Eliezer got up to wash before the meal, an angel switched his plate with that of Besuel's. They all ate, but it was *Besuel* who did not wake up the next morning!

7. Which twelve people entered Gan Eden (Paradise) alive?

(Kallah Rabbasi 5)

8. How old was Rivkah when she got married?

(See Yevamos 61b; Seder Olam, Maseches Sofrim, Haamek Davar)

9. Why did Eliezer give Rivkah new clothes?

(Maharil Diskin)

10. How do we know that when we pray we should tilt our head downwards and close our eyes?

(Tzror Hamor quoted in Shaarei Aharon 24)

11. When did a candle ignite "by itself"?

(Targum Yonasan ben Uziel; see Bereishis Rabbah 60:16)

12. How do we see that when a wicked person utters a blessing, it becomes a curse?

(Midrash Hacheifetz quoted in Shaarei Aharon 24:60)

---

7. The twelve people known to have entered Gan Eden alive are: Chanoch, Sarah Imeinu, Eliezer-Eved Avraham, Serach Bas Asher, Basya-Bas Pharaoh, Chiram, Eved Melech Kushi, Eliyahu Hanavi, Moshiach, Yaavetz - Rabbi Yehudah Hanasi's grandson, and Rabbi Yehoshua Ben Levi. Each one possessed a most extraordinary merit.

8. Some say Rivkah married at the age of three, and some say she was fourteen. Regardless, people were far more mature in the olden days.

9. Eliezer immediately gave Rivkah new clothes in case her old ones had *shatnez* in them.

10. As Rivkah was coming to Yitzchak, he was busy praying with his head downward and his hands raised heavenward. When he finished he had to lift up his head and open his eyes in order to see her. After all, when one prays, he must be concious that the *Shechinah* (Divine Presence) is before him, and it's respectful to close one's eyes and keep the head bowed in respect.

11. When Rivkah entered Sarah's house, the Shabbos candles (which used to miraculously stay burning from Friday to Friday) that went out after Sarah's passing, suddenly lit again, as if "on its own".

12. Lavan's family "blessed" Rivkah to have many offspring, saying, "You should increase to become 20,000,000. However, the wicked's blessing is

13. Which *tzadikim* in our time never leave Eretz Yisroel, even for a short visit, thus emulating Yitzchak Avinu?

(Eretz Avoseinu)

14. How do we know that Lavan had *chutzpah* (audacity)?

(See Rashi on 24:50)

15. How many trips did Rivkah make back and forth from the well to get drink for Eliezer's convoy?

(The Beginning, Tzror Hamor quoted in Shaarei Aharon; see Hoshea 9:14)

16. What did all the *goyim* say when Avraham Avinu passed away?

(See Bava Basra 91a)

---

really a curse, so she was barren for many years, except for one pregnancy in which she was carrying twins. Hashem did not want her wicked relatives to take the credit of Rivkah having many children, so she gave birth, only after Yitzchak the *tzaddik* prayed for her.

13. There are Jews in Israel who they refuse to go out of the holy land of Eretz Yisroel, even for a brief moment, due to their deep love for the holy land. They learn this from Yitzchak Avinu, who never left Eretz Yisroel, even when there was a severe drought.

14. When Eliezer proposed Rivkah's *shidduch* to Besuel, it was Lavan, his son, who voiced his opinion before his father. He should have known that it is not *derech eretz* for a son to speak up before his father does.

15. One camel drinks more than thirty men. It was startling for Rivkah to undertake feeding both the *minyan* of travellers, plus their camels. She had to fill up the buckets of water hundreds of times. Many people of great spirit do things that sometimes appear "insane" to ordinary folks. This was proof of the young Rivkah's greatness and strength. When one does far more than he is asked he proves his greatness.

16. Avraham Avinu was esteemed by the entire world, as the Prince of G-d! Avraham Avinu's passing impacted the whole world. All the great dignitaries of the day stood in a line, and proclaimed, *"Woe to the world that has lost its leader and woe to the ship that has lost its captain!"*

17. Is it better to pray at the time of "Mincha Gedolah" (earlier in the day, after 12:30 approx.) or at the time of "Mincha Ketanah" (later in the day, after 3:30 approx.)?

(Shulchan Aruch Orach Chaim 233:1)

18. Why did Hagar change her name to "Keturah"?

(Zohar 133b, Bereishis Rabbah 61:4, Yalkut Iyov)

19. How did Avraham Avinu change the color of the world?

(Maharsha on Bava Metzia 87a)

20. Why did Rivkah have to grow up like a "rose among thorns"?

(Shir Hashirim Rabbah 2:5, Bereishis Rabbah 63:4, Taam V'daas)

---

17. Although it is usually best to do a *mitzvah* as soon as possible, it is better to pray Mincha later in the afternoon (after approx. 3:30 pm, depending on the time of the year). The reason for this is because the *Korban Tamid* of the afternoon, which *Mincha* corresponds to, was usually sacrificed in the latter part of the afternoon. Some places pray earlier, just so that people don't forget to pray before sundown.

18. Hagar did complete *Teshuvah* after she returned to her father Pharaoh's home. She rejected *avodah zarah,* once and for all. Hagar changed her name, just as any genuine *ba'alas teshuvah* would. *Ketores* was the most pleasing offering in the Beis Hamikdash. By taking the name Keturah, she implied that *Teshuvah* turns sins into merits which are pleasing like the *ketores*. Therefore, Avraham remarried her. Others say that Ketura was a third wife: Sarah came from Shem, Ketura came from Yefes, and Hagar came from Cham.

19. Before the times of Avraham Avinu, old people did not get gray or white hair. But Avraham felt that there was a need to change elderly people's appearances so that they should receive more respect. So he prayed to Hashem, and from then on, older people started having white hair. This also reminded them to purify their ways while they were still in this world; white symbolizing cleanliness from sin.

20. We find many righteous people who had to grow up in wicked homes (Avraham, Rivkah, Rachel, Leah etc.). One reason was to show that no matter where a Jew lives in *galus,* he could rise above the evil influences, if he sincerely tries. Growing up in such an environment also fostered within them great humility.

Answers&Facts

---

21. Why *didn't* Avraham Avinu cry very much when his Eishes Chayil died?

(Ramban, Baal Haturim, Kehillas Yitzchak, Tanna d'Bei Eliyahu Rabbah 4)

22. What was Yitzchak praying for when Eliezer arrived with Rivkah?

(See Chiddushei Gaonim on Maseches Sotah, Chasam Sofer, Kli Yakar, Gemara Berachos 8a)

23. How late can we pray *mincha*?

(Shulchan Aruch Orach Chaim 233, Gemara Shabbos 32b, Yalkut Yosef, Ohr L'Tzion)

21. Surely Avraham cried bitterly over his beloved wife Sarah's passing. But the *Pasuk* has a small letter *chof* to indicate that Avraham held back some crying. This is because when righteous people die (*chas v'shalom*), the people don't cry from sadness for them, because it is known that they're going to a much better place, (the hope for everyone) *Gan Eden!* Rather the crying is for the living people, who will sorely miss them! Another reason why Avraham did not cry too much was so that so no one should think he was sad at having performed *Akeidas Yitzchak*. Others write that Sarah caused her own untimely death for challenging Avraham when she spoke harshly from her pain of child-lessness saying: *"Yishpot Hashem beini u'veinecha"* (16-5), which means that she wanted Hashem to judge Avraham for not having prayed enough for her to bear a child. One must never invoke judgment on another Jew, or *he* will be judged harshly instead. She also laughed at the angel's blessing for her to have a son. This laughter was held against her.

22. The *Gemara (Berachos 8a)* says that one should pray for a good wife who will help him grow in Torah. It was precisely at the moment of Rivkah's arrival, that Yitzchak was praying during *Mincha* that Hashem give him such a wife.

23. There are many different opinions as to how late one can pray *mincha*. As with all uncertainties in the area of *halacha* (Jewish Law), one must confer with his family's *Rav* and spiritual guide. The mishnah says to pray *mincha* before *erev* (evening). But there is much controversy regarding what is called *erev*. Most popular opinions agree: Thirteen-and-a-half minutes after sunset is the deadline. In case of emergency, some say you have twenty-five minutes. There are Chassidim who pray *mincha* quite late, as they are of the opinion that *shekiah* (sunset) is later than what others consider it to be.

24. Why is "Eretz Yisroel" so often referred to as "Eretz Canaan"?

(Mechilta on Parshas Bo)

25. Lavan wanted to rob Eliezer of his riches. What made him back off?

(Yalkut Shimoni 109)

26. When was the first Beis Hamikdash destroyed?

(The Beginning)

27. Which three miracles happened in Sarah's and Rivkah's homes which were similar to the miracles in the Mishkan?

(Rashi, Rabbeinu Bachya, Chiddushei HaGriz on Rambam, Teshuvos HaRashba 310, Bereishis Rabbah 60:16)

---

24. Eretz Yisroel is called Eretz Canaan approximately 70 times in *Tanach*. Some say, that since Canaan was cursed to be a slave and since what a slave owns belongs to his master, the *goyim* were reminded that Eretz Yisroel was their land only temporarily. Others say that the nation of Canaan was honored because when they heard that the Jews were granted the Eretz Yisroel, many of them left the land on their own accord!

25. Lavan wanted to mug Eliezer of the enormous wealth that he was carrying on the camels. Right then, Eliezer lifted a camel up over the creek! "Whoa!" thought Lavan. "Such superhuman strength! Never mind combat: I'll have to poison him."

26. Rabbi Avigdor Miller *zt"l* wrote that Sarah Imeinu's passing was the "first" *Beis Hamikdash's* termination, because her model home was to Hashem even a holier home than the *Beis Hamikdash* of Shlomo Hamelech! Indeed, Hashem wishes to reside in our homes even *more* than in the *Beis Hamikdash*! The actual Beis Hamikdash of Shlomo Hamelech stood for 410 years and was destroyed in 3338.

27. The Shabbos candles of Sarah and Rivkah stayed lit from Friday to Friday, the bread stayed warm and fresh all week , and a cloud was suspended over their tent. So too in the Mishkan, the *Menorah* stayed lit until the next kindling, the *Lechem Hapanim* stayed warm and fresh, while a Cloud of Glory stayed above it.

28. Why did Eliezer swear by Avraham's Bris Milah, and not by his Tefillin regarding his mission?

(Bereishis Rabbah 59:8, Eitz Yosef, Kli Yakar)

29. Which four things speed up the aging process (for example, the production of white hairs, baldness, and wrinkles)?

(Gemara Sanhedrin 52b and Tosafos there, Tanchuma)

30. How do we know that an idol worshiper would give up his gods for money?

(Maayanah Shel Torah, Alter of Nevardok on 24:31)

31. Which etiquette is contrary to the way of the Torah?

(Ramban 54:61, Bereishis Rabbah 60:14, Berachos 61a)

---

28. Avraham made Eliezer swear by his Milah that he would not pick for Yitzchak a bride from the girls of Canaan. This was because Milah was so special to Avraham since it was his first *mitzvah* given directly from Hashem, and it was acquired with *mesiras nefesh* (pain and sacrifice). Also Avraham implied that Milah helps control one from the *aveirah* of *zenus*. Cham, Cana'an's grandfather, was cursed as a result of his not controlling his desire in the *Teivah*. That happened because he didn't undergo *Milah*. "Don't pick a daughter from the girls of Canaan who are not holy as a result of their lack of self-control," ordered Avraham.

29. Fear, anger, war, and a bad wife make a person age quickly. These anxieties make a person look older than he actually is. However, Avraham looked old only due to his long life. It has been said, that man does not die with having enjoyed half of his desires. But Avraham died with great satisfaction.

30. Lavan took all his gods out from his house in order for Eliezer to stay there with all his wealth, because Eliezer refused to stay in a house with *avodah zarah* in it. Lavan's actions show that a *rasha* cares more about his money than about his gods.

31. The saying "ladies first" runs contrary to *halachah*. The *Gemara* tells us that a man must not walk behind a woman; rather, he should walk in front. Hence, Rivkah followed behind Eliezer, who led the way.

---

32. Why did Rivkah fall off the camel?

(Yalkut Shimoni, Tosafos)

33. Why didn't Avraham want a wife for Yitzchak from Malki-Tzedek's (Shem's) children—"a Rosh Yeshiva's daughter!"?

(The Beginning)

34. How do we see that when you speak in public, it is proper protocol to stand up?

(Rabbeinu Bachya, Shulchan Aruch Orach Chaim 690)

35. Who else is buried with the Avos, Imahos, Adam, and Chavah?

(See Chida quoting Yalkut Reuveini on Parshas V'zos Haberachah)

32. Rivkah saw with *Ruach Hakodesh* that Eisav *Harasha* was going to be born from her, and she fell from shock. Others say that she did not fall from the camel; rather, she looked down and lowered her head out of respect for Yitzchak.

33. Avraham did not want any *shidduch* from the land of Cana'an because their ways were evil and he did not expect any exception. Rabbi Mordechai Maslaton *shlit'a* comments that Shem was always *Sur MeRah* (turning away from evil), but Avraham wanted someone more than *Sur Me'rah*; he wanted someone who was always *Asei tov* (constantly doing good things). Rivkah was worthy of this, because she was always trying to do acts of kindness. Rabbi Avigdor Miller *zt"l* said that Avraham's ways of serving Hashem were innovative and unique. Had he married into a prestigious family like Shem's, he would have been prevented from serving Hashem in his way since they would have said, "That's not our way." He needed to be on his own in order to develop true Judaism.

34. When Avraham spoke to the men of Cheis, in order to purchase the *Me'aras Hamachpeilah*, he stood up. This is the proper way for someone to speak when in public: he should stand up in honor of those assembled.

35. Some say that angels carried Moshe Rabbeinu and his wife Tzipporah after their passing, to their burial place alongside the other *tzadikim* in the Me'aras Hamachpeilah! Also the head (and some say, even the body) of Eisav is buried in the Me'aras Hamachpeilah. (Perhaps it was due to his outstanding *Kibbud Av*.)

Answers&Facts

36. Why did Eliezer travel by camel and not by horse on his way to Aram Naharaim?

(Rokeach)

37. How was Rivkah a born princess?

(Pirkei d'Rabi Eliezer16)

38. Which of our three daily prayers probably "yields the best returns"?

(See Perishah on Shulchan Aruch, Orach Chaim Siman 232; Shaarei Aharon)

39. What was Eliezer's reward for successfully bringing Yitzchak a wife?

(See Pirkei d'Rabi Eliezer; Seder Hadoros, Zekeinim Baalei Tosafos, Maharil Diskin)

40. How fast did Eliezer travel back to Yitzchak?

(Pirkei d'Rabi Eliezer 16)

36. A camel in Hebrew is called *gamal*, so Eliezer hinted that what he was really looking for in a girl was that she be a *gomeles chesed*. It was this play on the word *gamal* which was the key to earn Yitzchak's hand in marriage. He needed his mate to have this quality of *chessed* just like Avraham had!

37. Besuel, Rivkah's father, was the king of Aram; hence, Rivkah was a genuine princess! Miraculously, the only time in her life that she personally went out to draw water was on that day. Ordinarily, the princess would have stayed in her palace, but Hashem arranged for her to go out on that day in order for Eliezer to find her.

38. *Tefillas Mincha* is said to bring the fastest results because *Minchah* is the hardest *tefillah* to pray. After all, people have to break away from work to pray. Since it is more difficult to pray then, its reward is much greater. As we learn in *Pirkei Avos* (5:26), *"Lefum tzaara agra"* (the reward is in proportion to the exertion).

39. Avraham freed Eliezer from being his servant in appreciation for his finding the best wife for Yitzchak. Eliezer went on to become the king of Bashan and was nicknamed Og Melech HaBashan because the people in Bashan used to call their kings "Og". (Don't mix him up with the *rasha* Og.)

40. It took Eliezer three hours' traveling time to bring back Rivkah. This was a miracle. Hashem shortened his trip both ways, in order that Eliezer would not have to spend the night with Rivkah, which would have transgressed the law of *yichud* (seclusion).

41. What happened to Avraham's daughter "Bakol"?
(See Bava Basra 16a; Bereishis Rabbah 59:7, Ramban)

42. Who were the four giants after whom Kiryas Arba was named?
(Rashi, Bereishis Rabbah 58:4)

43. Must Arabs undergo Milah nowadays?
(Rashi to Sanhedrin 59b, Rambam, Tosafos HaRosh)

44. Why was it good that Besuel died by eating "his own poison"?
(Yalkut Shimoni 109)

45. Why did Eliezer need ten camels when he traveled to bring Rivkah?
(Chizkuni, Tosafos on Kesuvos 7b, Shaarei Aharon quoting Rabbeinu Ephraim)

---

41. Some say that Avraham had a daughter named Bakol. There is a mystery about what became of her. It could be that there was no *tzaddik* great enough for her to marry, and therefore she went to *Olam Haba* early.

42. There were four *goyim* who were giants in Chevron at that time: Shashay, Talmay, Achiman and their father. Others say that the four giants refer to giants in stature; the four couples: Adam and Chava, Avraham and Sarah, Yitzchak and Rivkah, and Yaakov and Leah, all of whom are buried in Kiryas Arba, known today as Chevron. Others say it was nicknamed after the four *tzadikim* that were there: Avraham, Aner, Ashkol and Mamrei.

43. It seems that only the descendants of Ketura must observe *Milah* nowadays, but many Arabs do it anyway. We must thus be extra careful when we perform *Milah* to override their merit!

44. Besuel, King of Aram, had a terrible custom of taking all brides away from their husbands on the first night of their marriage, in order to do with them as he pleased. The men of Aram were furious at him for his terrible behavior. They said that if he were to take his own daughter, Rivkah, on her wedding day, he would be allowed to live, but if he did not, they would kill him and his daughter. To prevent any danger to Rivkah, Hashem saw to it that Besuel died before the wedding.

45. Eliezer needed ten camels to carry a display of Avraham's immense wealth. He also needed ten men for a *minyan* in order for him to pray, and make the *beracha* of *Eirusin* which is made when a couple is betrothed.

46. Why didn't Eliezer eat before proposing the *shidduch* for Rivkah?

(Alshich, Rav Binyomin-the father of the Maharal)

47. The Gemara (Kiddushin 70a) forbids one to use a girl for help, so why did Eliezer ask Rivkah for help?

(See Shaarei Aharon and Panim Yafos)

48. Why did Avraham absolutely refuse to allow any girl from Cana'an to become Yitzchak's wife; after all, were there absolutely no righteous ones around then?

(Atarah L'melech, Derashos HaRan, Rabbi Samson Raphael Hirsch zt"l)

49. Which *parshah* is beneficial for a *chosson* to read on his wedding day?

(Rabbeinu Bachya, Atarah L'melech)

50. Should women go out to work in order to add to their family's income?

(Midrash Shocher Tov 112:1, Mishlei 32, Rav Aharon Kotler zt"l)

46. Some say that just as one is not supposed to eat breakfast before doing a *Mitzvah D'oraysa*, such as taking *Lulav*, so too, Eliezer felt that this was a *mitzva*, and he chose not to touch food before he proposed a *shidduch* for Yitzchak.

47. The *gezaira* not to call upon a girl for personal assistance was not made until the times of the Talmud. Others say that Eliezer wanted to find out if Rivkah really had the *midah* of kindness, the *midah* that would qualify her as one of the matriarchs of our people, who are synonomous with kindness!

48. Avraham knew that the nation of Canaan was cursed by their grandfather, Noach. Hashem blessed our nation, and it is not proper for the blessed to mix with the cursed.

49. There is a nice custom for a *chosson* to read the *Parsha* of Rivkah's marriage to Yitzchak on his wedding day in order that it serve as a guide as to how he should conduct his life with kindness.

50. It says in *Eishes Chayil*, which is customarily sung on Friday nights, that a woman of valor works hard to try to increase her husband's income. This is especially important nowadays when many families lead *Kollel* lives, for they need an extra income. Such wives will help their husbands reach great heights in *Talmud Torah* and *Kiyum Hamitzvos* and will thus benefit the future of Judaism.

51. What is the greatest quality of a woman?

(Michtav M'Eliyahu)

52. Why did Rivkah cover her face with a veil? Should that be done nowadays?

(Kedushas Bas Yisroel)*

53. How old did the Roshei Yeshiva Shem and Eiver live?

(Bereishis 11:11 and 11:17)

54. What did Avraham reply when the citizens of Cheis called him both a god and a king?

(Bereishis Rabbah 58:6)

55. Besides Rivkah, for whom did water rise?

(Bereishis Rabbah 60:5)

56. In which merit did Avraham earn long life (until age 175)?

(Bereishis Rabbah 59:1, Mishlei 15:31)

---

51. The most noble quality of a woman is her selfless giving of herself on behalf of her family and others.

52. Rivkah covered her face in order to *badek* herself. This custom, prevalent among *Ashkenazic* Jews today, indicates to people that she is already taken and furthermore that they should not stare at someone else's wife.

53. Shem lived until 600 years, and Ever lived until 464 years.

54. When goyim tried to call Avraham both god and king, he responded, "The world is lacking neither its G-d nor its King!"

55. Just as water rose in the well for Rivkah, so too did it rise from the *Be'er Miriam* for the Jewish people when they left Mitzrayim and traveled in the desert.

56. No doubt, all Avraham's outstanding *mitzvos* contributed to his longevity. But the *Midrash* focuses primarily on his chesed and his learning of the Torah.

Answers&Facts

57. What was the symbolism of Rivkah's riding on a camel?
(Bereishis Rabbah 60:14)

58. When are you not allowed to start working before you pray Minchah?
(Mishnah Shabbos 1:2)

59. Why did they used to give a bride twelve months to prepare herself for marriage?
(Rashi to Kesuvos 53a, Bereishis Rabbah 60:12)

60. What document did Eliezer carry to Besuel's house?
(Bereishis Rabbah 59:11)

61. How was Eliezer allowed to engage Yitzchak to Rivkah if Avraham's son had never seen his *kallah* before?
(Kiddushin 41a, Emunas Chachamim)

---

57. Just as a camel has one sign of kashrus and one sign of impurity, so too Rivkah bore both a *tzadik* and a *rasha*.

58. The *Mishnah* lists many types of activities that should not be done before praying *mincha* lest they cause one to miss the davening: getting a haircut, going into a steam room, working at a tannery, eating lunch, and going to court. If one must work, he should have a monitor to remind him to pray.

59. The custom used to be to give the bride 12 months to prepare herself with clothing, jewelry, and cosmetics. In today's day and age, thanks to department stores, there is no need to push off the wedding date so much.

60. Eliezer carried the will of Avraham stating that all of Avraham's enormous wealth was to be given to his younger son, Yitzchak. I heard from a Rav that it is a good idea to impress the potential *mechutanim* (in-laws) in order to hasten the *shidduch*.

61. One may not send an agent to betroth a girl for him if he has never seen her, lest he come to despise her later. But Eliezer knew that Yitzchak would love Rivkah for her piety and beauty.

62.
Which three people were answered the moment they prayed?

(Pesikta Zutrasi 24:15, Bereishis Rabbah 60:4)

63.
On which day of the year did Sarah Imeinu pass away?

(Bereishis Rabbasi 94)

---

62. Sometimes a person must wait to see the fruits of his labor in prayer, but three people in history were answered the moment they prayed: Eliezer, when he prayed for Yitzchak to find his wife; Moshe, when he prayed that Korach be swallowed up; and Shlomo, when he prayed that a fire descend on the *mizbeiyach* of the new Beis Hamikdash. May we merit that Hashem answer our heartfelt cries for the *geulah*, may it come speedily in our days.

63. Sarah Imeinu passed away on Rosh Hashana. That's another reason we wail using a Shofar.

Answers&Facts

פרשת תולדות

?

1. How did Eisav trick his father Yitzchak into thinking he was a *tzadik*?

(Rashi to 25:27, Tanchuma 8, Bereishis Rabbah 65:1, K'sav Sofer)

2. Why didn't Rivka tell Yitzchak about the "real Eisav"?

(Ohr Hachaim 27:46, Ramban, Pachad Yitzchak, Lev Eliyahu, Me'am Lo'ez; see Bereishis Rabbah 65:15)

FUNdamental Answers!

"יגעתי ומצאתי!"

("I worked on these questions, and I found these answers!")

1. Eisav acted as if he were very meticulous in doing *mitzvos*. He would ask his father questions that implied that he was a very G-d fearing person. He would ask, "Do I need to take off *maaser* from salt in the house, or from straw in the field?" Eisav "acted" as if he only wanted to be in business so that he could give *maaser* to the Torah scholars, like the classic Yissochar and Zevulun deal, although that was never his intention. Yitzchak thought that Eisav was very meritorious for wanting to help Torah scholars. It is hard to believe that Eisav actually fooled his ingenious father Yitzchak, but Eisav must have been a very talented actor. Eisav was a type of Dr. Jekyl and Mr. Hyde. He pretended to be good in order to deceive his father, so that he not get a curse. Yaakov on the other hand was so perfect and straight that even when his mother told him to act like Eisav in order to get the *beracha*, he was worried of being a faker.

2. Rivkah didn't want to say *Loshon Hara* that Eisav was bad. She also figured that if Hashem wanted Yitzchak to know, He Himself would tell him. She also worried

3. **Why did Yaakov grab Eisav's heel during their birth?**

(Rashi; see Shaarei Aharon quoting Tosafos and Pirkei d'Rabi Eliezer)

4. **Why did Yitzchak want to bless Eisav more than he did Yaakov?**

(Radak, Toras Ha'olah)

5. **Why didn't Rivka go to Avraham Avinu to inquire about her extreme pregnancy pains?**

(Tur, Tosafos, Midrash, Seichel Tov, Seder Hadoros)

6. **How could the righteous Yitzchak and Rivka have the evil Eisav?**

(Riva)

7. **What did Hashem say when Eisav despised the *Bechorah* (Birthright & Temple Service), its privileges and obligations?**

(Midrash)

that if she told him, Yitzchak would say that it was her fault because she came from a family of *reshaim* and she didn't want to be blamed for Eisav's failings. Perhaps, she didn't want to tell him because she didn't want to cause him great heartache.

3. Some say that Yaakov wanted to tip Eisav over, to make the *rasha* fall! This was also because Eisav wanted to kill Yaakov and one may kill his attacker in self-defense. Others say that Yaakov was showing that the things that Eisav steps on with his heel are exactly the things that Yaakov grabs in life: Eisav stepped on *mitzvos & middos tovos*, morals and ethics. But the *tzaddik* Yaakov loved all those things. Indeed his name Yaakov has the word heel (*eikev*) in it, to imply that he loved the very things that Eisav despised.

4. Yitzchak knew that Yaakov was learning Torah all the time, so he didn't need his blessing, because Torah study itself would bring him blessings! But Eisav, who involved himself in the outside world, needed his blessing more!

5. Rivkah did not want Avraham Avinu to know that there might be a *rasha* inside her. She was embarrassed, so she preferred instead to inquire from Shem and Eiver, the elderly scholars of the generation.

6. Our Rabbis tell us that most children become like their uncles, and since Eisav's uncle was Lavan, he turned out to be just like him!

7. Hashem replied, "Eisav said, 'Why do I need this *Bechorah*?' I say, "Why do you deserve this *Berachah* (blessing)?" These are the same letters

8. Why did even the little children cry when Avraham Avinu passed away?

(Seder Hadoros 2133)

9. Who did only one Mitzvah?

(Bereishis Rabbah 82:15)

10. Why did Avimelech's Pelishtim clog Avraham's water wells?

(Ramban, Rabbeinu Bachya 26:14)

11. Why didn't Avimelech want Yitzchak to remain in his country?

(Ramban, Riva, Radak)

---

juggled around. Indeed, the one who *serves* Hashem gets the most *blessings!* And if Eisav didn't want to serve Hashem in the Beis Hamikdash, then Yaakov would receive the blessings instead.

8. Avraham Avinu was kind to the whole world. There was no one that didn't benefit from his kindness! Even the little children, who so often, people tend to ignore, were given his great attention, love, and kindliness, and that's why the children also cried when he passed away.

9. Eisav Harasha did only one *mitzvah*, that of *Kibbud Av*, honoring his father. (Apparently, he did not do the *mitzvah* of *Kibbud Eim*, honoring his mother. And any other *Mitzvos* that he did, such as "Speaking to his father in learning" or ritually slaughtering a bird with an arrow, were just acts, without any interest in fulfilling Hashem's *Mitzvos*.)

10. The Pelishtim were *jealous* of Avraham's success and popularity. Such is the craziness of jealousy that they clogged up the very water wells from which they would eventually have benefited. They did not want his wealthy son, Yitzchak to prosper either. It's weird that the rich are jealous of those who are richer than they are.

11. King Avimelech was so very jealous of Yitzchak that he wanted him to leave. When a person is jealous of another, he does not want to be around that fellow. Such a person feels there is not enough room in the world for the two of them. Avimelech lost out immediately, because much of the blessing that Avimelech had enjoyed in his country was a result of Yitzchak's presence. Once Yitzchak left, the fruits and vegetables deteriorated. Avimelech realized why this was happening, so he went to Yitzchak and begged him to join him in a treaty.

Answers&Facts

12. What made Yitzchak and Rivka sad and caused them a lot of pain?

(Bereishis Rabbah 65:4, Rabbeinu Bachya)

13. Why didn't Yitzchak make many *Geirim* (converts) as Avraham had done?

(Seforno)

14. Who ate like an animal?

(Bamidbar Rabbah 14:22 and 21:18, Tanchuma on Parshas Pinchas 13)

15. Why is Edom (Rome/America) such a ruling power in the world?

(Zohar)

16. Why did Hashem make Avraham, Sarah, Yitzchak, Rivka, Rachel, and Chanah barren?

(The Beginning, Mili d'Berachos 31b; see Bereishis Rabbah 60:13; Kol Yehudah)

12. Eisav married evil women who worshiped *avodah zarah* and they burnt incense for it, which caused smoke to rise. Yitzchak and Rivkah shouted at Eisav, but he wouldn't listen. It pained them to have a child who was wicked and didn't want to listen to their *mussar* (criticism). They were also sad because their *Ruach Hakodesh* left them due to their anger, and because they were in the company of those *reshaim*.

13. Avraham's mission was *to go out into the world* and bring people under Hashem's wings (as it were). Yitzchak's mission was to show that he could *remain in Eretz Yisroel* even when the going got rough, so Yitzchak was not allowed to leave Eretz Yisroel. His job was to show people that one must sometimes stay in Eretz Yisroel even if it is hard. His way of serving Hashem was different from that of Avraham.

14. Eisav said, "I am going to open my mouth wide, so pour the food in, as you would do with a camel." This was not proper manners. But then again, when did Eisav care about proper behavior??

15. Since Eisav excelled in *Kibbud Av*, as no one else had done, he merited that his descendants would become rulers in the world. The *galus* we are in now is called *Galus Edom* because he honored his father! We must make our *Kibbud Av V'eim* outdo Eisav's merit, in order to end this bitter *galus*!

16. Hashem loves the special prayers of the righteous. Hashem therefore challenged many great people by making them barren in order that they

17.
Why didn't Hashem let Yitzchak leave Eretz Yisroel during the famine - Avraham left during the famine in his time?

(Rashi)

18.
When did someone feel Gan Eden and Gehinnom in the same area, within a short period of time?

(Bereishis Rabbah 67:2, Seder Hadoros)

19.
When is it bad to love a son?

(Shemos Rabbah 1:1; see Sanhedrin 70b)

---

speak up, and He would then hear their voices. Also once they're praying for themselves, they would pray for so many others who need Divine assistance. In other words, their pleasant voices would bring redemption to others in need! They would also pray that any future children they will have will turn out to be saintly. That would cause the quality of their future children be that much greater as well! The Divine intervention to create our nation is a great encouragement, since the very existence of our nation came about through supernatural miracles. Therefore, no Jew should ever despair! Rather they should pray sincerely, and miracles will happen!

17. Yitzchak was sanctified like a *Korban Olah* once he was about to be sacrificed on the *Akeida*. Just as a *Korban Olah* is not allowed to leave the Beis Hamikdash, so too Yitzchak was not allowed to leave Eretz Yisroel. Hashem also said that outside of Eretz Yisroel, the people didn't deserve such an outstanding *tzaddik!*

18. When Yaakov came before Yitzchak in order to receive his *berachah*, Yitzchak felt the delight of *Gan Eden* there. When Eisav entered afterwards, Yitzchak felt the agony of *Gehinom*. The contrast was frightening!

19. If a son doesn't keep the Torah, *(Chas V'Shalom)*, he must be given *mussar* (constructive criticism). If parents don't criticize a child because they "love" him, this is not really "good love". That type of "love" just spoils the child! They should discipline the child in order to improve his ways, and their love will grow even stronger. Incidentally, the *Gemara (Makos* 8a) tells us a shocking thing: "Even if a child is good, the parent should discipline him, even with a *potch* (spanking), and he will become even better." That of course depends if it is administered in the right measure. (Just don't get carried away—that's child abuse!) Once in a while, the best thing for children is Vitamin N (No)!

Answers&Facts

20. Why did Yitzchak prefer food from a hunt if he owned plenty of cattle?

(Taam V'daas, Kli Yakar)

21. How do we see from Parshas Toldos that we shouldn't skip saying Korbanos?

(Seichel Tov 25:34)

22. Who enjoyed a kind of supernatural "Miracle Grow" with his crops during a time of famine?

(Toras Ha'olah 26:12)

23. Why was Eisav so hairy?

(K'sav Sofer)

24. How did people describe Yitzchak's extraordinary wealth?

(Rashi to 26:13)

20. Yitzchak wanted Eisav to trouble himself to get the food. By troubling himself for *Kibbud Av*, his favorite *mitzvah*, he would increase his merit to be able to receive the great blessing that Yitzchak wanted to bestow on him.

21. Eisav rejected and despised the *Avodas Beis Hamikdash*. We must not follow in his ways of ignoring and skipping Korbanos, which in a sense is a type of contempt. Every man must say at least the *pesukim* mentioning the *Olas Tamid and Ketores* every day. This is the minimal requirement!

22. Yitzchak went to Geror when there was a terrible famine in the world. But when he planted, the land produced a hundred times as much as it would have if there had been no famine! For example, if he planted one seed, it would grow a hundred times larger and taller than everyone else's. He became so wealthy that King Avimelech became envious. (Don't you wish that Hashem would grant you such "Miracle Grow" to be able to learn more Torah than you ever expected? After all, unfortunately there is a *spiritual famine* in the world today!)

23. Eisav was so hairy because he was just like an animal! His hairiness was a hint that he would live a very animalistic existence.

24. Men used to joke that they would rather have the money earned by selling the manure from Yitzchak's mules than to have the diamonds and gold of Avimelech. Yitzchak's wealth was thus far greater than we can fathom.

25. Who was born red like Eisav, but was so different from him?
(Bereishis Rabbah 63:80

26. Why did Yaakov go to learn at the Yeshivos of Shem and Ever for thirty-two years, if he could have learned from Yitzchak, his father?
(Bereishis Rabbah 63:6,10, Kli Yakar, K'sav Sofer)

27. How often should one go to a *tzadik* for a blessing?
(Maseches Sofrim, Rus Rabbah 6)

28. How was Yitzchak able to trust Eisav's *kashrus*?
(Torah L'daas)

---

25. Dovid Hamelech was also born red. Shmuel Hanavi feared that maybe he had murderous instincts, like Eisav Harasha. But, Hashem assured him that he had "good eyes" and would kill only with the consent of the *Sanhedrin* (i.e. the only blood he would spill would be the blood of those who threatened Am Yisroel.)

26. Yaakov knew the *Mishnah* in *Pirkei Avos* (1-7) that tells us to stay away from a bad friend, so he ran away from Eisav! He also knew that a person should exile himself to a place of Torah. When a person goes away from home to learn, he starts to shine brighter in Torah, because he's able to become greater than anyone had expected. Indeed, it is customary for a *Ben Torah* to travel away from home in order to achieve greater perfection in Torah knowledge.

27. A person should frequently ask *tzaddikim* for blessings. For instance, we find that Rus did not have a child before she was forty, but when Boaz blessed her, she immediately conceived a son. We find also that Avimelech's wife, the queen, was childless, but when Avraham prayed to Hashem to heal Avimelech and his household, his prayer caused her and everyone in the palace to have sons that year. So we see that a *tzaddik* can certainly make miracles happen through his blessings.

28. Eisav acted so well that he even fooled some into thinking that he was a "*Mashgiach*" (supervisor) of *Kashrus*.

Answers & Facts

29. What did Eisav gain by the two tears that he shed over missing the *tzadik's* blessing?

(Tanchuma on Parshas Kedoshim 15, Bereishis Rabbah 67:4)

30. Why did Yitzchak become blind [for 57 years]?

(Bereishis Rabbah 65, Megillah 28a, Rabbeinu Bachya, Tanchuma, Rashi)

31. Why didn't Eisav have a Bris Milah?

(Bereishis Rabbah 63:13, Daas Zekeinim Baalei Tosafos quoting Chullin 47b)

32. Who didn't want to go to Yeshiva (Torah school)?

(Seder Hadoros 2126)

---

29. When Eisav cried, it showed that he really valued his father's blessing. This was a great honor for Yitzchak. Therefore, Eisav merited gaining Mount Sa'ir and rulership over the Jews in *galus*. Therefore, in order to free ourselves from *galus*, we must shed tears when we pray, and do *teshuva* to counter the tears of Eisav.

30. Yitzchak was angry with Eisav's wicked wives, and anger dims a person's eyesight. Yitzchak *stared* at Eisav Harasha's face, and someone who stares at a *rasha's* face, loses his vision. (So don't stare at the wicked people on television and in sports!) The angels cried at *Akeidas Yitzchak* from seeing the amazing feat of a human being sacrificing his beloved and only son totally to Hashem, and their hot tears went into Yitzchak's eyes, thus affecting his eyesight. The smoke of the *avodah zarah* offerings of Eisav's wives also dimmed his vision. Additionally, he was not supposed to see that Yaakov was taking the blessings for himself. Also Yitzchak suggested to Hashem that man should suffer in order to atone for his sins and spare him suffering in *gehinnom*, so he got to suffer first. Yitzchak also stared at the *Shechinah* of Hashem during the Akeida. It was too overwhelming, and it affected his eyesight.

31. Eisav was born beet-red, and Yitzchak feared that maybe he wasn't healthy. He planned on making his *Bris Milah* just as Avraham had done with Yishmael, when he was thirteen. But, at thirteen, Eisav ran away and did not let anyone give him a *Bris Milah*. This was a clear sign that Eisav acted like a *goy*.

32. Until the twins Yaakov and Eisav became thirteen (their *Bar Mitzvah* year), it was really hard to distinguish their true nature, because they both went to school. But at thirteen, when Yaakov was running to Yeshiva while Eisav was running away from Yeshiva, it was apparent who was who!

33. Why didn't Rivka bear all twelve Shevatim herself?

(See Shaarei Aharon quoting Bereishis Rabbah 63:6; Tochachos Mussar)

34. What day of the year did Yitzchak wait for to give his most important blessings?

(Targum Yerushalmi)

35. What are three examples of Dama ben Nesina's wonderful Kibud Av V'em?

(Yerushalmi Peah)

36. From where do we see that we should not proudly display our wealth in front of the non-Jews?

(Seichel Tov 26:24)

---

33. Rivkah's wicked family, especially Lavan, blessed her that she should have millions of descendants. The wicked have no power to bless someone, and the wicked person's blessing thus turns into a curse! So she had fewer children than she should have had. Also she complained during her painful pregnancy, saying, "Why did I pray for a child, when it brings so much pain? If it's so painful, who needs it?" She should not have said that, because after complaining, she never had another pregnancy. It never pays to complain to Hashem! (The Jews in the *Midbar* complained about *Eretz Yisroel,* and they therefore never got to enjoy it!)

34. The night of *Pesach* is when Yitzchak waited to bless his sons, and that is a most auspicious time to bless your children.

35. Dama would not disturb his father's sleep, even at the expense of losing millions of dollars! Dama would not sit on his father's stone chair even after his death, because he valued it so highly. On one occasion, his mother humiliated him in front of all the Roman dignitaries, slapping him in the face with her shoe, and throwing his wallet into the sea, and he didn't even become angry at her. The *Gemara* says we should learn from this *goy* how to honor our parents!

36. Many times, great *tzaddikim* told their children not to show off their wealth, so as not to cause the *goyim* to become jealous. We see that when Avimelech saw Yitzchak's prosperity, he banished Yitzchak from the land. A similar event happened in Spain with the Jews in 1492, when Queen Isabella was jealous of a Jewish woman's wealth... (I'm afraid many people are not following this advice. People are building ostentatious homes, driving expensive cars, and taking extravagant vacations. Hopefully we won't suffer because of all this showiness, G-d forbid.)

37. How many years did Shem serve the *tzadik* Mesushelach?

(Seder Hadoros)

38. Why does a baby learn the Torah in the mother's womb?

(Niddah 30b, Toras Ha'olah)

39. Yitzchak ate *before* he blessed his sons. So why don't fathers eat the *seuda* Friday night before blessing their children?

(Seichel Tov)

40. What was so amazing about Nimrod's clothing, that Eisav coveted them, and robbed them?

(Bartenura quoting Bereishis Rabbah 63:13, Seder Hadoros)

---

37. It seems that Shem served Mesushelach for ninety-eight years. When one assists the Rabbis, he becomes much closer to them, and then he can see many more Torah applications and practices. So *serving* Rabbis will help you much more than just *learning* from them!

38. A baby learns the Torah in his mother's womb in order to survive as a Jew. The only way a Jew can live, is with the Torah. When a baby is submerged in water for nine months, Torah provides the oxygen and nutrients needed for its survival and development. Also it lets Torah become the person's subconscious mindset.

39. The reason we don't eat before blessing our children Friday night is because the starting of Shabbos is an extremely auspicious moment when the angels escort us to our homes, and we want the angels to see us bless our children before they leave. But, with Yitzchak, the angels still remained in his home, even after he finished his meal.

40. "Nimrod's clothes" were really the *Kasnos Ohr* that Hashem made for *Adam Harishon*, which had upon them designs of the animal kingdom. If an animal's image was touched, then that animal would come and obey the one wearing the clothes. These were supernatural clothes, and that's why Eisav coveted them, even murdering Nimrod to get them. Eisav didn't leave this clothing at home, for fear that his wives would be disloyal to him, and then use the clothes against him. He therefore entrusted these garments only to his mother, Rivkah. These very clothes were the ones that Yaakov wore to receive the *berachah* from Yitzchak.

---

41. For what reason were the firstborn sons originally supposed to serve in the Beis Hamikdash?

(Pele Yo'etz)

42. Why didn't Yitzchak insist that Eisav banish his evil wives?

(Targum Yerushalmi)

43. Is a blind person obligated to do all the Mitzvos?

(Bava Kama 84a, Shulchan Aruch Orach Chaim 473, Pri Megadim, Minchas Chinuch 26)

44. Why did Yaakov want to leave his mother's womb when passing by a Beis Midrash? After all, he was already being taught Torah by an angel!

(Rav Chaim Brisker zt"l, Toras Chinuch)

---

41. Hashem wanted the oldest in each family to serve in the *Beis Hamikdash* to be an example for all the younger siblings, thus impressing upon them that the fortunate way to live is to serve Hashem in His sanctuary. However, when even firstborn sons sinned in the incident with the *Eigel*, the privilege of serving Hashem was given primarily to the *Kohanim*.

42. Yitzchak and Rivkah told Eisav to get rid of his wicked wives. But Eisav went *"off the derech"* and refused to send away his evil wives. This was terribly painful for Yitzchak and Rivkah. Some say that Yitzchak hoped that by giving the *berachah* to Eisav, he would behave better.

43. There is a debate in the *Gemara* as to whether a blind person must do *mitzvos*. Most *Poskim* hold that a blind person is responsible for doing *mitzvos*. There are some who hold that a blind person may not do *aveiros*, but he need not do the *mitzvos* either, and whatever *mitzvos* he does, are considered "extra credit". But we hold like most *Poskim* who *pasken* that he really is responsible, for both *mitzvos* and *aveiros*.

44. Yaakov did not want to have a *chavrusah* like Eisav while he was in the womb. He did not want to learn Torah in the company of a hater of Torah and an evildoer. I also believe that Yaakov wanted to escape so that he could do the *Mitzvos* already and in order to teach Torah to others!! After all, Yaakov knew that there's no greater success than to teach others *Toras Hashem*!

Answers&Facts

45. When did Eisav "go off the *derech*" (abandon life as a religious Jew)?

(Shaarei Aharon quoting Tosafos, Bereishis Rabbah 63:10,11)

46. Who were the two hunters mentioned in the Torah?

(Noda B'Yehudah)

47. Why does marriage bring forgiveness for one's sins?

(Rashi, Taam V'daas)

48. Which woman named Yehudis was a *rashanta* (wicked woman)?

(Tanchuma 8, Bereishis 26:35)

49. Why didn't Yitzchak take another wife after ten years of not conceiving?

(Bereishis Rabbah 63:5; see Yevamos 64a and Tosafos Yeshanim to Yevamos 61a; Shaarei Aharon)

45. By thirteen, Eisav already had left *Yeshivah*. But at fifteen, he publicly violated the Torah and its commandments. The first two years after Eisav's *Bar Mitzvah*, Avraham Avinu was still alive, and Eisav wouldn't dare sin in public. When Eisav was fifteen, Avraham died, and Eisav began to sin publicly. It is interesting to note that the Avos were alive in this world together for fifteen years. Eisav was very foolish to miss that opportunity for growth!

46. The infamous Eisav and Nimrod are the only hunters mentioned in *Chumash*. We see from here that the sport of hunting is not a Jewish occupation. It was practiced by the wicked. Of course, Jews have much better ways to spend their free time.

47. Certain *mitzvos* bring a person *kaparah* for his sins. One mentioned in this week's *Parshah* is marriage. We learn that when Eisav married his cousin *Mochlas*, the daughter of Yishmael, Hashem was willing to forgive his sins in the merit of his marrying into a "fine family". It seems that Hashem wants a new couple to start with a clean slate, a new leaf, as a team to help each other serve Him better. That's why a *chassan* and *kallah* observe the day of their wedding by doing *teshuvah* and by praying.

48. Eisav's wife *Yehudis bas Bi'eiri* was a *rashanta* involved with *avodah zarah*.

49. Hashem wanted Yitzchak to already be an accomplished and perfect person before he had Yaakov. In that way, he could devote all his time and

50.
Which merit saves the Jews from being attacked by the non-Jews?

(Bereishis Rabbah 65:20)

51.
Which good deed of Eisav was Rabban Shimon ben Gamliel jealous of?

(Bereishis Rabbah 65:16, Devarim Rabbah 1:14)

52.
How old were Yaakov & Eisav when they received the *beracha* from Yitzchak?

(Bereishis Rabbah 65:19)

53.
Who died as a punishment for leaving Eretz Yisroel?

(Bereishis Rabbah 64:2)

---

energy to developing Yaakov into a *Gadol Hador*. If Yitzchak had been younger, he would have had to follow his own spiritual pursuits at the expense of Yaakov's. Therefore, Hashem preferred that Yitzchak was older and perfect when Yaakov was born so that he could now focus his energies on helping his son to grow. Moreover, Yitzchak and Rivkah realized each other's greatness, and they prayed to Hashem that all children they have should be from each other.

50.
If the voice of Torah is heard in the study halls, then the *goyim* will not attack the Jews. But if, G-d forbid, Torah study is *not* heard in the *Battei Midrashim*, then, G-d forbid, the *goyim* may indeed attack the Jews.

51.
Rabban Shimon ben Gamliel once said that no one ever honored his father more than he honored Rabban Gamliel and Eisav honored Yitzchak. However, Rabban Shimon ben Gamliel said he found one way in which Eisav had shown greater *Kibbud Av* than he had. Whenever Eisav served his father, he would clothe himself in royal garments so that his father should feel that much more important. Rabban Shimon ben Gamliel knew that we can learn even from the wicked Eisav.

52.
Yaakov and Eisav were 63 years old when they received the *beracha* from Yitzchak. One is never too old to get a *beracha* from a *tzadik*!

53.
Elimelech, along with his sons Machlon and Kilyon, died as a punishment for leaving Eretz Yisroel at a time of a famine. They should have stayed there to give hope and encouragement to their brethren.

Answers&Facts

54. Why didn't Hashem make Yaakov the *bechor* (firstborn) in the first place? Why did Yaakov have to purchase it?

(Bereishis Rabbah 65:15 and 63:13, Zevachim 112)

55. How did Eisav cause the Gadol Hador to die five years early?

(Bereishis Rabbah 63:11)

56. What did Rivka say was good about the two goats Yaakov offered Yitzchak?

(Bereishis Rabbah 65:14)

57. From when did Eisav want to kill Yaakov?

(Bereishis Rabbah 63:6)

58. What *beracha* should a father say upon the Bar Mitzvah of his son?

(Bereishis Rabbah 63:10)

59. How old were Yaakov & Eisav when Avraham Avinu died?

(Rashi)

---

54. More important than one's performance of a *mitzvah* is his attitude towards it. Hashem wanted to see Yaakov be *moser nefesh* in order to be able to have the *avodah*!

55. Avraham Avinu was the *Gadol Hador*, and he was supposed to live until 180. However, Hashem did not want him to die in grief over seeing a grandchild become such a rascal, so He had him pass away 5 years before his time.

56. The goats would enable Yaakov to receive the *Berachos*, and eventually the Jewish people would use two goats on *Yom Kippur* to achieve atonement.

57. Already from the womb, Eisav and Yaakov wanted to kill each other.

58. During the first 13 years of a boy's life, his father must train him to serve Hashem. Indeed, a father is held accountable for the behavior of his child. After that, he should say, "*Baruch... shepitarani mei'onsho shel zeh* (Blessed be He Who has made me exempt from this one's punishment)."

59. Yaakov and Eisav were 15 years old when Avraham Avinu died. Yaakov utilized those 15 years to learn from Avraham. It takes a smart person to glean wisdom from the generation's leading sage.

60. How was Eisav like a dirty pig?

(Bereishis Rabbah 65:1)

61. Yitzchak blessed Yaakov that his brother Eisav would serve him. Until when?

(Bereishis Rabbah 67:7)

62. Why did Eisav marry Yishmael's daughter Mochlas?

(Bereishis Rabbah 65:1 and 67:8, Rashi)

63. Who was the first Jew to act like a non-Jew?

(Bava Basra 16b, Midrash Shocher Tov 25:17)

---

60. A pig shows off its split hooves to indicate that it's kosher, when in reality it is *treif*. So too, Eisav married at 40 to act like his father Yitzchak, when in reality Eisav was quite immoral.

61. Yitzchak told Eisav that as soon as Yaakov's descendants stopped learning and keeping the Torah, he would be able to escape his obligation of having to serve him.

62. Some say that Eisav wanted to marry Yishmael's daughter in order to involve Yishmael in his feud with Yaakov over losing the *Bechorah* inheritance. He figured that Yishmael would then kill Yaakov in revenge. Afterwards, he himself would kill Yishmael as *Go'el Hadam*, and inherit both of them. Others believe that Eisav might have had a desire to do *teshuvah*, and thus Hashem actually forgave him for his previous sins. However, it's very difficult to believe he was doing *teshuvah*, since he did not divorce his wicked wives, Yehudis bas Be'eiri Hachiti, and Bosmas bas Eilon Hachiti, who were great sources of pain to his parents.

63. Yishmael was the first Jew on record to have acted like a *goy*. However, some say that he did *teshuvah* before his death and that he had severe stomach pains which atoned for his previous sins.

Dedicated in honor of my wife
ROBIN
Dr. Steven Haddad

Answers&Facts

פרשת ויצא

1. Why were angels rushing up and down a fiery ladder in Yaakov Avinu's dream?

(Bereishis Rabbah 68:12, Targum Yonasan ben Uziel, Chullin 91a, Az Nidberu)

2. Yaakov Avinu prayed the *Tefillah* of *Maariv* (Evening Prayer) when he was 77 years old. Why didn't he do so sooner?

(Berachos 27b, Bereishis Rabbah 68:9, Rokeach cited in Taamei Haminhagim based on Shabbos 11a, and see Tosafos there)

FUNdamental Answers!

"יגעתי ומצאתי!"

("*I worked on these questions, and I found these answers!*")

1. The face of Yaakov Avinu, the greatest of the Avos, is engraved on Hashem's *Kisei Hakavod*. When Yaakov was passing by the Har Habayis the angels down here ran up to tell the angels above "Come see that great *tzadik* whose very face is on Hashem's throne; he is resting right here!" Indeed, they were all rushing to see the *tzadik* up close! Harav Asher Rubenstein *shlita* noted that people hang up pictures of those whom they admire. Some hang up pictures of Gedolim *[lehavdil]* others hang up posters of sports stars. But Hashem, Himself, displays the picture of Yaakov Avinu! The angels were also the ones associated with Eretz Yisroel switching with the ones associated with outside of Eretz Yisroel.

2. The Gemara tells us a surprising thing: One who doesn't stop learning Torah for anything, doesn't need to stop and *daven* (pray) either! An example is

Questions&Riddles

3. Why did Yaakov Avinu place *stones* under his head—and not a pillow?

(Bereishis Rabbah 68:11 and 69:7, Rema on Orach Chaim 555, Sifri – Devarim 354, The Beginning)

4. How were the sleeping habits of Yaakov Avinu and Dovid Hamelech similar?

(Bereishis Rabbah 68:11, Me'am Lo'ez quoting Berachos 3b and 28a)

5. Why did Yaakov offer Lavan *seven* years of work in order to marry Rochel?

(Oznaim L'Torah based on Rambam Hilchos Ishus 15:19, Rabbeinu Bachya)

Rabban Shimon Bar Yochai whose constant occupation was learning Torah non-stop; therefore, he didn't need to pray. For in the merit of his Torah, Hashem provided him with all his needs. Until now, Yaakov had been learning Torah in the Yeshiva of Shem V'Eiver non-stop around the clock. So he didn't need to stop to daven *Maariv* (Sephardic Jews refer to the evening prayer as *Arbit*). But now that he was on his way to work with Lavan he needed to pray!

3. Yaakov foresaw with Ruach Hakodesh the Beis Hamikdash in its glory and in its destruction. He did not feel comfortable lying in a spot where the Beis Hamikdash would one day lie in ruins. He therefore put rocks under his head to mourn the *Churban* in advance! Miraculously, Hashem made that stone soft like a feathery pillow.

4. The Gemara tells us that the fourteen years that Yaakov studied in the Yeshiva of Shem V'Ever, he never slept on a bed. He learned Torah day and night all those years. What an outstanding sacrifice! Dovid Hamelech also hated sleep and preferred to stay up all night all the time singing *Tehillim* and learning Torah. Yaakov and Dovid slept very little. They only drowsed off for a brief moment to gain back their energy. (Note: We ordinary people, however, should try to sleep eight hours maximum or six hours minimum in order to be able to learn Torah with a clear head.)

5. Yaakov knew that one of the responsibilities of a husband is to bring joy to his wife, his partner in life. Yaakov knew that he would not be able to be sufficiently happy, since he knew that Eisav sought to kill him. He figured it would take seven years for Eisav to calm down and during that time he agreed to work for his uncle Lavan. After that time, he would be able to make his wife happy to fulfill the *mitzvah* of *"V'simach es ishto"* (to make his wife happy).

6. Why did the twelve stones turn into one big stone?

(Bereishis Rabbah 68:11, The Midrash Says)

7. Who was the mother of Rochel and Leah?

(See Seder Hadoros 2164)

8. Why are we allowed to pray *Maariv* before nightfall?

(Bereishis Rabbah 68:10, Taamei Haminhagim quoting Rokeach based on Sanhedrin 95b)

9. What do *Chazal* mean when they said that Leah was the first person to thank Hashem?

(Tosafos on Berachos 7b, Mili d'Berachos)

10. Who had a good name and a bad name at the same time?

(Bereishis Rabbah 71:3, Mili d'Berachos 7b, Tanchuma)

11. When is it okay to be jealous?

(Bava Basra 21a, Mishlei 23)

---

6. Yaakov took twelve stones from the Akeidas Yitzchak. He put them under his head and around him as well, to protect him from wild animals. All the rocks wanted to have a place under his head, and Hashem actually caused this to happen. This miracle symbolized that although Yaakov would have twelve sons they would come together as one unified nation dedicated to the Torah!

7. Adina was Lavan's wife, but she was barren. When Yitzchak told Yaakov to "go to Lavan's house and marry his daughters," Lavan was blessed to have daughters!

8. Yaakov really prayed Maariv before nightfall. Hashem had just made the sun set quicker that day so that Yaakov would spend the night at the *Makom Hamikdash*. So we too can pray Maariv while it's still daytime (and just repeat the Shema after nightfall).

9. Leah was the first person to name a child Yehudah, which can mean "thanks to Hashem (or literally, "he shall praise.") Surely, the previous *tzadikim* always thanked Hashem—but she was the first to name a child in this fashion!

10. Lavan is a good name for it means "white", but he was really a filthy crook with a bad reputation.

11. It is okay to be jealous of a *tzadik* or *tzadekes* if we admire their high level of fear of Hashem. This is known as: *Kinas Soferim tarbeh chochmah* (jealousy of the scholars increase wisdom). Just be careful that it doesn't turn into a *ruach ra'ah* like the one that Shaul suffered in regard to Dovid Hamelech.

Answers&Facts

12. How heavy was that massive boulder upon the well, which Yaakov so easily removed?

(Seder Hadoros 2185; see Toras Chinuch)

13. What did Yaakov do that was once fine but later became an aveira?

(See Sefer Hamitzvos: Parshas Shoftim #493 and Parshas Acharei Mos #206)

14. What did Rivkah warn her son Yaakov before she sent him to her brother, Lavan?

(Seder Hadoros)

15. Why did Rochel get a curse when she tried to prevent her father from doing *avodah zarah* and witchcraft?

(Bereishis Rabbah 74:5, Sefer Chassidim 924, Zohar 164b)

12. It seems that the stone that was upon the well required about thirty men to roll it off. Can you imagine that Yaakov had the strength to lift up a truck's weight? It was because Yaakov learned *Torah Lishmah*, that he possessed such energy and power!

13. Yaakov set up a stone pillar as a monument in honor of Hashem. Once this was a nice custom, but when the goyim started to use monuments in their idol worship, it became an unfavorable act. Also Yaakov married two (some say, four) sisters, an act that would later become forbidden.

14. Rivka warned Yaakov, her son, not to forget the *mitzvos* when he resided in Lavan's home. She knew that even with a strong Yeshiva education, one who leaves the protection of the "Yeshiva-oasis" and enters the territory of the *yetzer hara* is in trouble if he doesn't arm himself with caution. This is startling. Yaakov was a Gadol Hador, one of the strongest Jews in history and yet she was worried for him. This is a lesson in life. Don't take righteousness for granted. It must be a constant battle against evil until the day of death! (Unfortunately, even in the Yeshivos, we must take every step to make sure the *yetzer hara* doesn't come where he is not welcome!)

15. Although Rochel meant well in preventing her father from sinning, her action was a slight to her father's honor. A child must be sensitive never to hurt the feelings of parents. She also died sooner for acting on her own without consulting her husband, the *Gadol Hador!*

16. What did Yaakov keep saying when he was at Lavan's house?

(Bereishis Rabbah 68:11 and 74:8,11)

17. Why did Yaakov merit so many children (27, to be exact) and so many grandchildren?

(Bereishis Rabbah 79:1, Bava Basra 123a; see Tehillim 128)

18. How was Yaakov miraculously saved from Eisav's ambush at the Yardein River?

(Bereishis Rabbah 76:4)

19. Which five people are compared to the dead?

(Nedarim 64b, Berachos 18a, Bereishis Rabbah 71:6)

20. How could Yaakov marry two sets of sisters? Didn't the *Avos* keep the Torah perfectly?

(Ramban, K'sav Sofer; see Pesachim 119b)

21. Which *"no-goodnik"* told Lavan that Yaakov and his family had left?

(Baal Haturim, Seder Hadoros)

---

16. Yaakov kept on saying *Tehillim*. The pious always learn while they work!

17. Yaakov had extreme *Kedusha* and he was therefore blessed with so many offspring. The *Midrash* says that Yaakov did not leave this world until he saw 600,000 descendants! Indeed, the fear of Hashem is a tremendous merit for great children, in quality & quantity!

18. When Eisav realized Elifaz didn't do his mission, he himself went to murder Yaakov. Hashem miraculously allowed Yaakov to split the Yardein River with his stick and then created a tunnel for him to escape.

19. A blind person, a poverty-stricken person, a *metzorah*, and a barren person feel some-what dead. There is also a completely different group which is also included among the dead, and that's the wicked.

20. It seems that it was only in Israel that they had to keep the whole Torah completely. That is why Rochel Emainu, who was the second sister that he married, had to pass away before he entered Israel.

21. Amalek.

Answers&Facts

22. Why was Leah lucky that she suffered feelings of inferiority?
(The Beginning; see Sefer Chassidim 960)

23. How do we know that Lavan was "money hungry"?
(Bereishis Rabbah 70:13 and 74:11)

24. Why did Yaakov cry when he met Rochel?
(Bereishis Rabbah 70:12,13)

25. When should a person make a promise?
(Shabbos 30b, Bereishis Rabbah 70:1, Vayikra Rabbah 37; see Rambam Hilchos Nedarim 13:23; Tur Yoreh De'ah 203)

26. Why do are there 18 *berachos* in the *Tefillas Shemoneh Esrei?*
(Bereishis Rabbah 69:4)

22. Leah's suffering caused her to pray so much harder, which produced better results than any of the other wives of Yaakov were able to accomplish. Also people, who are ashamed for no reason, eventually are elevated and honored greatly.

23. Lavan kept on changing the terms of his deal with Yaakov concerning which animals to divide in their partnership. He changed the deal a hundred different times. Yaakov had to suffer shame from Lavan's conniving. (It was only temporarily, because the angels carried sheep to Yaakov turning them the way of his agreement.) Moreover, when he met Yaakov, he kissed his mouth in order to check whether there were any jewels in it, for many people carried jewels in hidden places to avoid paying tax on them.

24. Yaakov really cried tears of joy when he met Rochel! Yaakov was also sad that after a hundred twenty years they would not rest together in the Me'aras Hamachpelah. Yaakov also cried that he didn't have any gifts for her. Finally, Yaakov cried because the *goyim* suspected him of acting immorally by kissing Rochel, when they didn't know that she was his five-year-old first cousin.

25. If a person is in danger, he should promise that if Hashem saves him, he will give more *Tzedakah*, and increase his *Ma'asim Tovim*. As a result of this pledge, he will merit more Heavenly protection.

26. The names of the Avos are mentioned together in the Torah 18 times. It's in their merit that we can stand up to pray and petition Hashem these 18 *berachos*. The essence of these 18 *berachos* are praises to Hashem and requests for success in all areas of life.

27. Which *Maaser* (tithe) did Yaakov promise to give in gratitude for his safety?

(Bereishis Rabbah 70:7, Radak)

28. Why did Reuvein give his mother Leah *duda'im* (mandrakes, jasmine, or violets)?

(The Beginning; and see Bereishis Rabbah 71:2)

29. Why was *Rochel* a shepherdess but not *Leah*?

(The Beginning)

30. Why does the *Tefillin Shel Rosh* have two *Shins* on them, one with three heads and one with four heads?

(Minhag Yisroel Torah)

31. Why should expectant women gaze at the faces of *tzadikim*?

(Maharsha on Bava Metzia 84a)

---

27. Yaakov Avinu promised to give *Maaser* of his children, too! Levi was dedicated entirely to Avodas Hashem! Yaakov's grandsons, Ephraim and Menashe were considered like his own children. Four of his sons were firstborn who did not need to be dedicated for service to Hashem, since it was their birthright. Yaakov had ten remaining sons, of whom Levi was the representative of total dedication to Torah study and service to Hashem in the *Beis Hamikdash*.

28. Mandrakes were known to induce fertility. Even the righteous who trust in Hashem are required to utilize the means that are considered effective in their generation to have more children.

29. Leah's eyes were sensitive to the sun, because of her constant weeping. She was praying that she should not fall to the lot of Eisav. Therefore, Rochel her younger sister had to be the shepherd. Moreover, Rochel was active and industrious. She was therefore rewarded through Yaakov's decision to marry her.

30. The letter *Shin* – when it is spelled out "Shin Yud Nun" - is *b'gimatria* 360, which is the same numerical value of *Shas*. The tefillin remind you to learn *Shas*, as our three Avos and four Emahos so wished. It is important to contemplate our ancestors frequently. Even though women don't wear *tefillin*, we must recall that it was great women like our matriarchs who made our nation!

31. What a woman looks at before and during her pregnancy will indeed influence the looks and nature of her child. In the times of Rav Yochanan, one of the most handsome sages in the Gemara, many women would look at the holy Rabbi and pray that their children would be as physically and spiritually beautiful as he!

Answers&Facts

32. Why wasn't Rochel Imeinu buried next to Yaakov Avinu?

(Rashi quoting Bereishis Rabbah 72:3, Rashi 48:7)

33. Why did Yaakov have to get married "without a penny to his name"?

(Bereishis Rabbah 68:5 and 70:12,13, Toras Ha'olah, Seichel Tov; see Ibn Ezra on Parshas Ki Savo)

34. How does friendship with a *talmid chacham* bring someone blessing and good fortune?

(Berachos 42a, Mili d'Berachos, Bereishis Rabbah 73:8,12)

35. How can you tell what is it that you really love most in life?

(Chofetz Chaim referring to Shir Hashirim 3:1; see Sefer Chassidim 291)

---

32. Rochel's tomb had to be located at Beis Lechem so that when her descendants, the Jewish people, went into *Galus*, at least they would have encouragement seeing her tomb and knowing that she was praying for their welfare. Furthermore, Rochel gave up her chance to be in the company of Yaakov in order to acquire the fertility plant; her attitude toward keeping company was not as respectful as it should have been. Therefore, she was denied his company after death as well.

33. Truth to tell, Yaakov was extremely wealthy at first, before Eliphaz robbed his fortune. However, Hashem did not want Rochel or Leah to be influenced by his massive wealth as a motive for marriage. For each of them to marry such a *tzadik*, Hashem wanted their marriage to be one hundred percent *Leshem Shamayim*. Such a marriage that is for Hashem's sake will have the greatest success! Eventually, Yaakov became very wealthy again anyway. Yaakov initially cried that he did not have the jewelry that his father gave him to give his wife-to-be.

34. We find that as soon as Yaakov came to Lavan, Lavan's wealth increased immensely, and he was blessed with sons. We find repeatedly throughout T'nach that when a *tzadik* graces a home with his presence, that home is blessed so much more.

35. What a person dreams about is a clear indication of what the person really loves. The Gemara says that a person dreams what he thinks about. Yaakov Avinu dreamed about angels in heaven and the Torah. What do *we* remember dreaming about?!

36. How old were Leah and Rochel when they got married?

(Seder Hadoros)

37. How long did the *Imahos* Rochel and Leah live?

(Seder Hadoros)

38. Why did Hashem forbid Lavan to say even good things to Yaakov?

(Yevamos 107a, Me'am Lo'ez)

39. Why was Yehuda the most popular of all the *Shevatim*?

(The Beginning)

40. How do we see that it's always best to share your food with others?

(Chullin 4b, Mishlei 25:21, The Beginning, Seichel Tov)

---

36. Leah and Rochel were twenty-two years old when they got married. Some say that Rochel was twelve years old when she married Yaakov. When Yaakov met Rochel and kissed her, she was only five years old.

37. Rochel lived fourteen years after her wedding to the age of thirty-six (and according to some scholars, twenty-six). Leah lived to be forty-four.

38. The Gemara says that what *reshaim* call good, the *tzadikim* call bad! In life we find that righteous and evil people do not even share the same interests. Perhaps this is why Hashem did not want Lavan talking to Yaakov at all. Some explain that even if an idol-worshiper speaks words of goodness, he might use an *avodah zarah's* name in his speech, and Hashem does not want anything of that nature to be mentioned.

39. Yehudah's name means "he shall praise". In actuality, this was a prophecy that the Jewish people will always praise Hashem. Most Jews around us today come from Shevet Yehudah, and real appreciation of Hashem is what makes the Jewish people so very special.

40. The Talmud teaches us that if you want to persuade a person, you can do so by sharing your food and drink with him. It's for this reason that many business deals are closed over a lunch together. Yaakov fed Lavan, his opponent, in order to win him over. As the *pasuk* says, "If your enemy is hungry, give him bread to eat." When you bring a snack to school have your acquaintances in mind and share it with them, and they will probably become more friendly with you. It is for the same reason that it's also very important for husband and wife to go out to eat together, especially on a day like *Rosh Chodesh*, a "women's *Yom Tov*."

Answers&Facts

41. Who performed the *mitzvah* of *"V'ahavta L'rei'acha Kamocha"* (loving your fellow Jew) probably better than anyone else in history?

(Love Your Neighbor)

42. What did Hashem Yisborach reply when Yaakov answered Rochel sternly, *"Am I instead of G-d that I can give you children?"*

(Bereishis Rabbah 71:7)

43. Why didn't the strong, 63-year-old Yaakov just knock out the thirteen-year-old Elifaz when he came to attack him?

(Sichos Mussar)

44. How many angels surround each Jewish person?

(Tanna d'Bei Eliyahu Rabbah 18:55)

45. Did Rochel think she was going to lose Yaakov as her husband by giving him to Leah to marry?

(Bereishis Rabbah 70:17)

41. Rochel Emainu was probably the greatest example of one who selflessly loved another. She gave what she loved most in life— the great holy *tzadik*, Yaakov Avinu, and his home—to her sister so that she wouldn't be embarrassed! This act has got to be the greatest story of *"V'ahavta l'rayacha kamocha"* I have ever heard. In contrast, think about how little we sometimes want to share with our own brothers and sisters!

42. Hashem answered, "Is that the way you talk to a broken-hearted, barren woman? By your life, your children will have to bow down to her child"; indeed, they were humbled during a time of great famine.

43. The *tzadik* Yaakov was extremely powerful. But he knew that it was not worth lessening his sterling character traits by becoming angry even if he could have justified doing so. Anger ruins us all, and Yaakov would not let this negative trait scar his *neshama*.

44. *Chazal* say that the more Torah a person learns, the more angels surround and protect him. Actually, each *mitzvah* you do will create another angel who will defend you. When Yaakov was returning home, the Midrash mentions an astronomical number of angels who came to escort this *tzadik* home. We must try to create good angels from our deeds and not, Heaven forbid, evil ones! There is a tradition that four particular angels surround Jews: Gavriel, Michoel, Rafael and Uriel; interestingly, their initials spell: גמרי"א!

45. Absolutely. Rochel was willing to risk her entire future so that her sister, Leah, should not be humiliated. Wow! What *tzidkus!*

46. How do we see the awesome "power of prayer"?

(Bereishis Rabbah 70:13,15,16, Bava Basra 123b, Eitz Yosef)

47. Why didn't Yaakov marry at a younger age than 84?

(Bereishis Rabbah 68:5 and 70:18, Rav Chaim Pinchas Sheinberg shlit"a)

48. Why should someone never boast about what he is able to do?

(Radak, Bereishis Rabbah 68:12)

49. Why will there be two *Mashiachs*—one descending from Yehudah and one descending from Yosef?

(Maharal)

50. From which two *Shevatim* do most Jews today descend? Why?

(Bereishis Rabbah 73:6)

46. Leah cried her eyes out in prayer that she should marry a righteous person — and not the infamous, wicked Eisav. Not only were her prayers answered, but she also ended up marrying Yaakov even before he married his intended wife Rochel. She also lived much longer as Yaakov's wife. Why, she became the one who rests with Yaakov until now. The *Midrash* comments that Leah ended up being more successful than Rochel, as her descendants were greater!

47. Yaakov knew that his job was to establish a Jewish people. He knew he must have perfect sons without sins. He therefore knew that he had to learn Torah as much as he could, making him that much wiser and greater, so that his offspring would be that much better. (Nowadays, most *Poskim* say that even if you're in Yeshiva learning Torah with all your might, you should get married no later than age twenty-four if at all possible. See Kedushin 30a)

48. The angels Michael and Gavriel said, "We are going to destroy Sedom." That's why they were punished and lost their positions as Hashem's high ministering angels, and they did not regain their positions back for another hundred thirty-eight years. They were among the angels going up and down the ladder in Yaakov's dream. Arrogance causes one disgrace.

49. Yosef was supposed to be Yaakov's *bechor*, and Moshiach was supposed to come from Rochel. But Yehudah was also deserving. So one Moshiach will come from Rochel and one from Leah. May Hashem allow us to see them very happily and soon, Amen!

50. Most of us Jews are from Shevet Yehuda and Binyomin. Some of us (Kohanim and Leviim) come from Shevet Levi. The majority of the other *Shevatim* were punished and sent to the other side of the mysterious Sambatyon River. Yehuda and Binyomin lived in closest proximity to the Beis Hamikdash, which influenced them to be good. They were therefore saved from being exiled there.

Answers & Facts

51. What did Leah answer Yaakov when he said, "You tricked me into thinking you were Rochel"?

(Bereishis Rabbah 70:19)

52. What did Yaakov's dream about the fiery ladder really symbolize?

(Bereishis Rabbah 68:12)

53. What was the symbolism of Yaakov's removing the heavy boulder from the well?

(Bereishis Rabbah 70:12, Toras Chinuch)

54. Did Leah and her children know of Rochel's selflessness in giving Yaakov up to her? If Leah knew, why did she hesitate giving Rochel the fertility plant for free? Also, if the children knew, why did they despise Rochel's son Yosef?

(Sechel Tov)

---

51. When Yaakov saw in the morning that it was Leah he had married, he said, "Why did you trick me, daughter of a trickster?" She replied wittingly: "Doesn't a teacher have students? Just as you pretended to be your brother to do the will of your mother, so too I acted like my sister to do the will of my father!"

52. There were many allusions in Yaakov's dream about the ladder and the angels. One such allusion was to the various ups-and-downs that the Jewish people would experience in Galus!

53. Just as Yaakov removed the boulder in order to give water to the flocks, so too should parents and teachers remove the obstacles that prevent their children and students from learning Torah.

54. It seems that Leah and her sons did not know the extent of Rochel's kindness and selflessness. Because Rochel was very sensitive to Leah's feelings and she convinced Leah that she was really Yaakov's intended wife. Leah did not grasp the *mesiras nefesh* of Rochel. Had they known, they would not have been so mean to Yosef. Leah surely would have given the mandrakes without any conditions.

55. Why does the *Chumash* tell us only about *one* of the five *aveiros* which Eisav did when Avraham died?

(Darash Moshe)

56. When did burglars rob Lavan of all his wealth?

(Bereishis Rabbah 74:16, Eitz Yosef; see Bereishis Rabbah 70:19)

57. What does the *Midrash* mean when it says that ever since Hashem created the world He has been busy making ladders?

(Bereishis Rabbah 68:4)

58. Which four sins was Yaakov most afraid of when he was on the way to Lavan's house?

(Bereishis Rabbah 70:4)

59. How many angels came to greet Yaakov on his way back to Eretz Yisroel?

(Bereishis Rabbah 74:17, The Midrash Says)

---

55. Eisav committed five grave sins on the day on which Avraham Avinu passed away. He killed Nimrod, committed adultery, denied G-d, denied *techias hameisim,* and despised the service in the Beis Hamikdash. However, the Torah mentions specifically only the fact that he despised the *mitzvah* of the *Bechora.* But you should know that this hateful attitude gave rise to all the other sinful behaviors.

56. Right when Yaakov left Lavan's home to return to Eretz Yisroel, burglars came and taunted Lavan all night long as they "cleaned him out" of all his riches. Lavan merited wealth only as a reward for his having the *tzadik* Yaakov near him. Lavan should have appreciated Yaakov much more than he did, for there was a desperate need for water before Yaakov arrived— but as soon as he came, it started to rain. Moreover, his presence brought the blessing of sons upon Lavan.

57. Hashem is constantly raising and lowering people's status. So figuratively, He is constantly making ladders. For example, Hashem decides who will end up getting so-and-so's house, possessions, or position.

58. Yaakov feared Lavan's negative influence, especially regarding the sins of bloodshed, immorality, idolatry, and *lashon hora.*

59. Some say that 600,000 angels came to welcome Yaakov upon his return to Eretz Yisroel, while others say there were 1,200,000! This is no wonder, since the more one learns Torah, the more angels are created to protect him *(Tana D'vei Eliyahu).*

Answers&Facts

60. Which merit caused Hashem to defend Yaakov from Lavan's imminent attack?

(Bereishis Rabbah 78:11)

61. Why did Hashem finally tell Yaakov to leave Lavan's house?

(Bereishis Rabbah 73:12, Eitz Yosef)

62. How do you know that the "neighborhoods" used to be safer in the days of the Avos?

(Bereishis Rabbah 70:11)

63. How do we know that Yaakov dreamed about the Torah?

(Bereishis Rabbah 69:7)

---

60. Yaakov's exemplary honesty in business was the main merit that protected him from the attacking Lavan Ha'arami.

61. As long as Lavan was hospitable to Yaakov, Hashem did not order Yaakov to leave. On the contrary, Hashem said, "When someone opens his door to someone else in need, the recipient owes his life to him!" However, as soon as Lavan started being mean and not showing a kind, pleasant face to Yaakov, then Hashem told Yaakov to leave him.

62. In Yaakov's days, a girl was able to go to the well alone without any fear of harm. However, in the days of Moshe, seven girls went to the well and were endangered by the men who had gathered there.

63. The Torah says, *"Vayikatz Yaakov M'shenaso,"* which can be understood as follows: "Yaakov woke up from his learning Mishnayos." Well, what do you expect? You dream of what you think about! *tzadikim* always think of Torah, the will of Hashem. The ultimate in scholarship is when one sleeps, yet his mind is totally involved in Torah study! Yaakov was learning while he was sleeping, so let's try not to sleep while we are learning!

Dedicated in honor of
RABBI AND MRS. YISHAK DWEK
by Shelomo Dwek & Members of the Deal Synagogue

פרשת וישלח

1. How do we know that boys become *Bar Mitzvah* at the age of thirteen?

(Metzuveh V'oseh quoting Bereishis Rabbah 80:10, Toras Ha'olah)

2. Why did an evil angel attack Yaakov and not Avraham or Yitzchak?

(Kovetz Maamarim quoting the Chofetz Chaim, The Midrash Says)

FUndamental Answers!

"יגעתי ומצאתי!"

("I worked on these questions, and I found these answers!")

1. We learn the age of Bar Mitzvah from Shimon and Levi, who destroyed the wicked people in Shechem for being immoral. The Torah refers to one of them as a man for standing up against evil in his time. At that time, Shimon was thirteen years old and the first to be called a man. This is because the sign of being a man is to be able to stand up against evil.

2. The Yetzer Hara doesn't mind if you preoccupy yourself with acts of kindness or with prayers, just as Avraham and Yitzchak did. But let me tell you something: He hates when you learn Torah as Yaakov did, and that is what he really tries to prevent!

3. On which day of the year did Eisav's angel attack Yaakov Avinu?

(Seder Hadoros)

4. What did Yaakov wish that he had learned from Lavan, his father-in-law?

(Kovetz Maamarim quoting the Chofetz Chaim pg.97)

5. Why didn't Eisav's angel want to reveal his name to Yaakov?

(The Beginning, Az Nidberu, Rabbeinu Bachya, Ramban)

6. Why did Shimon and Levi massacre the city of Shechem?

(The Beginning, Shaarei Aharon citing Rambam Hilchos Melachim 9:14)

7. What does the name *"Yisroel"* (the name we share with Yaakov Avinu) mean?

(Rashi to 32:29, The Beginning)

---

3. Tisha B'av.

4. Yaakov wished that he would serve Hashem with a strong passion, *(lehavdil)* just as Lavan so energetically pursued evil.

5. The angel who attacked Yaakov was the angel who represented Eisav. This angel is essentially the Yetzer Hara, and he represents evil in this world. He could not tell Yaakov his name because the Yetzer Hara's name changes every day, since he constantly changes his strategies and tricks. He also didn't want Yaakov to know his name because he didn't want Yaakov's descendants to know how he was attacking. Others say that he didn't want his name to become an *avoda zara*, because angels are very sensitive to Hashem's honor.

6. The people who lived in the city of Shechem deserved death because they didn't have a real justice system. Why wasn't Shechem Ben Hamor brought to trial for kidnapping Dinah, an innocent girl? For covering up for Shechem, the people were considered accomplices to the crime.

7. "Yisroel" means that Yaakov will in the future gain the final power over all opposition. It can also be translated as "God rules". Or as "Prince of Hashem"! The angel stressed that Hashem would reveal Himself to Yaakov in Beis El and bless him in an official way. This would show that Yaakov didn't acquire the blessings through trickery or deception (as implied from the word *eikev*), but rather they were really Divinely bestowed on him.

---

8. Why was Yaakov afraid of Eisav's army; after all, hadn't Hashem promised to protect him? Don't we have a *mitzvah* of *Bitachon*, to put our trust in Hashem? Also, didn't Yaakov know that our secret defense system, "*HaKol Kol Yaakov*" (the sound of Torah study and *Tefillah*), protects us from "*Yadayim Yedei Eisav*" (the threatening violence of Amalek)?

(The Beginning, Bereishis Rabbah 76:2, Berachos 3a, Beis Halevi)

9. Yaakov told Eisav that Hashem had blessed him with great success because he kept all the 613 *Mitzvos*. But how could he have performed all the *Mitzvos* if he didn't live in Eretz Yisroel during the days of the *Beis Hamikdash?*

(Taam V'daas quoting the Chofetz Chaim)

10. Which parts of a kosher animal and beast are we forbidden to eat?

(Chullin 89b, Shulchan Aruch Yoreh De'ah 65:5)

11. What happened to the staff that Yaakov used to split the Yardein River while he was escaping from Eisav?

(Yalkut Shimoni)

---

8. Yaakov was scared that he might not be protected because he or his children could have sinned. In addition, Yaakov did not feel that he was learning Torah during that last period as vigorously as he used to.

9. Yaakov longed in his heart to fulfill all the mitzvos. He was therefore credited as if he had actually done them. Also, one who studies about a *mitzvah* is rewarded as if he actually performed it.

10. We are not allowed to eat the following parts of a kosher animal: *chelev* (certain fat), *gid hanasheh* (sciatic nerve), *shuman hagid* (the fat surrounding the *gid hanasheh*), and its blood.

11. The miracle-making staff of Yaakov was passed on to Yehuda and then to Moshe and Aharon and eventually to Dovid Hamelech. Moshiach is going to get hold of that staff and beat the enemies of Klal Yisroel with it very soon!

Answers&Facts

Questions & Riddles

12.
What type of house did Yaakov build?

(Targum Yonasan ben Uziel 33:17)

13.
What was Yaakov worried about during Eisav's threatening approach?

(Rashi, Targum Yonasan ben Uziel, Bereishis Rabbah 76:2, Ramban)

14.
Which blessing did Eisav's angel give to Yaakov?

(Shaarei Aharon, Rabbeinu Bachya, Midrash Avkir; see Taanis 6b)

15.
Yaakov's sheep were great in quality and in quantity. How much money were people willing to pay Yaakov to acquire even one of his 200,000 animals?

(Sefer Hayashar)

16.
Why is it ironic that Dinah is buried next to the *Tanna*, Rabbi Nitai Ha'arbeili?

(Mili d'Avos 1:7, Midrash Shocher Tov 34:1)

---

12. Yaakov built a Beis Medrash (House of Torah Study). That is the "house" that the *pasuk* tells us he built. Some say that he built a fortress so that Eisav wouldn't be able to attack his family.

13. Yaakov was concerned that Eisav was coming to fight him, assisted by the power of two Mitzvos that he did better than Yaakov—namely, *Kibud Av V'em* and *Yishuv Eretz Yisroel*. Yaakov was scared that someone in his family could be hurt, and that he might possibly have to kill Eisav in self-defense.

14. The angel blessed Yaakov that his sons should be *tzadikim* just like him!

15. Yaakov's sheep were so fat and fine that people pleaded with him to accept their powerful servants, horses, and camels, as a trade for any of his "blessed" sheep.

16. The Tanna Rabbi Nitai H'arbeili is noted for saying, "Stay away from a bad neighbor, and don't befriend a *rasha*." Dinah's downfall was caused by her going out to see what the *goyim* were enjoying. When Yaakov was learning in the Beis Midrash with all his sons, she strolled outside adorned with jewelry as if to call attention to herself. She was greatly disgraced. Therefore she was buried next to this sage, whose advice she should have heeded.

142   » *TorahShows' Questions & Riddles* ■ *Vayishlach*

17. Why is it inappropriate to watch a non-Jewish parade?

(Koheles Rabbah 10:8, Seder Hadoros, Pirkei d'Rabi Eliezer 38)

18. What is "good" about Anti-Semitism?

(The Beginning)

19. Why didn't the *Avos Hakedoshim* accept Princess Timna as a convert?

(Sanhedrin 99b)

20. For how long was Dinah kidnapped?

(Maseches Sofrim 21:9)

21. What was the symbolism of Yaakov's fight against the evil angel?

(Bereishis Rabbah 77:3)

22. Why did Yaakov's sons confiscate the money of the people of Shechem? Do we want non-Jews to call us robbers and thieves?

(The Beginning, Ohr Hachaim)

---

17. The goyim were making a parade and celebrating. When Rachel, Leah, and the Shefachos went out, Dinah was noticed by Shechem who took her.

18. Anti-Semitism subsequently distances us from the non-Jews. We are different! Through their anti-semitism they remind us of this fact, and that's much better for us, so as not to assimilate with them.

19. Princess Timna was prevented by the Avos from converting. They must have been concerned of negative tendencies in her character. However, she still wanted to be associated with our eminent Avos. So she married Eisav's son Elifaz, and gave birth to Amalek.

20. It seems Dinah was kidnapped for a short period of time. She was six years old when she gave birth to Osnas.

21. Just as Yaakov overcame his adversary victoriously, so too the Jewish people will prevail over those that want their harm!

22. Dinah's brothers expropriated all the city of Shechem's money because they collected *boshes* (humiliation fine). Chazal say, "*Hakol lefee hamevayesh vihamesbayesh.*" Can all their money atone for the atrocity they committed against *Beis Yisroel*? Now, even though, those *goyim* were executed, we don't say "*Kom lei bederabah minei*" (to forgo the lesser punishment) by *goyim*.

Answers&Facts

23. What did Yaakov cry about when Eisav was on the warpath?

(Bereishis Rabbah 75:13 and 76:6)

24. Who was physically stronger, Yaakov or Eisav?

(Bereishis Rabbah 77:3)

25. Why can't we eat the *gid hanasheh* (sinew on the upper joint of the thigh)? How can the *mitzvah* of not eating the *gid hanasheh* encourage us during this long exile?

(Sefer Hachinuch, Tur, Chizkuni, Daas Zekeinim)

26. When did Eisav experience *kefitzas haderech* (miraculously speeded-up travel)?

(Seichel Tov)

---

23. Yaakov cried for his immediate family's safety, and his future descendants as well. Yaakov prayed crying that the Jewish people not be endangered by Eisav's descendants. In addition, Yaakov prayed that if the Jews needed to suffer for their sins, at least let it be spread over the generations and not close together.

24. Of course, Yaakov was mightier than Eisav. Certainly, if Eisav's angel couldn't defeat Yaakov, do you think that Eisav could? Yaakov threw the angel into the dust! Yaakov got his supernatural strength from learning *Torah Lishmah* — with 100% sincere intentions!

25. The Bnei Yisroel were punished by never being to be allowed to eat the *gid hanasheh* of an animal or beast, since Yaakov's sons didn't escort him when he went back alone at night to retrieve some forgotten containers. Their father was wounded in that very part of his body. We, their descendants, are reminded eternally to honor and escort parents! There is another great symbolism in that ordeal. Yaakov was tormented by his sciatic nerve. But afterwards, Hashem made the sun shine special rays to heal him. This event symbolizes that in this night of *galus* although the goyim beat us, the *geulah* will appear as a sunrise, and Hashem will heal all the wounds and scars of his people, both physically and emotionally!

26. After Eisav met Yaakov and left for Seir, Hashem sped up Eisav's trip so that Yaakov would not have to suffer undue discomfort in the presence of that frightening and wicked terrorist, Eisav Harasha.

27. What happened when Eisav tried to bite his brother Yaakov?

(Bereishis Rabbah 78:9, Pirkei d'Rabi Eliezer, Targum Yonasan ben Uziel, Targum Yerushalmi)

28. How was Yaakov punished for flattering the *rasha* Eisav by calling him "my master" eight times?

(Bereishis Rabbah 75:11 and 83:2, Bereishis 36:31)

29. What did Yaakov's sons do before burying the *avodah zarah* that they found in Shechem?

(Bereishis Zuta, Gemara Avodah Zarah 52b)

30. Why is it good that Jews are dispersed throughout the lands instead of residing together as one nation?

(Pesachim 87b, Chofetz Chaim)

31. Why did Rochel Imeinu have to pass away during childbirth?

(Zohar)

---

27. When Eisav tried to bite Yaakov's neck (like a vampire!) he discovered that Yaakov's neck became as hard as marble, and Eisav cracked his teeth. This was in fulfillment of the *pasuk:* "Sheenei reshaim shebarta" (the teeth of the wicked will be smashed). (He cried that now he needed dentures!)

28. Since Yaakov flattered the wicked Eisav, calling him "master" *eight* times, Eisav had *eight* descendants who were kings long before any of Yaakov's descendants became kings.

29. Yaakov's sons crushed and ground up the *avoda zara* before they buried it.

30. That we Jews are dispersed all over the globe is a blessing in disguise. Hashem has seen to it that the *goyim* are unable to wipe us all out.

31. The Zohar says that Rochel didn't get to enjoy Binyomin in her lifetime, since she had pained her father when she confiscated his ridiculous *avoda zara*. (It seems that this is proof to the opinion in *Shulchan Aruch* (Yoreh Deah 240:18) that declares even if a parent is a *rasha* one must honor and fear him.]

Questions & Riddles

32. What did Mordechai tell Haman about their ancestors?

(Me'am Lo'ez)

33. What did Shimon and Levi rely on as they waged war against Shechem?

(Bereishis Rabbah 80:10)

34. Why was Yaakov punished with Dinah's abuse as a result of not having given her as a wife to Eisav? After all, even Dinah's mother, Leah, had cried her eyes out because she did not want to marry him!

(Bereishis Rabbah 76:9 and 81:1-2, Rabbi Avigdor Miller zt"l, Eitz Yosef)

35. Why was the *Kodesh HaKodashim* built on Binyomin's territory?

(Kol Eliyahu, Chida quoting Rabbanei Ashkenaz, Seichel Tov)

36. How many Rabbis do we know about who had the privilege of learning privately with angels?

(Maggid Meisharim)

32. Mordechai told Haman, "Just like my grandfather, Binyomin Hatzadik, never bowed to your grandfather, Eisav Harasha, so too, I am not bowing down to you either!"

33. Shimon and Levi counted on their *zechus Avos* as they fought the enemy.

34. We find in the Gemara that Rav Yochanan gave his sister to a Jewish gangster in order to make him the famous Baal Teshuva and Amora Reish Lakish. She obviously brought him to Torah. However, Yaakov hid Dinah away in a crate so Eisav shouldn't take her. We can understand Yaakov's trepidation. However, he should have cried when he knocked in the nails into the crate, because he should have wished to be of greater assistance to his brother.

35. Binyomin was harassed by his brothers when they suspected him of stealing the goblet from Pharaoh's viceroy (Yosef). They hit him between his shoulders. Hashem ultimately defends the honor of those who are hurt for no reason. Hashem sympathizes with someone who has been socially degraded, and that's why His *Shechinah* was in Binyomin's portion! Another reason is that Binyomin never bowed to Eisav Harasha.

36. The Tur had an angel help him write his popular commentary known as the Baal Haturim in one night! Moshe Rabbeinu wrote thirteen Sifrei

37. What was so important about the containers that Yaakov went back over the river to get?

(Chullin 91a)

38. Of whom was Dinah a *Gilgul?*

(Toras HaChida quoting Mekubalim)

39. Yaakov divided his family into two groups so that the attacking enemy would not be able to kill all of them. Who constitutes the *"P'leitah"* (remnants) of Yaakov's family today?

(See Bereishis Rabbah 76:3, Novominsker Rebbe shlit"a, Kol Haneshamah)

40. Why do many Jews wrap a red string around Kever Rachel as a *segulah?*

(Toras Ha'olah)

Torah on his last day in this world, with angelic help. The Beis Yosef, the Arizal, and their colleagues also benefited from angels who aided them in their growth in Torah and Yiras Shamayim. It's no wonder—because these *tzadikim* were themselves such angels! As the Gemara says regarding Gedolim of previous generations: *"Rishonim k'malachim"!*

37. Yaakov wanted the forgotten containers because they were purchased with kosher/clean money. That kind of money is hard to acquire, but it buys much more blessing than does ill-gotten money.

38. Dinah was a reincarnation of her great-great-grandmother, Amtelai bas Carnevo, Avraham Avinu's mother.

39. After the Holocaust, Jews who are alive today must feel that they are the remnant who must make up for all the millions of victims of violence by their study of Torah and their adherence to Hashem's Mitzvos. (I'm reminded of a story that happened to a friend in an airport. He was blessed with a large family and his numerous children were running around the waiting area of the terminal. A German woman who was obviously impatient with her wait, kept on looking at the family with disgust. Finally she rudely asked the father of the children, "How many kids do you have? When are you going to stop?" He answered brilliantly, "When I have six million!")

40. Red signifies the shame that Rachel spared her sister, Leah. Such self-sacrifice for another Jew is an everlasting merit which is symbolized by a red string.

Answers&Facts

41. How were the 400 soldiers of Eisav rewarded for running away and not battling Yaakov?

(Shmuel I 30:17, Bereishis Rabbah 78:15)

42. How do we see that curiosity can be a bad trait?

(Seder Hadoros)

43. Why was Shechem's father called Chamor (donkey)?

(Midrash, Seichel Tov 33:19)

44. How do we see the names of the *Avos* and *Imahos* alluded to in the name 'Yisroel'?

(Tuvecha Yabi'u)

45. What does it mean that Yaakov was *shaleim* (complete)?

(Rashi, Bereishis Rabbah 79:5)

41. Since the 400 powerful soldiers of Eisav fled, choosing to leave Eisav all alone, and not to combat Yaakov, 400 Amaleki soldiers escaped in a battle later on in history when Dovid Hamelech fought against the Amalekim who had burned down his town Tsiklag.

42. Curiosity can be a detrimental trait if it motivates a person to learn how the wicked live and act. After all, curiosity will then contaminate the mind of its possessor. Dinah should not have gone out to observe the festivities of the *goyim* in Shechem, and she would have lived happily ever after.

43. Shechem's father was called Chamor because his intelligence was no better that that of a donkey. Why, he even had to appoint his son to make all the decisions for him.

44. The *Yud* in *Yisroel* stands for Yitzchak and Yaakov. The *Sinn* stands for Sarah. The *Reish* stands for Rivka and Rachel. The *Alef* stands for Avraham. And guess what? The *Lamed* stands for Leah!

45. Yaakov survived Lavan's home, and he even arrived to Eretz Yisroel "complete". This means he had been healed from his limp, that none of his children were hurt by Eisav; that he was healthy; that he was wealthy; and that he remembered all the Torah that he had previously learned!

46. How old was Yaakov when he returned to Eretz Yisroel?

(Seder Hadoros)

47. Why did Dinah marry Iyov?

(Bereishis Rabbah 76:9 and 80:4, Seder Hadoros)

48. What was Reuven's "sin"?

(Shabbos 55b, Midrash Talpios; see Karnei Re'em, Zera Yitzchak)

49. Which *pesukim* in *Parshas Vayishlach* are appropriate to read before traveling so as to merit a successful trip?

(Beis Tefillah by the Chassid Yaavetz)

50. How many angels, disguised as powerful soldiers and cavalry, did Yaakov send against Eisav and his 400 warriors (or generals)?

(Bereishis Rabbah 78:11 and 75:10,12, Seder Hadoros)

---

46. Yaakov was 99 when he returned to Eretz Yisrael. I guess it's never too late to make *Aliyah!*

47. Dinah's incident with Shechem occurred when she was but a young girl. (Between 6-10) She was so humiliated that she refused to leave Shechem's house until Shimon had promised to marry her. Afterwards, however, he divorced her, and Yaakov gave her to marry the righteous Iyov. As you can plainly see, Dinah suffered on account of her curiosity.

48. Reuven didn't really sin. He just tried to defend his mother's (Leah's) honor. He saw that Yaakov was going to move into Bilhah's (Rachel's maid's) house. He thought that it was an insult for his mother that a maidservant should become her *tzarah* (rival) as well! He moved Yaakov's bed into Leah's house. This is called a sin because a child must respect a parent's decision.

49. On Motzoei Shabbos before leaving on a trip one can read Parshas Vayishlah as a *segulah* for a successful trip.

50. Yaakov sent (approximately) four million angelic soldiers against Eisav! Eisav was overwhelmed. He asked the ones clothed in armor to whom they belonged, and they said, "Yaakov." He saw the horsemen and charioteers and they said, "We are Yaakov's." They so agitated Eisav's army that Eisav felt compelled to beg for his life, and he even called himself Yaakov's brother. They shook the hatred out of him, albeit temporarily! When Eisav met Yaakov, he asked, "Where did you get such an army?"

Answers&Facts

---

51. Why did the righteous General Avner insist that Shaul Hamelech and his son, Ish-Boshess, reign as kings before Dovid Hamelech?

(Bereishis Rabbah 82:4)

52. Which grandson(s) of Eisav tried to kill all the Jews?

(Eitz Yosef, Bereishis Rabbah 83:2)

53. When did hate temporarily turn into love?

(Bereishis Rabbah 78:9 and 54:1)

54. From where do we learn that you should patronize your own country?

(Bereishis Rabbah 79:10)

55. Why was it imperative that the *Nasi* (President) of Klal Yisroel be wealthy?

(Berachos 27b, see Rashi 32:9)

---

51. Avner reasoned that Ish-Boshes should be king after Shaul, his father, instead of Dovid. Yoav and most of Shevet Yehuda sided with Dovid and crowned him king. But, Avner, Shaul's mighty general, opposed them. He understood the *pasuk* "*And kings will issue from you*" to refer to Shevet Binyomin who was yet to be born. So at least two kings had to come from Shevet Benyomin. In reality, this prophecy referred to kings from Shevet Yehuda as well.

52. Haman and Hitler tried to annihilate the Jews. (We don't know for sure if Hitler was a direct descendant of Eisav, but it sure seems so!) Let's always remember: you can defeat Amalek with Torah and Tefillah!

53. Yaakov sent presents to Eisav and cried to Hashem for peace. Consequently, some say that Eisav's attitude toward Yaakov turned *from hatred to love* for that one day. Why, his bite even turned into a kiss!

54. When Yaakov arrived in Shechem, he showed his appreciation and helped its economy. He minted a coin, had stores opened, and sent gifts to the town leaders. We must show appreciation to the country and city that hosts us in our exile.

55. The elected *Nasi* needed to be a man of means so that people would respect his word. As the saying goes, "the wisdom of the poor is despised" (Koheles). Also, he would need funds to be able to establish good public relations with the government and bribe them if need be.

56. How do we see that Yosef had the strength to overpower Eisav?

(Shemos 17:13)

57. To whom was Yaakov bowing seven times when Eisav came to attack him?

(Bereishis Rabbah 78:8)

58. Yosef was missing for 22 sad years as a punishment for Yaakov Avinu's not having fulfilled the *Mitzvah* of *Kibud Av V'em* for 22 years (from the age of 77 to 99). Why was this Yaakov's fault? After all, he had to leave his parents in order to get married and build his family!

(Chasam Sofer, Kesher Shel Kayama quoting Kiddushin 30b)

59. What miracle happened to Yaakov Avinu at the Jordan River?

(Bereishis Rabbah 76:5)

---

56. Yehoshua, a descendant of Yosef was the one Moshe sent to battle and defeat Amalek.

57. When Yaakov appeared to be bowing to his brother Eisav, in reality, he was only concentrating on Hashem. [Interestingly, in Shemoneh Esrei we bow to Hashem seven times.]

58. Yaakov was punished by not being able to enjoy his son Yosef for 22 years, since Yaakov himself wasn't in touch enough with his parents for the 22 years he resided at Lavan's house. Rivkah never got to see her religious grandchildren in her lifetime. She died just as Yaakov was returning to his parents home 36 years later.

59. Eisav tried to corner Yaakov by the water and cause him to drown. Hashem dug him a route to safety. Then Yaakov hit the water and it split allowing him a safe escape.

60. Was Yaakov afraid of the fiery angel that came to attack him?

(*Bereishis Rabbah 77:2, Ovadyah 1:18, Yirmiyah 23:29, Tanchuma on Parshas Yisro 17, Devarim Rabbah 3:13, The Midrash Says*)

61. Which *Mitzvah* did Yaakov perform as soon as he arrived in Shechem?

(*Bereishis Rabbah 79; see Mishnayos Eiruvin chapter 5*)

62. What will the sun do in the future days of *Mashiach*?

(*Bereishis Rabbah 78:5, Malachi 3:19-20, Avodah Zarah 3a*)

---

60. The evil angel was disguised as a shepherd or a gangster. He originally acted as if he was assisting Yaakov, but then he showed his fire. Yaakov was not nervous at all, as he replied, "You want to scare me with fire, when I am all fire, as the Navi Ovadia will later say 'the house of Yaakov is fire that will consume Eisav'!" Yaakov represented Torah which is fiery.

61. Yaakov arrived in Shechem just before Shabbos. He marked the *Techum* limits so that none of his children should walk outside this area on Shabbos. Just as Shabbos differentiates between the holy and mundane, Yaakov wanted to instill in his children the carefulness not to intermingle with the neighbors that were not G-d fearing.

62. When Moshiach comes soon, Hashem will make the sun burn the wicked and heal the righteous. May this happen in our time, *Amen!*

פרשת וישב

? 1. Why did Yaakov love his son Yosef more than he loved all his other sons?

(*Bava Basra 123a, Targum Yonasan, Tanchuma 2, Ramban, Bereishis Rabbah 84 and 94*)

2. Why did Yosef's brothers throw him into a pit?

(*Malbim*)

FUNdamental Answers!

"יגעתי ומצאתי!"

(*"I worked on these questions, and I found these answers!"*)

1. Aside from the fact that Yosef was born from Yaakov's main wife, Rochel, and that he was born when Yaakov was very old (at age 91), Yosef was extraordinarily brilliant, and he used his gifted mind for Torah. He absorbed the decades worth of Torah that Yaakov had learned at the *Yeshivos* of Shem and Ever at the young age of 17! He also loved him more because he looked exactly like him, which was a sign of his uniqueness. They had so much in common: Both were born *mahul*; both had mothers who initially were barren; both had brothers who hated them; both had dreams of greatness, etc.

2. Yosef's brothers felt that Yosef was showing off, as though he were superior and they were inferior. By throwing him into a pit, he would be humbled; his spirit would be crushed. They were also worried that just as Avraham had Yishmael and Yitzchak had Eisav, maybe Yosef thought, that he was a *tzadik* and all the other brothers were wicked sons. They felt he was belittling them before Yaakov in order

3. Why did Yosef's brothers buy shoes with the money they received from selling Yosef?

(Chida)

4. Why was Yosef the first Jew to have to go into *Galus* (exile)?

(Maayanah Shel Torah)

5. Why was Yaakov beset by many hardships in his life although he had prayed for tranquility?

(Bereishis Rabbah 84:3, K'sav Sofer, Taam V'daas, Rashi)

---

that he be blessed and they be cursed. Because they saw him as a threat, they tried to get rid of him. As the *Gemara* says: "If someone comes to kill you, you are allowed to kill him first in self-defense."

3. Because of *Sinas Chinam* there would have to be a long exile, before the Jews could come back to Yerushalayim, their home. The shoes symbolized that the Bnei Yisroel would be doing a lot of walking until they return to Eretz Yisroel. As the Gemara says in Yoma, (9b) the Beis Hamikdash was destroyed because of senseless hatred.

4. Yosef had exceptional ability to stay holy, even in an environment that was impure and corrupt. Knowing that the Jewish people would someday have to be sent into exile, it was needed that someone with this tremendous quality of holiness would lead the way so that later on we too could be pure even in an immoral society and corrupt environment.

5. Indeed, the Mishnah in Sanhedrin tells us that tranquility is good for righteous people because they use their time to learn and teach Hashem's Torah to everyone around them. So really, asking for tranquility is a perfectly fine request. However, since Yaakov, our forefather, was to be the role model for all generations for us to emulate, he needed to endure hardships, so that we could all learn how he stayed faithful to Hashem and to be the shining example for us to follow throughout the trials we have to face in our own lives. It was for this reason that Yaakov was unable to have a totally serene and peaceful life. He had to have hardships with his own children- whether it was Dina's kidnapping or Yosef's kidnapping - in order to show us how to stay firm and have bitachon in Hashem that all will turn out well. Another explanation is that the Satan complains that *tzadikim* are going to have so much peace, tranquility, pleasure and delight in the World-to-Come that they have no need for these qualities in this world also. Hashem is teaching us that the righteous should not be worried about their comfort in this world because they ought to be focused on the real world, the World-to-Come, which is so much better.

---

6. **What was the last *halachah* that Yaakov taught Yosef before his disappearance?**

(Riva)

7. **Why did Yosef reveal his "dreams of self-glory" if he knew that doing so would cause jealousy?**

(Moshav Zekeinim quoting Sanhedrin 89a, Ohr Hachaim quoting Berachos 56a)

8. **Why did Yaakov give Yosef the regal *kesoness pasim* (multi-colored cloak) if doing so would arouse jealousy and sibling rivalry?**

(Bava Basra 21a, Chasam Sofer)

9. **What did Yosef's brothers often give him?**

(Bereishis Rabbah 87:4)

---

6. The last *mitzvah* that Yaakov discussed with Yosef before his disappearance was *mitzvah* number 530, the *mitzvah* of *Egla Arufa*. This *mitzvah* revolves around what Beis Din must do if they find a dead body without any trace of the killer. They must take a young calf and break its neck by the river in order to make everyone shiver that here a man was plucked out of this world at such a young age when he could have accomplished so much. Knowing this, people would become more sensitive and careful to prevent murder in their midst. Interestingly enough, Yosef also was a young man, only 17 when he was plucked away from his family. There was so much that he and his family could have done together.

7. Yosef thought that this was a prophecy, not just a regular dream, and the Torah says that a *Navi* is not allowed to hold back a prophecy; rather, he must utter it, or else he's punished by death. Yosef felt that he had no choice, and perhaps he didn't want to tell them, but he felt that doing so was his obligation. Also Yosef knew that you're supposed to tell your dreams to your friends so that they can interpret them positively.

8. Yaakov really felt that since Yosef learned Torah so well, he would serve as a splendid example for his other sons to follow. Yaakov figured that if he gave Yosef a special gift, this would cause "jealousy of the scholars," which the Gemara says increases their wisdom because each one tries harder to achieve more. But the painful reality is that favoritism in class does not cause the other boys to try harder; it just causes animosity toward that exceptional student.

9. When Yaakov saw a nice portion, he would save it for Yosef. Yosef's brothers were jealous, and they would give him an *Ayin Hara*.

10. What *Lashon Hara* did Yosef say about his brothers because he suspected them of evil deeds?

(See Me'am Lo'ez; Shaarei Aharon, Bartenura, Re'em, Yefas To'ar, Pesachim 113b)

11. To what were the *tzadikim*, Yosef and Gidon compared in their dreams?

(Rabbeinu Bachya citing Sefer Shoftim 7:14)

12. Why did the sons of Yaakov pasture their sheep in Shechem, of all places?

(Shaarei Aharon)

---

10. Yosef was *Motzi Shem Rah* on his brothers. He saw them doing suspicious things, and he should have given them the benefit of the doubt. What did he see? a) He saw them eating an animal which seemed to be alive (*Ever Min Hachai*) without having been properly 'slaughtered' first. In reality though it was a calf that was in its mother's stomach at the time of *Shechita* and the law is that the *shechita* of the mother permits the calf to be eaten without its having been slaughtered itself. b) He saw that they were degrading the sons of the *Shefachos* - namely, *Gad, Asher, Dan,* and *Naftali.* He said that they called them slaveboys. C) He said that they were gazing at the girls of the land, but in reality, they were merely involved in business transactions with the *goyim.* Yosef was punished measure for measure. When the brothers sold him, they 'slaughtered' a goat whose blood they used for dipping his coat. He said that they called the sons of the *Shefachos,* slaves, and he himself was sold as a slave. He said that they were staring at women, and his punishment was that he was put into a terrible situation with an immodest woman.

11. Yosef was compared to a stalk of wheat, and Gideon was compared to a loaf of barley. The reason that Yosef dreamed about wheat was because later the brothers would need wheat during a time of famine, during which time they would come down to Mitzrayim and bow down to Yosef. Sometimes, people bow down and are forced to humble themselves before others in order to get food to eat. In Gideon's time, it was in the merit of their bringing the barley of the *Korban Omer* that the Jewish people were saved and that's why he was compared to barley.

12. The brothers had just finished destroying Shechem after the episode with Dinah. They went to graze their sheep there to show that they were not scared of the people who lived there because they deserved punishment, and they showed trust in Hashem that He would protect them for standing up to evil people.

13. **What happened to the shepherd dogs that were sent to attack Yosef Hatzaddik?**

(Bereishis Rabbah 84:14, Rokeach quoting Pesachim 118a, Ramban, Tur)

14. **Why are goats used on *Rosh Chodesh* and *Yom Kippur* to atone for our sins?**

(Moreh Nevuchim 3:46)

15. **Why were ten outstanding *Tannaim* (Rabbis of the *Mishnah*) tortured to death? ה' ינקום דמם**

(Rabbeinu Bachya on Parshas Mikeitz; see Rambam Hilchos Geneivah 9:5)

16. **What did a wolf say to Yaakov Avinu?**

(Seder Hadoros)

---

13. Some say that the brothers wanted to send their shepherd dogs to attack Yosef Hatzadik, since the Gemara says that one who speaks *Lashon Hara* deserves to be thrown to the dogs. But when they tried to send the dogs to attack him, Yosef's righteousness protected him and they didn't attack him.

14. The brothers sold Yosef and dipped his beautiful coat in goat's blood (which resembles human blood). We must always remember this act of "sibling rivalry." This is why on Rosh Chodesh and Yom Kippur we must use a goat to atone for our sins. We are thus reminded to do *teshuva* for this common sin of not getting along within our own family. (It would be a good idea for us to accept upon ourselves that every Rosh Chodesh we pause and send a loving letter to our family, or some other treat.)

15. We find in the history of our people ten tragic occurrences in which Tanaaic Rabbis were murdered in cold blood. The Rabbis were: *Rabbi Shimon ben Gamliel, Rabbi Yishmael ben Elisha-Kohen Gadol, Rabbi Akiva, Rabbi Yehuda ben Bava, Rabbi Chananya ben Tradyon, Rabbi Yeshovev Hasofer, Rabbi Elazar ben Dama, Rabbi Chanina ben Chachinoi, Rabbi Chutzpus Hametorgemin, and Rabbi Elazar ben Shamua.* Their deaths were required to atone for the 10 great *tzadikim* - the sons of Yaakov - who had participated in Yosef's sale. The reason that death was their punishment is that the Torah warns that if someone kidnaps another and sells him, he is punished by death. It seems that those great *Tannaim* were in some way the *Gilgulim* of the 10 *Shevatim*.

16. Brokenhearted, Yaakov demanded that his sons search for the body of Yosef, who seemed to have been attacked by a beast. He said to bring the first wild animal that they were to see; maybe that will be the predator. They brought Yaakov a wolf, and Yaakov cried out bitterly, "Why did you eat Yosef, my son!? Why didn't you fear Hashem!? Why did you kill my son, my innocent son!?" Hashem made a miracle and the wolf spoke and said, "I swear to Hashem

---

17. What happened when the Arabs beat Yosef near *Kever Rochel* (his mother's grave)?

(Seder Hadoros)

18. When did an eleven-month-old baby argue with its mother?

(Seder Hadoros)

who made me and by the life of you my master that I did not see your son. I come from a faraway land because my son also is missing. Many days I have searched for my son and did not find him, and now they capture me to add more misery!? I never tasted human flesh in my life!" Yaakov was astonished by its speech, and the wolf was sent away in peace.

17. When the Arabs were taking Yosef down to Mitzrayim, he kept on crying and screaming, "Father! Father!" And the Arabs beat him in the face. Yosef kept on crying uncontrollably until he could not cry anymore. They beat him and threatened him that he had better stop crying. Hashem saw the pain of Yosef, and Hashem made the hands of those who hit him become paralyzed; they didn't know what had happened to them. When they passed by Rochel's grave, Yosef ran to his mother's grave and cried, "Mommy! Mommy! Wake up and see your son — how he was sold as a slave — and no one has pity on me. Cry with me in my pain, and see what my brothers have done to me. Wake up, Mommy, and fight for me! They tore me away from my father without pity!" Yosef cried a great cry until he was silent, and he then heard a voice come from under the ground: "My son, my son, Yosef, my son, I've heard your cry and your scream. I've seen your tears. I know your pain, my son, and it hurts me greatly. But my son, now you must wait for Hashem and pray to Him; don't be scared because Hashem will be with you. He will save you from all tragedy. Go, my son, to Mitzrayim and don't be scared." Rochel strengthened Yosef and encouraged him. Yosef still cried until one of the Arabs pulled him away again and hit him and cursed him. Yosef begged, "Take me back to my father, he is very rich, and he will ransom me" but they said, "Quiet, you're a slave," and they began to beat him again. Hashem defended Yosef's honor by creating a storm replete with lightning and thunder. The ground trembled, and all the people were scared; they couldn't even move on. They wondered what sin they committed that made G-d do this to them. And then they realized it must be because they were mean to that servant, and they begged his forgiveness. Yosef prayed to Hashem, and the storm stopped. They then decided that Yosef was not worth the consequences that they would have to suffer, so they sold him to a different group of Arabs.

18. Osnas, the step-daughter of Potifar, defended Yosef. Zolikah, Potifar's wife, charged Yosef with abusing her. Potifar was furious, and about to kill Yosef, when Zolika's little baby spoke up and said "No, it's Mommy who's lying, not Yosef the righteous." Wow, what a miracle!

19. Which wives saved their husband's lives?
(Midrash, Yalkut Shimoni 146)

20. Why did Yehuda lose his wife and his children?
(See Sotah 13b; Bereishis Rabbah 85:3, Sefer Chareidim)

21. How many incidents of "deadly jealousy" can be found throughout T'nach?
(Midrashim)

22. What was Yosef's reward for objecting to Potifar's wife Zulika's immoral, evil behavior?
(Zohar)

---

19. Yosef married Osnas, the girl who had saved his life. Some say she was Dinah's daughter from Shechem. We find many examples that a wife saved her husband's life. Moshe Rabbeinu's wife, Tziporah, saved his life on the way to Mitzrayim when he was almost punished with death for delaying the Bris Milah of his son Eliezer. Esther saved Mordechai's life from Haman's evil schemes.

20. Yehuda lost some popularity after Yosef was sold, because anyone who starts a *mitzvah* and doesn't finish it, lowers his own status. Yehuda lost his first wife and children as a punishment for not saving his brother Yosef.

21. The T'nach contains several accounts of deadly jealousy. There are too many examples for me to enumerate here, but I wish to mention some. Kayin was jealous of Hevel; Eisav was jealous of Yaakov; the *Shivtei Kah* (brothers) were jealous of Yosef; the Meraglim were jealous of the leaders who were supposed to take over after they entered the Land of Israel; Korach was jealous of Moshe; Shaul was jealous of Dovid; Yoav was jealous of Avner; Yeravam was jealous of Rechovam; Achav was jealous of Nevayos; the king's officers were jealous when Daryaveish appointed Daniel a head minister. The reason Hashem created Adam Harishon alone was so that no one would say, "My father is greater than your father." We hope that Hashem will remove the *Ruach Ra'ah* (evil spirit) that makes one hate another just because he's a good person!

22. Yosef was rewarded with *Malchus* (kingship) because he stayed holy and controlled his Yetzer Hara, which had tempted him to sin through *zenus*.

Answers&Facts

---

23. How do we see that one never loses out by keeping the *mitzvos*?

(See Menachos 44a, Even Sheleimah 2:10, Eitz Yosef on Parshas Mikeitz)

24. What beautiful benefits come to a woman who behaves with *tzenius* (modesty)?

(Megillah 10b, Yoma 47a, Bamidbar Rabbah 1:3)

25. Why didn't Dovid Hamelech become king before he was thirty years old?

(Sefer Chassidim 504)

26. What does the story of Yosef have to do with the story of *Chanukah*?

(Pardes Chanukah)

27. When the *Sanhedrin* had to administer capital punishment (that the accused should be punished by death), they fasted. So why did Yosef's brothers eat bread after they punished him by throwing him into a pit?

(Taam V'daas)

23. Osnas, the step-daughter of Zolikah (Potifar's wife) was even more beautiful than her mother. Yosef refused to take an *Eishes Ish*, and Hashem rewarded him by giving him even a more beautiful wife in the end. Hashem makes sure that those who keep His Torah never lose out.

24. The Talmud tells us that a woman who is modest in her appearance will merit descendants who will be kings! (Remember: *Talmidei Chachamim* are the kings of today!)

25. Since Yehudah sold Yosef to be a slave and Yosef didn't marry until he was thirty, Yehudah's descendant Dovid Hamelech did not rise to his power until he was thirty years old.

26. Just as oil floats to the top and doesn't mix with any other liquid, so too did Yosef did not mix with the immoral Egyptians, and that's why he rose to the top (as we will see in the next *Parsha*).

27. Yosef's brothers ate only bread after throwing him into the pit. They felt that he was telling Yaakov that they were evil, like Eisav or Yishmael. They ate now that they were relieved that he couldn't prevent them from becoming the *Shivtei Kah*.

28. Why is a *Pidyon Haben* accomplished through five shekalim?
(see posuk 37:28 Bereishis Rabbah 84:18, Yerushalmi Shekalim 2:3)

29. Why was Zarach's hand destined to come out first even though Peretz was destined to be born first?
(The Beginning, Harchev Davar, Emes L'Yaakov)

30. What type of jealousy *should* Yosef's brothers have possessed?
(Pele Yo'etz citing Bava Basra 21a, Tanna d'Bei Eliyahu Rabbah 25)

31. Why did Yehuda marry Tamar, his daughter-in-law, after she was widowed?
(Bereishis Rabbah 85:2,8, Ramban, Sefer Chassidim 504)

32. How did the fact that Yosef cared for other people enable him to save his own life?
(The Beginning)

---

28. Yosef, Yakov's firstborn, was sold for 20 silver *selaim*, which equal 5 silver *shekalim*. As a penalty for such a hateful act, every father must redeem his firstborn son for 5 *shekalim*.

29. Peretz needed to be born first in order to be assured of being the Royal Family. Peretz's almost not going first symbolized that *Malchus* Yehuda would also almost get lost but in the end it would prevail. Also it hinted that many times in *Galus*, Klal Yisroel might "see" the hand (actually the imminent arrival) of Moshiach, only to realize he will come at an unexpected time.

30. Yosef's brothers should have had "positive jealousy", known as "*Kinas Soferim*." They should have reasoned that he was successful because of his higher level of fear of Hashem. By increasing their service of Hashem, they too would become more successful.

31. Yehudah knew through *Ruach Hakodesh* that he must marry Tamar. In those days, "*Yibum*" was permitted with any relative. Some say that the angel Michoel made him go to her. Since he caused Yosef's marriage to be delayed twelve years, his own marital situation was not so comfortable.

32. Yosef's caring about the prisoners' mysterious dreams helped him eventually to be remembered as an able interpreter of dreams. His success in interpreting Pharaoh's dreams led to his promotion.

Answers&Facts

33. Why didn't Yosef send a message to his father, Yaakov, that he was alive and well in Egypt?

(Ohr Hachaim 45:26; Shach on Parshas Vayechi)

34. How did Yosef's descendants suffer because he acted superior to his brothers?

(Bereishis Rabbah 84:10, Eitz Yosef; see Nedarim 81a)

35. How do we know that if you raise a child, it is considered as though you gave birth to that child?

(Bereishis Rabbah 84:11)

36. What was Yosef whispering while he was working for Potifar?

(Bereishis Rabbah 86:5, Tanchuma 8)

37. Why shouldn't a parent or a teacher "play favorites"?

(Bereishis Rabbah 84:8, Shabbos 10b)

38. Why was Potifar's wife compared to a wild bear?

(Maharzu on Bereishis Rabbah 84:7,19)

---

33. Yosef didn't want to tell his father if Hashem hadn't done so. Also, Yosef's brothers made him promise he would never tell.

34. Yosef was really as humble when he rose to majesty as he was when he was a slave. However, since he made his brothers feel inferior, some of his royal descendants were wicked and arrogant - namely - Yeravam and Achav.

35. In Yosef's dream, he referred to 'Bilhah' as his mother, because she had raised him after Rochel's passing.

36. Yosef always whispered words of *Torah* and *Tefillah* while serving Potifar. At first, Potifar thought that Yosef was speaking witchcraft, but then he realized he was really speaking words of endearment to Hashem.

37. Yaakov gave Yosef an exquisite and colorful cloak in recognition of his effort and achievement in Torah knowledge. It cost two coins. But it created such hatred that from that time onward, his brothers treated him harshly.

38. A bear is not bashful. Even the mighty lion possesses a little shyness, but not the bear. One must be shy not to do evil deeds (but not shy to do good deeds)! Zolika was not bashful when it came to immoral acts.

---

39. Why did Yaakov want Yosef to inquire how the sheep were doing?

(Bereishis Rabbah 84:13)

40. How did Zolika (Potifar's wife) threaten Yosef in order to force him to give up his morals?

(Bereishis Rabbah 87:10)

41. What happened to the snakes and scorpions in the pit into which Yosef was thrown?

(Seder Hadoros, The Midrash Says)

42. Who was the first genuine *"Baal Teshuvah"*?

(Bereishis Rabbah 84:19, Eitz Yosef)

---

39. The *Midrash* tells us that one must always inquire about the welfare of those things which have benefited him. This is why Yaakov was inquiring how the sheep were doing.

40. Zolika spoke harshly to Yosef in an attempt to seduce him. She wanted to kill her husband so that she could marry Yosef. She said "I will torture you." Yosef replied "Hashem does justice on behalf those who are oppressed." She said "I will starve you." He answered, "Hashem gives food to those who are hungry." She said, "I will shackle you." He said, "Hashem frees those who are tied up." She said, "I will bend you." He said, "Hashem straightens those who are bent." She said, "I will blind you." He said, "Hashem gives sight to the blind." Finally, she had a razor sharp iron brace put on his neck which would force his head to point in her direction. What did Yosef do? He closed his eyes not to see her *p'ritzus* (disgusting behavior).

41. When Yosef was thrown into the pit he screamed in horror. What was the result? Hashem made a miracle, and all the snakes and scorpions squeezed themselves into cracks so as not to harm him.

42. Reuvein sincerely regretted that he had disturbed his father, Yaakov. He felt bad that he had not given his father the maximum *Kibud Av* that he should have, he fasted and wore sackcloth to show his pain. Reuvein became the first authentic *Baal Teshuva*. Adam and Kayin repented only from fear of punishment. Moreover, they repented because of their sins, while he repented because he had not performed a *mitzvah* in the preferred fashion.

43. In the attack at Ai, why did Yehoshua Bin Nun have to tear his clothes in grief?

(Yehoshua 7:6, Bereishis Rabbah 84:20)

44. Why did Yitzchak pretend to cry and mourn over Yosef's absence?

(Bereishis Rabbah 84:21)

45. Why did the children Er and Onan die so young?

(Rashi, Yevamos 34b)

46. Who merited giving birth to twins as a reward for their *tzenius* (modesty)?

(Bereishis Rabbah 85:7)

47. Why didn't Yosef wrest his coat away from that seductive Zulika, who was going to "frame" him with it?

(Ramban, Sichos Mussar)

---

43. Yosef's arousing his brother's jealousy, caused his brothers to sell him. Then Yaakov tore his clothes in grief and mourning. Because of this, Yosef's descendant Yehoshua also had to tear his clothes in grief and mourning when he suffered losses at the battle with Ai.

44. Yitzchak knew the truth that Yosef was not killed by a wild animal. But he didn't want to tell his son Yaakov, since Hashem hadn't told him. To share in his pain he cried and mourned. But when they weren't watching, Yitzchak would wash his face, anoint himself, and eat and drink as usual.

45. Er and Onan were not acting *b'kedusha*, even though they were only about seven years old. They were therefore punished by death.

46. Two famous women covered their faces with veils, thus showing their extreme modesty: Rivkah and Tamar. Both were therefore blessed with twins.

47. Yosef could have pulled his jacket away from Zolika in order to prevent her from framing him. But he didn't want to be close to an *aveirah* for even a split second, and fled as fast as he could from there. One must always outrun the snares of the *Yetzer Hara*.

48. Why must we give a half-shekel annually?

(Yerushalmi Shekalim 2:3)

49. How old was Yosef when he was tested as to whether or not he would surrender to his desire?

(Bereishis Rabbah 87:6, The Midrash Says)

50. How did Yaakov accept all the troubles that he had to face in his lifetime (for example, Eisav's terrorism, Lavan's crookedness, Dinah's humiliation, Rochel's early passing, and Yosef's disappearance)?

(Zohar, Eitz Yosef on Bereishis Rabbah 87:4)

51. Why is it very important to gaze at *tzadikim*?

(Tanchuma 8, Zohar, Rosh Hashanah 16b, Chida in Devar Kedumos under 'Tziyor')

52. Why shouldn't Yosef's brothers have been so jealous of him?

(see Chovos Halevavos Shaar Hachna'ah 10, Pele Yo'etz, Orchos Chaim L'Rosh 59 & 111)

---

48. In the times of the Beis Hamikdash, every Jewish male over age 20 was required to pay a *Machatzis Hashekel* tax. The money was used to purchase *korbanos* to atone for Jewish sins, especially the sale of Yosef Hatzadik.

49. Yosef was a 17 years old teenager when he prayed that Hashem test him. He was tested for 12 months. His self-control was indeed extraordinary.

50. Yaakov accepted all life's challenges with love and trust in Hashem.

51. When one stares at something, the object makes a lasting impression on him. One should therefore get in the habit of looking at *tzadikim* which will improve his character. Yosef saw his holy parents in his imagination, and it prevented him from sinning. (It's a tragedy and a pity how youngsters watch TV and other *treife* media and are contaminated by gazing at the ways of *reshaim*.)

52. Yosef's brothers shouldn't have hated Yosef for accomplishing more than they did. They should have been happy that he was accomplishing so much good. They should have realized that Hashem was pleased with him, since Yosef was so highly recognized and honored. They should have just increased their determination to accomplish their own missions as best they could. After all, people are different, and everyone has his own unique task. It helps to look at people who are not as fortunate as you and then you will be happy with your lot. One must ask Hashem to cure him from the disease of jealousy.

Answers&Facts

53. Why didn't Pharaoh's Chief Bartender remember to put in a good word for Yosef, as Yosef had originally wanted him to do?
(Tanchuma 9, Beis Halevi)

54. Why is Yosef Hatzaddik mentioned during Heaven's judgment of a person after his death?
(Yoma 35b)

55. Why did our ancestors, the Bnei Yisroel, have to suffer such cruelty in Mitzrayim?
(Shabbos 10b, Tosafos, and Maharsha there)

56. What did Yosef mean when he told the angel, "I am searching for my brothers"?
(Rav Reuven Elbaz shlit"a)

57. When was a descendant of Rochel jealous of a descendant of Leah?
(Shmuel I chapter 18)

53. Yosef should have trusted solely in Hashem and not have asked the non-Jewish Chief Bartender to speak up for him. Because of displaying this slight lack of trust, he had to wait several hundred days to become a free man.

54. Yosef was put to the ultimate test of passion and temptation. He overcame his natural drives and instincts even though there were no Jews watching him. In life, man is tested daily — and many fail. On their Judgment Day they will be asked why they didn't learn self-control and fear of Hashem from Yosef.

55. The Jews had to go to Egypt, since Avraham doubted he would have offspring in his old age. Hashem responded to this slight lack of trust with a promise that "your descendants will be numerous, and they will be servants in a foreign country." But it turns out that they really would not have had to work so hard during those years. Actually, the bitter slavery was a punishment for Yosef's being sold into captivity in Mitzrayim!

56. When Yosef was searching for his brothers to inquire of their welfare, he told the angel, "*My brothers I am searching for.*" This can be interpreted as, "*I am looking for brotherhood!*" It is so important to show friendship and love to your own brothers.

57. In the Torah we find that Leah's children were jealous of Rachel's child, even to the extent of nearly killing him. In Navi we find the opposite; that a descendant of Rachel (Shaul) was jealous of a descendant of Leah (Dovid), and nearly killed him.

58. How could the *yetzer hora* have almost caused Yosef to stumble; after all, aren't immoral desires found only in the hearts of people who are empty of Torah wisdom (see Rambam Isurei Biah 22:21)?

(Nefesh Hachaim)

59. Why did Rav Amrom Chasidah scream for help by saying, "There is a fire in the house of Amrom" if there really wasn't a fire there?

(Kiddushin 81a)

60. Why did even the great Torah scholars pray to Hashem to save them from their *Yetzer Hara*?

(Kiddushin 81b)

61. Why is it important not to let three days go by without talking to a Jew whom you might not like?

(Mishnah Sanhedrin 3:5)

---

58. Generally, the temptation for evil is only manifest in the mind of one empty of Torah wisdom and discipline. Nevertheless, daily, the *yetzer hara* tries to creep into the minds of the righteous *tzadikim* also. Only they know how to disintegrate impure thoughts right away.

59. The Gemara relates incidents where the Satan tested big *tzadikim* in the area of immorality. One such case was with the pious Rav Amrom, where Jewish women who were captives were rescued and staying in his attic. He felt an urge to do an *aveira*. He lifted an extremely heavy ladder to do so. On the way up the ladder, he caught himself, and he shouted "help, there's a fire in the house of Amrom". He wanted people to come running as it would cause him embarrassment to dare continue his plan. We see from here that the Satan tries to test man, and man must devise strategies to outsmart him!

60. Since tefillah can make miracles, one must employ this powerful method in his battle to subdue his *yetzer hara*. Hopefully, together with the pursuit of Torah and fear of Hashem, *tefillah* can save one from downfall.

61. Chazal speak about someone who is called a hater. That title refers to someone who did not talk to his fellow for three days, due to contempt. It is important to talk to each other to iron out any misunderstandings.

Answers & Facts

62. What should Internet users learn from the story of Yosef in Potifar's house?

(Tochachos Mussar)

63. How can the destiny of the Jewish people be compared to those of Yosef and Tamar?

(Torah Mi'Tzion)

62. Internet is a form of Eishes Potifar. It presents itself as an information super-highway, but many of the things it shares are absolutely forbidden to the Jew. Many Rabbis forbid its usage at home, while permitting it for office use if needed to make a livelihood. You need a lot of *Yiras Shamayim* to have Internet. Even Yosef who prided himself with his fear of Hashem was put to the test for a year and he almost failed. What can one say today, when the spiritual fiber of the Jew is being worn down day after day?

63. Just as Yosef was enslaved and suffered terribly, but was saved and rose to greatness and glory, so too will the Jews be saved from all the suffering of Galus and everyone will merit prestige and honor. Similarly, Tamar suffered being widowed twice and she was sentenced to being burned, but in the end was saved and mothered the ancestor of Moshiach, so too will Am Yisroel, who endured the sadness of the Churban Beis Hamikdash twice, and the fires of Galus, merit to see Moshiach and live happily ever after!

Dedicated in honor of
MY WIFE NATALIE AND KIDS:
ROCHELLE, MORRIS, VIVIANE,
DEBRAH, ISSAC AND SOLOMON
by Max Mizrahi

פרשת מקץ

1. Why was Yosef originally imprisoned for ten years?

(Shemos Rabbah 7:1; see Torah Mi'Tzion)

2. Why does the Torah refer to Yosef's additional two years in the dungeon as "two days"?

(Sifsei Cohen)

FUndamental Answers!

"יגעתי ומצאתי!"

("I worked on these questions, and I found these answers!")

1. Yosef spoke *lashon horah* about his ten righteous brothers, and therefore had to remain in prison for ten years. The additional two years in prison was a punishment for counting on the Sar Hamashkim to get him out, when he should have counted only on Hashem!

2. Yosef's faith and trust in Hashem were so strong that even the two long years of darkness felt like a short time, because he knew that everything Hashem does is for the best. When one knows that Hashem does everything for our benefit, it's much easier to accept and to cope with tough times.

3. How can you contrast the dreams of Pharaoh and *lehavdil* the dreams of the *Avos*?

(See Sefer Chassidim 165, Torah Mi'Tzion)

4. How are the dreams of kings different from the dreams of ordinary people?

(Bereishis Rabbah 89:4)

5. Why did Pharaoh dream about cows and wheat? How many times did he dream about them?

(Midrash Hagadol)

6. Egypt's famine was supposed to be for 42 years, but on account of Yaakov's and Yosef's prayers, the time was reduced to only 2 years. When were the Egyptians re-punished with hunger, this time for 40 years?

(Yechezkel 29:12, Bereishis Rabbah 89:9)

7. How are the miracles of *Chanukah* hinted at in *Parshas Mikeitz*?

(Iturei Torah, Torah Mi'Tzion)

---

3. Pharaoh dreamed of food and animals; *lehavdil*, the *Avos Hakedoshim* dreamed of Hashem and His Torah! It is not surprising that Yosef dreamt of the sun and the stars but Nevuchadnetzar dreamed of gold, silver and precious metals. A Jew must always dream of loftier and holier things, as that is our focus. The pursuit of things that rise us above the gravitational pull of this physical planet.

4. Kings' dreams are concerned with the welfare of the whole world.

5. The Egyptians used to worship cows as gods. They figured that whenever cows plow, food grows, so they thought it was divine. Pharaoh dreamed of what he thought about and valued. Pharaoh kept on having these nightmares for two straight years every single night! He was going mad from not understanding their meaning.

6. The *Chachamim* held that Mitzrayim was supposed to suffer a hunger for 42 years. When Yaakov came to Mitzrayim the famine stopped. In the days of Yirmiyahu, Egypt suffered a famine for 40 years. Since they never did *teshuva* in the first place, the punishment was not *cancelled*, it was just *postponed*.

7. Just as the weak, scrawny cows devoured the fat, strong ones and the thin wheat stalks consumed the thick ones, so too a small group of *talmidei chachamim*, known as the Chashmonaim, overcame the larger and more powerful

8. What did Hashem say when Yaakov cried out to his children, "Why did you do such evil to me"?

(Bereishis Rabbah 91:1)

9. Which secret did Binyomin keep?

(Bereishis Rabbah 92:8, Esther Rabbah 86:8)

10. How was the *Sar Hamashkim* (Chief Bartender) similar to the wicked Haman?

(Bereishis Rabbah 89:7, Seichel Tov)

11. What finally motivated the *Sar Hamashkim* to speak up to Pharaoh on behalf of Yosef?

(Bereishis Rabbah 89:7, Riva)

Greek oppressors. Also, just as the nations appeared strong and invincible but through the passage of time have become virtually extinct, the relatively weak and small Jewish nation continues to outlive their enemies and oppressors.

8. When Yaakov asked his sons, "Why have you done such evil to me?" Hashem said, "At this very moment I am crowning your son monarch of Egypt (and the entire world, for that matter), and you are complaining, 'Why have you do such evil to me!'" So we must never be quick to complain when what seems to be bad might actually be covering a great deal of good in Hashem's caring Master Plan.

9. Binyomin knew the treachery that his brothers had performed by selling his brother Yosef. However, he never gossiped about them to their father Yaakov.

10. Just as Haman had not wanted to see Mordechai promoted in the kingdom of Achashveirosh, so too did the Sar Hamashkim not want to see Yosef promoted in Pharaoh's kingdom. They slandered the Jews, implying that they were not competent. In the end, just as Haman himself would give Mordechai a haircut before he rose to high stature, so did the Sar Hamashkim give Yosef a haircut before his ascent to royalty.

11. The Sar Hamashkim saw Pharaoh losing his mind on account of his mind-boggling dreams. It was as if Pharaoh was going to die of misery. The Chief Bartender rationalized that if Pharaoh died, a new King Pharaoh might not regard him as highly, so he had better speak up in order not to lose his job. From here we see that the wicked are "kind" when they have an ulterior motive for doing so.

Answers&Facts

12. How did Yosef know that his brothers were sincerely doing *teshuvah* for having sold him?

(Bereishis Rabbah 91:7, Tanchuma 8)

13. Why did even the Egyptians call Yosef "*Chacham*" (Wise Sage)?

(Bereishis Rabbah 90:3, 91:5, The Midrash Says)

14. How did Pharaoh know that Yosef had *Ruach Hakodesh*?

(Me'am Lo'ez, Maayanos Hanetzach)

15. Why was the letter ה added to Yosef's name (יהוסף)?

(Tehillim 81; see Sotah 10b and 36b)

16. Why did Yosef cry (privately) when his brothers arrived?

(Rashi)

17. Why did Pharaoh dream on *Rosh Hashanah* about the future famine?

(See Megillah 3a; Malbim)

---

12. Yosef tested his brothers' sincerity by asking if they would be willing to ransom their missing brother even for an enormous sum of money. They said, "Of course, that's just what we want to do."

13. Since Yosef always kept his mind pure, Hashem promised that he would become famous as a sage! In addition, the Mitzrim realized that he must have been supernaturally brilliant, because he had told them to save up food before the famine, yet it was only his food that didn't become moldy or rotten!

14. Pharaoh tried changing details of his dream in order to test Yosef's credibility. Yosef however, corrected Pharaoh and stated the real facts. "Wow!" Pharaoh said, "Not only does he know how to explain dreams, but he even knows my dreams!"

15. The letter *Heh* represents Hashem's Name. It was added to Yosef's name to testify that he was constantly faithful to Hashem.

16. On the one hand, Yosef was so happy to see his brothers that he privately cried tears of joy, on the other hand, he also felt their pain and worry, so he cried tears of sympathy for them as well.

17. On Rosh Hashana, Hashem judges the world. That's why Paraoh's conscience was aware of Divine judgment during his sleep on that day.

18. Why did Yosef merit kingship for eighty years?

(Yerushalmi Berachos 2:33)

19. How did Yosef master seventy languages, and why was Pharaoh nervous about this skill?

(Sotah 36b)

20. Why did Yosef marry *Osnas Bas Potiphera* the priest of On?

(Rabbeinu Bachya, Chizkuni quoting Midrash)

21. Pharaoh switched Yosef's name to *"Tzofnas Paneiyach"* (Decoder of Mysteries). Which names did Nevuchadnetzar give Daniel, Chanania, Mishael, and Azaria—and why?

(Daniel 1:7)

---

18. Yosef merited a long reign of kingship, because he totally feared Hashem and overcame extreme temptation!

19. The angel Gavriel taught Yosef the 70 languages of the nations of the world in order that Pharaoh should honor him, because one can't appreciate another person's intellect and wisdom if he can't communicate with him comfortably. [This is one of the reasons why the *Sanhedrin* had to know seventy languages.] Pharaoh was nervous that Yosef would become more popular than he himself, since Yosef knew even Hebrew, which Pharaoh did not. He made Yosef swear that he would not reveal that he knew more languages than Pharaoh.

20. When Yosef was raised to great authority many people threw things at him when he was on parade. Osnas realized he was a Jew, and she threw her *kabbalistic* amulet that she had received from her grandfather, Yaakov Avinu. When Yosef read about her relationship to Yaakov, (which was stated on the amulet) he chose her to be his wife. We see from here that Hashem prepares one's *shidduch* for him. (Incidentally, the Torah tells us that her stepfather, who had been an executioner, became a priest! Her decency in behavior must have caused him to renounce his immoral ways.)

21. Nevuchadnetzar called Daniel - Beltshazar, Chananya - Shadrach, Mishael - Meishach, and Azarya - Aveid Nego. These youths were from the Royal Family of King David. Nevuchadnetzar wanted to assimilate them into his culture, so he switched their names to non-Jewish ones in attempt to make them forget their true Jewish identities.

Answers&Facts

22. What did Pharaoh mean by referring to Yosef as an "Avreich"?

(Rashi, Bava Basra 4a, Tur)

23. Why did Pharaoh admit that "there is no one as smart and as understanding as Yosef!"?

(Alter of Kelm)

24. Why was it good for Bnei Yisroel that there was a dreadful hunger in the world in 2236?

(See Berachos 9b; Zohar 1:196, Malbim)

25. Why did Yosef force upon the Egyptians the *mitzvah* of *Milah*?

(Taam V'daas, Bereishis Rabbah 90:6 and 91:5, Eitz Yosef, Ya'aros Devash)

26. Why did Yosef call his first son "Menashe"?

(Bereishis 41:51, Bereishis Rabbah 79:5 and 86:6)

22. "Avreich" is an affectionate title given to one who is young in years, but old in wisdom. We call *Kollel* members by this name, since they devote their time to discerning Hashem's will, and diseminating it to others.

23. When Yosef replied that only Hashem could reveal to him the dream's message, even Pharaoh admitted that *there is no wisdom like the fear of G-d!* When Nevuchadnetzar and Belshazar needed Daniel to interpret their dreams, he also credited Hashem as the only Knower of All! Truly great people know who their Sponsor is!

24. It was beneficial for the Jews that there was a famine in the world, because everyone had to come and give all their money to Yosef in order to receive food. This money was kept in Egypt's royal treasuries. When Am Yisroel were leaving Mitzrayim it was much of this money that was given to them in fulfillment of Hashem's promise that they would leave their slavery with a *"rechush gadol"* (great fortune)!

25. Yosef knew that the Bnei Yisroel would have to live in the spiritual wasteland known as Mitzrayim. He knew that the lowliness of the Egyptians would destroy the pure Jews born there, for they would be embarrassed to do *mitzvos*. He therefore ordered the non-Jews there to do the very *"mitzvah"* that defines a Jew and increases *kedusha*, so that in the future Jews would proudly retain their Jewishness.

26. Yosef bemoaned that he forgot some of his Torah in exile. So he named his first son "Menashe", which means "forgotten" to inspire himself to gain back that which he had forgotten. He also wanted to thank Hashem for making him forget his suffering and loneliness.

27. Why are the Bnei Yisroel often referred to as *Ephraim*, as in: "My precious son Ephraim" (Yirmiyah 31:19)?

(Vayikra Rabbah 2:3)

28. Why was *Shevet Menasheh* split into two when the Jews returned to Eretz Yisroel under Yehoshua's leadership?

(Haamek Davar, Chizkuni)

29. How can you merit incredible blessings, just as Yosef Hatzaddik did?

(See Torah Temimah; Sanhedrin 92a)

30. In what way did Yosef hold like *Beis Shamai* while Levi held like *Beis Hillel*?

(Chizkuni, Yevamos 63b)

31. How do we see that ignoring *Kibud Av V'em* shortens one's lifespan?

(Vilna Gaon 42:23)

---

27. Menashe was busy doing errands for Yosef, the monarch. However, Ephraim stayed out of the limelight and focused on learning Torah. Ephraim eventually became the *Rosh Yeshiva* in Egypt. Hashem therefore said, "I will call my devoted children after Ephraim!"

28. Menashe caused the *Shevatim* to tear their clothes in grief when he arrested them. So too, his descendants were torn into separate parts - those in the Land of Israel and those outside of Israel.

29. When you teach others Torah you merit a form of kingship! As *Chazal* illustrate, "Who are the Jewish kings? The Talmidei Chachamim!"

30. During a famine in the world, one may not have children unless he had not yet fulfilled the *mitzvah* of *Piryah V'rivyah* (Be fruitful & multiply). Yosef held like Beis Shamai that with two sons you have already fulfilled the *mitzvah*. Levi held like Beis Hillel that you need a boy and a girl to fulfill the *mitzvah*. That's why Levi had Yocheved at the time of the famine.

31. Yosef was quiet when the *Shevatim* referred to Yaakov Avinu as "our father your servant." Since he had not defended the honor of his father 10 times, he lost 10 years of his life. Wow! Just think about the importance of honoring your parents.

Answers&Facts

---

32. Why did all ten brothers have to go to Mitzrayim?

(See Rashi, Rabbeinu Bachya quoting Yerushalmi Berachos 7:3)

33. Why didn't Yosef's brothers recognize his voice or his appearance?

(Bereishis Rabbah 91:7, Rashbam, Ohr Hachaim, Rashi)

34. Which other famous *tzaddikim* were imprisoned, and why?

(See Berachos 61b, Ahavas Chaim)

35. What did Shimon do to the seventy strong men whom Yosef had advised Pharaoh to send to hold him in custody?

(Bereishis Rabbah 91:6, Midrash Avkir, The Midrash Says)

36. What *aveira* did Yosef pretend to do?

(Bereishis Rabbah 92:5 and 91:6, Radak, Chizkuni, Tur, Ramban, Tosafos)

---

32. The brothers knew they would need to pray to Hashem to be able to find their missing brother. So they wanted ten to go so they could pray in a *minyan*. A minyan really increases the strength of your tefillah!

33. Yosef's brothers did not recognize his voice because he spoke through an interpreter, and in a foreign language. Also usually Yosef was one who spoke gently, and now he spoke harshly. Regarding his appearance, they could not tell how he looked because now he had a beard.

34. To list a few famous *tzadikim* that were imprisoned: Avraham Avinu; Moshe Rabbeinu; Rabbi Akiva; Ma'haram M'Rutenberg; Baal Ha'Tanya and many other great Jews were all imprisoned at different times throughout history. Perhaps it was to solidify their commitment to Hashem, by showing that they couldn't be swayed from the service of Hashem regardless of their predicament.

35. Shimon screamed at the approaching guards whom Yosef had ordered to arrest him. His shout was so fearsome that they fell down and their teeth fell out. So Menashe had to give him one powerful blow, and then it was possible to subdue Shimon.

36. Yosef pretended that he was able to see what was going around him through the use of a magic cup. Now really *Aveirah # 249* forbids a Jew to practice sorcery. I guess that his fake prop also made it appear that this ruler was a *goy*; therefore, they would never suspect that he was Yosef.

---

37. Why wasn't Yosef's harshness toward his brothers considered revenge?

(Vilna Gaon, Sichos Mussar; see Bereishis Rabbah 91:8)

38. What did Reuvein intend by guaranteeing the safety of Binyamin with the lives of his own two sons?

(Bereishis Rabbah 91:9, Chasam Sofer)

39. Did the *Shevatim* get to say *Tefillas Haderech* before Menashe pursued them?

(Mayanah Shel Torah)

40. How could Yosef's brothers have eaten *"kosher meat"* from an Egyptian kitchen?

(See Maharsha on Chullin 91a)

41. In which way was Yaakov concerned about an *Ayin Hara*?

(Rashi, Bereishis Rabbah 91:6, Eitz Yosef, Ramban, Michtav M'Eliyahu)

---

37. Yosef wanted his brothers to do *teshuva*. By making them feel regret about selling him (since they saw that one's sins can indeed make the sinners and their victims suffer), he would be saving them from Heavenly punishment. Also Yosef's brothers made him swear that he wouldn't return home to their father Yaakov, nor was he ever allowed to inform Yaakov that he was alive and well. So he had to cause Yaakov to hear it from them.

38. Reuvein meant that his sons would lose their firstborn-inheritance rights, if he didn't return Binyomin home safely. To this Yakov said, "fool, you already lost your rights when you disrespected me regarding Bilhah."

39. Yosef told Menashe to stop his brothers before they were well on their way, since he knew that once they said *Tefillas Haderech*, Hashem would spare them from attacks on the way, and it would then be impossible to capture them.

40. Perhaps Yosef ordered a *mashgiach kashrus* to work for his Jewish guests.

41. Yaakov's sons were extremely handsome and well-built. He therefore did not want them entering the city through one gate, lest doing so would cause jealousy and bring about the evil eye.

Answers&Facts

42. Why did Yosef first arrest all ten brothers for three days?

(Bereishis Rabbah 91:7; see Baal Haturim)

43. How did Reuvein try to defend Yosef's poor relationship with the Shevatim so that they wouldn't harm him?

(See Ramban)

44. Yosef's brothers abstained from wine after Yosef's "misfortune" so why did they drink it later at Yosef's banquet?

(Bereishis Rabbah 92:5; see Gur Aryeh)

45. What was the name *"Tzofnas Paneiyach"* an abbreviation of?

(Bereishis Rabbah 90:4)

46. When did Yosef tell his brothers that *"Zechus Avos"* (ancestral merits) had helped them?

(Bereishis Rabbah 92:4)

---

42. Yosef put his brothers in jail for *three* days. He wanted his brothers to have a *kapara* for *three* things: Undressing him; throwing him in the pit; and selling him. Also Hashem doesn't let a *tzadik* feel distress for more than three days in a row.

43. Reuvein really tried to persuade his brothers to be *dan* Yosef *l'kaf zechus*. He tried to arouse their compassion and brotherhood for Yosef. When he saw they weren't accepting his attempt at *Shalom*, he pleaded with them not to kill him but rather to just throw him in the pit. Reuvein hoped that afterwards he would return to the pit and bring Yosef home.

44. Yosef would not enjoy wine during the brothers distress. But now that it was coming to an end they made a *"l'chaim"*.

45. Tsofnas Paneiyach stands for: T'sofeh-Seer; P'odeh-Redeemer; N'avi-Prophet; T'omech-Sponsor; P'oter-Interpreter; A'rum-Clever; N'avon-Understanding; C'hozeh-Visionary. These were all terms to describe Yosef's supernatural wisdom.

46. Yosef told his brothers that surely finding their money back in their sacks was a courtesy that G-d had performed for them owing to their exceptional ancestral merits.

---

47. When Yosef demanded that one brother be left in his custody, why weren't the *Shevatim* allowed to choose which one?

(See Yerushalmi Terumos 8:4; Bereishis Rabbah 91:6,8)

48. Why did Yosef put Shimon in jail?

(See Yerushalmi Terumos 8:4; Bereishis Rabbah 91:6,8, Tanchuma Yashan 17, Maskil L'Dovid)

49. When the Shevatim realized that they were in big trouble, why did they say, "What is this that Hashem did to us?" Shouldn't they have said, "Everything Hashem does is for the best!"?

(Mili d'Berachos 54a)

50. When did a slave rise to royalty?

(Bereishis Rabbah 89:3)

51. Where do we find an example of the Gemara's concept that "every forbidden flavor has a kosher parallel"?

(Chullin 109b, Even Sheleimah 2:10, Bereishis Rabbah 90:3)

---

47. The *halacha* is that if the goyim insist on taking one Jew we don't have the right to pick. Only they can pick, Heaven forbid.

48. Yosef picked on Shimon since he was the one that pushed him into the pit. He needed *kapara* for that.

49. When one sees himself suffer he is supposed to know that it's for his own benefit, and usually it's a message from Hashem to do teshuva.

50. Yosef went from slavery to kingship. (*Lehavdil*, Haman, who was really a slave to Mordechai, also was raised to a royal position; but not for long!)

51. The Gemara lists many kosher foods that taste the same as non-kosher foods. Similarly, Yosef did not marry the attractive Zolika, the wife of the Chief Executioner. So Hashem gave him her step-daughter, Osnas, who was even more beautiful than her step-mother. Hashem enables the Jews to derive pleasure from permissible things instead of forbidden things!

Answers & Facts

Questions & Riddles

52. Why did Yosef arrange to have the money of the Shevatim put back into their luggage?

(Malbim)

53. Why did King Nevuchadnetzar completely forget his dream before the prophet Daniel arrived?

(Tur)

54. Why did Nevuchadnetzar order the death of his royal advisors for not having interpreted his dreams satisfactorily?

(Tosafos)

55. What was Yosef's reward for not allowing himself to sin with Potifar's wife?

(Bereishis Rabbah 90:4, The Midrash Says)

---

52. Yosef's replacing the Shevatim's money in their bags alluded to the future, when after the Jews would leave Mitzrayim, their money would be returned and they would be wealthy.

53. Hashem made Nevuchdnetzar forget his dream again and again, so that when Daniel would tell him the exact dream and its message he would honor and respect Daniel all the more. When all of his advisors tried to interpret his dream he grew enraged, and was forced to realize that no one is like the Jewish people.

54. Nevuchdnetzar went into a rampage and wanted to kill all of his advisors since they were useless at deciphering his dream that was making him so scared. He was over-demanding since he expected them to discover what the dream was that he kept forgetting.

55. Hashem rewarded Yosef in both worlds for his self-control and self-discipline. The reward for those who keep themselves holy is astronomical! Yosef's lips that did not kiss temptation were to dictate the world. Yosef's body that did not touch sin was clothed with royal fine linen. Yosef's neck that did not bow in sin was to be decked with a royal necklace. Yosef's hands that did not sin were to wear Pharaoh's royal signet ring. Yosef's feet that did not sin were to be carried on the royal carriage. Yosef's mind that did not think of sin was to be called wise. Hashem rewards each and every facet of one's *mitzvah* observance!

56. When did Dovid Hamelech ask Hashem to have pity on mankind just as Yosef Hatzaddik had?

(Bereishis Rabbah 91:5, Tehillim 80:2)

57. Did the Egyptians listen to Yosef's warning to stock up on food before the famine?

(Bereishis Rabbah 91:5)

58. How old was Binyomin when his brother Yosef was taken away from him?

(Sotah 36b)

59. Were the Shevatim scared to wage war against Mitzrayim?

(Bereishis Rabbah 92:8)

60. What warning did Yaakov Avinu send to the mighty ruler Tzofnas Paneiyach?

(Sefer Hayashar)

---

56. During the hunger in the days of Dovid Hamelech, he asked Hashem to provide for everyone even if they were not deserving, just as Yosef provided for everybody in his generation regardless of how deserving they were.

57. Pharaoh shouted at his people that they should have listened to Yosef and stocked up food before the hunger. Some did, however, their food rotted.

58. Binyomin was nine years old when Yosef was kidnapped.

59. The Shevatim were not scared to battle the world-power Mitzrayim, if need be, because they knew Hashem would be on their side.

60. Yaakov Avinu sent a letter warning King Tzofnas Paneiyach not to distress his family, because Hashem always defended his Avos and Imahos from dangerous kings.

Answers & Facts

61. What warning did Yaakov give his sons about wealth?

(Rashi, Torah Mi'Tzion, Ya'aros Devash)

62. What did Yosef do on Shabbos?

(Yalkut Shimoni 146)

63. Why are Yosef's descendants protected from *Ayin Hara?*

(Bamidbar Rabbah 14:6)

61. Yaakov warned his sons not to flaunt their wealth in front of Eisav or Yishmael, in order that they not become jealous. History shows us that many Jews fell victim to the hate and violence of the goyim, when they became jealous. Holocaust and havoc were caused due to Jews arousing the envy of the nations. It is therefore imperative that Jews live humbly and modestly and then they will enjoy safer havens in the long run.

62. On Shabbos, Yosef was very careful to review all the Torah he had learned from Yaakov Avinu, his father. (We see from this Midrash that even if someone works for others during the week and can't make his own work hours, on Shabbos when all work stops, the "work" of studying Torah must continue!)

63. Just as Yosef did not sin with his eyes by looking at Potifar's wife or the other Egyptian women, so too his descendants are spared any harm that eyes sometimes cause-such as *Ayin Hara!*

Dedicated in honor of my Eishet Chayil,
MARGALIT.
May she continue to be a source of inspiration for me and our children. May G-d grant her many happy years for her dedication and constant pursuit of Chesed for the entire community.
Love, Joseph, and our children:
Yehudit, Rivka, Yael, Shalom, Avraham and Daniel Saka

פרשת ויגש

?

1. Why did Yaakov send Yehuda to open a Yeshivah in Goshen? Couldn't Yosef have opened it himself?

   (Shimush Talmidei Chachamim, Bereishis Rabbah 95:3; see Bamidbar Rabbah 79:5)

2. What did Yehuda and Shimon want to do to the land of Egypt?

   (Bereishis Rabbah 93:8, Tanchumah, Seder Hadoros)

FUndamental **A**nswers**!**

"יגעתי ומצאתי!"

("I worked on these questions, and I found these answers!")

1. Although the Torah refers to Yosef as the paradigm *tzadik*, in one respect, Yehuda was greater than Yosef. Yosef was once the most brilliant son of Yaakov, but after many years in Egypt, he had forgotten some of the *Torah* that he had learned. Of course, he was still an incredible *talmid chacham*, but he was missing the all-important ingredient known as *Shimush Talmidei Chachamim* (Serving the Rabbis). By not being in Yaakov's presence, he did not see how the *Gadol Hador* lived his life on a daily basis, so even the *Torah* that he remembered was not comparable to that of Yehuda, since Yehuda had been a constant eyewitness to Yaakov Avinu's actions. Hence, Yehuda was more qualified to open a Yeshiva before *Klal Yisroel* came down to Mitzrayim.

2. Yehuda was about to destroy three of the twelve neighborhoods in Egypt, and the other nine brothers would each destroy one, in revenge of Egypt's injustice to Shimon and Binyomin. However, the brothers said that Egypt is not insignificant like Sedom. If they would destroy Egypt, it would jeopardize the entire world.

3. When did music and song play a role in someone living forever?

(Seder Hadoros 2336, Me'am Lo'ez)

4. Why did Rabbi Elazar cry when he read *Parshas Vayigash*?

(See Chagigah 4b and Bereishis Rabbah 93:10; Tehillim 50:21)

5. Why did Yosef give Binyomin 300 silver pieces?

(Chida quoting Rokeach, Vilna Gaon, Birchas Yitzchak; see Megillah 16b)

6. How was Goshen like Monroe, Skvere, Williamsburg, Telz, Vilna, Radin, Lakewood, and Boro Park?

(Darash Moshe; see Pirkei Avos 6:9)

---

3. When Serach the daughter of Asher informed Yaakov that his son Yosef was still alive, she did so through song and music while Yaakov was praying. She therefore spared him the shock that might accompany such news and did not endanger Yaakov's health. It was almost as if she had merely asked the question: "Is Yosef still alive in Egypt?" This pure act of kindness earned her everlasting life even in this world! Since she had protected the *tzadik's* life through her thoughtfulness, her own life was extended in this world (probably over two thousand years), and only later did she enter *Gan Eden* alive. (I don't know any other person that lived longer than her.)

4. When Yosef's brothers realized that Tzofnas Paneiyach was none other than their own brother Yosef, whom they had betrayed, their shame was so great that they were speechless, and they passed out. Rabbi Elazar cried out that if in front of another human being a person could feel such shame for having behaved so disrespectfully, what will happen when Hashem will reveal Himself to us in the World to Come? How great will be our shame and embarrassment for not having respected Hashem enough! Who then will be able to talk?!

5. There is a rule in the Gemara (Gittin 44a) that if someone sells his servant to a gentile, he is fined that he must purchase him back for even up to ten times his value. The standard cost of a servant was thirty shekelim. Thus ten times that price is three hundred. By Yosef giving this handsome sum to Binyomin and not to his brothers, it was a pain to them which would atone as if they paid that fee to Binyomin themselves. Others say that Yosef paid this sum since he had almost taken Binyomin as his slave.

6. Goshen was a thoroughly religious city! Of course, the ultimate place for a Jew to live is in an environment that is 100% Torah–true. Some rare communities today still shelter their residents from the negative influences of the world. One who resides in such a community is most fortunate. That place becomes like an island

---

7. Why did our Nation have to be born in Mitzrayim and not in Eretz Yisroel?

(The Beginning)

8. How do we see that complaining can be dangerous to one's health?

(Daas Zekeinim Baalei Tosafos)

9. Why do we eat *chazeress* (lettuce) on Pesach night?

(Yerushalmi Pesachim 2:5)

in *Galus*, an oasis in the spiritual desert out there. Our greatest challenge today is to keep negative influences out of our homes and out of our hearts!

7. There are many reasons why *Am Yisroel* started off in Egypt, and not in their own land. One reason is that Egypt was a land ruled by just one king. In the Land of Israel, however, there were several kings. Bnei Yisroel had to have the message driven home that there is only one King—not Pharaoh, but Hashem! Also, once they were slaves under a king of flesh and blood, they would be better prepared to achieve their goal of being slaves of Hashem, the Supreme King. Another reason we had to go to Mitzrayim was as a punishment for our ancestors having sold Yosef, which eventually brought him to Mitzrayim. It was good for the Jews to live among people who hated shepherds; therefore, there would be no assimilation.

8. Yaakov Avinu told Pharaoh that the reason he looked very old was because he had a difficult life. His very own brother Eisav, was a scoundrel who was waiting to kill him; his intended wife, Rochel, was switched for Leah; his father-in-law always tricked him in business; his daughter, Dinah, was kidnapped; Yosef was probably killed; he did not get to see his mother Rivka the last 36 years of her life; and so forth. We might even justify Yaakov's complaining; however, just because he complained, he was punished. We find so many examples throughout *T'nach* about people who complained and were punished for doing so! On Tisha B'av the Jews complained about Eretz Yisroel when the spies claimed how dangerous it was to live there, so they died in the desert, never reaching their destination. One's trust in Hashem must be so strong, that he doesn't complain even when he deeply desires things to be better. The result of Yaakov's complaint was his premature passing, and that resulted in the slavery in Egypt beginning many years earlier. Could any pain of Yaakov's have been worse than the 33 extra years of his descendants enduring slavery in Mitzrayim?! (See Vayechi #33, that some say Yaakov's earlier passing was a result of his having cursed Rochel, albeit inadvertently.)

9. Lettuce, especially Romaine lettuce, at first tastes fine, but afterwards it leaves a bitter taste in one's mouth. So it was with us Jews as well: When we went down to Egypt at first all seemed pleasant; after all, we were guests in the land of Egypt. But, later on, the Egyptians were so mean to the Jews that life became extremely bitter for them.

10.
Why did Yosef and Binyomin cry over the destruction of both *Batei Hamikdash* and the Mishkan even though these calamities hadn't happened yet?

(Bereishis Rabbah 93:12, Rav Yechezkel of Kozmir quoting Megillah 16b)

11.
Where do we find the righteous elderly woman Serach Bas Asher showing up again in history?

(Sotah 13a, Shmuel II 20:22, Pesikta d'Rabi Kahana 10:117)

12.
Why did Yehuda say that Yaakov would die if something happened to Binyomin? After all, Rabbi Yochanan tragically lost ten sons, עליהם השלום but he still kept going strong?

(The Beginning)

---

10. Yosef and Binyamin cried over the future destruction of the *Batei Hamikdash* because they saw through *Ruach Hakodesh* that it would be destroyed because of *Sinas Chinam* (hatred for no reason). They shed tears because they realized that Yosef's exile to a land far away from his father was caused by senseless hatred, and they realized that this hatred had not disappeared and would resurface many times in the future. Now that's something to cry about! [Incidentally, in 2001, some Arabs went to burn the building housing the grave of Yosef Hatzadik in Shechem. Rebbitzen Jungreis wisely commented that this was a message that the rampant fire of *Sinas Chinam* has not been put out yet!]

11. Serach shows up again when Yoav, the general of Dovid Hamelech's army, was coming to attack the city where she lived in order to punish a rebel that was within it. Even after 690 years, Serach was still there to tell Yoav and his men how best to accomplish their task. Even much later in history, we learn that Rabbi Yochanan was teaching about the miracles of the Exodus from Egypt; as he was describing how the walls of water looked at *Keriyas Yam Suf,* a woman in the *Ezras Nashim* screamed out, "I was there, and this is how it looked... ." So we see that she had incredible longevity, and only at some later time did she enter *Gan Eden* alive.

12. You can't compare the great *tzadikim*—that is to say, the *Shevatim*—to other *tzadikim*. After all, Yaakov had envisioned each son as being a kind of Beis Hamikdash! Now, can someone be consoled over the destruction of a Beis Hamikdash? Well, one son seemed to indeed have been destroyed (Yosef's disappearance)! Could Yaakov survive a second *Churban Beis Hamikdash*? That's why Yehuda declared that if he were to take Binyomin away from their father, the strain on Yaakov Avinu would be too great for him to bear.

13. What *Mitzvah* can one perform when something "bad" happens?
(Berachos 54a, Shulchan Aruch Orach Chaim 230:5)

14. Why did Yehudah's brothers tell him not to demolish Egypt?
(Bereishis Rabbah 93:8)

15. Why did Yaakov start saying *Shema* when he saw Yosef after an absence of so many years?
(Maharal, Sfas Emes)

16. Yehuda pleaded to be taken as a slave instead of Binyomin. What did Yosef tell him?
(Bereishis Rabbah 93:8)

17. Why did Yehuda, who was only the fourth son of Yaakov, merit the kingship of our nation?
(The Beginning; see Yalkut Shimoni Esther 1053)

---

13. There is a *Mitzvah* to love Hashem, no matter what measure He grants you. Indeed, this Mitzvah can ultimately be performed when a person's lot is not necessarily to his liking. Also, the *Shulchan Aruch* says that a person should be in the habit of saying, "Everything that the All-Merciful does is for the best." When uttered after something bad happens, this statement indicates genuine *bitachon* (trust in Hashem).

14. Yehuda's brothers talked him out of an attack, saying that it would endanger the whole world that was relying on Egypt's food banks.

15. Yaakov recited the Shema as he was about to reunite with his long-lost son Yosef. He wanted to channel all the love in his heart - which was so enormous at the time - to the One who creates love- Hashem Himself.

16. Yosef asked Yehuda why *he* talked so much in order to save Binyomin. He replied that he guaranteed to protect Binyomin. Yosef asked, "Why did you not protect your other brother, Yosef?"

17. Yehuda displayed genuine leadership quality when he suggested that they sell Yosef instead of killing him, and now again when he put his life on the line to fight for Binyomin's life. A leader is the one who is willing to fight for the welfare and benefit of others!

Answers&Facts

18.
What happened to Rabbi Chanina Ben Chachinai's wife when her husband suddenly returned from Yeshivah after 13 years?

(see Rashi 45:26, Doresh Tov quoting Kesuvos 62b)

19.
In what merit did Yosef become so great a ruler?

(Zohar Bereishis 93b, Yerushalmi Berachos 2:3; see Sefer Chassidim 960)

20.
Why did Hashem grant Yosef righteous sons?

(Doresh Tov quoting Chida)

21.
Who went out to welcome Yaakov to Mitzrayim? What did they do?

(Seder Hadoros)

22.
How many descendants were born to Dan's deaf son, Chushim, in a span of 250 years (2238-2488)?

(See Chofetz Chaim on Parshas Pinchas 26:42)

---

18. Rabbi Chanina's wife died from shock when her husband appeared suddenly after thirteen long years of being away in *Yeshiva*. The surprise was too much for her heart, and she had cardiac arrest. He cried out, "Is this the reward for one who supports the learning of Torah?" A miracle happened and she lived again!

19. Yosef was despised wrongly by his brothers. Hashem has special pity for people that are degraded even when they're good. Amazingly, Hashem will promote a person like that to a great and honorable status. Also, Yosef kept the *mitzvos* and guarded his thoughts and his *bris milah*, which enables a person to become a ruler!

20. As a proof of Yosef's *kedusha*, Hashem granted him righteous sons. (See Bereishis 6:1.)

21. Yosef himself harnessed his chariot to escort his father. He was accompanied by all the mighty officers of Egypt. A decree was issued that whoever doesn't go out to greet Yosef's father, would be killed. The entire Egyptian nation went out in an enormous parade, with music and uniforms, to welcome Yaakov to Mitzrayim.

22. An astonishing 64,400 descendants came out from Dan's deaf son Chushim, within a couple hundred years! Even though Dan had the smallest *Shevet* at first, bearing only a deaf child, eventually his tribe ranked among the largest! In the end, everyone sees that Hashem is fair!

23. What method did the furious Yehuda use to soften the ruler Tzofnas Paneiyach's heart?

(See Ohr Hachaim 44:18 and Mishlei 27:19)

24. How did Yosef show he cared about his brothers' feelings?

(Chullin 60b, Tanchuma 5)

25. Who was born when the Jews went down to Egypt— and died when the Jews left 210 years later?

(Bava Basra 15a)

26. Which special *Berachos* did Yaakov say when he was reunited with his son Yosef in 2338?

(See Berachos 58a)

27. What did Yehudah say when his sword wouldn't come out of its sheath?

(Bava Basra 75a)

---

23. Yehuda put love in his heart for the ruler, *Tzofnas Paneiyach*, because there is a phenomenon that if you love someone, that person will love you back (*k'mayim hapanim l'panim!*). We see from here that you can better someone's attitude towards you by bettering your attitude towards them.

24. Yosef sent out all the Egyptians (even his guards) when he revealed himself to his brothers, in order to spare them humiliation before the *goyim*. Yosef told his brothers, "Just as I don't have any hate for Binyomin, I have no hate for you, either. It was all Heaven's will." Additionally, Yosef moved the Egyptians around into different neighborhoods, so that his family shouldn't have to feel like *they* were foreigners.

25. Iyov, the mysterious *tzadik*, was born when the Jews went to Mitzrayim, and he died when they were on their way out 210 years later. Moshe related the saga of Iyov's life to encourage the Jews in Mitzrayim. Moshe Rabeinu authored the story of the righteous Iyov's suffering to illustrate that although sometimes *tzadikim* suffer, in the end they enjoy much happiness and blessing!

26. When Yaakov saw Yosef, he most likely made the following blessings: 1) *Shehecheyanu*, 2) *Mechayei Hameisim*, 3) *Hatov V'Hameitiv*, and 4) *Shecholak Mik'vodo L'basar V'dam*.

27. When Yehuda was about to draw his sword against the antagonizing *Tzofnas Paneiyach*, the sword wouldn't come out. (This was no lack of skill, as *Chazal* tell us of Shaul Hamelech, that every time he drew his sword, it always met its mark!) Yehuda said, "This ruler must fear G-d, and that's why I can't harm him".

Answers&Facts

28. Why did Yehuda burn the wagons that Pharaoh had sent to pick up Yaakov?

(Bereishis Rabbah 94:3)

29. Why did Yosef send *calves* with the wagons? Wouldn't horses have been more appropriate?

(Hevel Tashbar, Rashi)

30. Why wouldn't Yaakov kiss his son Yosef after their long separation?

(Rashi, Kallah Rabbasi 3; see Bereishis Rabbah)

31. Why did Yosef lose ten precious years of his life?

(Midrash Hacheifetz on Parshas Shemos, Berachos 55a, Vilna Gaon)

32. Why did the Jews settle in the land of Goshen?

(Midrash Hagadol 46:34, The Midrash Says)

33. What did Yosef command his family to do regarding their names?

(Baal Haturim on Parshas Shemos)

---

28. Yehuda burned the wagons that Pharaoh dispatched to pick up Yaakov, since they had pictures of *avoda zara* engraved on them.

29. The mighty ox, the king of the domesticated animals, symbolized Yosef. The calves hinted to this. Also, the last *Mitzva* Yaakov discussed with Yosef, was that of *Eglah Arufa*. He wanted to show his father that he still remembered much of the Torah that he taught him!

30. When Yosef embraced his father and he kissed him, Yaakov was saying *Shema*. So Yaakov didn't kiss him then. Some say that Yaakov suspected that gentile women kissed the handsome and attractive Yosef, and he therefore did not kiss his beloved son ever again. In reality, though, Yosef stayed clean and pure all along.

31. When Yosef finally saw Yaakov, he was on his chariot. Since he appeared not to be rushing to greet his father, this slow reaction caused years of his life to be lost. Honoring parents lengthens lives! Also, he should not have kept quiet when they referred to Yaakov as "your servant". In addition, although Yosef was truly humble in his leadership, somehow he acted superior to his brothers, and therefore died before them.

32. Goshen belonged to Sarah Imainu. Pharaoh wrote it to her as a gift when she was released from his palace.

33. Yosef told his family not to change their Hebrew names, although Pharaoh changed *his* Hebrew name to *Tzofnas Paneiyach*.

34. How do we know that coffee has a soothing effect to relieve anxiety and worry?

(Bereishis Rabbah 94:2, Maharzu)

35. What did Potifar tell Pharaoh when Yosef was raised to a position of royalty?

(Midrash Aggadah 49:24)

36. Why don't Torah scholars have to pay the city tax for security and welfare?

(Bava Basra 7b, Yerushalmi Chagigah 1:7)

37. Why didn't Yosef also take the land belonging to the Egyptian priests in return for giving them food?

(Targum Yonasan 47:22)

38. Who was the greatest real-estate agent in history?

(Bereishis 47:20)

39. Why did Yaakov live thirty-three years fewer than Yitzchak?

(Daas Zekeinim Baalei Tosafos)

---

34. Yosef ordered them to bring Egyptian coffee to their father Yaakov. He said that it has a soothing effect to expel worry and anxiety.

35. Potifar asked Pharaoh, "How could you raise my slave - whom I bought for 20 silver coins - to royalty?" Yosef responded to Potifar, "You had no right to buy me, since I am not from the Canaanim, who were slaves. On the contrary, I am from the royal family of Avraham and Sarah. And to prove it, let Pharaoh take out the sculpture that he made of Sarah Imainu, and you will see that I look just like her." And so it was!

36. Real *talmidei chachamim* need not pay the local security tax, because it's really their merits that protect everyone else.

37. The Egyptian priests defended Yosef when Potifar wanted to kill him, so Yosef showed appreciation by not making them sell their property to buy food.

38. Yosef managed all the land in the world!

39. See answer #8. Yaakov complained to Pharaoh that he had a hard life. There were 33 words in the dialogue between Yaakov and Pharaoh discussing his extremely old appearance. Since Yaakov sounded pessimistic, (even though he intended to just avoid *Ayin Hara* from Pharaoh,) he lost 33 years of his life.

Answers&Facts

40. Where is Serach bas Asher today?

(Derech Eretz Zuta 1, Tosafos on Bava Basra 121b)

41. Why did the Egyptians worship sheep?

(Midrash)

42. When were there famines throughout the entire world?

(Bereishis Rabbah 40:3)

43. Why didn't Yosef's brothers trick the "mean" ruler *Tzofnas Paneiyach* by bringing him some other boy named Binyomin?

(Bereishis Rabbah)

44. What does Hashem say about one who comes up with original Torah ideas or about one who builds a *Beis Midrash*?

(Tanna d'Bei Eliyahu Rabbah 10:8)

45. What must a city have before a Torah scholar can move there?

(Sanhedrin 17b)

40. Serach bas Asher eventually went into *Gan Eden* alive.

41. The Egyptians thought that many stars formed the shape of a sheep and they assumed that maybe sheep were gods, so they worshiped sheep.

42. Ten times there were hungers throughout the entire world. One of those times was during Yosef's reign. This is a historic fact: a Jew saved the world from starving to death!

43. The Shevatim didn't want to bring a fake Binyomin, because if Shimon wouldn't recognize him, they would really be in trouble.

44. Hashem proclaims of one who thinks Torah and of one who establishes a *Beis Midrash*, "The great reward that I have in My treasure house will be yours, and in your merit I will save the Jewish people!"

45. There are ten things that a city must have before one settles there: A *yeshiva* to teach the children Torah, a *Beis Din* to execute justice, a *Shochet*, a *Mohel*, a *Sofer*, a *Gabai Tzedaka*, a doctor, a bathhouse, a restroom, and fresh fruits.

46. During their dialogue, Yosef and Yehuda were compared to what?

(Tanchuma, Bereishis Rabbah 93)

47. Who acted like a lawyer?

(Daas Chachamim, Bereishis Rabbah 93:5)

48. Why did the predicted seven-year-long famine stop after only two years?

(Rashi)

49. Who was the seventieth one to travel down to Egypt with Yaakov Avinu?

(Yalkut Shimoni based on Pesikta, Bereishis Rabbah 94:9)

50. How did Yosef reveal his secret identity?

(Bereishis Rabbah 93:8)

51. Why didn't Yosef want to show his mightier brothers to Pharaoh?

(Bereishis Rabbah 95:4, Eitz Yosef)

---

46. Yosef and Yehuda were compared to a lion and an ox, with each one standing up to the other. Their dialogue was both forceful and witty.

47. Yehuda passionately defended all of Binyomin's rights.

48. When Yaakov came to Mitzrayim, the hunger stopped in his merit.

49. The seventieth one that went down to Egypt with Yaakov's family was Yocheved, Serach, or Hashem Himself. Hashem told Yaakov, "I will be with you even when you go into *galus*."

50. When Yosef finally revealed his identity, he said, "Do you think your brother is lost? I will call him to appear before you. '*Yosef ben Yaakov, Yosef ben Yaakov*'." They gazed at all the entrances, until they realized it was none other than he himself. They collapsed in complete shock.

51. Yosef did not want to show Pharaoh his stronger brothers, lest he draft them into the army. He didn't want his brothers endangered, nor did he want them away from Yaakov.

Answers&Facts

52. How do we know that Yaakov Avinu was a king in Canaan?

(Bereishis Rabbah 93:6)

53. Why was Yaakov frightened to go down to Egypt until Hashem encouraged him?

(Rashi)

54. What did Yaakov mean when he said, "I never dreamed of seeing your face, and now I am even being shown your children"?

(Rabbi Zlotowitz z'tl)

55. Why did Yehudah have to offer himself as a slave to *Tzofnas Paneiyach*?

(Abarbanel)

56. Who died and was miraculously revived?

(Tanchuma, Bereishis Rabbah 93:8, Shabbos 88b, Melachim II chapter 4, Yechezkel chapter 37, Megillah 7b, Kesuvos 62b, Bava Kama 117a, Pirkei d'Rabi Eliezer 33)

---

52. When Yehuda threatened Tzofnas Paneiyach to free Binyomin, he said, "Pharaoh is the king of Egypt and you are the second in command, so too, Yaakov is a king in Canaan and I am second in command…"

53. Yaakov was frightened to have to leave Eretz Yisroel and go to exile into Egypt. He feared what might become of their religious status. Hashem had to come to Yaakov in a dream to encourage him that He would be with him.

54. Yaakov was so surprised to see true *Yiddishe nachas* (Jewish pride) from Yosef's grandchildren, considering how challenging it must have been to maintain a high moral standing in a land filled with corruption. He proclaimed, "I didn't expect to see you again, and now I even see my character in your children!" Yaakov was very happy to see that his personality was apparant in Yosef's children as well.

55. It was befitting that Yehuda offer himself as a slave to Yosef, since he was the one that proposed that Yosef be sold as a slave in the first place!

56. Yosef's brothers died from shock when they learned his secret identity. Hashem miraculously revived them. (There are many other instances of the revival of the dead mentioned in T'nach and Shas: During Matan Torah; the daughter of the Shunamis; the dry bones in the days of Yechezkel; Rav Zera; Rabbi Chanina ben Chachinai's wife; Rav Kahana and others.)

57. Why did Yosef give Binyomin extra garments?

(Megillah 16b, Vilna Gaon, The Midrash Says)

58. Which sin caused Yosef's brothers to hate him?

(Rashi)

59. Why didn't Yaakov believe that Yosef was alive in Mitzrayim?

(Kedushas Levi, Avos d'Rabi Nosson)

60. What happened to all the money that Yosef accumulated during the famine?

(Pesachim 119a)

---

57. Yosef hinted to Binyomin that some day, his descendant, Mordechai, would go through the streets clothed in royal garments, as he would rise to power and save the Jews. Yosef also wanted to test his brothers to see if they would be jealous of Binyomin or if they would be happy for him. Some say that the garments were of cheaper material, and it really was the same value of the garments the brother's had received.

58. It was *lashon hora* (badmouthing) that caused the brothers to hate Yosef.

59. Yaakov did not believe his sons that Yosef was still alive, because they had lied previously, saying that he was killed by a wild animal. Also, Yaakov could not believe that his son Yosef was alive spiritually in that spiritual wasteland.

60. Yosef amassed all the money in the world into his treasury. When the Jews left Mitzrayim, they took it with them. It remained in Jewish hands until Rechovam, the son of Shlomo Hamelech. Sheishak, the king of Mitzrayim, took it from Rechovam. Zarach, the king of Ethiopia, took it from Shaishak. Asa, the king of Judah, took it from Zarach, and he sent it to Hadrimon, the son of Tavrimon. The Nation of Amon took it from Hadrimon. Yehoshafat, the king of Judah, took it from the nation of Amon, and it was held until the Jewish king Achaz. Sancheriv came and took it from Achaz. The Jewish king Chizkiyahu took it from Sancheriv, and it was possessed until the Jewish king Tzidkiyahu. The Kasdim took it from Tzidkiyahu. The Persians took it from the Kasdim. The Greeks took it from the Persians. The Romans took it from the Greeks, and it is still in their possession.

Answers&Facts

---

61. About what did Yehuda warn *Tzofnas Paneiyach?*

(Rashi, Sefer Hayashar)

62. Whom did Yosef cry about when he was reunited with his brothers?

(Iturei Torah quoting Korban Ani, Midrash Shocher Tov, Mishlei 1:13)

63. Where does it say in the Torah that one ought not to be depressed?

(Daas Chachamim quoting Rav Yisroel of Ruzhin)

61. Yehuda warned Yosef that Hashem would punish him if he threatened any of Avraham & Sarah's grandchildren, just as Hashem smote Pharaoh when he took Sarah Imainu. Yehuda also threatened to kill Tzofnas Paneiyach, Pharaoh, and all of Egypt.

62. Yosef cried over the future murder of the *Asara Harugei Malchus*, who were to pay the price for that sale - to atone for the *shevatim - tzadikim* that mistakenly kidnapped their brother.

63. Yosef encouraged his brothers not to be sad that they tried to harm him, because it all turned out for the best. He said, "Don't be depressed..." The way to serve Hashem is with joy and happiness!

Dedicated in loving memory of
AL DWEK CHALOUSI A"H
by Hal Dwek

פרשת ויחי

1. Which seven *Mitzvos* are most effective in speeding up the *Geulah Sheleima* that will get us out of this *Galus* once and for all?

(See Otzar Ha'aggadah: 'Geulah')

2. What were some of the unique qualities of each of Yaakov's sons, the Shevatim?

(Shivtei Yisroel)

fUndamental Answers!

יגעתי ומצאתי?

("I worked on these questions, and I found these answers!")

1. The Midrash mentions a number of super-special Mitzvos which are most powerful to bring the end to all suffering, and the return of our people to our homeland with joy and happiness. The first is the mitzva of Emunah - strong belief in Hashem; the second is the mitzva of Teshuva - repentance; the third one is Learning Torah for Hashem's sake- especially Mishnayos; the fourth is Ahavas Yisroel - loving your fellow Jew; the fifth is Tefillah - sincere prayers; the sixth is Tzedakah - charity; and the seventh is Shabbos! Galus started in Parshas Vayechi, as the Bnei Yisroel went down to Mitzrayim. It's up to us to get out.

2. The Roshei HaShevatim each had extraordinary qualities that made them unique and beloved. Their greatness is beyond the scope of our imagination, and each Shevet deserves a work by itself. However, we must observe some of the things they are known for, so that we can emulate them, as well. Reuven was a model Baal Teshuva, sincerely repenting a misdeed; Shimon opposed and punished the evil-doers; Levi was devoted to the full-time learning of Torah; Yehuda was a natural leader, step-

3. How did Yehudah's family earn kingship?

(Tosefta on Berachos 4:16, Rabbeinu Bachya)

4. Why does one bless his sons to be like Ephraim and Menashe? After all, wouldn't it be better to bless them to be like the *Avos*?

(Igra d'Kallah, Mayanah Shel Torah)

5. How may *Tefillah* be compared to a bow and arrow?

(See Mayanos Hanetzach quoting the Kotzker Rebbe; see Bereishis Rabbah 97:6 and 99:2)

ping forth to defend his brother; Yissochar was always learning Torah, non-stop; Zevulun supported Yissochar, enabling him to learn Torah without interruption; Dan was brave to fight against the wicked ; Naftoli was always fast to do *kibud av*, running to do errands for Yaakov or for his brothers whenever they requested; Gad was a mighty warrior (Eliyahu Hanavi who will soon bring the tiding of Moshiach's arrival is from Gad); Asher was extra devoted to mastering Mishnayos; Yosef was able to stay holy, even against odds; and Binyomin wouldn't speak lashon horah to tell of Yosef's sale. *Zechusam yagen aleinu!*

3. There are many experiences in the history of Shevet Yehuda where the Shevet showed a natural leadership. One of the most famous of these episodes took place when Nachshon ben Aminadav of Shevet Yehuda was the first to jump into the waters of the Yam-Suf, confident that Hashem would save us. This demonstration of faith showed that he was a natural leader, perfect for the Jewish people. Yehuda also spoke up to sell Yosef, instead of killing him by throwing him into a pit, which showed caring when others didn't. Even more so when Binyomin was going to become a slave, Yehuda offered to become a slave in his stead. Such humility- offering to let himself be a slave so that his brother will live- is a compassionate trait fit for a king.

4. Ephraim and Menashe were so righteous, even as the first Jews in Galus, that they were ranked together with the *tzadikim* of the previous generation; they became Shevatim! Every father's prayer is that his child shall also be so righteous to the extent that he be ranked as the great Jews of the previous generation. Additionally, they deserve such honor, because they were not jealous of each other. Menashe, the older son, did not feel bad that Ephraim went before him. Parents wish that there not be jealousy between their children, because jealousy is the most common cause of sibling rivalry. Yaakov knew that jealousy is what caused the galus, and stopping jealousy can get us out of exile!

5. Just as one has to aim a bow and arrow, so too by *tefillah*, you need to aim your prayers towards Yerushalyim to the Beis Hamikdash above it in Heaven. Also, just as by a bow and arrow, the more effort you have in pulling the string

6. **Why did Yaakov give Yosef the city of Shechem?**
(Bereishis Rabbah 97:6)

7. **Why did Reuvein lose all three distinctive positions: Bechorah, Kehunah, and Malchus?**
(See Bereishis Rabbah 98:4 and Malbim 49:5; Sforno, Kuzari)

8. **How did Yaakov curse Shimon's & Levi's anger?**
(Tur, Chizkuni; see Bereishis Rabbah 99:7)

9. **Why did Yaakov choose Shimon's descendants to be schoolteachers if the teaching profession requires a good deal of patience?**
(Bereishis Rabbah 99:6, Emes L'Yaakov, Toras Hachinuch)

---

toward you the further the arrow will go, so too, the more you "pull" the words to your heart the further your prayers will accomplish.

6. Yaakov said that Yosef deserved the land of Shechem more than those who inhabited it. While they were morally corrupt, he was pure and holy. After the Mabul of 1656, even the *goyim* realized that they better not upset Hashem by being immoral, and they guarded themselves. The people of Shechem were first to breach that purity and therefore Yosef who upheld the purity was better chosen to own that city.

7. Reuven lost his birthright to Yosef, the kingship to Yehuda, and the priesthood to Levi. It was due to his anger that he removed Bilha's bed and replaced it with Leah's. This was an act of *chutzpa*, as he did not consult with Yaakov. These traits of anger and *chutzpa* cannot be present in a king or in a kohen, so he lost these great privileges.

8. Yaakov cursed the anger of Shimon and Levi that it should never be fruitful. They acted like brothers in their defense of Dinah, but not when it came to their attack on Yosef. They should have realized on their own that it doesn't pay to be angry, and in that way they would be able to stop this bad habit.

9. Yaakov knew that the best way to rectify a sin is by making a *tikkun* - changing that bad action. Since Shimon was short tempered, as he massacred the city of Shechem, becoming a schoolteacher would force him to be extra patient, and that would be a *tikkun*. The first of the "Ten Commandments of Being a Good Teacher" is to have lots of patience. The reason, however, that it was good for Shimon to have a potential temper is that a teacher also needs to be able to discipline his students, as Rabbi Yehuda Hanasi said to his son: "*Zerok marah betalmidim*"- Put a fear in the students. "Be tough, but be fair."

Answers&Facts

10. What was Yaakov's blessing to Ephraim and Menashe?

(*Taam V'daas, Berachos 20a, Bereishis Rabbah 97:3*)

11. Why isn't there a letter *"ches"* or *"tes"* in the names of the Shevatim?

(*Zohar 2:230a*)

12. Why are there twelve months, twelve constellations, and twelve hours of the day and the night respectively?

(*Pesikta Rabbasi 4, Bereishis Rabbah 100:9*)

13. Which two Shevatim did Yaakov proclaim to honor the most, since he considered them the most important tribes?

(*Bereishis Rabbah 98:2, Eitz Yosef*)

---

10. Yaakov said that just as Hashem saved me from bad thoughts and helped me to stay holy, so too, you youths, who will be in an immoral society, may Hashem bless you to have clean thoughts and stay righteous. May you be fruitful in the land like the fish. Just like fish are not curious to know what's going on outside of their waters, so too you, as Jews, should keep your eyes in the waters of Torah, and not be curious to know what's going on in the outside world- the world of the gentiles. [This is a great lesson for the upcoming week, the start of the "Days of Shovavim" (Repentance on Thoughts).]

11. The letters ח or ט are not found in the names of the *shevatim*, hinting that they were entirely righteous, clean from any sin (חטא). The *pasuk* in Shir Hashirim (4-7) refers to them as, "My beloved is beautiful without any fault."

12. Hashem made the 12 constellations in the merit of the 12 Shevatim. That's also why there are 12 months of the year, and 12 hours of the day and the night.

13. Yaakov told his children to honor Shevet Yehuda and Shevet Binyomin most. This is because the future kings would come from them, namely, Shaul Hamelech, Ish Boshes Hamelech, Dovid Hamelech, Shlomo Hamelech, etc. Both Rochel's and Leah's descendants were kings. Also, the main tribes that most Jews today come from is Shevet Yehuda and Binyomin. The tribe of Levi would automatically earn respect, because they were most devoted to learning Torah, which brings honor to those who study it. (The rest of the Shevatim are temporarily trapped behind the Sambatyon River.)

14. Shaul knew that Hashem promised that kings would come from Binyomin, the son of Rochel. Even though it was promised that kings were to come from Yehuda, it seemed that now was the term of Binyomin's family's rulership,

14. Why did Shaul Hamelech try to kill Dovid if the *Malchus Yisroel* really belonged to Shevet Yehudah in the first place?

(Mussar Haneviim)

15. Why did Yaakov initially hesitate to bless Ephraim and Menashe?

(Tanchuma 6, Pesikta Rabbasi 3)

16. Why was the Beis Hamikdash built on Binyomin's portion?

(Bereishis Rabbah 99:1, Mechilta on Parshas Yisro)

17. Why are all Jews called "Yehudim" after Shevet Yehudah?

(Bereishis Rabbah 98:6, Rashi)

18. Why did Yaakov put his right hand over the head of his younger grandson, Ephraim?

(Rashi, Bereishis Zuta)

---

and anyone who would try to take that away was considered a *mored bemalchus*- a rebel to the king- to be disposed of.

15. After Ephraim and Menashe sat learning Torah before Yaakov, he was proud of them and was about to give them great *berachos*. Suddenly, because of seeing through Ruach Hakodesh that Yeravam Ben Navat and Achav Ben Omri would descend from Ephraim, and Yehu and his sons from Menashe, he lost his Ruach Hakodesh and froze. Yosef immediately prostrated himself on the floor and prayed to Hashem for mercy. The Ruach Hakodesh returned, and he blessed them.

16. Binyomin was never involved in hatred (*sinas chinam*). He wasn't part of Yosef's sale to Mitzrayim. His property was therefore most suited for the Beis Hamikdash, which brought Shalom to the world. Also Binyomin was the only son of Yaakov that was born in Eretz Yisroel.

17. "*Modeh*" means admit, and it means thanks. Yehuda admitted a wrongdoing, and that took power. Yaakov wanted that all Jews should have that quality- to admit to Hashem that we must serve Him better, and we need him and must frequently thank Him. This therefore became our namesake as Yehudim. Also since Yehuda saved Yosef when Shimon and Levi were about to kill him, Hashem said, "You saved your brothers from sinning with bloodshed and you thus saved them from Gehinnom, all Jews will be therefore called after your name."

18. Yaakov placed his right hand over the younger son Ephraim to show that he was more special, since he devoted more time and effort into Torah study. It was due to Ephraim running away from the limelight that he got the limelight.

Answers&Facts

---

19. Why did Yosef embalm Yaakov; after all, *tzadikim* don't decompose anyway?
(*Bereishis Rabbah 100:3, Bava Basra 17a*)

20. Which acts of kindness are called *"Chessed shel Emes"* (true kindness)?
(*See Rashi, Sifsei Chachamim, and Mo'ed Kattan 28a*)

21. Why did Yaakov compare Yissochar to a donkey? Wouldn't it have been proper to compare him to a more respectable creature?
(*See Shaarei Aharon quoting Zohar 49:14; Bereishis Rabbah 99:10*)

22. Why was Zevulun blessed before Yissochar if Yissochar was older?
(*Bereishis Rabbah 99:9, Sforno*)

19. The Talmud tells us that Yaakov Avinu never really died. Yosef was punished for having him embalmed, by dying before his brothers, even though he was younger than they were. [Maybe he allowed that, because that practice showed the importance of the deceased, since it was the way of the Pharohs to mummify their great rulers.]

20. The Chevra Kadisha - who bury the dead- don't expect any benefit in return from the dead, and this is true kindness. Unfortunately, due to the recent tragic terrorist acts, a new team of special volunteers called "Zaka" tries to rescue victims, but also work to recover body parts from the scene of the crime and bring them to a proper dignified Jewish burial.

21. A donkey has a special quality that it will carry its load for its master faithfully. It does not complain nor does it seek comfort when it crouches down. So too, Yissochar, the epitome of a *talmid chacham* does not look for comforts in this world but rather looks to carry the heavy precious load of the Torah.

22. Zevulun was known as a supporter of Yissochar's family so that Yissochar could concentrate on his studies. As it says without "dough" there's no learning. So we give credit to the supporters of the Torah who make it possible for others to learn.

23. Which is greater nowadays—to learn Torah continually as part of a Yissochar-Zevulun relationship or to learn Torah part-time while supporting yourself?

(See Biur Halachah 231; Chiddushei HaRim on Avos 2:12)

24. How did Yissochar help Zevulun's business prosper while also causing many non-Jews to convert to Judaism?

(Bereishis Rabbah 98:12, Matnos Kehunah, Eitz Yosef)

25. What do our Chazal mean when they say, "Torah scholars don't rest in this world or in the next world?"

(Maharsha on Berachos 64a)

26. In what respect did the *Shofeit* Shimshon act like a snake (remember, the snake is the symbol of Dan, Shimshon's tribe)?

(Bereishis Rabbah 99:12 and 98:19)

---

23. Once upon a time people were able to carry on a business and think of Torah while they worked and reach great achievements in the work place. But today with the drastic shortage of *talmidei chachamim* - of true Torah scholars - knowledgeable in all areas of Torah, we must turn to Yissochar-Zevulun deals and Kollels (Torah Academies for married men) to try as much as we can to develop competent leaders for tomorrow.

24. The fruits (cows) of Yissochar were so gigantic, in the merit of their Torah learning, that Zevulun used to travel selling these remarkable items and everyone wanted to buy them. As a matter of fact many *goyim* were so impressed with the "secret" of Yissochar & Zevulun's success (prioritizing service of Hashem, which brought them to success spiritually and materialistically) that they converted to Judaism!

25. In this world *talmidei chachamim* don't have time to rest. They wake up early in the morning and they go to sleep late at night. In their pursuit of Torah excellence, they barely get to rest or take it easy. In the next world also they don't get to rest in one location, since they left writings and students in this world and children whose merit increases their merit, which causes them to go higher and higher all the time in Gan Eden without getting to rest in one spot.

26. Just as a snake has camouflage skin and sneaks upon its victim, so too did Shimshon act as if he did not care for his people and lived amongst the Plishtim. In this way he was able to attack the enemy so much more cunningly.

Answers & Facts

27. Why was Asher selected to save all those who study the *Mishnah* from *Gehinnom*?

(Midrash Talpios quoting Arizal, Kuntrus L'olam Hevei Rutz L'Mishnah)

28. What did Yaakov's sons assert when he suspected them of being sinners?

(Bereishis Rabbah 98:3, Baal Haturim 49:1)

29. Why didn't Yosef invite his brothers to dine with him after their father, Yaakov, had passed away?

(Bereishis Rabbah 100:8)

30. How did the tribe of Ephraim produce a great man like Yehoshua so soon in their history?

(See Taam V'daas quoting Bereishis Rabbah 91:6, and see Bereishis Rabbah 98:18)

---

27. Asher showed the greatest effort to study the Mishnayos. He was therefore selected to be present by the gateway of Gehinom to rescue those who study Mishnayos diligently in their lifetime that they should be spared from that dreaded punishment. (Speaking of Mishnayos, if you set yourself a goal to study and review a chapter a week, you can complete Shas Mishnayos in 10 years!)

28. Yaakov wished to inform his children of the final day of salvation for the Jewish people. But right then he blanked out and forgot the date. He worried that perhaps maybe his sons were not as righteous as he thought. Could they have sinned? They assured him of their faith to Hashem. *"Shema Yisroel, Hashem Elokeinu Hashem Echad"*, "Listen Yisroel (Yaakov was also called Yisroel), Hashem our G-d is the only Power we serve." Yaakov felt so proud hearing their commitment, that he said, "Bless the name of Hashem's Honorable Kingdom forever and ever.

29. Yosef had good intentions in not inviting his brothers to dine with him, after the passing of Yaakov. He reasoned that during his lifetime Yaakov placed Yosef at the head of the table, but now he didn't want to show himself more honor than Yehuda the official family of kings, nor did he want to make Reuven the oldest feel inferior, so he didn't invite them. But, they were paranoid, assuming he hated them. For the sake of Shalom they lied and said "Yaakov, our father said not to hold a grudge against us."

30. Ephraim was always concentrating on his Torah learning, whereas Menashe, although he learned as well, was busy with the affairs of the kingdom. If a person wants outstanding sons, they must see their father always toiling in his learning. Ephraim therefore produced a leader such as Yehoshua to succeed Moshe quicker

---

31.
Why did Yaakov pray to be sick before he passed away?

(See Bava Metzia 87a; Maskil L'Dovid)

32.
Why did Yaakov make Yosef swear that he would bury him in Eretz Yisroel?

(Bereishis Rabbah 96:5; see Ramban and Shaarei Aharon

33.
What happened to Yaakov as a result of the curse that befell Rachel?

(Moshav Zekeinim)

34.
In the days of the Mishkan, *Maaser Sheini* and *Kodshim Kalim* (sacrificial meats) could be eaten in any location from which one could see Shiloh, whereas in the days of the *Beis Hamikdash* they could be eaten only inside the city of Yerushalayim. Why?

(See Zevachim 118b; Chiddushei HaRim, Megillah 9b)

---

than Menashe produced Gideon. Incidentally, there is a Midrash that states that Gideon was not really a high caliber *tzadik* or *talmid chacham*, but that he merited being the savior of the Jewish people of his time due to his devotion to the *mitzvah* of honoring his father. It was the *mitzva* of honoring his father that somehow paralleled Menashe's helping his father that actually made Gideon a leader as well.

31. Yaakov was scared that if a person would die suddenly without ever being sick, he would never have a chance to do *teshuva* before he left this world. He would also never get the chance to tell his family his last wishes. When a person gets sick in his or her old age, it is really a benefit for everyone. Yaakov also wanted to be sure he would bless his children one more time before he passed away.

32. Yaakov knew he could trust Yosef to do his will, but he was concerned that Pharaoh might resist this permission. By forcing Yosef to swear to his father Pharaoh would not be able to object a son who wanted to keep his father's promise.

33. Since Yaakov uttered a curse at the one who stole Lavan's crazy idols, and a Jew none other than his own wife suffered the fate of that curse, he too lost out. If someone causes another Jew suffering they do not get let off the hook either. It's for this reason that Yaakov didn't live as long as his father Yitzchak did.

34. Yosef was very careful that his eyes should not "see" *tamei* things, therefore Shiloh which was his property was blessed in that anyone who could "see" Shiloh could still eat the Masser Sheni and the Kodshim Kalim. This area was pronounced holy whereas in Yerushalyim you could only eat these things in the city proper itself.

Answers&Facts

35. Which *Shevet* carried out the *mitzvah* of *Hashavas Aveidah* (returning a lost article to its owner) most often?

(Rashi)

36. How many crowns were placed on Yaakov Avinu's *Aron* (coffin) while it was en route to its final destination in Eretz Yisroel?

(Rashi to Sotah 13b, Bereishis Rabbah 100:5)

37. Yosef said that the *Go'el* (Savior) of the Jews would utter the key sentence: *"Pakod yifkod"* ("He – Hashem – will certainly remember.") Why such a repetitious phrase?

(Iturei Torah, Torah L'daas, Mayanos Hanetzach)

38. What are *Mashiach's* eight names?

(Otzar Hayedios)

39. Which holiday *was* supposed to honor the Shevatim?

(Tur Orach Chaim 413)

35. Dan was placed in the back of the Jewish people. They were therefore able to find many things that the Jewish travelers left behind. Obviously they got to do this *mitzvah* of returning lost items more than anyone else did.

36. Thirty-six crowns. This is to symbolize that *talmidei chachamim* are the true princes. When all of the kings of the land heard of Yaakov's arrival, they put their crowns on top of his coffin. This was very appropriate because Hashem calls the Jewish people "His children", and since Hashem is the King of Kings, then we are the "princes of princes"! Not only that, but a Cloud of Hashem's *Shechinah* accompanied the coffin back to Eretz Yisroel! This symbolized that just as the Cloud would later escort the Aron Kodesh with the Torah, from Egypt to Israel, now too, the Cloud escorted the Aron Kodesh and Torah, namely Yaakov Avinu.

37. The message of the true Moshiach of Klal Yisroel is Pakod Yifkod, "Hashem has surely remembered to save you." The reason the words are repeated is because there are two types of redemptions that we need. Our physical needs must be taken care of and so too our spiritual needs. Only then is it considered the real Geula.

38. Yinon, Tzemach, Menachem, Peleh, Yoetz, Kal, Gibor, Abi-Ad and Shalom.

40. When returning from burying Yaakov in Chevron, Yosef traveled by way of Shechem. Why?

(Tanchuma, see Berachos 54a; Bereishis Rabbah 100:8, Maharzu)

41. From where can we see that when you show respect to another person, you receive from him much more respect than you yourself have given?

(See Rabbeinu Bachya)

42. What lesson can we learn from the 2001 terrorist arson attack upon *Kever Yosef Hatzadik*?

(Rebbitzen Jungreiss)

43. From where do learn the importance of a world organization, such as *Agudath Israel*?

(See Malbim; Bereishis Rabbah 98:2)

---

39. The three Moadim (Pesach, Shavuos and Sukos) are in honor of the Avos. The twelve Roshei Chodesh are in honor of the 12 Shevatim.

40. Yosef wished to say the Beracha one must say when a miracle happens to him. He therefore went past the pit which he was thrown into in order to thank Hashem for the miracle of saving him in that very place.

41. Yaakov asked Yosef to bury him in Israel. Yosef agreed. So too, Yosef was given the merit that Bnei Yisroel carried his coffin throughout the desert all those years back to Israel. When you respect the will of others - especially your parents - you'll be surprised how much respect you'll get back in the future.

42. Some want to suggest that the reason the Arabs burned Yosef's stone monument recently was a message that just as Yosef suffered from hatred, so too we must stop the pointless hatred burning amongst us in order to end the terrible Arab crisis, *Rachmana litzlan*.

43. called his children together before he passed away, and ordered them to be united as a group, and never fight. We must be one nation, and only then can we expect the Geulah. (Politics and strife among schools, Shuls, neighborhood, and different Jewish sects is not what Yaakov had in mind.)

Answers&Facts

44. How was *Malchus Yehudah* compared to the cycle of the moon?

(Shemos Rabbah 15:56)

45. Why didn't Yosef order that his coffin be buried in Eretz Yisroel immediately after his demise?

(Rashi)

46. What can one do to save himself from an *Ayin Hora*?

(See Tamid 32a; Berachos 20a)

47. Why should one request to be buried in Eretz Yisroel (after 120 years)?

(Bereishis Rabbah 96:5, Me'am Lo'ez quoting Zohar)

48. Why is learning in *Kollel* a most wonderful, "rich" career?

(Mishnas Rav Aharon)

---

44. The 15th day of the month is when the moon is complete and brightest. So too the 15th generation from Avraham Avinu was King Solomon, whose kingdom was greatest. After that, the kingdom of Klal Yisroel became smaller, until it disappeared after the 29th generation. We must be encouraged though, since it is only temporary. Just as the moon renews itself, so too will the renewal of the kingdom of Yehuda come very soon.

45. The Egyptians wanted Yosef's coffin to stay there by the Nile, so that in his merit the waters would flow well. It seems therefore, that he didn't have a choice.

46. Don't show off! A person should frequently say "Beli Ayin Hara" whenever he merits something extra special. One should also not show off things that he has more than anyone else. It seems that controlling ones eyes from seeing things that he shouldn't is also a *segulah* not to be harmed by the Ayin Hara. We find that Yosef was blessed with this great security since he always controlled his eyes by not giving in to temptation. Yosef did not let his eyes feast on the illusions of the Satan.

47. Its much more comfortable by Techias Hamesim to come out of the ground in Israel than anywhere else, because in other lands one must roll in tunnels which doesn't sound so comfortable. Also the land of Israel atones for one's sins, and the ones there will probably be the first ones to be reborn.

48. Kollel affords young and old men the best of both worlds. It lets them amass great wealth of Torah knowledge and at the same time their needs for their families to be taken care of. One who learns in Kollel is really like a Kohen of the Bet Hamikdash. How fortunate is his lot.

---

49. Why was Yosef called a *Nazir*?
(Bereishis Rabbah 98:20, The Beginning; see Bereishis Rabbah 97:6 and Eitz Yosef there)

50. Why shouldn't people predict the date of *Mashiach's* arrival?
(Yalkut Shimoni on Chavakuk 562; see Bereishis Rabbah 98:2 and Daniel 12:4)

51. Who did Yaakov think would be the future *Mashiach*?
(Bereishis Rabbah 98:14)

52. When should we say: *"Li'shuascha Kivisi Hashem"* ("I hope for Your salvation, O G-d")?
(See Mishnah Berurah 230:7, Gilyon HaShas on Bava Metzia 87a, Pirkei d'Rabi Eliezer 52; Kaf Hachaim)

53. To which angel was Yaakov referring when he blessed Yosef's sons: *"Hamalach Hagoel Osi…"* ("The angel that saved me should bless these youths…")?
(Eitz Yosef on Bereishis Rabbah 97:3)

---

49. Yosef demonstrated the greatest amount of self-control. Just as a Nazir restrains himself from drinking wine (representing the pleasures of life) and guards himself from becoming tamei, so too Yosef earned the title Nazir, which also means crown, because of his holiness.

50. The Rabbis curse one who announces the date of Moshiach's coming. This is because if he doesn't come the predictor is going to do more harm than good by discouraging people's hopes. Even though many dates were announced of Moshiach's coming, it just really meant that it was a special time, which could have merited Moshiach. We must therefore not proclaim a specific date, we must just say: "He is on the way!"

51. Yaakov thought Shimshon from Shevet Dan was Moshiach.

52. After you sneeze, it is a good custom to say, "I hope You will save me Hashem." When a person sneezes, hopefully the body extracts germs and undesired elements. Therefore, a person should say a prayer to Hashem that he should be healthy. This custom can be more appreciated if you recall the olden days. When someone sneezed his neshama would leave and he would die. That's why when someone sneezes you're supposed to bless him "Chaim tovim", "Gezuntheit" or "G-d bless you", which are all wishes that he stay healthy.

53. Mattatron was the angel that went before Yaakov to protect him. Wherever that angel appeared, so did Hashem. Yaakov blessed them that this angel be with them as well, and ultimately Hashem Himself would protect us.

Answers&Facts

54. When is the only time that one may become angry?

(See Kesef Mishnah on Rambam Hilchos De'os, and see Ben Yehoyada on)Pesachim 119b

55. Which *Shevet* was/is the poorest? Why?

(Bereishis Rabbah 98:5 and 99:7, Pesikta d'Rabi Kahana 32)

56. What did the *Beis Yosef's Maggid Meisharim* (guiding angel) tell him were the dangerous consequences of anger?

(Maggid Meisharim)

57. Why was *Malchus Beis Dovid* split up in 2964, during the reign of Shlomo Hamelech's son, Rechavam?

(Melachim I chapter 11)

58. Who is fit to be called *"Chacham"*?

(Meiri; Bereishis Rabbah 90:3)

54. The only time you can get angry is if you see someone making a Hillul Hashem, To defend Hashem's honor you may get angry, but one should never get angry over physical needs. Even in regard to spiritual needs one should not bring himself to anger. (When rebuking a sinner, anger is often not effective. You can accomplish more with honey than with vinegar.)

55. Shimon was, and probably still is, the poorest tribe, since they did not get the blessing of Yaakov due to their anger. They also did not receive the blessing of Moshe (in Sefer Devarim) since he was upset about the shameful incident in which 24,000 members of Shevet Shimon sinned after Bilam's temptation. Shevet Shimon did not only lose out materially by not getting the blessing of their Gedolim, they even lost out spiritually. No Shofeit (judge) descended from them to lead the Bnei Yisroel.

56. The heavenly angel warned Maran Rabbi Yosef Kairo, that one should never get angry because it destroys the soul, Heaven forbid.

57. Shlomo Hamelech married too many wives. Many were converts and they continued their Avoda Zara practices. Since he didn't protest this enough, the kingdom was torn away from him and given to Yeravam.

58. In Pirkei Avos we are told, a Chacham is somebody that learns from everyone, and someone who can perceive the ramifications of everything. However, to be properly titled the honored name of Chacham, one must know at least three *sedarim* of the six sedarim of Shas. The Midrash tells us that the reason Yosef earned this prestigious title was not merely for his extraordinary knowledge of Torah, but because he kept his thoughts pure. Hashem testified, "The mind that did not entertain improper thoughts will be called Wise!" Indeed Yosef was called the wisest in the land.

59. Which great couple came from the tribe of Binyomin who saved the Bnei Yisroel in 3406?

(Megillah 12b)

60. Did Yaakov ever find out about the kidnapping of Yosef?

(See Ramban 45:27; Bereishis Rabbah 97:4,6)

61. When did 301 Jewish soldiers defeat 135,000 enemy attackers?

(See Rashi to Sefer Shoftim 7:8)

62. Who died in this *Parshas Vayechi*?

(Sotah 13a; see Taanis 5b)

63. Why is it most appropriate to read the story of Yosef's exemplary purity during the week before *Shovavim*?

(Bereishis Rabbah 49:2, Rav Yaakov Hillel shlit"a)

64. Who was smaller but bigger—and second but first?

(Bereishis Rabbah 97:5)

---

59. Mordechai HaYehudi, the famous member of the Sanhendrin, and his beautiful wife Esther saved the Jewish people from the Amalek of their time.

60. It's not certain if Yaakov ever found out that Yosef was sold.

61. Menashe's descendant Gidoen also became a great leader. Yaakov prophesied that Hashem would make a miracle through him when his 300 innocent soldiers defeated the 135,000 soldiers of the Midianite army as if they were one person!

62. Eisav died in Parshas Vayichi. Yaakov on the contrary did not die as Chazal say Yaakov Avinu never died!

63. The weeks from Parshas Shemos through Mishpatim (and through Tetsaveh in a leap year) are designated as days during which one can fix the damage that has been done by not staying holy. What better inspiration can there be then that of the young teenager Yosef, whose blood was hot and who was all alone, yet did not let himself become impure, thereby causing a great Kiddush Hashem. Yosef cheered his brothers up, by showing them that it was the merit of Shemiras Habris that earned him kingship in the world!

64. Ephraim was younger than Menashe, but he was a bigger *tzadik*. Also he was born second but placed first in the proverbial *beracha*: "May Hashem make you like Ephraim and Menashe."

Answers&Facts

65. When did Jewish slavery begin in Mitzrayim?

(Bereishis Rabbah 96:1)

66. To whom did Yaakov give Adam Harishon's priestly clothes?

(Bereishis Rabbah 97:6, Eitz Yosef)

67. Which two *tzaddikim* almost revealed the date of Mashiach's arrival?

(Daniel 12:4, Bereishis Rabbah 98:2)

68. Why did Yaakov characterize his children by using animal imagery?

(Bereishis Rabbah 99:2-3 and 100:9, Pirkei Avos 5:23)

---

65. Right after Yaakov Avinu's demise, the slavery started in Mitzrayim. It seems that as long as Yaakov was alive the Jews knew how superior they were, but once he passed away most of them went to work for Pharaoh. Had they maintained a greater self-esteem they never would have sunken into slavery and sin.

66. Yaakov Avinu gave the wondrous clothes of Adam Harishon (which he bought from Eisav) to Yosef. This was because Yaakov transferred the *bechora* (Birthright and Temple service) from Reuvein to Yosef. These clothes we're worn by Adam Harishon as *bigdei kehunah* when he sacrificed a *korban*, and Yaakov wanted Yosef to merit this service.

67. There were two *tzadikim* that knew the future date of Moshiach's arrival but it became disclosed from them right when they wanted to reveal that secret to others. Yaakov Avinu and Daniel.

68. Some say that the nations that oppressed the Jews throughout Galus were likened to animals and beasts. Yaakov was alluding to the inherent strength of each Shevet to be able to defeat a particular enemy. May we be *zoche* to see the merits of the Shevatim defeat our enemies very soon, Amen.

Dedicated in memory of
ROZA MASLATON KADA a"h
from Gabriel & Sara Ahdut and children

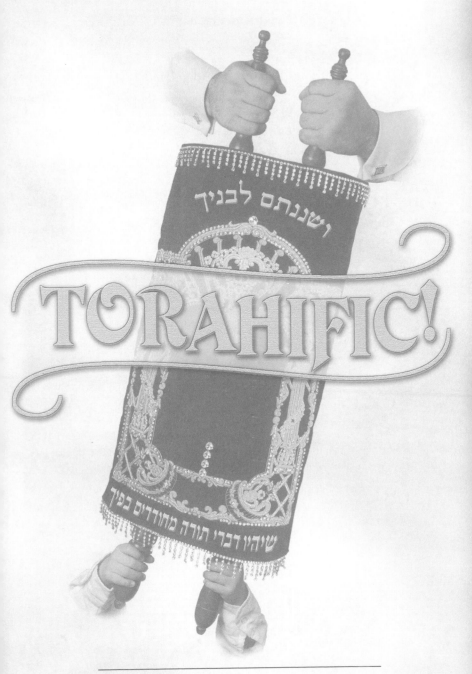

TORAHIFIC!

sefer shemos

פרשת שמות

1. Why did Am Yisroel have to reside in Egypt and not in any other land?

(Netziv; See Doresh Tov quoting Ben Ish Chai; Torah Mi'Tzion)

2. Who was the youngest Hatzalah member ever?

(Shemos Rabbah 1:13)

FUNdamental Answers!

"יגעתי ומצאתי!"

("I worked on these questions, and I found these answers!")

1. The commentaries give many reasons why the Bnei Yisroel had to be enslaved specifically by the Egyptians (the descendants of the slave Canaan):

a. Egypt would be a place that Jews would not mingle with the non-Jews, since the Egyptians greatly despised Jews.

b. They would oppress the Jews so harshly that the Jews would finish their exile sooner than was originally decreed!

c. The Jews would be more thankful for the wonderful land Hashem gave them after having lived in such an immoral land before entering Eretz Yisroel. They would appreciate the contrast of the two lands - like sunlight over darkness!

d. Idolatry was more rampant in Egypt than anywhere else. The Bnei Yisroel had to go to Egypt and see all the Avodah Zarah eradicated and witness Hashem as the only Power (through the Ten Plagues and the Exodus from Egypt), so that they would serve only Hashem!

2. Miriam was only five years old when she saved Jewish babies from Pharaoh's murderous clutches!

3. Why did Pharaoh want to kill the young girl Miriam?

(Shemos Rabbah 1:13)

4. Why was the young Miriam nicknamed *Bish Gadeh* (bad luck) and *Azuvah* (rejected)?

(See Shemos Rabbah 1:17, and see Me'am Lo'ez)

5. What did Shifrah (Yocheved) and Puah (Miriam) pray for?

(Shemos Rabbah 1:15; see Eitz Yosef; Doresh Tov)

6. Which special merits brought about the Bnei Yisroel's rescue and freedom in that incredible year in history – 2448?

(Yerushalmi Taanis 1, Vayikra Rabbah 32:5, Shir Hashirim Rabbah 12:1, Shemos Rabbah 1:28 and 3:4)

3. Miriam received prophecy even as a youngster. She defied Pharaoh when he gave her and Yocheved his new decree to kill the Jewish boys. Miriam said to Pharaoh, "Woe to the man when Hashem makes him pay for this." Pharaoh was furious and wanted to kill her. Yocheved saved her by telling Pharaoh, "You're worried about a toddler - she doesn't know anything!"

4. The last eighty-six years of the Jews' enslavement in Egypt were the most horrific. During that time, the Egyptians increased their oppression against the Jews by killing their newborn baby boys. Miriam was born just as everything was beginning to turn for the worse. Many Jews called her "Bad Luck". She answered optimistically, that it was actually a good sign, and that their rescue was near. Just as a pregnant woman feels the greatest pain just before delivery, these years of undue hardship were a prelude to the Exodus. Well, eighty-six years later, she sang at Keriyas Yam Suf jubilantly, saying, "Didn't I tell you so?!"

5. Shifra and Puah prayed to Hashem that all the newborn Jewish babies should be born healthy without any defect so no one would blame them for the baby's deficiency.

6. The main merits the Jews had for leaving Egypt - even though many Jews abandoned their religion in that spiritual wasteland - were: A) They kept their Hebrew names. B) They didn't change their holy way of speaking. C) They didn't speak Loshon Hora about each other. D) They kept their Jewish way of dress. E) They were not morally corrupt. F) They would eventually accept the Torah at Har Sinai.

7. Why do we say in the Kiddush of Shabbos night זכר ליציאת מצרים? (that Shabbos should remind us of the Exodus from Egypt)?

(Tosafos on Pesachim 117b; see Shemos Rabbah 1:28)

8. Why didn't Moshe pray to Hashem to cure his childhood speech impediment?

(Shemos Rabbah 1:26, Ramban, K'sav Sofer)

9. How were Yocheved and Miriam fundraisers?

(Shemos Rabbah 1:15)

10. Which disastrous mistake took place in the year 2418?

(Sanhedrin 92b, Shemos Rabbah 20:10, Pirkei d'Rabi Eliezer 48, Seder Hadoros)

---

7. Pharaoh ordered the Jews to perform thirty-nine types of work. Moshe persuaded Pharaoh to let the Jews rest one day a week from their backbreaking work so they could rejuvenate themselves. Hashem later gave the Jews the gift of Shabbos – a day on which we are totally free from performing these specific duties that we had to do as slaves in Egypt over three thousand years ago.

8. Moshe didn't want to cure himself, even at Matan Torah (when all sick people were cured), to remind himself to stay humble. Humility was his greatest quality, and he didn't want to become arrogant about the fact that he was the greatest leader in history.

9. Yocheved and Miriam compassionately went around collecting from the rich Jews in Egypt for the needs of their poor and less fortunate brethren.

10. 30,000 mighty warriors who descended from Shevet Ephraim decided that it was time for them to leave Mitzrayim. They reasoned that the since they stemmed from Yosef they were not required to remain in Mitzrayim the full term of 210 years. After all, the Jews had to experience agonizing slavery as a punishment for selling Yosef. Why should Yosef and his family suffer? They left with only weapons and money, but no food. They thought that they could buy food from their enemies or prevail upon them to give them their necessities. However, when they reached the people of Gat, they refused to give them food, and instead they called upon the neighboring Pelishtim (Philistines) to wage war against the Bnei Ephraim. The Bnei Ephraim fought them and suffered catastrophic losses. Only ten people survived. We see from here that even the one who causes another to be jealous will suffer. Yosef did indeed need atonement for arousing his brothers' jealousy, so the Bnei Efraim needed to be enslaved as a *Tikkun* like everybody else.

Answers&Facts

---

11. Who frequently administered C.P.R. (Cardio Pulmonary Resuscitation) in Egypt?

(Baal Haturim quoting Sotah 11)

12. How does the Yetzer Horah try to harm us like Pharaoh?

(Mesillas Yesharim, Shemos Rabbah 5:18)

13. How were the *Zekainim* (Elders) punished for not going with Moshe to speak to Pharaoh?

(Shemos Rabbah 5:14)

14. Why did Moshe call Aviram a *rasha* if he was the one getting beaten by Dasan?

(Rashi, The Midrash Says)

15. When did anti-Semitism begin in Egypt?

(Yalkut Shimoni, Sforno)

11. Yocheved used a tube to blow air into the lungs of newborns who required oxygen. She was therefore nicknamed *"Shifra"*, which alluded to her skill to save with a *shefoferes* (tube).

12. Pharaoh tried to keep the Jews working so hard and long that they would not have time to contemplate rebelling against him. Similarly, the *Yetzer Horah* (also known as the Satan) wants people to be so occupied with the physical pleasures of this world that they would not have the opportunity to scrutinize their ways and overcome the *Yetzer Horah*.

13. Hashem told Moshe to be in contact with the *Zekainim* (Elders), because all good projects would need their presence and guidance. Moshe gathered the elders and informed them what Hashem told him. However, when Moshe went to Pharaoh, they were afraid to stand before Pharaoh. They slipped away one by one until only Moshe and Aharon were standing before him. Hashem punished them by not inviting them to go up with Moshe on Har Sinai to receive the Torah.

14. Moshe criticized Dasan and Aviram for fighting. He said, *"Rasha,* why are you hitting a *rasha* like yourself?" Moshe called both of them *reshaim*, because as the saying goes, "It takes two to tango!" (Rabbi Yomtov Azatchi *shlit'a*)

15. As long as the Jews lived secluded in Goshen, life was comfortable. However, when "curious" Jews went to observe their Egyptian neighbors in their theaters, circuses and malls, anti-Semitism broke out and became rampant. Throughout

16. Who did Moshe think would be better than him to save the Jewish people?

(Shemos Rabbah 5:23, Ramban)

17. Why didn't Moshe get to see the victory over the 31 gentile kings that ruled in Canaan during his lifetime?

(Sanhedrin 111a)

18. Why did Hashem speak from a fire in a thorn bush?

(Shemos Rabbah 2:5, K'sav Sofer, Tanchuma 14, Shaarei Aharon)

19. Which three fires gave light and warmth but did not destroy?

(Rabbeinu Bachya)

---

history, Jews have gotten constant reminders that we are different. We should be proud of our distinction, and not mingle with people who do not cling to Hashem.

16. Moshe did not want to lead the Bnei Yisroel if his older brother Aharon, who was worthy in his own right, would feel slighted that his younger brother was appointed over him. Some say that Moshe was so exceedingly humble that he felt anybody would be better than he to be Hashem's messenger to lead the Bnei Yisroel in their ascension to greatness.

17. Moshe questioned Hashem's fairness for allowing the Egyptians to add to their already harsh decrees toward the Jews. Hashem criticized Moshe for challenging His constant mercy, which is sometimes camouflaged. Hashem said, "It's a pity that the *Avos* are not present here. They were promised great things, and although I tested their faith, they never questioned Me, yet you question Me? You will see how I will punish this cruel king Pharaoh, but you will not see how I punish the 31 kings that reside in Israel."

18. A thorn bush is a small, insignificant plant. Hashem demonstrated that He loves dwelling with the humble! The thorns also symbolized that Hashem shares our pain in exile.

19. The fires of Har Sinai, the S'neh (thorn bush), and the Mizbaiyach gave light and warmth, but did not destroy. Hashem, Who controls everything, took away one of fire's basic properties in those places, to show that when Hashem is present, there is no danger. As much as many enemies try to destroy the Jews, the Jewish nation will still endure, because with Hashem standing near us, we are invincible!

20. Why did Moshe ask Pharaoh permission for only a "three-day leave"?

(Shemos Rabbah 3:8)

21. What happened to the many baby boys that were cast into the Nile River or that were born in the fields?

(Shemos Rabbah 1:12, Pirkei d'Rabi Eliezer 42, Tanna d'Bei Eliyahu)

22. Why didn't Pharaoh also kill the Jewish girls?

(Maharsha on Sotah 11b, Ohr Hachaim, Lekach Tov, Shemos 1:14,18, The Midrash Says)

23. Why did Levi's descendants remain the most religious people while the Jews were enslaved in Egypt?

(Shemos Rabbah 15:4, Rabbeinu Bachya)

24. Which *tzaddik* married Basya bas Pharaoh when she converted to Judaism?

(Vayikra Rabbah 1:3, Seichel Tov)

---

20. Moshe wanted to trick the Egyptians into chasing the Jews after they would not return following their three-day break. He wanted them to chase the Jews to the Red Sea, to pay them back for drowning Jews in the Nile. This would be an appropriate punishment, to lure the Egyptians to drown in the Red Sea.

21. Angels descended from heaven and rescued many of the babies that were thrown into the Nile River. The babies were placed on land with stones that miraculously nursed them with milk and honey. The babies that were in the fields were protected in deep tunnels underground. At the Exodus, those surviving victims ran after their fathers in joy!

22. Pharaoh didn't kill the girls because the Egyptians were immoral people and they wished to take them as wives. Also, the astrologers predicted that a boy would be born who would save the Jews, so the boys were targeted.

23. Levi lived the longest of all Yaakov's sons (Levi lived until 137 years of age). Therefore, *he* was more able to guide his great-grandchildren to fear Hashem more than the other *Shevatim*.

24. Kalev married Basya. She was a very righteous convert, who merited entering *Gan Eden* alive!

---

25. How can we see the importance of Bris Milah from Moshe Rabbeinu?

(Nedarim 32a, Shemos Rabbah 5:8, Onkelos, Bach on Hilchos Milah)

26. On which day of the year was the baby basket that contained Moshe placed into the Nile River?

(Shemos Rabbah 1:24, Rabbeinu Bachya)

27. Who escorted Moshe and Aharon when they went to speak to King Pharaoh?

(Seder Hadoros)

28. Who was the youngest and most successful marriage-counselor ever?

(Sotah 12a)

---

25. Moshe rushed back from Midyan to Mitzrayim to save the Jews from their agony and slavery. He postponed his newborn's *Bris Milah* while traveling. Yet, he almost died for that, because *Milah* is so important that it must not be postponed unnecessarily. His wife Tzipporah performed the *Bris Milah* and saved the day! The Bach stresses that it is the *mitzvah* of Milah that gives the Bnei Yisroel the merit to live in Eretz Yisroel. By Moshe not being careful enough to do it right away, he may have delayed the Jews' entry into Eretz Yisroel!

26. Some say that Moshe was placed into the Nile on the 6th of Sivan. The angels said to HaKadosh Baruch Hu, "Should the one who will receive the Torah on Har Sinai upon this date drown in water?" Others say Moshe was placed in the Nile on the 21st of Nissan. The angles pleaded to HaKadosh Baruch Hu, "Should the one who will sing to you at the sea on this day [the day Hashem split the *Yam-Suf* and the Bnei Yisroel sang *Az Yashir*] perish by water?" It seems that the acceptance of Torah and singing to Hashem saved Moshe and Klal Yisroel.

27. The Elders were supposed to accompany Moshe, but it seems they were hesitant to meet Pharaoh face-to-face, and left one by one. Mighty lions that guarded the palace and were supposed to scare away intruders miraculously changed their nature, and humbly escorted Hashem's messengers before Pharaoh.

28. Miriam was the youngest and most influential marriage counselor ever! You see, after Pharaoh decreed death on all newborn boys, Amram, and all the men of that time, divorced their wives. Miraim said to her father Amram, "Your decree is worse than Pharaoh's! Pharaoh, who is wicked, only targeted boys, but you, who are righteous, are stopping boys and girls from being born!" Amram remarried Yocheved. All the Jews followed their leader and remaried their wives, thanks to little Miriam. Miriam and Aaron danced in front of their parents at their wedding!

Questions & Riddles

29. What happened to Pharaoh's three advisors?
(Rashi, Seder Hadoros, Seichel Tov)

30. When did all the staff members of Pharaoh's palace become temporarily handicapped?
(Yerushalmi Berachos)

31. Why did Moshe execute the Mitzri who visited Shulamis bas Divri?
(Shemos Rabbah 1:28, Shaarei Aharon)

32. Why was the name that Moshe received from Basya more accepted than the names given by his parents Amrom and Yocheved?
(Shemos Rabbah 1:26)

33. Why did Moshe's staff turn into a snake?
(Shemos Rabbah 3:12, Yechezkel 29:3, Yeshayah 27:1, Pesikta Zutrasi 9:9)

29. Pharaoh had three royal advisors: Yisro, Iyov, and Bilam, with whom he consulted regarding the "Jewish Problem". Yisro suggested that he shouldn't harm them. He ran away and was rewarded by Hashem with great honor. Iyov, who was quiet, suffered. Bilam suggested killing them, so he was later executed.

30. When Moshe was approximately twelve years old, he went out of the king's palace to feel the pain of his tormented people. He saw a Mitzri beating a Jew (Dasan) to death so he could take his wife for himself. Moshe used the Holy Name of Hashem to kill that wicked Mitzri. The unappreciative and infamous Dasan and Aviram informed Pharaoh, and now Moshe was "wanted" on murder charges. When Moshe was sentenced to death, the executioner was shocked that his neck miraculously turned to marble. Some say that the executioner, grabbed an angel disguised as Moshe while the real Moshe ran away. At that time, Hashem made all of the king's staff members become blind, deaf, and dumb so that Moshe could escape.

31. Moshe killed the Egyptian taskmaster for harming Shelomis bas Divri.

32. Interestingly, although Moshe had ten Jewish names, Hashem and the Torah recognized him by the one that his 'lifesaver' gave him! Basya was kind, and the reward for kindness is eternal.

33. When Moshe was talking with Hashem, Moshe's staff turned into a snake, to frighten him for speaking *loshon hora* about Klal Yisroel. He said, "They won't

34. How do we see that Hashem helps one if he sincerely wants to do a *mitzvah*?

(Seichel Tov expounding on Sotah 12b, Shabbos 104a, Yoma 38b, Zohar 1:54)

35. Why was Moshe wearing Egyptian clothing when he rescued Yisro's daughters?

(Ibn Ezra, Abarbanel, Haamek Davar, Shaarei Aharon quoting Rabbeinu Ephraim)

36. Who gained by losing?

(Sotah 12b)

37. Why did Moshe name his first son Gershom (lit. stranger there), which refers to his being a stranger in Egypt? Eliezer would have been a nicer name for his first son, since it refers to Hashem saving his life from danger!

(Shemos Rabbah 1:33, Abarbanel, Chizkuni, Chofetz Chaim on Parashas Yisro, Toras Habayis)

---

believe me when I tell them that You will take them out of Mitzrayim." Hashem said, "Don't act like the snake that spoke *loshon hora*. The Jewish People are *Ma'aminim B'nei Ma'aminim* (Believers, the sons of Believers)!"

34. Basya wanted to save the baby, but it was out of her reach. She stretched out her hand anyway to do as much as she could. Hashem made it stretch very far, to show that one can do more than they expect to, if they sincerely try!

35. The young Moshe wore royal clothing in Pharaoh's palace. When escaping, he wore Egyptian clothing as his disguise. Some say he was punished for this and was therefore not buried in Israel. If Moshe was criticized for wearing these clothes even though he did it to save his life, we certainly must think twice before purchasing the latest fashions!

36. "Bas-Ya" means, "Daughter of G-D". When she rejected her father's kingdom and all the privileges of the royal family to become a Jew, Hashem said, "You will be part of Klal Yisroel, the children of My Royal Kingdom instead!"

37. Moshe did not want to forget for even one moment that he was only a visitor in Egypt. He did not want to forget that he was in Galus. Nor did he want to forget that we are only visitors in this world. With this awareness, he would live his life as a more spiritual person. He therefore named his first son Gershom, which means "I was a stranger there," to keep him constantly aware of his temporary status there. It also served as a reminder for his children to realize that they didn't belong amongst the *idolaters*.

38. Which seven *tzaddikim's* lifetimes span all of world history (almost 6,000 years!)?

(Bava Basra 121b)

39. Which *tzaddikim* never sinned? (Hint: one is alluded to in this Parshah.)

(Shabbos 55b)

40. On whose back did the young Moshe ride?

(Me'am Lo'ez, Netziv, Shemos Rabbah 1:26)

41. How did Basyah know that the baby she found in the basket (Moshe) was Jewish?

(Shemos Rabbah 1:24, Midrash Avkir, Pirkei d'Rabi Eliezer, Yalkut Shimoni)

42. Why did Pharaoh order the Jewish women (Yocheved and Miriam) to kill the Jewish baby boys?

(Mussar Hamishnah on Avodah Zarah 2:1)

---

38. 1) Adam, 2) Mesushelach, 3) Shem, 4) Yaakov, 5) Amram (Moshe's father), 6) Achiyah Hasheloni, & 7) Eliyahu Hanavi (who never died) each lived to see each other in succession. Together, their lives span all of human existence.

39. Amram (Moshe's father), Binyamin (Yaakov's son), Yishai (Dovid's father), and Kilav (Dovid's son) never sinned at all.

40. Pharaoh used to give young Moshe rides on his back. He also used to hug him and kiss him, because he was so cute and adorable. Hashem demonstrated that even if the non-Jews try to prevent the *Geulah* by enacting evil laws, the redeemer will flourish amongst them!

41. Moshe was born circumcised. Also, Basya felt that he was crying for the Jews, so she figured he must be Jewish. Others say that she saw Aharon crying for his brother, and the *middah* of crying for a brother in need is a Jewish trait. We must learn from this to cry for our Jewish brothers in distress!

42. The *Mishnah* (Avoda Zara 2-1) tells us not to use an idol-worshipper as a midwife, lest she kill the baby and claim it was a stillborn. This Pharaoh knew that only a Jew could have easy access to the Jewish labor-rooms. That's why he tried to manipulate Jews to do his dirty work.

---

43. Why was Princess Basya going to the Nile River?

(Sotah 12b, Shemos Rabbah 1:23)

44. Who was instantly healed when touching Moshe's baby basket?

(Shemos Rabbah 1:23, Targum Yonasan, Pirkei d'Rabi Eliezer 48)

45. Which people in *Tanach* are recorded as having had multiple births of sextuplets?

(Shmuel II 6:11, Bamidbar Rabbah 10:8, Yalkut Shimoni)

46. Why was Moshe chosen to be the greatest Jewish leader in history?

(Chochmah U'Mussar, Shemos Rabbah 1:27 and 2:2)

47. Why did Yocheved take a chance sending baby Moshe off into the dangerous river?

(Shemos Rabbah 1:26)

---

43. Some say Basya had leprosy, and was going to the Nile to bathe. Others say she was using the Nile River as a *Mikveh*, to convert to Judaism.

44. When Basya touched the basket, she was instantly cured from her leprosy. She thus knew that this was a very special baby!

45. Oveid Edom Hagiti's wife and their (eight, or some say) nine daughters-in-law were blessed with multiple births "of six in a womb" giving him a great quantity of offspring quickly (64a). The Gemara tells us that he was rewarded because he was scrupulous to honor the dignity of the *Aron HaKodesh*, which he safeguarded for a while after the Pelishtim returned it.

46. Moshe cared for Klal Yisroel more than anyone else! When Moshe was able to leave the palace, he went out to see their oppression first-hand. He cried for them saying, "It pains me to see your suffering, if only I could die for you!" He would then lend his shoulder to help everyone with their heavy cement loads. He acted as if he was doing it to help get Pharaoh's orders completed. Hashem said, "You left your comfort to see the pain of the Jews and acted like their brother, so I will leave My place in the upper heavens to speak with you..."

47. Yocheved wanted to fool the Egyptian astrologers by throwing the baby they were targeting into the Nile River. She reasoned that once they would report to Pharaoh that the Jewish savior was already cast in the water, he would end his decree against the Jewish newborn boys.

Answers&Facts

48. How did Moshe kill the cruel and wicked Egyptian taskmaster who committed adultery?
(Shemos Rabbah 1:29)

49. Who stated so humbly: "Who am I? (Pasuk 3:11)"?
(See Chullin 89a)

50. Why didn't baby Moshe want to accept milk from Basyah's wet-nurse?
(Gemara Avodah Zarah 26a, Rambam Hilchos Avodah Zarah 9:16, Tur, Shemos Rabbah 1:25, Ritva Yevamos 114a, Emes L'Yaakov)

51. Why did Moshe ask Yisro for permission to go to Mitzrayim if Hashem ordered him to go?
(Shemos Rabbah 4:3, Rashi)

48. Some say that Moshe killed the evil Egyptian by saying one of the holy Names of Hashem. Others say he physically killed him by punching him with his mighty fist. A third opinion maintains that he hit him with a cement shovel.

49. Hashem encouraged Moshe to save the Jews. Moshe was so humble that he asked sincerely, "Who am I?" He didn't deem himself worthy of such a prestigious position. Moshe did not possess low self-esteem, nor did he have an inferiority complex. Rather, he did not want to ruin his qualities with arrogance.

50. Although the *Mishnah* permits a non-Jewess to nurse a Jewish baby, it is only in the case where the baby would be endangered without it. In practice it should be avoided, since the non-Jew eats non-kosher food, it would cause *timtum halev* (a defect that dulls the heart from spirituality) to the baby if he drinks the milk that was produced from non-kosher food. Also, it wouldn't be appropriate that Moshe's mouth which would later converse with the holy *Shechinah* should have nursed from a *tamei* (impure) person.

51. When Moshe married Tzippora he swore to Yisro that he would not leave Midyan without his permission. In addition, Moshe felt a deep appreciation to Yisro for saving him when he was a baby, and for sheltering him when he was fleeing Pharaoh. The Midrash says one must be so grateful to one who opens a door to help him that he should be indebted with his life to him!

52. Were visitors to the Beis Hamikdash permitted to wear shoes there?

(Berachos 54a)

53. Why did Yisro make his daughters become shepherdesses?

(Shemos Rabbah 1:32)

54. What was the punishment of any Jewish parents that hid their newborn baby boys?

(Malbim)

55. Why did Amrom marry his aunt, Yocheved, if the Torah would later forbid a Jewish man from marrying his aunt?

(Ramban to Bereishis 26:5, Yalkut Reuveini, Rabbeinu Bachya on Parshas Chayei Sarah)

52. *Kohanim* were not allowed to wear shoes in the Beis Hamikdash, so there would be nothing separating them from the holy ground. This law also applied to any Jew entering the Beis Hamikdash. This *halachah* is learned from the story of the Burning Bush. Hashem told Moshe, "The ground you are standing upon is holy," and Hashem told Moshe to take off his shoes there.

53. Before Moshe arrived in Midian, Yisro wanted to repent from idolatry. He took all his priestly artifacts and gave them to his townsmen. He told them that he was too old, and they should pick someone else to care for them. The townspeople excommunicated him and told all the shepherds in town to boycott him. He had no choice but to use his daughters as shepherds. He merited such an extraordinary son-in-law due to his brave devotion to Hashem!

54. Parents who attempted to hide their newborn boys from Pharaoh's Secret Service were executed.

55. *Before* the Torah was given, one was not prohibited to marry a close relative (i.e. sister or aunt).

Answers&Facts

56. What did Moshe believe was the reason the Jews suffered slavery more than any other nation?

(Shemos Rabbah 1:30)

57. Whose merit caused the *Geulah* (redemption) from Mitzrayim?

(Shemos Rabbah 1:34,35 and 1:12)

58. How do we know that Hashem doesn't raise someone to greatness without first testing him with something small?

(Shemos Rabbah 2:3)

59. When did the Jews' crying out with prayers alleviate much heartache, pain and suffering?

(Shemos Rabbah 1:34, Esther Rabbah 5, Zohar, Pesachim 118a, Berachos 32)

---

56. When Moshe saw that the wicked Dasan and Aviram were going to inform Pharaoh of his killing of the evil Egyptian, he knew why the Jews deserved to suffer so terribly in Mitzrayim. Speaking lashon hara is so severe that it is enough to cause the Jewish people to suffer in exile.

57. It was due to the combined merits of the Avos (Avraham, Yitzchok, and Yaakov) that Hashem was ready to save the Jews from Mitzrayim. When the Jews cried out, they activated the *Zechus Avos!*

58. Before Moshe was selected to be the *Manhig* (Master Leader) of his generation and all subsequent generations, Hashem tested him by seeing how he would shepherd sheep. Would he be compassionate, honest and sensitive? It was only when Moshe proved his fine character with the sheep that he was raised to be the ultimate role model and savior of the Bnei Yisroel!

59. When the Jews cried out in Egypt, their tears abolished the decree of exile against them. The Zohar says that Eisav's tears (when Yitzchak gave the berachos to Yaakov instead of him) caused the Jews to go into exile, but the Jews can stop the danger and trouble with their cries of prayer! A practical lesson to learn from this is that we must cry out to Hashem to save us from this long, painful Galus. What better time to pray then while saying *Shemoneh Esrei* every day with true *kavanas halev* (concentration and feeling in the heart)!

60.

The Jewish women miraculously carried six, twelve, or sixty babies during each pregnancy! Why those specific numerations?

(See Maharam Shif in Derushim Nechmadim)

60.

A guppy fish can give birth to fifty-plus offspring at a time, and a scorpion can give birth to seventy-plus at a time. Similarly, the righteous women of Egypt also gave birth in great volume. This was an encouragement to the Jews not to fear Pharaoh's decree to lessen them, as Hashem already promised to Avrohom that his descendants would be very numerous. The reason they had those specific numbers at a time (six, twelve or sixty) was to repair all the previously born souls that needed *Tikkun* by being reborn as *gilgulim*, in order to speed up the *Geulah*. That's one of the reasons Chazal said that it was thanks to the righteous women, who raised families even at such turbulent times, that the geulah came about.

וילך איש מבית לוי
Dedicated in honor of
MY DEAR WIFE YVETTE
by Mayer Lati

פרשת וארא

?

1. What did Hashem tell Moshe Rabbeinu before he started to lead the Jewish people?

(Doresh Tov, Shemos Rabbah 7:3, Zohar)

2. What did Hashem tell the octopus to do in Egypt?

(Seder Hadoros 2447)

FUNdamental Answers!

"יגעתי ומצאתי!"

("I worked on these questions, and I found these answers!")

1. Hashem appointed Moshe and Aharon as leaders with the following warning and demand: "My sons are stubborn, hot-tempered and troublesome. With this in mind, their leaders must be strong and able to tolerate them, even if they curse or stone them!"

2. When Hashem sent cobras, scorpions and all sorts of dangerous wild things to punish the Egyptians, they locked all their doors to prevent the wild creatures from getting in. Hashem ordered giant squids and octopuses to use their long arms to pull off the roofs and open the locks of the doors, so that all the wild animals would be able to continue their attack. This demonstrates that nothing can stop the will of Hashem!

3. Why did Moshe merit to receive more prophecies than his older brother Aharon?

(K'sav Sofer, Ruach Chaim)

4. How do we see that one who becomes angry also becomes crazy?

(Birchas Peretz on Nedarim 22b)

5. Egyptian school children knew how to turn sticks into snakes, so what made Pharaoh scared of Moshe's staff?

(Shemos Rabbah 9:7)

6. What did one frog say to the other?

(Shemos Rabbah 10:6)

---

3. One of the prerequisites to attain divine prophecy is to be **happy**. It is a quality that comes naturally after a person perfects his character in the service of Hashem. Aharon witnessed the agony and hardship of the Jews more than Moshe, so he was unable to be happy and meditate successfully. Moshe, on the other hand, was generally secluded from the horrors of Mitzrayim, first in Pharaoh's palace and then in Midyan, so he had a better frame of mind to connect with the *Shechinah*.

4. The more the Egyptians hit the frogs, the more they multiplied. They did not stop beating them immediately, because they got **angrier** as the frogs multiplied. This drove them to even act more irrationally; they lost their mind and just kept on hitting! When a person acts out of anger, he acts **irrationally**.

5. Pharaoh mocked Moshe's miracle of turning a staff into a snake. He called for school-children ages four and five to perform such a phenomenon. Then Moshe had his staff swallow all the other staffs, and Moshe's staff still looked the same. It didn't get any fatter. *That* scared Pharaoh, because then he realized, *"What if he tells it to swallow me and my throne!"* Nevertheless, inspiring impressions do not often last long, and Pharaoh did not relent.

6. Pharaoh sat on his throne adorned in his royal clothes surrounded by his royal officials. Suddenly the frogs started going up **into his body** and out through his mouth. The frogs then did the same to his officials. Some frogs shouted out from inside their stomachs saying, *"When are we going to get out of here?"* to which other frogs replied, *"When Ben-Amrom [Moshe] comes to pray for us!"* That's when Pharaoh called for Moshe and Aharon to come quickly.

7.
Which plague made the Jews very wealthy?

(Yalkut Tehillim, Shemos Rabbah 9:10, Tanchuma)

8.
When is it good to cry?

(Yerushalmi Taanis 2:1, Ramban 12:42)

9.
Why is wine used on the night of Pesach to commemorate *Yetziyas Mitzraim*?

(Netziv)

10.
How is it beneficial for you to care for your friend when he has problems?

(Torah Mi'Tzion, Chasam Sofer, Reb Levi Yitzchak Mi'Berditchev)

---

7. Even if an Egyptian tried drinking with a straw from a Jew's water, the Egyptian received blood. The only way that an Egyptian was able to get water was by purchasing it from a Jew. (Do you know how much you could charge an oppressor for bottled water?) It was one of the ways that the Jews became very wealthy, and this was the beginning of their promised - "Rechush Gadol", a guarantee to Avrohom Avinu centuries earlier that the Bnei Yisroel were going to amass a fortune when they left Mitzrayim.

8. Tears are precious! When one cries out to Hashem, his prayers are given more attention. Tears don't cost money, and they are not harmful to the body. Thus, the Bnei Yisroel were redeemed from Egypt with prayers and tears. We just might be redeemed from this exile with tears as well! Let's learn from the Bnei Yisroel's manner of ending Galus in Egypt, and end this long and bitter Galus. In fact, all trouble can be alleviated using our mouths and hearts in an outpouring of sincere prayers!

9. Wine is a phenomenal drink. It can actually change a person's spirits, transforming him from from being sad to becoming happy, and vice versa. So when we commemorate our freedom from Egyptian slavery, Chazal instituted that it be done with wine, to show that we were transformed from a lower state to a higher state - from sadness to joy!

10. Hashem saw that although the Jews were moaning and groaning from their own pain, they still felt the pain of their fellow Jews. They prayed for each other's salvation. This gave them great merit and enabled Hashem to hear their cries and to save them. Some say that they were able to reduce their original sentence of 430 years of slavery to 210 (about half), because they felt the pain and sorrow of their fellow Jews, which made it as if they had suffered doubly already! Today, if we really feel the pain of our fellow Jew, we could reduce the period of this exile as well.

Answers&Facts

Questions & Riddles

11. **What lesson did some *tzaddikim* take from the frogs of Mitzrayim?**

(Shemos Rabbah 10:2, Tosafos on Pesachim 53b, The Midrash Says)

12. **What else turned into blood besides the water in Mitzrayim?**

(Shemos Rabbah 9:11)

13. **What happened to the *barad* (fire & ice meteors) that were left suspended in the sky when the *makkah* ended in 2448?**

(Shemos Rabbah 12:7)

14. **Which species was the dreaded *Tzfardei'a*?**

(See Haamek Davar)

15. **What were the four stages of our freedom from Egyptian slavery?**

(Yerushalmi on Pesachim 10:1, Rabbeinu Bachya, Torah Temimah)

---

11. Chanaya, Mishael, and Azaryah chose to be thrown into a fire rather than to bow down to a statue that was made in the image of Nevuchadnetzar. Even though it wasn't a real *Avodah Zarah*, they preferred to give their lives for *Kiddush Hashem* lest anyone think that they idolized that *rasha*. They were inspired by the frogs: They didn't have a *mitzvah* to die for Hashem, but nevertheless, many jumped into the hot baking ovens in Egypt. We, who have a *mitzvah* to make a Kiddush Hashem, should surely defend Hashem's honor!

12. All houses of Avodah Zarah turned bloody. If one sat down in one, his clothing became stained with blood. In the future, Hashem will humiliate all idols along with their worshippers.

13. Some of those miraculous hailstones (consisting of fire and ice) stayed suspended in space until Yehoshua's war with the Emori forty-one years later, when they came crashing down on the enemy. There are still many more that will come crashing down on Gog and Magog when Mashiach battles them soon!

14. Some say that the second plague was frogs, while others maintain they were crocodiles. (After all, Egypt is famous for the ferocious Nile crocodiles!)

15. Our ancestors were saved from Mitzrayim in four stages: a) They (and as a result, us!) were saved from the slave-torture of those cruel Egyptians; b) They were freed from being even respected servants; c) Hashem took revenge on our persecutors (with the numerous plagues); d) Hashem then gave us his Torah, which makes those who study it truly free!

---

16. How do we see the importance of always showing appreciation?

(Tanchuma 14, Shemos Rabbah 10:4 and 20:1, Bava Kama 92b)

17. What famous storybook did Moshe Rabbeinu write for the Jews to read in Egypt?

(Malbim, Shemos Rabbah 5:22)

18. Which *mitzvah* did Moshe and Aharon teach the Jews in *Mitzrayim* in 2447, one year before they left *Mitzrayim*?

(Yerushalmi on Rosh Hashanah 3:5, Midrash Halachah, Sefer Hamitzvos #42)

19. Why did Moshe keep hesitating to go to Pharaoh, if Hashem had told him to? After all, what would he lose?

(Torah Mi'Tzion, Kli Yakar)

---

16. Moshe would not hit the water or the dust because they were once instrumental in saving his life. (He was placed in the water to trick the Egyptian astrologers into believing that the Jewish leader was already cast into the water, and he buried in dust the immoral and attacking Egyptian who was killing a Jew). This shows us how careful we should be not to degrade anything that we benefited from!

17. The book of Iyov was written by Moshe Rabbeinu. It is a fascinating story of a righteous man who was tested with suffering to see if he would stay faithful to Hashem. In the end, there was "a light at the end of the tunnel", and Iyov came closer to Hashem and was given great fortune. There is doubt if the story ever took place; it may be a fictional parable to teach us a lesson. Regardless, it gave the Jews enormous hope that if they wouldn't doubt Hashem in tough times, all would turn out wonderfully!

18. Moshe Rabbeinu taught the Bnei Yisroel the laws of "freeing slaves". In the merit of this Torah-learning, the Bnei Yisroel were saved! They learned that sometimes one can buy a Jewish slave, but never on a permanent basis, and they must treat him with much respect. This strengthened the Jews to be able to hang in there, because soon they could possess their own slaves, and they wouldn't have to work as slaves to goyim any longer.

19. Moshe was reluctant to go and save the Jews from Egypt, because he felt that his brother Aharon deserved that privilege. He didn't want Aharon to feel bad that he wasn't given this great opportunity.

Answers&Facts

20. Which plague was the harshest on our Egyptian persecutors?

(Shaarei Aharon citing Seichel Tov and Be'er Yitzchak, Taam V'daas quoting Zohar)

21. How could Moshe and Aharon be considered <u>equal</u> if no prophet was ever as great as Moshe?

(Darash Moshe, Sh'lah, K'sav Sofer)

22. Why did Moshe's staff turn into a snake, and not into a horse, a bull, a lion, or a wolf?

(Rabbeinu Bachya, Shemos Rabbah 9:3)

23. Why couldn't the *Mitzrim* hide in trees or on rooftops during the plague of *Arov* (wild animals)?

(Shemos Rabbah 11:2)

20. Some say that the frogs, with their constant croaking, were the most unbearable plague for the Egyptians. It was most frightening, because the frogs were alive inside their bodies. Frogs emerged wherever there was water, even from the sweat of the Egyptian's body! It was a truly horrifying makkah. It gave the Egyptians a taste of their own medicine.

21. Moshe actually accomplished more than any other human. He conversed with Hashem as his best friend, and he received all the lessons of the Torah directly from Hashem! However, since Aharon also maximized his potential, he was considered equal to Moshe in the sense that they both maximized their true potential!

22. Pharaoh "sinned with his tongue" when he said, "Who is Hashem that I should listen to Him?" So he was terrorized with a snake, which was the symbol of "sinning with the tongue", since it once spoke lashon hora in the days of Adam and Chavah. [It is very interesting to note that when archeologists discovered a golden mummy of King Pharaoh, they revealed two golden serpents above his forehead. It is very likely that Pharaoh used the snake as his symbol of power, as the Neviim even referred to Pharaoh as a serpent! So Moshe humbled him by showing that our Power can devour all of his power!

23. When the lions, tigers, bears and other wild animals attacked the Egyptians, they could not escape into trees or to the rooftops. Even dangerous birds participated in this plague to inflict revenge upon the Egyptians for afflicting the Jews.

24. If Hashem promised to bring the Bnei Yisroel into Eretz Yisroel, why did most of them pass away in the desert?

(Ohr Hachaim)

25. Which merit enabled the Jews to live safely during the Ten Plagues?

(Bamidbar Rabbah 9:14)

26. Which plague accompanied each of the other plagues?

(Shemos Rabbah 10:2)

27. When did enemies become peaceful in order to punish our foes?

(Shemos Rabbah 10:2, The Midrash Says)

28. Why was the Nile River afflicted with the first plague?

(Shemos Rabbah 9:11, Tanchuma)

---

24. Hashem promised to bring *those* special Jews into Israel on condition that they remain faithful to Him. But since they complained too often during their journey through the desert, they lost their beautiful appearance. It was as though they were not the same ones who were destined to arrive.

25. All the safety and security that Hashem gave the Jews during that gruesome year of plagues was in the merit of them guarding themselves from immorality even while living in such a perverse society. During these days, when everyone can use extra protection from the dangers of the enemies, it is important to beware from the Yetzer Hara and not lead an immoral lifestyle so that the *Shechinah* and Divine protection should not leave us!

26. Pestilence, a deadly disease (perhaps a virus), broke out along with each of the ten plagues, as revenge on the Egyptians for all of the bloodshed and cruelty they dealt the Bnei Yisroel.

27. Fire and water are opposites by nature. You might refer to them as "enemies" since they work against each other. But when it came time to do the will of Hashem: to punish our enemies, they worked in harmony. Pharaoh was so awed by this that he said "viduy" (confession). He thought that since the moral Jews' lifestyle completely contradicted the immoral Egyptian culture, they could not co-exist together, and he tried to eliminate the Jewish Nation. But now after witnessing the plague, and seeing that opposites could exist together after all, he regretted plotting against the Jews.

28. When Hashem punishes a nation, He also humiliates their gods. Therefore, since the Egyptians thought the Nile was divine, it was smitten first.

Answers&Facts

29. When will *barad* (ice-fire hail) rain down again?

(*Shemos Rabbah 12:2*)

30. Why did Egyptian culture have vegetarian tendencies?

(*Ibn Ezra*)

31. Why is there a *mitzvah* for Jewish men to remember our Exodus from Mitzrayim, every single day & night?

(*Ramban, Toras Ha'olah*)

32. What happens when you're happy because of your friend's success?

(*K'sav Sofer*)

33. How does magic work, if we know that all power is solely Hashem's?

(*Shaarei Aharon, Rambam*)

---

29. In the near future, *barad* will fall down on our archenemies, Gog and Magog. We can't wait to have those miracles performed! We pray that it shall bring national security for the Bnei Yisroel.

30. Egyptians worshipped animals thinking that they were divine, so they didn't dare eat them. [There are still some foolish Hindus who live in India today who follow this absurd belief.]

31. We must recall day and night, (during our Prayers, Kerias Shema, Birkas Hamazon, Mezuzah, Tefillin, Shabbos, Succah, etc.) Hashem's enormous kindness for saving us from Egyptian slavery! We must express our appreciation that we are not slaves to other people. This is also a 'chizuk' to us, that no matter how bad times might be [G-d forbid], Hashem will save us! Also, we must contemplate how to achieve our redemption. Our task is to escape the 'tumah' around us, just as we left the 'tumah' that was rampant in Mitzrayim.

32. When you are happy for another's "spiritual success" you become greater as well. Since Aharon rejoiced at Moshe's leadership, he too earned an equal status to Moshe at that time.

33. Magic is often an illusion, a mere trick. But in reality, Hashem made a balance in the world of positive and negative charges. We are ordered to do only holy practices, but the *Satan* and those wishing to be evil, tap into impure charges to fool people. Amazingly, it is permissible to use the Torah to make "magic"! For example, Rav Chanina and Rav Hoshia used to make a calf every Friday, so they would have what to eat on Shabbos, but one is not allowed to use the power of *tumah* to make something.

34.
Which human beings made themselves into *avodah zarah*?

(Shemos Rabbah 8:3, Midrash Hagadol on Parshas Noach 11:28, Megillah 10b)

35.
What does the magical incantation *"abra kadabra"* mean?

(Sefer Yetzirah)

36.
Which emperor was devoured by a crocodile when he tried banning the Jews from saying *Kerias Shema*?

(Beis Yosef on Tur Orach Chaim 423 quoting the Gaonim)

37.
How long did each of the *makkos* last?

(Rabbeinu Bachya, Shemos Rabbah, Seder Hadoros, Rosh Hashanah 11b)

38.
Why don't we make a *Berachah* on the *mitzvah* of *"Arba Kosos"*?

(Avudraham, Midrash Halachah)

---

34. Nimrod, Pharaoh, Chiram, Nevuchadnetzar, Haman, and Yoash were all haughty men who deemed themselves gods. Later, Yushka also acted as if he was a god. They all eventually suffered great shame for their preposterous behavior.

35. You can actually create things by using certain words of the Torah! This can be found in the hidden words of the *Kaballah*. *"Abera"* means "I can create" and *"Kedabra"* means "with my words", but no one who hasn't mastered Torah knowledge in its various aspects can do this.

36. When *Yuzgider*, the king of Persia, forbade the Bnei Yisroel to recite the *Shema* everyday, he posted guards by the synagogues to enforce his tough decree. The Rabbis prayed to Hashem to stop that madman. Indeed, Hashem stopped him by sending a crocodile (*tanin*) from the moat to climb up the palace wall to eat the king, and the decree was annulled.

37. Some say that the Egyptians were warned one week per plague and smitten for three weeks, while others say vice versa. Here is the ancient calendar of events, (according to some *Rishonim*): 15 Nissan 2447, Hashem spoke to Moshe from the thorn bush. All *Pesach* of 2447, Moshe was hesitating to be the messenger. The end of *Nissan*, Moshe arrived in Mitzrayim to encourage Klal Yisroel and warn Pharaoh. For three months, he was not seen. During *Av*, the plague of Blood occurred; *Elul*, the plague of Frogs; *Tishrei*, 2448, the plague of Lice; *Cheshvan*, the plague of Wild Animals; *Kislev*, the plague of Pestilence; *Teves*, the plague of Boils; *Shevat*, the plague of Hailstones; *Adar*, the plague of Locusts; *Nissan*, the plague of Darkness. *Makas Bechoros* occurred on Pesach night, the fifteenth day of *Nissan*.

38. We don't make a *berachah* on the four cups of wine that we drink on *Pesach* night, since they are not drunk consecutively, as there are interruptions between each one.

Answers & Facts

39. Who went to outer space in 2447?

(Rashi to 9:22)

40. Why don't we drink a fifth cup of wine Pesach night?

(Torah Mi'Tzion, Shemos Rabbah 6:5, Taam Vodaas, Torah Temimah)

41. Why were the Egyptians afflicted with 50 additional plagues by the sea?

(Tanchumah 5)

42. Where was Pharaoh going when Moshe and Aharon came to speak to him?

(Doresh Tov; see Shemos Rabbah 9:8)

---

39. Some say Hashem lifted Moshe to Heaven before he lifted his hand upward to bring down the hail. This showed us that Moshe beat the Egyptian administering angel above, as well. [I bet you thought astronauts were the first living people in space.]

40. We don't drink a fifth cup of wine on *Pesach* since it corresponds to our entering Israel - which was unfortunately only temporary! We call this cup "Eliyahu's Cup." When Eliyahu heralds in the *Moshiach*, we will enter our Promised Land and then drink the fifth cup on Pesach. Interestingly, even born-and-bred Israelis don't drink the fifth cup today, because having a *"Medinah"* ("State") without a Torah-based government is not enough of a reason to celebrate, especially with all this "peace talk", giving up "pieces" of Israel to blood-thirsty Arabs, רחמנא ליצלן. We yearn for the day that Eliyahu Hanavi, *Moshiach*, and Moshe Rabbeinu will orchestrate the affairs of Israel by having the *K'nesset* run by the rabbis of the *Sanhedrin* according to the exact will of Hashem!

41. Pharaoh was *chutzpadik* by asking, "מי ה'?" ("Who is Hashem?") The *gematria* of מי is 50, so he was smitten with 50 more plagues!

42. Pharaoh proclaimed himself a god. He even said he never eats or has the need to eliminate waste. In truth, he used to visit the Nile every morning to relieve himself when no one would see him. To humble this brazen ruler who didn't even want to give Moshe an appointment to hear his message, - precisely when he had to go to take care of his needs, he was stopped and ordered: "Let my people go!" To put him in his place, twelve rats bit him in the bathroom and he screamed so loud that every one in the palace heard him.

43. Hashem sent the *tzirah* insect (a sort of poisonous hornet) to poison the evil nations that were residing in Israel in 2488. Also the wicked Titus,

---

43.
At which other time in history did Hashem send bugs to defeat our enemies?

(*Shemos Rabbah 10:1, Shemos 23:28, Yehoshua 24:12, Gittin 56; see Bamidbar Rabbah 18:22*)

44.
Why was Moshe the king of Midyan for many years?

(*Seder Hadoros, Ibn Ezra*)

45.
What must a penniless person do if he can't afford wine for the *Arba Kosos* of *Pesach*?

(*Rashbam to Pesachim 99b, Bi'ur Halachah 656*)

46.
When in history were there plagues of mice besides the *makkah* in *Mitzrayim*?

(*Yerushalmi Demai 1:3, Shmuel I 5:6*)

---

who destroyed the second Beis Hamikdash, met his match; he died because a bug devoured his brain. There is a *Midrash* that says that in the future Hashem will defeat our enemies with little insects! The *Navi* (*Yeshayah* 7-18) wrote: "It shall be on that day that Hashem will whistle to the fly that is at the far end of Egypt's rivers and to the bee that is in the land of Assyria…" (Who hasn't heard of the dreadful West Nile mosquito? It just might have a major role in the *Geulah Sheleimah!*)

44. It seems that Moshe was drafted as a general for Midyan. After all, he was tall, strong, handsome and regal! Eventually he was promoted to be king in Ethiopia. He was famous for his righteousness and purity since he would not assimilate with the local population. Later on, out of reverence for him, the local citizens sent him off with presents. This experience, along with his childhood upbringing in a royal palace, prepared him to eventually be our king!

45. If someone is very poor, he must still arrange for four cups of wine to drink on Pesach. He should take from the charity administrator, borrow, work, or even sell his clothes, in order to acquire the required wine. There is no one who does not need to commemorate Hashem's endless kindness! A good person must always feel: "How can I thank Hashem enough?"

46. In the days when Eli was Kohen Gadol, the Bnei Yisroel waged war against the Pelishtim. Goliath the Giant stole the golden *Aron Hakodesh*. Hashem sent **rats** and hemorrhoids against our enemies to show their frailty and helplessness. *L'havdil*, at a different time, there was a Jewish town that was not giving Terumah and Maaser to the Kohanim and Leviim. So mice were sent to take their crops away, until Rabbi Pinchas ben Yair got the townspeople to do Teshuvah.

47. Why did Hashem let His spokesman – Moshe Rabbeinu – keep his speech impediment?

(Ran, Toras Ha'olah, The Midrash Says)

48. Why didn't Moshe remain the Kohen Gadol?

(Shemos Rabbah 37:1)

49. Why were these particular ten plagues given to the Egyptians as punishment?

(Midrash Tanchuma, Abarbanel)

47. Hashem did not want anyone to claim that Moshe made up the Torah himself in order to start a cult for his honor, Heaven forbid. To prove that it wasn't Moshe's dynamic public speaking that persuaded people to follow him, Moshe was left with a sort of slur in his speech. This way it would be known that the Jews accepted Moshe because Torah is the truth. They had heard Hashem Himself authorize Moshe as the messenger to teach us His will and based their acceptance on this fact, and not on his rhetoric. Others say that it was to give encouragement to everyone to teach Torah without fear of their less than perfect speaking abilities. Hashem will cause that His Torah will be understood through good people, regardless of their oratorical skills.

48. When Moshe humbly declined the honor to become the agent to save the Bnei Yisroel – however noble his intentions – he lost the prestigious position of *kehuna* (priesthood). Instead, it was given to Aharon. [Ironically, the *midda* necessary to be a *Kohein* is *zerizus* (speed).]

49. There are many reasons that the Egyptians were crushed with these particular ten plagues. This is one explanation:

1) BLOOD - for not allowing Jewish women to go to the *mikvah* (to cleanse themselves from the blood of *Niddah*) in order to have children.
2) FROGS / CROCODILES - for ordering Jews to catch all types of creepy creatures just to humiliate them.
3) LICE - for making the Jews sweep and scrub the streets like janitors.
4) WILD ANIMALS - for making Jews capture lions and bears, thus endangering Jewish lives for Egyptian amusement.
5) PESTILENCE - for making the Jews shepherd their cattle, livestock, sheep and camels in the mountains, valleys and deserts, which kept them away from their families.
6) BOILS - for ordering the Jews to heat and cool water for them to bathe, as if the Jews were bathhouse attendants.

50.
How many years ago were the Bnei Yisroel rescued from Egyptian slavery?

(Seder Hadoros)

51.
At which other time in history was there a plague of locusts?

(Yoel 1:1)

---

7) Hail Rocks - for making the Jews plant gardens, orchards, vineyards and trees.

8) Locusts - for making the Jews plant wheat and barley.

9) Darkness- for making Jews holds candles throughout the night (often upon their heads).

10) Firstborn deaths- for murdering so many newborn Jews.

Others explain the ten plagues as reciprocation for ten other ways they caused the Jews to suffer. (Hashem could have squashed the enemies of Klal Yisroel like you would get rid of a cockroach, but the slower method of punishment was meant to pay back measure for measure.)

1) The Egyptians murdered Jewish babies in the Nile.

2) The Jewish women wailed and cried out because of the mass murder of their children.

3) The Jews were forced to work with dirt to make cement.

4) The Egyptians went into Jewish homes grabbing children for slave work at the labor camps.

5) The Egyptians stole cattle and livestock.

6) The Egyptians called Jews *tamei*, now *they* were *tamei* with *tzora'as*.

7) The Egyptians hit the Jews with fists and stones, screaming at them.

8) The Egyptians confiscated crops from the Jews.

9) The Egyptians exiled the Jews, and exile is like darkness.

10) The Jews are called Hashem's first born children, so the Egyptians lost their first born children.

50.
The Bnei Yisroel were rescued over thirty-three centuries ago (from the year 2,448 until 5,766 over 3,318 years have passed). I wonder how many generations there have been since that amazing epoch in Jewish history. *(Rabbi Tatz, in his book, "The Jewish Thinking Teenager's Guide to Life," writes that if you figure that each generation is 40 years, then it's about 80 generations. 80 x 40= 3200!)*

51.
In the days of the wicked king Menashe, Yoel Hanavi prophesied of a plague of four types of locusts devouring the crops in Israel as a punishment for their sins.

---

52. How do we see צדיק גוזר והקב"ה מקיים ("Hashem fulfills the decree of the righteous person")?

(Shemos Rabbah, Shabbos 59b)

53. Why do we wear *tzitzis* on a four cornered garment?

(Rashi to Parshas Shelach 15:38)

54. Why did Pharaoh say *"Viduy"* after the plague of *barad* (fire/ice hailstones)?

(Daas Zekeinim)

55. Why did Moshe leave the city in Egypt to pray after the plague of *barad*, and not after the other plagues?

(Ramban, Daas Zekeinim)

56. Why didn't the Jews believe Moshe that the time had arrived to leave Mitzrayim?

(Shaarei Aharon)

52. We see that Hashem fulfills the decree of the righteous **immediately**, because as Moshe prayed for the hail to stop, the hail stayed suspended in the air, defying the rules of gravity! (Become an extraordinary *tzadik* and maybe you can decree the end of our long and bitter *Galus!*)

53. The four corners of our *tzitzis* should remind us of the four stages of redemption that Hashem granted us: A) He stopped the terrible slavery; B) He spared us from even serving the *goyim* respectably; c) He avenged our suffering by punishing our oppressors; D) He gave us the gift of Torah.

54. By the plague of hailstones, Pharaoh really realized how wicked he was. He felt so guilty that he said *viduy*: "I sinned *this* time. Hashem is the *Tzadik*, whereas I and my nation are the wicked". Pharaoh voiced this confession more by this *makka* (plague) than any other, because Hashem had warned the Egyptians to take in their cattle and they had refused to listen.

55. Moshe did customarily leave the Egyptian city when he prayed. However, he had no choice during *barad*, since some Egyptians brought their sheep in from the fields lest they get killed. The city was full of sheep. Since those animals were worshipped, it made the city disgusting, and therefore Moshe wouldn't pray there.

56. There were many Jews who were so tangled with *Avodah Zarah* that they did not want to believe the news that they could go now and serve the One and Only Living G-d.

57. How do we see from *Parshas Vaera* that Hashem is going to revive the dead in the future (*Techias Hameisim*)?

(Sanhedrin 90b)

58. When was there a plague of snakes against the Bnei Yisroel?

(Parshas Chukas 21:6)

59. What was the hidden meaning of Moshe's staff swallowing Pharaoh's staffs?

(Rabbeinu Bachya)

60. Were Pharaoh's snakes able to move?

(Sforno)

61. What happened when the original Pharaoh took Sarah to his palace?

(Daas Zekeinim)

---

57. Hashem said, "I appeared to Avrohom, Yitzchok and Yaakov… and I will fulfill My promise to give 'them' Eretz Cana'an…" It is a sure thing that *they* will personally receive it soon, alive and well, when Moshiach comes once and for all.

58. During the long journey in the desert, many of the Bnei Yisroel complained about the Manna. Snakes were sent to bite them. They complained about something that tasted so good, so they were taught a lesson with a snake, to whom everything tastes like dust.

59. Moshe's staff swallowing Pharaoh's staffs symbolized that the Mitzrim were going to be swallowed up by the sea.

60. Pharaoh's snakes were illusions and could not move. Only Hashem can create a living, moving organism. It's been stated that even all the scientists and inventors in the world cannot create a small living insect! *(Chovos Halevavos)*

61. The Pharaoh that took Sarah from Avrohom was immediately stricken with severe leprosy, which prevented him from touching the *tzaddekes*. Moshe's snake alluded that, to the Pharaoh of his day, by showing the leprous skin on the snake. It was a warning to Pharaoh not to start up with the Jews, the descendants of Avrohom and Sarah!

Answers & Facts

פרשת וארא ■ ושננתם לבניך » 245

62. Which six Nevi'im are mentioned in Parshas Vaera?

(Rabbeinu Bachya)

63. How many years after the Bnei Yisroel went to Mitzrayim did their slavery begin?

(רש"י, שפתי חכמים) *(Rashi, Sifsei Chachamim)*

62. Six *Neviim* are mentioned in *Parashas Vaera*: Moshe, Aharon, Pinchas (who is Eliyahu), and Korach's three sons, Asir, Elkana, and Aviyasof.

63. Levi was 43 when he went down to Mitzrayim. He lived there 94 years. It was only after his passing that the slavery began. Thus, the actual period of bitter slavery in Mitzrayim was **116** years long. There is a question among the commentators why exactly the original decree of exile in Egypt was for a period of over **400** years. But one thing is for sure: *Teshuvah* and *Tefillah* can get us out of there!

פרשת בא

1. Which two firstborn Egyptians were spared from *Makkas Bechoros?*

(Shemos Rabbah 18:3, Mechilta 13)

2. What was the "great wealth" that Hashem promised *Avrohom Avinu* that the Jews would receive after they were freed from slavery?

(Berachos 9b, Torah Mi'Tzion quoting Dubno Maggid)

FUNdamental Answers!

"יגעתי ומצאתי!"

("I worked on these questions, and I found these answers!")

1. During Makkas Bechoros all first-born Egyptians died, male and female. Only two survived: Basya, the daughter of Pharaoh, because she saved Moshe, and Pharaoh, in order to bear testimony to the world of Hashem's infinite power.

2. Hashem assured Avrohom Avinu that the Bnei Yisroel would receive a *rechush gadol*, an immense fortune after their slavery. This fortune was really referring to the Torah, which is our most valuable acquisition. However, since no one can fully grasp the greatness of the Torah and some may be disappointed with that gift, the Jews were also given monetary wealth.

3. Why did *Hashem* want the Jews to sacrifice sheep before their *Geulah* (redemption)?

(Shemos Rabbah 16:3)

4. From where can we deduce the incredible merit we earn when we place a *Mezuzah* on our door?

(Torah Mi'Tzion based on Zohar, Midrash Halachah quoting Mechilta)

5. Why must men wear two *Tefillin* – one upon the head and one upon the arm?

(Maran in Shulchan Aruch Orach Chaim 25:5, Toras Ha'olah)

3. The Egyptians worshipped sheep as Avodah Zarah. Hashem wanted their god slaughtered before their eyes before the Jews left. In addition, it served as a punishment for the Egyptians, since they would hunt deer and rams and cook their meat without even offering it to the starving Jews who had only bread (*matzah*) to eat.

4. Hashem ordered the Bnei Yisroel to put blood of the Korban Pesach on their doorposts. The blood of this *mitzvah* would protect them during the devastating final plague. If that which was temporary, brought them safety and security, the Mezuza which has Hashem's Name and is permanently affixed on our doors will surely protect us!

5. There are many reasons given why we need to wear two Tefillin. Ten are listed below:

1. The two Tefillin are supposed to serve as signs and reminders for two things: a) We must always appreciate how Hashem compassionately freed us from the slave-camp of Mitzrayim, and made us His Chosen People! b) The reason Hashem took us out of Mitzrayim was so that we accept the Torah and become His faithful servants.
2. We must serve Hashem with our heart and mind.
3. We should serve Hashem out of love and out of fear.
4. We must do *mitzvos* and not *aveiros*.
5. We must observe the *mitzvos Bein Adam L'Makom* (between man & G-d) and *Bein Adam L'Chavero* (between man & his fellow man).
6. We must learn the *Torah She'biksav* (Written Torah) and the *Torah Sh'Baal Peh* (Oral Torah).
7. We must serve Hashem with our body and our soul.
8. We must learn Torah day and night.
9. We are privileged to serve Hashem in this world and in the world to come.
10. We should study Torah and teach it to others!

6. When should a man wear *Tefillin* even on Shabbos?

(Mishnah Eiruvin 10:1, Shulchan Aruch Orach Chaim 301)

7. Why does Hashem want us to give the *Kohein* a sheep in exchange for a first-born donkey?

(HaTorah V'hamitzvah)

8. Why does the right strap of the *Tefillin-Shel-Rosh* hang down lower than the left strap?

(Zohar Bamidbar 228, Davar B'ito)

9. Why was our first *mitzvah* as Hashem's nation about time – Rosh Chodesh (The New Month)?

(Davar B'ito)

6. If you find Tefillin abandoned in a field or on a street and you surmise they would get ruined or be treated in an undignified manner if they were left there, you are allowed to wear them on Shabbos and walk home with them. The Rabbinical prohibition of muktza (carrying items which are forbidden to use on Shabbos) is suspended to preserve the Tefillin's dignity.

7. Giving a sheep to a Kohen to redeem a first-born donkey has a very deep symbolic meaning. Before the Bnei Yisroel accepted the Torah, Hashem sent seven prophets to offer the Torah to the idolaters. They rejected it. Hashem therefore chose the Jewish people as His own nation, instead of the idolaters. This is symbolized by the Kohen (who represents Hashem) taking a sheep (a kosher animal) for himself, and giving away the donkey (a non-kosher animal).

8. The straps coming down from the Shel Rosh signify the blessing that flows to this world from Hashem. The leather straps reach the stomach and the Milah in order to remind us that it's in these two areas where we are tested to see if we will conduct ourselves with *kedusha* to merit Hashem's blessings in the world.

9. This *mitzvah* emphasizes that since our primary goal as Jews is to serve Hashem, then we should make the most of our time to perform as many *mitzvos* as possible. We are also reminded to renew our commitment to the Torah's *mitzvos* every month with fresh enthusiasm!

Answers&Facts

10. Which *mitzvos* can give a person merit to live longer?
(Menachos 44a, Taanis 20b, Megillah 27a; see Kiddushin 39b)

11. When did the Egyptians want to assassinate King Pharaoh?
(Shemos Rabbah 18:10)

12. For how many days did the Egyptians suffer from a "blackout?"
(Shemos Rabbah 14:3)

13. Which *mitzvah* (mentioned in *Parshas Bo*) cannot be performed, unless a different *mitzvah* is fulfilled first?
(Mechilta 12:48)

14. Why did many wealthy Jews die during the Plague of Darkness?
(Shemos Rabbah 14:3, The Midrash Says)

10. All *mitzvos* are known to increase one's lifetime even on this world. Certain *mitzvos* bring greater merit. One *mitzvah* mentioned in Parshas Bo that is said to lengthen one's life is the *mitzvah* of Tefillin. A number of Rabbis attributed their long life to their great devotion to this *mitzvah*.

11. When the Egyptians saw their powerful civilization dissolving before there eyes due to Pharaoh's stubborness, they wanted to kill him.

12. The plague of physical darkness lasted six days. During the first three the Egyptians were able to move, but not during the last three. One more day of darkness enveloped the Egyptians when they chased the Bnei Yisroel at the Yam-Suf.

13. The Korban Pesach may not be eaten by someone who neglects the *mitzvah* of Bris Milah.

14. There were a number of influential and wealthy Jews in Mitzrayim who assimilated with the Egyptians and did not want to leave with the Bnei Yisroel. They had their way, and stayed in Mitzrayim! They died during the darkness. It has been said that even when Moshiach comes there may be Jews that don't want to leave their comfort and luxury in Galus to return to Eretz Yisroel. One's desire for materialism can make him lose focus of what's really important.

15. How many Egyptians converted to Judaism after seeing the phenomenal miracles in Mitzrayim?

(Meir Tov)

16. Which *mitzvah* is equal to all of the other *mitzvos?*

(Yerushalmi Peah 1, Pesikta Zutrasi 13)

17. Why are *Bris Milah* and *"Korban Pesach"* the only *"Mitzvos Asei"* that if someone disregards he is punished with death?

(Shemos Rabbah 17:3, Bnei Yissoschar)

18. Why do we put *Tefillin* on our weaker hand?

(Torah Mi'Tzion, Menachos 36b, Mishnah Berurah 27:1)

19. What do the seven (or eight) wrappings of the *Tefillin* upon our arm correspond to?

(K'zeh Re'ei V'kadeish)

---

15. There is a question exactly how many Egyptians converted to Judaism after witnessing Hashem's absolute power. Some say 2,400,000 converted, others say 3,600,000, while some say even a higher number.

16. There are several *mitzvos*, which are so fundamental that they are considered equal to all *mitzvos* combined! Tefillin is one such *mitzvah*. We must be careful to wear our Tefillin properly by making sure they are in place in order to fulfill this important *mitzvah*.

17. Hashem gave two *mitzvos* - Bris Milah and Korban Pesach - to the Bnei Yisroel to perform before they left Mitzrayim because they didn't possess enough merits to leave Mitzrayim. These *mitzvos* are so crucial to our nation that a person would forfeit his life if he chose to neglect them.

18. The Tefillin are placed on the weaker hand to remind a person that he is powerless without Hashem's help! Also, we do *mitzvos* with our right hand, and since the tying of the Tefillin is the main *mitzvah*, we tie it with our right onto the left.

19. The seven times we wrap the black retzuah (leather strap) around our forearm is supposed to remind us to master all the seven branches of Torah: Chumash, Navi, Kesuvim, Mishnah, Gemara, Halacha & Kabbalah!

Answers&Facts

20. What incentive did Hashem send the Bnei Yisroel to make them want to perform the *mitzvah* of Bris Milah?

(Shemos Rabbah 9:6)

21. If one didn't put on *Tefillin* in the morning, how late can he still put them on to properly fulfill the *mitzvah*?

(Bi'ur Halachah 30:5)

22. When is there a national custom to raise funds in order to enable the poor to fulfill a particular *mitzvah*?

(Yerushalmi Bava Basra 1:2, Pri Megadim 469)

23. Why must the owner of a first-born donkey break its neck if he doesn't want to give the *Kohen* a sheep for its *pidyon* (exchange)?

(Tanchuma)

---

20. Many Jews in Mitzrayim did not want to perform a Bris Milah! Hashem made strong winds blow the fragrance of Gan Eden into the meat of the Korban Pesach. The Jews were so anxious to enjoy the food with its delectable aroma that they pleaded with Moshe for a piece. He said, "Only one who is circumcised may enjoy it." They rushed to have themselves circumcised. Sometimes all we need is an incentive to do great things!

21. One who for any reason did not put on Tefillin all day may still put them on until dark. During Bein Hashemashos (twilight), he must put them on without a *beracha*.

22. There is an old Jewish custom to raise funds for the poor to have wine and matzah for the Seder when we commemorate Yetzias Mitzrayim. It is known as "*Kimcha D'Pischa*."

23. If a Jewish owner does not wish to give a sheep (lamb or kid) to the Kohen in return for his first-born donkey, he is punished with the loss of that donkey. It is killed, and the owner may not derive any benefit from it. If one does not give charitably, he loses out in the end too!

24.
May women put on *Tefillin?* Which girls donned *Tefillin* regularly?

(Midrash Halachah, Ben Yehoyada Eiruvin 96a, Rama Orach Chaim 38:3 and Mishnah Berurah there)

25.
Why should we buy expensive *Tefillin?*

(Kitzur Shulchan Aruch of Rav Raphael Baruch Toledano 10:1, see Pesachim 50b)

26.
Why was every *Avodah Zarah* destroyed during the *makkos* in Mitzrayim, with the exception of one idol – the *Baal Tzefon* statue?

(Shemos Rabbah 15:15, Mechiltah on Parshas Beshalach 2:2)

27.
What wonderful relief does *Rosh Chodesh* bring?

(Kuzari)

---

24. Shaul Hamelech's daughter, Michal, and Rashi's daughters, are known to have donned Tefillin. However, since most women are not on their spiritual level, they should not wear Tefillin. Michal believed that the merit of wearing Tefillin would help her bear sons.

25. As good shoppers we always look for quality when we buy a car, stereo or any other product. Surely, then, we must invest in a pair of quality Tefillin that will be used for a lifetime! If someone thinks they can buy a kosher pair of Tefillin for $50, they don't realize how much meticulous work a good pair of Tefillin needs. A pair of Tefillin written by a G-d fearing and skilled scribe costs closer to $1,000! It's a pity how so many people err by buying a cheap pair when it may not even be kosher! Consider the Tefillin as your battery charger that can charge your soul with Yiras Shamayim. Isn't it worth investing to get the best charge possible?!

26. When Hashem retaliated against the Egyptians for enslaving the Bnei Yisroel, He also disintegrated their many idols. Hashem left the *Avodah Zarah* of Baal Tzefon standing so people should still be tested by free choice to see if they will recognize the only G-d, Hashem. Pharaoh foolishly didn't get the hint. He worshipped that Avodah Zarah on the way when he chased the Bnei Yisroel to the Yam-Suf.

27. There are many auspicious times when Hashem forgives the sins of the Bnei Yisroel. One such time is Rosh Chodesh. We say in the Mussaf of Rosh Chodesh that, "It's a time of forgiveness for all of them [the Bnei Yisroel]." This is a great encouragement for those who wish to be clean from sin. One must look at each new month as an opportunity to serve Hashem with a clean slate!

Answers&Facts

---

28. Hashem completed the world in *Tishrei*, on *Rosh Hashanah*. Why, then, is *Nissan* referred to as the first month?

(Yerushalmi Rosh Hashanah 1:1)

29. How was *Rosh Chodesh* celebrated back in the 3000's, in the times of the *Nevi'im*?

(Shmuel I 20:24, Melachim II 4:23, see Mishnah Rosh Hashanah 3:7)

30. How do we see Hashem's love and affinity for the Bnei Yisroel?

(Shemos Rabbah 15:5)

31. When is there a *mitzvah* to give away something kosher to receive back something not kosher?

(Yoreh De'ah 321:1, Sefer Hamitzvos #22)

32. How is it possible that Tefillin appear beautiful, yet they are absolutely *passul* (disqualified)?

(Tanchuma 14, see Mishnah Berurah 32:103)

28. Hashem created the world at Rosh Hashana. But it was in Nissan that we became a nation. Therefore, Nissan is considered the first month with regard to celebrating our holidays, for all the Yomim Tovin are *zecher li'yitziyas Mitzrayim*, as a remembrance that we were taken out of Mitzrayim which took place in Nissan.

29. Rosh Chodesh would be celebrated by visiting the leaders of their generation, such as the King, the Navi, the Av Beis Din or the Kohen Gadol. It was a most inspiring way to begin the new month. Perhaps this is why many Chassidic Rebbes make a special Rosh Chodesh tish.

30. We can see Hashem's total devotion to the Bnei Yisroel, for He Himself went down to the spiritually impure land of Mitzrayim to save His children!!

31. There is a *mitzvah* of Pidyon Peter Chamor to give a kosher sheep to the Kohen to receive back your first-born non-kosher donkey.

32. Sometimes things are not as kosher as they seem. For instance: you might see wine with a *hechsher* on the bottle, but it became *yayin nesech* (for it was touched by a idol-worshipper), so the wine is now forbidden to use. Tefillin may be beautifully written, but they might have been written out of

33. Which Rabbi never walked four *Amos* (cubits) without his *Tefillin* upon him?

(Succah 28a)

34. The Vilna Gaon's mother, Rebbitzen Treina Kramer, ע״ה, appeared to him in a dream after her passing, and she quoted *pasuk* 11:26 of *Parshas Bo*. What was she implying?

(Otzar Chaim)

35. Why does the *Tefillin-Shel-Rosh* have four compartments, while the *Tefillin-Shel-Yad* has only one compartment?

(Rosh and Me'iri to Menachos 32b)

36. What is loved and enjoyed one minute, and despised and rejected the next minute, even though it didn't change?

(Imrei Binah of the Ben Ish Chai 89)

---

order and are therefore invalid. That's why you should only buy Tefillin from a Ben Torah who has a G-d fearing reputation!

33. Rabbi Yochanan Ben Zakai was never seen going four Amos without wearing his Tefillin.

34. The Vilna Gaon's mother paraphrased what Moshe Rabbeinu said to Pharaoh: "We won't know with what to serve Hashem until we get there!" She implied that just as the Bnei Yisroel said they wouldn't know which Korbanos to bring until they reached the desert and heard Hashem's commandments, people don't fully realize how much to serve Hashem until they "get there," arriving in Heaven (after 120 years) to see exactly what Hashem really values, and wants everyone to do.

35. Tefillin remind us to use our five senses to solely honor the One who grants them to us. The Tefillin of the head has four sections to remind us to properly use the four senses situated in the head: seeing, smelling, hearing, and tasting. The Tefillin of the arm should remind us to properly use the sense in the hand, the sense of touch. If only we would use these gifts and resources the way their Sponsor intended!

36. Chometz is loved until Erev Pesach and is then rejected.

Answers&Facts

---

37. Which food has three different *Berachos* at different times of the year?

(The 'Sephardi Berachos Bee')

38. While wearing our *Tefillin*, we must not be in a light-headed mood. What is a most common (*kalus rosh*) lightheadedness that people have?

(Od Yosef Chai on Parshas Chayei Sarah 3)

39. Why must a Jewish father pay a *Kohein* five silver *shekalim* for his first-born son?

(See Yerushalmi Shekalim 2:3; Shimushah Shel Torah)

40. What should a man do if he forgot to don *Tefillin* one day?

(Yalkut Yosef Hilchos Tefillin 30)

41. Why is the day before *Rosh Chodesh* called "Yom Kippur Katan"?

(Pri Chadash 407 quoting Rav Moshe Cordovero zt'l)

---

37. The *beracha* on matzah is *borei minei mezonos* for Sephardim; *hamotzi* if they make a meal out of it; and *Achilas Matzah* when they eat it at the Seder.

38. Praying without concentration is a form of lightheadedness that is common and wrong. We may not put our minds and lips on "autopilot" when we pray! That constitutes *hesach hadaas* from the Tefillin as well.

39. A father of a *bechor* must realize that his son essentially should be with a Kohen who can train him to live on a higher standard as befits a potential servant in the Beis Hamikdash. The father's "buying" the boy back demonstrates that he understands his awesome responsibility to train him to live a holy life as befitting a first-born.

40. If one forgot to put on Tefillin, he lost out on eight *mitzvos*. He should: do Teshuva, have his Tefillin inspected for mistakes, wear Tefillin d'Rabbeinu Tam from then on, learn with his Tefillin everyday and give *tzedakah* to the best of his ability.

41. Hashem graciously forgives some of the sins of Bnei Yisroel on Rosh Chodesh. Therefore, many devout Jews spend that day and the day pre-

42. Why do we display three *Matzos* upon the table during the *Pesach Seder*?

(Ohr Zarua)

43. Which Jews didn't have light during the Plague of Darkness?

(Nachal Kedumim; see Shemos Rabbah 14:2)

44. Why do non-Jews base their calendar on the sun (365 days per year), while we base our calendar on the moon (354 1/3 days per year)?

(See Shemos Rabbah 15:28; Sefer Yereim 103, Iturei Torah)

45. What is the appropriate prayer to say while we burn our *chometz*?

(The Chassidic Haggaddah)

---

ceding it amid feelings and supplications of repentance. Some synagogues even have special prayer services called Yom Kippur Katan the day before each Rosh Chodesh, and especially before Rosh Chodesh Elul.

42. A Korban Todah is brought with three types of bread. On Pesach we all celebrate the Seder as a Seudas Hodaah that Hashem took us out of Mitzrayim; therefore, we use three matzos.

43. The wicked Jews who died during the plague of darkness did not get to behold the light that the Bnei Yisroel enjoyed. It was the special Ohr Haganuz (Hidden Light) that is reserved for the truly righteous. It was with this supernatural light that the Jews had "x-ray vision" and could see through walls to discover Egyptians treasures!

44. Any idol-worshipers that don't fear G-d will be consumed in fire, which is represented by the sun. Whereas the moon, which has light but does not burn, symbolizes that Am Yisroel will ultimately enjoy light. Also the sun is not seen in the night, as a sign that undeserving non-Jews won't have Olam Haba, but the moon which can be seen in the day is a sign that the deserving Jews will prosper in both worlds.

45. When many pious Jews burn the chametz, they pray that Hashem burn away their Yetzer Hara as well!

Answers&Facts

---

46. What is written inside the *Tefillin* of *Hashem Yisborach?*

(Berachos 6a)

47. Why don't we wear *Tefillin* throughout the day?

(See Menachos 36a, Pesikta Rabasi 22, Minhag Yisroel Torah 25)

48. What is a person missing if he doesn't learn *Torah* while wearing his Tefillin?

(Ben Ish Chai on Parshas Chayei Sarah 1:11)

49. Why were three stalks of the small hyssop plant used to color the doorposts of the Jewish homes in Mitzrayim?

(Shemos Rabbah 17:2)

---

46. Our Tefillin bear witness about our total love to Hashem. Likewise, Hashem's Tefillin testify to His eternal love of the Bnei Yisroel and their uniqueness!

47. Ideally, a Jewish male should wear his Tefillin all day. However, since one would find it too difficult to keep himself in the required pure state all day, it was decided that one should only wear Tefillin for Shacharis so he can say Kerias Shema and pray with them. There are some great Jews who wear Tefillin all day, such as the venerable sage Hagaon Harav Chaim Pinchos Scheinberg *shlita*. We should long for the days of Moshiach, when it will be customary to wear Tefillin all day long as it used to be done.

48. One can only perfect his soul if he learns Torah while wearing his Tefillin! Unfortunately, there are those who rush to take their Tefillin off immediately after Tefillah. It is a pity to waste such a wonderful opportunity!

49. The hyssop was used to protect Klal Yisroel, because Hashem wanted to show that although something seems small and insignificant, it could be so powerful. The *ezov* (hysopp) was used to purify a *metzora* (leper), to make the Para Aduma formula, and in Mitzrayim to save the Jews through the miracles. Big and small things are equal before Hashem!

---

50. Why are donkeys privileged to be used for the *mitzvah* of *Pidyon Petter Chamor?*

(Rashi, Tanchuma on Parshas Beshalach 25, see HaTorah V'hamitzvah pg. 438)

51. What was the popular custom in European *Yeshivos Ketanos* every *Rosh Chodesh?*

(Bach)

52. Which *pasuk* warns us never to procrastinate in the performance of a *mitzvah?*

(Mechilta; see Berachos 64a)

53. Which *mitzvah* can save a person from *Gehinnom?*

(Otzar Ha'aggadah)

54. Why do we need *Tefillin* on us during the week, but not on Shabbos and *Yom-Tov?*

(Menachos 36, Eiruvin 96, Maran in Shulchan Aruch Orach Chaim Hilchos Tefillin 31:1)

---

50. Since the donkeys carried the Bnei Yisroel's immense wealth out of Mitzrayim, the donkeys were rewarded by being part of a *mitzvah*. Amazingly, just by associating with our holy nation, the *tamei* animal became a *cheftza* d'*mitzvah* (object of holiness)!

51. On Rosh Chodesh the school children would bring gifts for their Rebbeim who devoted their lives to teach them Torah. (Perhaps this was their tuition.)

52. Matzos and *mitzvos* are spelled with the same Hebrew letters. This implies that just as we must guard our matzos and bake them in a hurry lest they become chometz, so too, we must not delay the performance of *mitzvos* lest they lose their quality as well.

53. A number of *mitzvos* can help spare a person from suffering in Gehinom. One such *mitzvah* is wearing Tefillin properly.

54. A Jewish man must always have two signs of his allegiance to G-d. Usually the signs are Tefillin and Bris Milah. However, on Shabbos and Yom Tov, these holy days themselves declare that testimony so we don't need the tefillin as a sign.

Answers&Facts

---

55. When is it virtuous to wear *Tefillin* only upon the arm?

(Birkei Yosef, Yesod V'shoresh Ha'avodah)

56. How do we see that you should show some good deeds in public, but should keep other good deeds private?

(Emes V'emunah)

57. Will *Bechoros* (first-born boys) serve in the Beis Hamikdash in the future?

(Aruch Hashulchan Ha'asid)

58. When will there be another Plague of Darkness?

(Shemos Rabbah 14:3, Yeshayah 60:2)

59. From where can we see the "power of prayer"?

(Toras HaTefillah, See Rambam Hilchos Teshuva 7:7)

---

55. One may not do *mitzvos* to "show" that he is more pious than he really is. This is called *yuhara* (false pride). There have been many devout *talmidei chachamim* who have worn just their Tefillin-Shel-Yad under their shirt-sleeve clandestinely.

56. Just as we cover the Shel Yad but uncover the Shel Rosh, so too, one should perform many *mitzvos* publicly but should do good deeds in private too!

57. Bechoros are holier than regular Jews. They will be privileged to serve in the final Beis Hamikdash. They will also serve as great examples for their younger siblings how life should revolve around the privilege to serve Hashem!

58. At the future redemption, Hashem will engulf the nations that did not obey Him in darkness, and He will shine upon Klal Yisroel. May it happen in our time!

59. It is known that Tefillah can annul a bad decree. In Mitzrayim, Hashem cancelled half the time of their enslavement since they cried out in prayer. During these days of crisis, it is incumbent upon us to pray for our brethren in Eretz Yisroel and throughout the world.

60. From what age can a boy wear Tefillin?
(Yalkut Yosef)

61. When is it improper to write a number?
(Chasam Sofer, Yabi'a Omer)

62. Why did the five *Tannaic Rabbis* stay up all *Pesach* night at the *Seder*, isn't there a *mitzvah* to relax and enjoy *Yom Tov*?
(Maharal, Shimush Talmidei Chachamim)

63. Why did *Moshe* accept the (2,400,000 Egyptian magicians) as converts without asking permission from *Hashem Yisborach*?
(Introduction to Shimush Talmidei Chachamim)

64. If someone drank the *Arba Kosos* without reclining, must he drink them again?
(Mishnah Berurah 480:8)

---

60. Usually a boy is not mature enough to wear Tefillin with the proper required cleanliness until he is about twelve and a half. Some Poskim permit an orphan even as young as ten to wear Tefillin earlier so that it be a merit for the deceased parent.

61. Some say you shouldn't write the date in numbers (i.e. 1/20/71=January 20, 1971), for Hashem designated Nissan as the first month. Writing in such a manner implies that another month other that Nissan is the first month.

62. For the Tannaim who were on such a high spiritual level, staying up and reminiscing about the multitude of wonderful miracles that took place in Mitzrayim was not a chore or an inconvenience, but rather, a pleasure and a delight!

63. Moshe wanted to make the converts welcome to Judaism so it would be a Kiddush Hashem, but sometimes the Rav must be skeptical to make sure the converts don't negatively influence the Bnei Yisroel.

64. Some Poskim maintain that if a man drank the Arba Kosos without reclining, he must drink them again while reclining. So sometimes one would be required to drink eight cups of wine on Pesach night!

Answers & Facts

65. Why is *Rosh Chodesh* celebrated more by women than by men?

(Tur quoting Pirkei d'Rabi Eliezer)

66. Which *beracha* is supposed to be said only once a month, and some people miss it anyway?

(Sanhedrin 42a, Shulchan Aruch Orach Chaim 426)

65. Originally, the three *Moadim* (holidays) were in honor of the Avos, and the 12 Roshei Chodesh were in honor of the 12 Shevatim. But after the sin of the Eigel, that holiday was taken from the tribes and given to the women instead, since they did not partake in that sin. This publicizes that the faith of the women was greater than that of the men, for they did not willfully contribute to make the Eigel.

66. We thank Hashem every day and night for light and its various outlets, but the actual blessing upon the renewal of the moon is once a month.

Dedicated in honor of

OUR PARENTS AND GRANDPARENTS

by Issac, Moses & Benjamin Hidary

פרשת בשלח

1. How do we see that the Jewish people are more precious to Hashem than His angels?

(Chagigah 12b, Shemos Rabbah 23:7, Rokeach, Chullin 91b)

2. Why did Hashem let Pharaoh frighten the Bnei Yisroel like a pirate pursuing them trapping them between the raging sea and the wild desert animals?

(Shemos Rabbah 21:6 and 17:5)

fUNdamental Answers!

"יגעתי ומצאתי!"

("I worked on these questions, and I found these answers!")

1. When *Malochim* sing to Hashem, they must first utter three words before saying Hashem's name. They say *"Kadosh, Kadosh, Kadosh, Hashem…"*. On the other hand, the Jews were able to say *"Ashira La'Hashem"* with Hashem's Name being the second word - because Hashem's loves when *we* sing more than when the angels do! In addition, Hashem does not let the angels above sing *Shira* until the Jewish people first sing *Shira* on this world. (We must be more careful to come early to *Shul* so that we don't delay the angels singing *Shira* to Hashem.)

2. Hashem loves to hear our voice in prayer! The Bnei Yisroel were saved because they cried out in *tefillah* to Hashem to save them. Once they left Mitzrayim they were quiet. Hashem let Pharaoh scare them in order to give them a reason to raise their voices in *tefillah* once again.

3. Why did Moshe tell the Bnei Yisroel to turn back to Mitzrayim?

(Ohr Hachaim)

4. How many flavors did the miraculous *Mann* have?

(See Yoma 75b; Me'am Lo'ez quoting Yalkut Shimoni on Shir Hashirim)

5. Why didn't the *Ananei HaKavod* (miraculous clouds) carry the Bnei Yisroel instantly to *Eretz Yisroel* instead of them tarrying in the desert?

(Shemos Rabbah 20:15, Mechilta, Tanchuma, Rashi, Torah Mi'Tzion)

6. Why were the waters of *Marah* first bitter and then sweet?

(Netziv)

---

3. Moshe had the Bnei Yisroel make a sort of U-turn as a ruse to trap the Egyptians, so they would be drawn out of Mitzrayim and meet their end at the Yam Suf. Upon seeing them turn around, the Egyptians would believe that the Bnei Yisroel were lost and they could overcome them. That's exactly what happened. When the Egyptians saw the Bnei Yisroel turn around, they exclaimed, "Those Jews don't even know where they're going! They are going in circles and coming back!" The Egyptians were infused with renewed vigor to attack the Jews. The Egyptians chased them to the Yam Suf where they received their well-deserved punishment.

4. The *Mann* tasted naturally like a type of honey wafer, but it could also taste like anything you wished. Some say, it possessed 546 innate flavors!

5. The Miracle Clouds did not take the shortest route because Hashem wanted them to spend time in the desert to prepare for life in Eretz Yisroel. They needed training in the laws of Terumos and Ma'aseros, and other mitzvos that one must keep in Eretz Yisroel. The desert served as a form of a *Kollel* to teach them Torah and all the *mitzvos* that they would have to perform in Eretz Yisroel. Also, when the Cana'anim who resided in Eretz Yisroel heard that the Bnei Yisroel were coming, they chopped down the fruit trees and fields of crops just to make life hard for them when they would arrive. The Bnei Yisroel stayed in the desert to give the Cana'anim time to cultivate the land again; they would now enter a land that was suitable for farming.

6. When the Jews arrived at *Marah*, the water was not drinkable. You can imagine how bitter they felt! They had traveled for so long and had nothing to drink! Moshe cast a *Hordafni* stick - which has a bitter taste - into the water. Miraculously, the bitter water and the bitter stick together became sweet! This symbolizes that even if someone finds it difficult to learn the Torah (which is compared to water) at first, he should know that the sweet times follows the bitter times. Don't give up before you feel how sweet Torah-learning can be!

---

7. *Chazal* say that Am Yisroel committed ten transgressions on their way to Eretz Yisroel. What are six failings that the Bnei Yisroel exhibited that are mentioned in *Parshas Beshalach?*

(*Avos 5:5; see Shemos Rabbah 25:4*)

8. How did Moshe prove to all that his staff was not a sort of magical wand?

(*Shemos Rabbah 21:6,9, Rabbeinu Bachya, Tur, Rosh*)

---

7. 1. When the Bnei Yisorel were trapped at the Red Sea, they questioned Hashem: "Were there no graves left in Egypt that you brought us to die in the desert?"

2. When they arrived in Marah, the water was bitter, and they complained angrily, "What are we going to drink?"

3. When they arrived at the Sinai Desert, they had no food to eat. "If only we had died by the hand of Hashem in the land of Egypt where we sat near the pot of meat", they moaned.

4. Hashem sent them Mann to eat and commanded them not to leave any leftovers for the following day, for they would receive new Mann each day. A couple of Jews, the infamous Dasan and Aviram, broke the rule, thereby demonstrating their lack of confidence in Hashem's ability and generosity.

5. Those same two people, Dasan and Aviram, went out on Shabbos carrying containers to collect Mann, even though Hashem told them that no Mann would fall on Shabbos.

6. When the Bnei Yisroel arrived at Refidim, they had no water to drink. They again challenged Moshe. Hashem told Moshe to hit a rock and water would then flow from the rock. Hashem tested the Bnei Yisroel many times to teach them one important lesson: Am Yisroel should feel comfortable and relaxed by counting solely on Him for everything that they need. We should heed this lesson too!

8. Moshe split the Yam-Suf with a wave of his hand. He did not use his staff (contrary to some artistic renditions that portray Moshe holding up his staff). Actually, Hashem told Moshe, "Lift the stick away from you." When Moshe lifted up his hands to split the sea, he proved that the water split because he was the Eved Hashem, the messenger of Hashem, and not because he used some type of magical wand, which some cynical Jews and Egyptians had suspected.

9. Why did Moshe insist on keeping the Bnei Yisroel away from gathering the Egyptian treasures after the Splitting of the Sea?
   (Be'er Yitzchak)

10. Which ten *mitzvos* were given in *Marah*?
    (Rashi, Ramban, Mechilta, Sanhedrin 56b)

11. Why did the Egyptians act so irrationally and chase after the Jews into the sea?
    (Rambam, Chizkuni; see Shemos Rabbah 23:14)

12. Which *pasuk* in *Parshas Beshalach* teaches us that learning Torah saves a person from suffering?
    (Berachos 5b, Od Yosef Chai on Parashas Ki Sisa)

9. The Egyptians filled their chariots with expensive jewels, gold, silver and treasures with which Pharaoh had bribed them to pursue the Bnei Yisroel. The Bnei Yisroel took that wealth when the Egyptians drowned. What an immense fortune it was! Moshe quickly led them away from the Yam Suf to continue on toward Har Sinai and receive the Torah. Moshe showed them that they had to run away from the pursuit of material gains to receive the much greater treasure: spiritual wealth. Now is not the time to amass money when such a treasure is awaiting them! We could learn from Moshe's lesson too, that we must pursue the ultimate wealth—Torah knowledge! Moshe epitomized the dictum that Torah is more precious than gold. (Tehillim 119:72)

10. The Bnei Yisroel were given Ten Commandments in Marah. It was a "warm up" for the Aseres Hadibros, that they were to receive at Har Sinai. They were commanded to keep the 'Seven Mitzvos B'nei Noach' (Seven Noachide Laws which even non-Jews must keep): not to eat from a living animal; not to curse Heaven; not to steal; to have a justice system; not to kill; not to lead immoral lives; and not to serve Avodah Zarah. Three more mitzvos were added: the laws of Shabbos, the laws of Kibud Av V'em, and civil laws.

11. The cloud that separated the Jews from the Egyptians blocked the Egyptians from seeing the sides of the sea; in their frenzy and hatred they ran full-speed into the water after the Jews, thinking it was still dry land. By the time they realized where they were, it was too late; they were already in the sea and could not get out. The Medrash offers another explanation, that Hashem put a drive in the horses to chase the Jews and not fear the water.

12. Moshe said, "If we listen to the voice of Hashem and do what's right by following His mitzvos and guarding His statutes, all of the diseases that Hashem inflicted in Mitzrayim will not be put on you, because Hashem will heal you." (Shemos 15-26) The Gemara learns from here that if a person is experiencing pain and suffering, he should study Torah, and it will help alleviate his troubles.

13. Why did the Mann melt each morning by 10:00 a.m.?
(Berachos 27a, Rabbeinu Bachya)

14. Why must we read from the Sefer Torah publicly within every three days?
(Mechilta, Dorshei Reshumos)

15. How many *Mitzvos* do you get when you sing *Zemiros, Pizmonim,* or *Bakashot?*
(Rabbi Yaakov Kassin zt'l in the intoduction to Shira U'Tehillah)

16. Who made up the youngest choir in history?
(Shemos Rabbah 23:8)

17. Hashem gave the Bnei Yisroel water from stones in the desert. When in history did Hashem give water from a dry bone?
(Bereishis Rabbah 98:13, Sefer Shoftim 15:19)

---

13. Hashem wanted the Jewish people to be able to fulfill the fundamental *mitzvah* of *tzedakah* even when all their needs were being taken care of. Since the Mann melted early, those who woke up late did not get their portion. They would now have to rely on others who would be willing to share their portion with them. Hashem loves the *mitzvah* of *tzedakah*, for it ensures the world's continuity.

14. Torah is compared to water. Just as a person cannot survive three days without any water, a person's *neshama* (soul) cannot survive without Torah-learning for three days! Therefore, we publicly read the Torah for everyone to hear *Divrei Torah* at least once every three days.

15. You get a *mitzvah* for every letter that you sing to Hashem in gratitude and appreciation! In one song, you can actually acquire hundreds of *mitzvos* by singing to Hashem!

16. The unborn fetuses in their mothers' wombs also joined in the *Shira*, singing to Hashem at the splitting of the Red Sea. Some chorus!

17. After Shimshon killed a thousand Pelishtim (Philistines) with the jawbone of a donkey, he became overconfident about his strength and ability. Hashem made him suffer from severe thirst to make him realize that even he must depend on Hashem. Hashem gave him water by showing him that water flowed out from the very bone with which he killed the *Pelishtim*. Everything is a miracle of Hashem!

Answers&Facts

18. Why did Hashem make the Jews thirsty in the desert?

(Ramban, Netziv, Ohr Hachaim, Zohar on Parashas Naso 124)

19. Hashem told Moshe at the *Yam Suf*, "Why are you crying out in prayer? Just tell the Jews to travel!" What else should Jews do when in danger if not pray?

(Shemos Rabbah 21:2,4, Targum Onkelos, Ohr Hachaim)

20. How can reading the *parsha* of the Mann [Ch.16, pesukim 4-36] help you financially?

(Doresh Tov)

---

18. Hashem tested the Jewish Nation with thirst to determine whether they would complain or whether they would show trust in Hashem and speak to Moshe with respect. Life is a series of tests to prove our faith in Hashem. He wants us to realize how much we need Him and that we can depend on Him!

19. Hashem wanted to perform miracles to save the Bnei Yisroel, but they did not merit them, since they were on such a low spiritual level (the 49th level of tumah) in Mitzrayim. But when they showed that they trust in Hashem, it served as a great merit for them. Hashem told them to enter the raging sea: Their trust in Hashem by following his order would give Klal Yisroel the merit that they needed to be saved! Many times Hashem wants to reward the Bnei Yisroel, yet the Satan speaks against them. He mentions all the *aveiros* the Bnei Yisroel commit and says to Hashem, "Are they really worthy of receiving Your reward?" To counter his evil intentions, the Bnei Yisroel need to do something that shows they trust Hashem so that He can say defiantly to the Satan, "Look! They trust Me!" That forces the Satan to be quiet, and the Bnei Yisroel receive their due reward. In addition, Hashem meant, "Moshe, you need not pray now, because the Bnei Yisroel have already prayed and I accepted their Tefillah already."

20. One who says the *Parshas HaMann* daily - or even occasionaly - and takes to heart the incredible kindness that Hashem provided for the Bnei Yisroel by sending them food and jewels in the arid desert, will strengthen his bond with Hashem. In the *zechus* (merit) of that faith and trust that one places in Hashem by affirming that all sustenance and support comes from Him, Hashem will guarantee that his needs will be met.

21. When did Moshe Rabbeinu teach the Bnei Yisroel natural medicine?

(Rabbeinu Bachya)

22. Why did some of the water turn into rocks during the splitting of the *Yam Suf*?

(Doresh Tov)

23. Did the nations of the world know about Am Yisroel's amazing forty-year odyssey in the desert and all of the phenomenal miracles that took place?

(Shemos Rabbah 20:16 and 25:7)

24. Who were the fifteen special guests at the *Yam-Suf* (Red Sea)?

(Rashi to Tehillim 78, Me'am Lo'ez)

25. When did Moshe and the Bnei Yisroel fast?

(Ran on Mesechta Taanis)

---

21. When the Bnei Yisroel arrived at *Marah*, Moshe gave them a "science class" to show how all Hashem's creations can be used in many different ways. For example, certain herbs and plants can actually provide cures and better health for mankind. Indeed, this demonstrates that all wisdom can be found in the Torah, as the Mishnah in *Pirkei Avos* (5:22) states: "Delve into it [the Torah] and delve into it, because it is all in it!" Then Moshe told them that, ultimately, they should rely on praying to Hashem and keeping His *mitzvos* to ensure good health!

22. Hashem punished the Egyptians at the sea in two ways – drowning them and crushing them – because they wanted to both drown the Jewish children and crush the Jewish people.

23. The non-Jews did see and hear about Klal Yisroel's protective clouds, the heavenly fire, and their heavenly food – the *Mann*. Hashem wanted them to be filled with awe of the Bnei Yisroel before they entered Eretz Yisroel.

24. The *Avos*, and Yaakov's twelve sons, the *shevatim* (tribal heads), stood and witnessed the Splitting of the Sea when their great-grandchildren were leaving Mitzrayim.

25. When the terrorizing Amalekim attacked the Jews, Moshe declared war against them in self-defense, and Klal Yisroel fasted. In a time of war, the Jewish people fast in order to show Hashem that they are humble and count solely on Him.

Answers&Facts

26. Which *aveirah* (sin) is as bad as all the other *aveiros* combined?

(*Shemos Rabbah 25:12*)

27. Why does the Mishnah state that there are "forty-minus-one" *melachos* (forbidden types of work) on Shabbos, rather than state clearly that there are "thirty-nine" *melachos*?

(*Tosafos Yom-Tov on Shabbos 7:2*)

28. Do we say the special 'beracha upon a place where a miracle happened' if we visit Egypt today?

(*Doresh Tov, Chasam Sofer*)

29. Why is the *mitzvah* of Shabbos mentioned twelve times in the *Torah* in seven different *parshiyos*?

(*Aruch Hashulchan 242*)

30. What does "*Zeh Keili V'anveihu*" mean?

(*Shabbos 133a, Mechilta*)

---

26. The reward for Shemiras Shabbos (Shabbos observance) is as great as all of the *mitzvos* combined. Conversely, the punishment for one who transgresses the holy day- by working, is as severe as that of all the punishments combined!

27. There are really forty types of labor that you are not allowed to do on Shabbos: The 39 types of labor, plus a 40th prohibition—that you are not allowed to leave the techum. The difference between them is that one who performs one of the 39 forbidden activities is punished with stoning, while one who leaves the techum receives lashes. Shabbos is a gift from Hashem - but a very serious and expensive gift- because if one doesn't treat it with care, he is severely punished.

28. If a person visits Mitzrayim today, he should make a special beracha thanking Hashem for all the miracles he did there for our ancestors.

29. The better we keep Shabbos, the better our seven days of the week and the twelve months of the year will be. Our overall success is determined to a large degree by how well we honor and guard Shabbos Kodesh!

30. We glorify Hashem by beautifying our *mitzvos* (i.e. - by buying a beautiful Tallis, *Yarmulka* (Kippah), Mezuza, Sefer Torah, Kiddush cup, Lulav, Succah, or even by praying a beautiful Tefillah.) Everything that we do should have that

---

31. Why didn't the *Ananei HaKavod* (Heavenly clouds) protect some members of Dan's tribe?

(Mechilta, Targum Yonasan)

32. Which specific mitzvos protected the Jews from the raging Red Sea?

(Doresh Tov, Midrash Avkir, Mechilta)

33. Which five weapons did the Jews possess when they left Egypt?

(Shemos Rabbah 15:3, K'sav Sofer)

34. What did a non-Jew taste when he attempted to eat the supernaturally delicious Mann?

(Tanchuma 25, Shemos Rabbah 5:9, Yalkut Shimoni)

---

special sparkle and shine, thereby showing that we are honoring the King! Another explanation is that the word *"Ve'anvehu"* can be read *"Ani Vehu"* (I am like Him!) by emulating His ways. We should try to emulate the ways of Hashem: just as Hashem is merciful, we should act with mercy to our fellow man; just as Hashem is compassionate, we should be compassionate to all as well.

31. One of the people from the tribe of Dan smuggled an *Avodah Zarah* out of Egypt. The holy clouds would not protect that sinner. It was a pity that he didn't take to heart the message to do teshuva and dispose of the *Avodah Zara*, so he became vulnerable when Amalek attacked the Bnei Yisroel.

32. The mitzvos of Mezuza, which is on our right, Tefillin, which is on our left, and Tzitzis, which is before and behind us, were the three mitzvos that protected the Bnei Yisroel when they entered the dangerous waters of the Red Sea, keeping them completely safe and secure. [Interestingly, our Rabbis say that someone who is careful with these *mitzvos* will be safe from sin, and, if a person is safe from sin, he is saved from other dangers and problems!]

33. The merits of Avrohom, Yitzchak, Yaakov, Moshe, and Aharon, our righteous leaders, protected, and keep protecting the *Bnei Yisroel* like powerful weapons!

34. When a non-Jew tasted the *Mann*, it tasted bitter and horrible.

Answers&Facts

---

35. Why did Moshe appoint Yehoshua to combat Amalek?

(Shemos 26:3, Ramban, Pirkei d'Rabi Eliezer, Zohar, K'sav Sofer)

36. Why was Yosef's coffin disrespectfully referred to as "Yosef's bones"? After all, the (holy) bodies of *tzadikim* don't rot, nor do they turn into skeletons!

(Sotah 13b, Shach)

37. How do we see that the women of Klal Yisroel possessed more faith in Hashem than the men?

(Yad Sh'lah 15:21)

38. Why did the sea split when it saw Yosef Hatzaddik's coffin?

(Midrash, Emes L'Yaakov)

---

35. Moshe said, "Let (Yehoshua) the descendant of the one (Yosef) who said 'I fear Hashem', destroy the ones who don't fear Hashem!" Also, the strength of Torah would defeat Amalek, and since Yehoshua was Moshe's most faithful student, he would be the most appropriate general to beat Amalek. Moshe also wanted to prepare Yehoshua for his future responsibility of removing the enemies of the Bnei Yisroel when he became their leader and led them into Eretz Yisroel. Some say that as Yehoshua fought Amalek in this world, Moshe's hands were subjugating the administering angel of Amalek above.

36. Yosef remained silent when his brothers referred to Yaakov Avinu as "your servant." This was considered an act of disrespect to his father's honor. Therefore, he was referred to in a disrespectful way – as "Yosef's bones" – when the Bnei Yisroel took his remains out of Mitzrayim.

37. The women brought out musical instruments from Mitzrayim to sing *Shira*, because they knew Hashem would make great miracles. The men sang, but didn't come as prepared as the women. They did not have musical instruments that would have enhanced their singing to Hashem.

38. It's not natural for a body of water to split. But when the sea saw Yosef's coffin, the angel of the sea deduced that if a boy in his prime – at the age of 17, when the *Yetzer Hara* is so strong – was able to control himself against Potifar's wife and go against his instinct, the sea can also go against its natural instinct and split. It's interesting to note that it was partially because of Yosef that the *Bnei Yisroel* went down to Mitzrayim (since he aroused the jealousy of his brothers who hated him and sold him to Mitzrayim), and ultimately, it was thanks to Yosef that we got out of Egypt and that the waters split.

---

39. From which *aveira* is one unable to do *teshuvah* (return)?

(Mishnah Eiruvin 4:21)

40. How did Pharaoh and Haman benefit us?

(Taam V'daas, Shemos Rabbah 21)

41. Which famous *tzadikim* split bodies of water?

(Chullin 7b, Yehoshua 3:16, Yerushalmi D'mai 3:3, Melachim II : 2, Tanchuma Vayeitzei)

42. When would Moshiach have come if only *Am Yisroel* had sung *shirah*?

(Shir Hashirim Rabbah 4:8)

43. Which three Jewish communities were uprooted when some Jews settled in Egypt?

(Gittin 57a)

---

39. One is not allowed to leave the *techum* on Shabbos (the 2000 *amah* limit starting after the last houses of a city). If one does leave the *techum* on Shabbos, he is punished. He is not allowed to move from that spot until the end of Shabbos. He is kind of "frozen" in his *daled amos* (6 feet); he can't "return" until after Shabbos.

40. Pharaoh and Haman were cruel to us, causing us to humble ourselves before Hashem by doing *Teshuva*. By scaring us, they caused us to come closer to our Father in Heaven. The *Gemara* says that Haman "accomplished" more than all the Prophets that warned the Bnei Yisroel, for the Bnei Yisroel did a complete teshuva in his times!

41. Moshe Rabbeinu split the Red Sea when he took the Bnei Yisroel out of Mitzrayim; Yehoshua split the Yarden River when he brought the Bnei Yisroel to enter Eretz Yisroel; Eliyahu Hanavi split a body of water right before he rose to Shamayim, and so did Elisha after he took over his Rebbe's role. We also find that Rav Pinchus ben Yair split a river on his way to the Yeshiva and to perform a *Pidyon Shevuyim*. The first one mentioned is the Torah is yaakov when fleeing from Eisav.

42. During the days of Chizkiya and Yeshayahu Hanavi, Sancheriv, the king of Ashur, wanted to conquer Yerushalayim, but he and his army were destroyed by a miracle. Had the Bnei Yisroel sung *Shira* to thank Hashem for saving them from that largest army in history, Hashem would have sent Moshiach right away.

43. The Jewish towns of Alexandria, Kfar Sechania, and Kfar D'charia were destroyed because many Jews settled in Mitzrayim and did not sufficiently mourn the *Churban* of the Beis Hamikdash.

Answers&Facts

44. Why did many great Rabbis live in Egypt if the Torah says never to return there?

(Yerushalmi Sukkah 5:4, Ritva, Ridvaz, Shaarei Aharon, Tzitz Eliezer 14:83)

45. Are we permitted to go tour Egypt and see the Great Pyramids in order to thank Hashem for saving us?

(Responsa of the Chavos Daas 3:81)

46. Why are marriage and making a livelihood compared to the Splitting of the Sea?

(Zohar, Sanhedrin 24a, Sotah 32a, Doresh Tov)

47. Why do many Jews feed the birds on *Erev* Shabbos *Parshas Beshalach*?

(Minhag Yisroel Torah)

44. It seems that Rabbi Moshe ben Maimon, the *Rambam,* was forced to live in Egypt to use his skills as a physician to help the sultan. Some *Poskim* hold that the prohibition to go from Eretz Yisroel to Mitzrayim was in force only during the time that the Egyptians were reputed to be the most immoral and perverse society in civilization (*Toras Kohanim P' Acharei* 18). Now that Sancheirev mixed up all the nations of the world during the period of the First Beis Hamikdash, that immoral Egyptian society no longer lives there; therefore, it wouldn't be forbidden to live there nowadays. (My father-in-law, Mr. Aharon Salem, grew up in Egypt. He told us that Goshen still possesses an extraordinary beauty, and tourists are always impressed when they go there.)

45. One is permitted to tour ancient Egypt, assuming there is an experienced armed escort as security from any hostile neighbors.

46. The real miracle of *Kerias Yam-Suf* is not that it split for a second, but that it stayed split for a while. The same is true of marriage: it's not enough to initially be nice to one another; the real job is to always be kind to each other! Making a living is also analogous to Kerias Yam Suf. When the Bnei Yisroel approached the sea, the angel of the sea did not recognize many of them as grandchildren of the *Avos* because they didn't conduct themselves accordingly, and therefore, did not want to split the sea for them. The same holds true with *parnasah:* sometimes a person changes his ways and doesn't act anymore like the same person who originally deserved the money. He therefore needs special mercy from Hashem to receive financial assistance.

47. There were two very wicked Jews, Dasan and Aviram, who did not believe that Hashem would send *Mann* every day to the Bnei Yisroel. They saved

48. Why wasn't it tiring for the Bnei Yisroel to travel through the night?
(Shaarei Aharon)

49. If Hashem hates Amalek so much, why doesn't He just obliterate them in a split second? Likewise, why didn't Yehoshua eliminate them when he battled them?
(Alshich based on Shemos Rabbah, Tanchuma)

50. What would have happened if all the Jews had kept the very first Shabbos after Matan Torah?
(Shabbos 118b)

---

some for the next day, something that Hashem said they shouldn't do. Moreover, they went out with a container to collect Mann on Shabbos. No Mann fell on Shabbos, so they scattered some of the Mann that they had from *Erev* Shabbos around the field to make others believe that Mann did come down that morning. The birds foiled their plans by eating those portions of Mann. We express our appreciation to the birds for preventing this *Chillul Hashem* by giving them food before *Parshas Beshalach*, the *parasha* that discusses the Mann.

48. The Clouds of Glory carried the Bnei Yisroel, and they moved along effortlessly (just like a moving sidewalk). Thus, even traveling at night was easy.

49. Before a nation is defeated, its representative angel in heaven must be defeated as well. The representative angel of Amalek is the Satan (the *Yetzer Harah*) himself. Only when we destroy the Satan who tries to influence us, can we bring about the downfall of his nation, the terrible Amalek! Also Yehoshua could not eliminate the Amalekim, because the Satan was not yet defeated either.

50. Had the entire Jewish people kept that first Shabbos, no nation or people would ever have been able to conquer them. But since Dasan and Aviram went to collect Mann on the first Shabbos, and Tzelafchad desecrated the second Shabbos by gathering sticks, the Jewish people as a complete nation never kept an entire Shabbos. This is very embarrassing, because Shabbos is a gift from Hashem—why didn't many Jews appreciate it? If the entire Bnei Yisroel would keep one Shabbos properly, Moshiach would come and bring the *Geulah* instantly! It is most meritorious to respectfully request of storekeepers who are open on Shabbos to observe this commandment of the Torah. Try to explain to them that Hashem will bless their lives more. Just as one would not stand idly if someone is taking poison, one must not be apathetic to those who transgress the *mitzvah* of Shabbos. Most of the violators never received a proper Jewish education, which is all the more reason to treat them with love and consideration.

Answers&Facts

51. When was it deadly to jump off a diving board by the pool?
(Shemos Rabbah 21:7, Mechilta)

52. How do we know that there will be Techiyas Hameisim (Revival of the Dead) for Am Yisroel?
(Sanhedrin 91)

53. The *Gemara (Taanis 7a)* compares Torah to water! What are some of the similarities between them?
(Devarim Rabbah 7:3)

54. How can we best overcome our Nation's numerous enemies today, like: Sadam Hussein, Hamas, Yassir Arafat, Osama bin Ladin, Hezbala, neo-Nazis etc.?
(Sanhedrin 106, Tanchuma Ki Tetzei, Shabbos 118b, Shemos Rabbah 26:2)

51. When the *Yam-Suf* split, all the waters in the world split - even the waters in people's teacups - in order to publicize the miracle. It showed that Hashem was saving his people and punishing their enemies. Obviously, this would not have been an exciting time to dive off a diving-board when there was no water to jump into; one who would do so would get a "splitting" headache.

52. The *pasuk* says, *"Az Yashir Moshe U'Bnei Yisroel Es Hashira Hazos,"* Moshe and the Jews will sing this song. The future tense of the pasuk implies that not only did they sing it at the Splitting of the Sea, but also they will sing it when Moshiach comes.

53. The Gemara compares Torah to water: Why? a) It gives us life; b) We need it; c) It makes us tahor (spiritually pure) like a mikvah; d) It reaches the low and humble like water that always goes to the lowest point; e) It puts out the *fire* of the *Yetzer Hara*; f) It refreshes us; g) It gets lost if it's not kept in a container (so too, we should take good notes of the Torah so we don't lose it).

54. The Bnei Yisroel are protected from their enemies when they are devoted to learning Torah. Amalek was able to attack the Bnei Yisroel after they left Mitzrayim because they did not continue learning about the mitzvos with the same enthusiasm as before. Yeshivos are our battle fortresses! The Beis Midrash is our "Pentagon!" When Moshe Rabbeinu and later Dovid Hamelech sent soldiers to war, they also sent the same number of Bnei Torah to learn Torah and pray so that the soldiers in battle would be victorious in their merit!

55. Which other time did a pillar of fire extend from Heaven to earth, besides when the Bnei Yisroel were in the Midbar?

(See Tosafos on Berachos 17b)

56. Why may we not ride a horse or camel on Shabbos or on Yom-Tov?

(Mishna Berurah, Mishnas Eliezer on Eiruvin)

57. What lesson should we learn from the amount of Mann the Bnei Yisroel collected each day?

(Abarbanel, Malbim)

58. What "props" did Yirmiyahu HaNavi use when he spoke to the Bnei Yisroel about making a living while being fully devoted to Torah-study?

(Yirmiyah 4:31, Mechilta, Rashi)

---

55. There was a custom during the times of the Gemara for the laymen to come learn Torah with the leading Rabbis during the months of Elul and Adar. It was known as *Yarchei Kalah*. At that time, there was so much Torah study going on that a pillar of fire used to come down from Heaven over their Beis Midrash. The Gemara criticizes the gentiles who lived in the host city Masa Machasya for not converting after witnessing such an awesome miracle.

56. The best-known reason why horse riding is forbidden on Shabbos is because we might come to break a branch (which is forbidden by the Torah to do on Shabbos) to hit the animal to make it go faster. Another reason is that if we would ride a horse or camel, we would be traveling very quickly, and might unknowingly leave the city's techum, which is forbidden to do on Shabbos.

57. Each person received the same amount of Mann no matter how much he collected. Even if he took extra Mann, he still came home with the same amount. The same concept holds true with parnasa. Hashem decides on Rosh Hashanah how much we will earn during the upcoming year. We don't have to be workaholics at the expense of learning Torah and doing mitzvos. If we do Hashem's will, He will provide us with our needs, regardless of how much time and energy we exert ourselves with.

58. Yirmiyahu showed the Bnei Yisroel the clay jar of Mann that was preserved by Aaron Hakohein hundreds of years earlier, to teach them that just as Hashem gave the Bnei Yisroel Mann in the desert, He would take care of all their needs nowadays too if they devoted themselves to Torah.

Answers & Facts

59. What benefit do we get when we say (or sing) Az Yashir daily?

(Zohar, Doresh Tov, Chareidim, Ben Ish Chai, Torah Mi'Tzion, Shemos Rabbah 24:3)

60. How were the protective *Ananei Hakavod* more effective than bullet-proof vests? *(Mechilta 14:27)*

61. Which non-Jews pursued the Bnei Yisroel at the Yam-Suf, but nevertheless, survived the drowning?

(Siftei Kohein 42)

62. Why didn't those Jews who were idolizing *Pesel Michah* (an idol) die while crossing the Yam-Suf?

(Baal Haturim)

63. Why did the Mitzrim merit being swallowed up by the ground and getting a burial? *(Mechilta 15:12)*

---

59. Saying *Az Yashir* with great enthusiasm and appreciation atones for our sins and gives us merit to sing by the *Geulah,* may it come in our time!

60. The *Ananei Hakavod* not only swallowed the arrows of the attacking Egyptians, but they also deflected the arrows back at them! Hashem sent angels to fight for the Jews! May Hashem send our enemies missles, back at them.

61. Pharaoh drafted soldiers from other nations that he ruled in order to overcome the Jews. Those "guest soldiers" were left alive so that they would return home to their countries and relate the greatness of Hashem to their countrymen.

62. There were some Jews guilty of idolatry for worshipping an idol called *Michah,* but were not killed at the *Yam-Suf* together with the idol-worshipping Egyptians. This prevented a *Chillul Hashem,* lest the non-Jews say that Hashem could not differentiate between His people and the enemy.

63. Since the Egyptians showed respect to Yaakov Avinu when they escorted him to his burial place in Chevron, they were given proper burial after they drowned in the sea. The sea kept on spitting them out, so they were washed ashore and covered by the sand. Also, Pharaoh was spared the shame of his soldiers not being buried, since he called *Hashem the Tzadik,* after the plague of *Barad* (Ice-fire Hailstones).

---

64. Why did the wicked nation of Amalek attack the Jewish people?

(Shabbos 118b, Tanchuma, Sanhedrin 106, Shemos Rabbah 26:2)

64. The ruthless nation of Amalek attacked when many Jews were slacking off in their Torah study. Let's not forget that our greatest defense is heartfelt Tefillah and Torah achievement!

Dedicated to

ALL THE CHILDREN OF KLAL YISROEL.
May they grow up in the ways of the holy Torah.
by Mr. and Mrs. David Shwekey, & Mr. and Mrs. David Shriqui,
& Mr. and Mrs. Ezra Debbah

פרשת יתרו

?

1. How were Yisro's sons treated after they converted to Judaism?
(*Zohar 3:196b*)

2. Why did Moshe Rabbeinu request that Yisro help lead the Bnei Yisroel through the desert?
(*Divrei Yoel, Rav Amnon Yitzhak shlita*)

fUNdamental Answers!

"יגעתי ומצאתי!"

(*"I worked on these questions, and I found these answers!"*)

1. Yisro's sons were initially looked down upon since they were sons of an idolater. They therefore left the Bnei Yisroel's camp in the desert and went to study Torah on their own. Hashem saw how they persevered in their study of Torah despite all the hardships they had to endure. He rewarded them by bringing about that their descendants would become outstanding Talmidei Chachomim who became very popular amongst the Bnei Yisroel!

2. Moshe expected to encounter all types of religions while the Jews travelled through the desert. He was afraid they would try to negatively influence the Bnei Yisroel. He offered Yisro the privilege to help him lead the Bnei Yisroel, for he had knowledge of every religion and yet decided that Judaism is the only true religion. He would therefore be the best candidate to keep the evil influences of other cultures at bay by knowing how to refute them.

3. If the *mitzvah* of learning Torah is the greatest of all mitzvos, why isn't it one of the *Aseres Hadibros?*

(Emes V'emunah)

4. Why was the Torah given in the month of Sivan?

(See Sefer Haparshiyos)

5. Why did Yisro deserve such an illustrious son-in-law, Moshe Rabbeinu?

(Mechilta, Rashi Sotah 11, Shemos Rabah 1:26)

6. Why is it that at *Matan Torah*, in addition to hearing the words of Hashem, we saw His words too?

(Torah Sheleimah 78, Torah Mi'tzion; see Rokeach)

---

3. When Hashem stated that He is the One who took Klal Yisroel out of Mitzrayim, He implied that the purpose He took us out was so we should do His will. That automatically requires us to learn His Torah, since only then we can know how to fulfill His will!

4. The zodiac sign for Sivan is twins. This alludes to the tradition that Torah should be learned with a *Chavrusa* (study partner). One must always learn Torah with another person, or at least from the *seforim* written by great Jewish leaders.

5. Yisro saved Moshe's life when he was a child growing up in Pharaoh's palace. Hashem doesn't let any good deed go unrewarded. Moshe eventually *saved* Yisro's daughters from harm too, by way of *midah k'neged midah*. Since Yisro saved the greatest leader the Bnei Yisroel ever had, it was only fitting that he should enjoy a close relationship with him as well.

6. When one sees the letters of Torah it makes him wiser *(Osiyos Machkimos)*. We are fortunate nowadays that many *seforim* and publications are produced with visual aids to help us better understand the *mitzvos*. Some say that seeing the words also symbolized that it is not enough for parents or teachers to preach; the children must see them practicing what they preach! The motto, "Do as I say, not as I do," is unacceptable in successful education. Who knows how much more a child learns by just observing his parents and teachers, than through the material they actually teach! The *Gemara* makes this point by saying, "*Gadol shimusha yoser milimudah.*" It is greater to serve your teachers than to learn from them, because then you have the opportunity to study close-up what they really value.

---

7. How did Hashem show the Jewish people that they are His princes?

(Panei'ach Raza)

8. What did the *Ger Tzedek*, Rav Avrohom Pototsky, Hy'd, (the famous convert, Avrohom ben Avrohom) consider was the main reason why he became a Jew?

(Otzar Hachaim)

9. Why do some Jews know more Torah than other Jews?

(Yalkut Yosef; see Berachos 58a)

10. Why is the *mitzvah* of *Kibud Av V'em* (honoring parents) mentioned next to the *mitzvah* of Shabbos in the *Aseres Hadibros*?

(Baal Haturim, Nachal Kedumim)

11. Why was the Torah given to us on Shabbos?

(Ben Ish Chai, Yerushalmi Shabbos 15, Pesikta Rabbasi 23)

---

7. Every Jew was adorned with two crowns at Har Sinai. This demonstrated our close relationship to Hashem as His princes!

8. Avrohom ben Avrohom (who lived in Vilna during the Vilna Gaon's lifetime) said that he believes there were some non-Jews in the world who really wanted to accept the Torah individually. They were later reincarnated as gilgulim to be given the chance to practice Judaism. He was one of those people. On the other hand, there might have been some Jews that really didn't want to accept the Torah wholeheartedly. Those were the ones who later turned away from Judaism.

9. Some say that your soul was granted Torah knowledge in comparison to the enthusiasm your neshama expressed when it said "Naaseh v'nishmah"!

10. Just as one should think of 'honoring Shabbos' throughout the week by reserving precious items for Shabbos, one should also think all week of ways how to honor one's parents.

11. Shabbos is very holy; therefore, it was the best day to deliver the holy Torah to the holy Bnei Yisroel. It also hints that workingmen should set much more time to learn Torah on Shabbos than they are able to do during the week!

Answers&Facts

12. If Hashem despises *avodah zarah* (idol worship), why doesn't He just make it disappear?

(Mishnah Avodah Zarah 4:7, Tanna d'Bei Eliyahu Zuta 21)

13. What three things did the Bnei Yisroel speak about with Moshe Rabbeinu?

(Ramban, K'sav Sofer)

14. Why did Moshe Rabbeinu originally want to judge the Jews without any assistance?

(Shimush Talmidei Chachamim)

15. Why do the rocks of Har Sinai have lots of thorn bushes on them, still visible even today?

(Megaleh Amukos)

12. Some Greek astrologers challenged the *Tana'im* with this question: "Why doesn't Hashem eliminate all forms of *Avodah Zarah* from the world?" The *Chachomim* answered, "There are idolaters who worship the sun, the moon, and the stars that illuminate the world. Do you want Hashem to destroy the world by removing them?" They then persisted: "At least He could rid the world of the idolatrous objects that *don't* benefit the world?" The Rabbis answered, "Doing that would lend credibility to the ones that weren't destroyed. Hashem lets the world exist in a natural order, and those who sin will be punished!"

13. Jews generally went to Moshe for advice, blessings and prayers, and to learn Torah.

14. Moshe, in his exceptional humility, wanted to personally judge the Bnei Yisroel. He wanted everyone to have a direct association with him, the messenger of Hashem. In addition, it would be better for everyone to hear the holy words of Torah directly from him, and not from someone who heard it from him, thereby eliminating mistakes. Similarly, nowadays, one should try to hear Torah directly from the Rosh Yeshiva and *Manhig* in his generation.

15. The stones of Har Sinai are very distinguishable, even today. They have a greenish-brownish image of a thorn bush all over them. This should remind us of Hashem's special affinity for the humble and the modest!

16. Why did the women receive part of the Torah before the men?
(*Tur, Shemos Rabbah 28:2, Rabbeinu Bachya*)

17. Why did Yisro offer *Korbanos* (sacrifices) when he came to visit the Bnei Yisroel?
(*Ramban, Malbim*)

18. What is the first *mitzvah* you do when you're *Bar/Bas Mitzvah*?
(*See Rambam Hilchos Yesodei HaTorah 1:1, Vilna Gaon, Rav Tzaddok Hakohein*)

19. During which of the Ten Commandments did the entire world shake?
(*Shavuos 39a; see Chayei Adam 5*)

20. How many of the 613 *Mitzvos* can we still perform nowadays?
(*Chofetz Chaim, Rav Saadya Gaon on Shir Hashirim 5:2*)

---

16. Women were given the Torah first, since it is the good wife or mother who can encourage the entire family to learn and keep the Torah! Women by nature are more vigorous in performing mitzvos once they understand them. In addition, when Hashem commanded man (Adam Harishon) the mitzvos without his wife being present, there were devastating results.

17. Some say Yisro offered an Olah as his conversion offering, and a Shelamim as a Todah in appreciation for the miracles that transpired for the Bnei Yisroel.

18. The first *mitzvah* you must perform immediately upon becoming Bar/Bas Mitzvah is to believe that Hashem is the One-and-Only, High Power! Don't take the *mitzvah* of Emunah (belief in Hashem) for granted! The Rambam writes that he enjoyed discussing the *mitzvah* of Emunah more than any other *mitzvah*, for it forms the foundation of our service to Hashem. We recite the Shema morning and night to remind ourselves twice a day that Hashem is our King. We must constantly internalize this belief within ourselves.

19. When Hashem warned us not to mention His Great Name in vain, the entire world trembled, showing the gravity of this sin. Some great tzadikim even have the habit to tremble as they mention Hashem's Name while they daven or say a *beracha*.

20. Of the 613 *mitzvos*, 270 of them are still possible to perform today (approx. 42%)! All the other *mitzvos* will be performed when Moshiach comes - when the Bnei Yisroel will return to do the service of the Beis Hamikdash.

Answers&Facts

---

21. Why are there so many different opinions in *Halacha* (Jewish Law)?

(See Shabbos 139a; Tanna d'Bei Eliyahu Zuta 16:44, Vilna Gaon)

22. Which is greater: to build a *shul*, write a Sefer Torah, or support a Torah Scholar?

(Me'il Tzedakah)

23. Why was the Torah given in the desert before the Bnei Yisroel entered Eretz Yisroel?

(Bamidbar Rabbah 1:7, Eitz Yosef)

24. Which non-Jew was renowned for his exemplary *Kibbud Av V'em?*

(Yerushalmi Peah, Gemara Kidushin 31a)

---

21. We need great merits to fully comprehend the Torah's laws. While we're in *Galus*, due to our many sins, and tragedies that we had to endure, our understanding of the laws has diminished. If we would fear Hashem more, we would better understand the mitzvos, and would not be as confused. Soon when Mashiach comes, Eliyahu Hanavi will come and clarify all our doubts and uncertainties.

22. It is more meritorious to sponsor a Torah scholar's learning (such as one who learns in a Kollel) than to write a Sefer Torah or build a Synagogue! You can remember this rule with the following scenario: If you had to choose between saving a Sefer Torah, a shul or a *talmid chacham*, which one takes precedence? Surely a Jewish person, who is dearer to Hashem than any building or Sefer Torah!

23. The Torah was given on ownerless land to show that Torah isn't limited to the privileged few; everyone can study Torah. In addition, Hashem did not want the Bnei Yisroel to abandon the Torah for financial pursuits. Therefore, Hashem provided them with everything they needed in the desert so that they could delve into His Torah undisturbed by life's many financial pressures!

24. Damah ben Nesinah, a non-Jew, displayed extraordinary respect for his parents. The Gemara lauds him as the role model for this *mitzvah*! He would never cause his parents any discomfort, even if it meant losing an enormous sum of money. As in the instance when the Kohanim sent a delegation to him to purchase a rare and expensive jewel that they needed for the *Choshen Mishpat*. The key was under the pillow, which his father was resting on. He refused to get the key lest he wake his father, even at the cost of losing the enormous profit. Moreover, no matter how despicably his parents treated him, he still treated them with humility and awe. He once was sitting with the dignitaries of the land and his

---

25.
Why did Hashem lift Har Sinai above the Jewish people to threaten them to accept the Torah if they had already lovingly stated *"Na'aseh V'nishmah"*?

(*Maharil, Chofetz Chaim, Tosafos on Shabbos 88a, Tanchuma, Chiddushei HaRim*)

26.
Why did the Bnei Yisroel make a bigger Kabbalas HaTorah at the time of the miracle of Purim than at Har Sinai on Shavuos?

(*Shabbos 88a, Shevuos 39a*)

27.
How do we see that Jewish stories known as *Aggados* endear people to Hashem and His Torah?

(*Rashi, Rav Nachman of Breslov*)

---

mother went over to him, spit at him and hit him over the head with her shoe. She dropped her shoe and he picked it up and handed it back to her. She then threw his wallet in the river and he still didn't offend her. He held his father in such high regard that he treated him as if he were divine. When his father died, he placed his favorite chair in a temple because he felt it was too special to remain in his house. Surely *Chazal* could have found a Jewish person who excelled in this *mitzvah*, but they used a non-Jew as an example to illustrate that even common sense should dictate that we should treat our parents with utmost respect and honor.

25.
It's true that the Jews accepted the Torah happily. However, Hashem threatened them by suspending the mountain over their heads to make them realize the seriousness of this union between Hashem and the Jewish People. They needed to accept the Torah out of fear, and not solely out of love! True, serving Hashem out of love is superior to serving Hashem out of fear, but you need both emotions. Also, they had to be coerced into accepting the Torah She'baal Peh (Oral Law), as it is the indispensable commentary to the Torah Sheb'ksav (Written Law). Finally, they needed to realize that a life without Torah is as if one is dead and buried!

26.
On the sixth of Sivan, Shavuos 2448, the Jews accepted the Oral Torah (Mishnayos & Gemara) mainly out of fear of Hashem. However, on Purim 3406, the Jews recommitted to the Torah She'baal Peh out of their love to Hashem! Naturally, serving Hashem out of love is far superior.

27.
Yisro was moved to convert to Judaism after Moshe recounted to him the amazing story of Yetzias Mitzrayim. As the legendary storyteller, Rabbi Hanoch Teller says, "There's nothing like a great story to *wake up* the soul!"

Answers&Facts

28. In what tone and in which language did Hashem speak the first *Dibros?*

(Shemos Rabbah 29:1 and 28:6)

29. Where did the Jews find a *mikvah* to purify themselves before *Mattan Torah?*

(See Seder Hadoros)

30. Can you say the *Kiddush* on Shabbos in English, Spanish, French or in any other language?

(See Tosafos on Sotah 41a and Tiferes Yisroel)

31. What was the color of the *Luchos* (tablets)?

(Ohr Hachaim on Devarim 11)

28. Each person heard Hashem's voice in the tone that he/she would best appreciate. Men prefer one tone, women like another tone, and youngsters like a third one, so Hashem enabled each person to hear His voice in the tone that would best resonate with them. The key to effective teaching is to teach in the tone students will want to hear and appreciate. Remarkably, another miracle occurred - Hashem's voice was heard simultaneously in all seventy languages!

29. Hashem made a river flow by *Har Sinai* in which the Jews could immerse themselves before receiving the Torah. Purity is a prerequisite to attaining Torah scholarship. The power of the *Mikvah* cannot be overstated. Just as a non-Jew can rise to the status of a Jew with just one immersion, a Jew can rise to much higher spiritual heights every time he immerses as well!

30. Technically, Kiddush may be recited in any language. After all, you recite Kiddush so you and your family can internalize Hashem's awesome power - to create and maintain the complete universe, and you may choose to do this in your natural tongue. However, the custom is to say it in Hebrew as a preventative measure for those who would wish to reform the Torah.

31. The *Luchos* were sapphire (blue). (Perhaps Hashem's throne and the sky are also blue, so that we should always be reminded of *Matan Torah!*)

32. Why did Hashem start the Ten Commandments by saying, "I am Hashem Who took you out of Mitzrayim…," wouldn't it have been more powerful to say, "I am Hashem Who created the world!"?

(Aruch Hashulchan)

33. Which two *tzaddikim* were buried beside Har Sinai?

(Seder Hadoros 2448)

34. Why won't a non-Jew be able to excuse himself for not keeping the *"Sheva Mitzvos B'nei Noach"* (The Seven Noachide Laws) by saying that "no-one ever told me about them"?

(Ran; see Makkos 9b)

35. Why was Har Sinai chosen as the site for *Matan Torah?*

(Sotah 5a, Bereishis Rabbah 99:1, The Midrash Says)

---

32. Hashem did not start the Ten Commandments by saying that He created the world, because many nations already believed that; they just claimed that Hashem lets the world run on "autopilot" since creation and doesn't run the world on a day-to-day basis. Therefore, Hashem mentioned that He took the Bnei Yisroel out of Mitzrayim to emphasize that He Himself is in complete control of everything that occurs in day-to-day life, for He manipulated the laws of nature to bring each Makkah.

33. Rav Saadia Gaon and Rav Hai Gaon are buried right next to Har Sinai.

34. The seven mitzvos of the non-Jews are really common sense, so how could they excuse themselves by claiming,"We didn't know?" Of course one must figure out that: 1) There is a G-d, 2) Who demands justice, 3) No cursing of Heaven, 4) No stealing, 5) No immoral activity 6) No killing, 7) and no persecuting creatures unreasonably!

35. Many high mountains had Avodah Zarah erected upon them, so they were disqualified to be the platform for Matan Torah, whereas Har Sinai was a lower mountain that was never used for worship. The Gemara says that all the mountains fought amongst themselves for the honor to be the stage where Hashem revealed Himself to man, but Hashem chose the humble one, Har Sinai, instead.

Answers&Facts

36. Which four sculptures may never be made together?
(Rosh Hashanah 24b, Tosafos on Yoma 54b)

37. Who is guaranteed to merit the crown of Torah?
(Kli Yakar in his Derush L'Pesach)

38. How do we see the importance of being quiet when a Rabbi or teacher is talking?
(Shemos Rabbah 29:8, Mili d'Avos)

39. Why did the angels want to keep the Torah in heaven?
(Shemos Rabbah 28:1, Dubno Maggid, Shimush Talmidei Chachomim)

40. Why doesn't the Torah begin with the Ten Commandments?
(Rashi to Bereishis 1:1, Mechilta)

---

36. We are not allowed to make a sculpture of a man, lion, eagle, and ox alongside each other. Since these were chosen to be on Hashem's throne, we don't want anyone to mistakenly think of them as being divine.

37. Someone who travels away from the comfort of his own home to acquire Torah knowledge will merit that he or his son will receive the crown of Torah! That is why it is a time-honored practice to go "out of town" to learn in Yeshiva.

38. Just as Hashem quieted the whole world when He spoke to Klal Yisroel, not even allowing an echo to emanate from His voice, so too, teachers, who impart the sweet, holy words of Torah to the Bnei Yisroel, need absolute silence when they teach their students!

39. The angels did not want humans to receive the Torah, because they felt that man would not know how to sufficiently honor it.

40. The Torah does not begin with its 613 laws, because Hashem wanted to first illustrate that He created this entire world for the Bnei Yisroel to keep the Torah and give Him His due honor. Rashi adds another reason: If the non-Jewish nations ever accuse the Jews of stealing Eretz Yisroel from the nations that had previously lived there, the Jews can respond, "The Torah says Hashem created the world; He decided to give Eretz Yisroel to us."

41.
Is a Jew allowed to learn secular wisdom?
(Amudei Olam quoting Chida)

42.
In learning Torah, which is greater: "quality", (in-depth knowledge) or "quantity" (knowing a lot)? (או בקיאות)
(סיני או עוקר הרים or בעיון)?
(See Berachos 64a; Chikrei Lev)

43.
What are the frightening statistics about students' success in Torah?
(Rashi to Koheles 7:28, Baal Haturim, Haamek Davar, Pele Yo'etz)

44.
Which seven *mitzvos* can we – and must we – perform continuously?
(Chayei Adam, Kitzur Shulchan Aruch of Rav Raphael Baruch Toledano zt'l)

---

41. One should not spend time studying secular wisdom unless it will directly enhance his service of Hashem.

42. Some suggest that *before* the advent of the printing press, the quantity of wisdom was more important since seforim were so rare. Nowadays, one really could look up any topic with the proliferation of *seforim* in Judaica stores and libraries; therefore, qualitative wisdom is superior. We must try to seek out a Rav who possesses both strengths who we can rely on to teach us authentic Torah applications to practical life.

43. Global statistics of Torah achievement and scholarship are heartbreaking. It was said in the olden days that out of a 1000 students entering a Yeshiva, only 100 students would know Mishnah, and 10 out of 1000 would know Gemara and 1 out of 1000 would know Halacha! Oy vey, who knows what the statistics are today? Case in point: Of the 524 chapters of Mishnah, how many chapters does the average teenager know? It is *yechidei segulah* (special individuals) that struggle to master all the various parts of the Torah. There are some optimistic authorities who believe that nowadays the odds are better, since Hashem has great pity on a Dor Yesomim.

44. The seven mitzvos that we must strive to perform all the time are: Belief in Hashem; denial of all foreign deities; to do everything solely for Hashem's honor; to love Hashem; to fear Hashem; not to look at immoral things; and to love every Jew!

Answers&Facts

45. What should one do if he does not understand Torah?
(See Niddah 70b)

46. Why is it most wise and virtuous to hire tutors to teach your children Torah?
(Gemara Beitzah 16a, Vilna Gaon, Ben Ish Chai, Mili d'Avos, 1:6, Maasei Tzadikim)

47. Why is it said, that we have "*Sheva Mitzvos from the Rabbanan*" (Seven *mitzvos* that *Chazal* instituted), if really we have so many more?
(Shimush Talmidei Chachamim)

48. When do the stones of the *Mizbeiyach* cry?
(Gittin 90a)

---

45. If one does not understand Torah, he should: a) Find a better teacher; b) concentrate better; c) pray to Hashem; d) give tzedakah, but, most importantly, e) never give up!

46. Unfortunately, teachers all too often cannot give enough individualized attention to each and every student. This causes many children to develop low self-esteem, poor confidence, and mediocre accomplishments. It is very helpful for a child to get extra coaching from a talented tutor. The *Talmud* tells us that a father will be handsomely reimbursed for any expenses he spends on teaching his son Torah. One mother related that the reason she merited a son who is a reputable *Gadol Hador* is because "even when we didn't have money to put bread on the table we still hired a *melamed* to teach our son Torah." [It should be stated that by no means should a tutor substitute for the father who *could* teach his son. Rather, the tutor should be the extra coach to help complete the task when the father is preoccupied.]

47. The Rabbis instituted countless mitzvos and halachos. But they instituted seven mitzvos upon which we make a *beracha*: *Hallel, Birchos Hanehinin* (berachos that we make on food), *Netilas Yodayim, Megillas Esther, Ner Chanukah, Nairos Shabbos,* and *Eruvin.*

48. The stones of the Mizbeiyach cry when a man divorces his wife.

---

49. Who died at Har Sinai sanctifying the Name of Hashem? Why?

(Bais Tefillah Tehillim 119)

50. After concluding *Shemoneh Esrei,* we say *Yehi Ratzon.* Why do we *first* ask there that the Beis Hamikdash should be rebuilt and *only then* do we ask for our due portion of Torah?

(Ben Ish Chai on Vayishlach 1:11)

51. When were Yisra'elim called Kohanim?

(Shemos 19:6; see Shmuel II 8:18)

52. From where do we learn that you should always begin a conversation with a peaceful introduction?

(Shabbos 89a, Avos 4:20)

---

49. Chur was killed at *Har Sinai* when he tried to defend the honor of Hashem by protesting when the Bnei Yisroel worshipped the *Eigel*, the Golden Calf. His death was not in vain. In the merit of his extreme loyalty to Hashem he merited to have a descendant [Betzalel] who made the Mishkan, which atoned for the sin of the Golden Calf.

50. We pray that we should receive our portion of Torah only after we pray that the Beis Hamikdash should be rebuilt, because we cannot really know many halachic decisions of the Sanhedrin, nor can we perform most of the mitzvos until the Beis Hamikdash is rebuilt!

51. Hashem called the Bnei Yisroel, "*Mamleches Kohanim*" (Kingdom of Priests). This gesture of honor shows the importance of every Jew. We also find that Dovid Hamelech's sons were so distinctly praised – they were called Kohanim - even though they descended from *Shevet Yehuda*.

52. When Moshe welcomed his father-in-law Yisro, the Torah says that he started the conversation with peaceful pleasantries before he told him about Hashem's great miracles. Peace is so important, that Moshe started with it even before telling of Hashem's greatness! Even when Moshe went up to Heaven, Hashem commented that Moshe should say *Shalom* to the angels. The *mishnah* in *Pirkei Avos* insists that we should always greet people by saying, *Shalom*. It's a pity how often people don't take the extra second or two to give Shalom or say "Hello" to one another! Are we strangers in our own families?!

Answers&Facts

---

53. When were all the handicapped people healed?

(Rashi, Mechilta; see Gur Aryeh)

54. Why didn't Rav Shmuel bar Sheilas inspect his garden for thirteen years?

(Pele Yo'etz citing Gemara Bava Basra 8b)

55. Why is it customary to *"shuckle"* when learning Torah?

(Baal Haturim, Rama Orach Chaim 48:1, Sefer Chassidim, Sh'lah, Kaf Hachaim)

56. How could the Bnei Yisroel have overslept that awesome morning of *Matan Torah* when they knew that Hashem would speak to them?

(Pirkei d'Rabi Eliezer 41)

57. Why do Jews have the custom not to sit on their knees?

(Emes V'emunah)

53. All blind, deaf, crippled, and ill people were healed at *Matan Torah*. This shows that when we follow the Torah faithfully, we bring wellbeing to the world, besides receiving our due reward in *Olam Habah*.

54. Rav Shmuel bar Sheilas was the Rebbe *par-excellence*! His *talmidim* were such a priority to him, that he avoided tending to his own needs out of his total devotion to his *talmidim*. Rav once saw him in his garden and asked him why he was not in school teaching. He replied, "For thirteen years I did not see my garden, and even while I am in it, my mind is thinking of my *talmidim*!"

55. When Hashem gave the Torah to the Bnei Yisroel, they all trembled. It is customary to '*shuckle*' (sway) while we learn to demonstrate our awe of Torah. In addition, one must really learn Torah with a *bren* (fiery passion) and get himself physically involved in his learning for it to really refine his character! The swaying is also symbolic of a flickering flame since Torah is compared to fire.

56. Hashem had to wake up the Bnei Yisroel with thunder so they could receive His Torah. They slept because they assumed the best way to receive the prophecy of Hashem's revelation at Har Sinai would be in a semi-conscious state.

57. The Jewish custom is not to sit on our knees, even while playing on the floor. The idolaters worshipped *Avodah Zarah* while sitting on their knees, and we don't want to do anything that is associated with *Avodah Zarah*.

58. Why did Hashem let the Bnei Yisroel see His honor if it was too much for them to handle, to the point that they had to be revived?

(Shemos Rabbah 29:4)

59. What does the *pasuk* mean when it says that we are Hashem's *segulah*?

(Onkelos)

60. Which seven prophets did Hashem send to the non-Jews to offer them the Torah?

(Bava Basra 16b)

61. How can we thank Hashem enough for the gift He gave us, His Torah?

(Toras Chinuch)

62. When does one really start learning Torah?

(Toras Chinuch, see Gemara Taanis 7a, Makkos 10a)

---

58. Hashem knew that some Jews were going to worship *Avodah Zarah* and defend themselves by saying, "If only we saw Hashem's honor and heard His voice, we wouldn't have sinned". Hashem therefore let them feel His Presence at *Har Sinai*, to refute that claim. In addition, Hashem wanted to demonstrate that it is not an exaggeration when it says in *Tehillim* (19-8): "Hashem's Torah is perfect; it revives the spirit!" [Literally.]

59. The Jewish people are Hashem's favorite people. He cherishes us!

60. Hashem sent the *non-Jews* the following seven prophets to offer them the Torah: Eliphaz, Tzofar, Bildad, Elihu, Iyov, Be'or and Bilam. All the nations rejected the offer, but the Bnei Yisroel accepted it. We must never forget our commitment and our good fortune!

61. The best way to show Hashem gratitude for granting us His wonderful Torah is by sharing it with others, as often, and as best we can!

62. The Gemara says that one will learn most when he starts to teach others. As one Rabbi put it: "I learned much from my Rebbi, more from my *chavrusas* (friends), but I learned the most from my students!"

Answers & Facts

63. Which three famous non-Jews converted to Judaism after being awed by the miracles Hashem did for the Jews?

(Shemos Rabbah 27:4)

63. When the nations of the world heard of the miracles that transpired for Am Yisroel at *Yetzias Mitzrayim*, some converted. Yisro joined Klal Yisroel when he heard of the miracles of Yetzias Mitzrayim. When Rachav heard of the miracles that occurred when the Bnei Yisroel were on the way to Eretz Yisroel, she converted. The Queen of Sheba visited in the days of Shlomo Hamelech. Hashem loves converts so much that He sent down a "V.I.P." portion of Mann after the regular time it came down each morning just for Yisro!

Dedicated in Honor of our parents and grandparents
MR. & MRS. ISAAC AND EMELIE MOGRABY
AND
MRS. MARGALIT SASSON
By Moshe and Rachel Shaya-Mograby and children

פרשת משפטים

1. How much is one fined if he insults a *Talmid Chacham*?

   (*Rambam Hilchos Chovel U'mazik 3:5,6*)

2. In which case is one liable only for damages that occurred at night, and not for those that occurred during the day?

   (*Mishnah Bava Kama 5:6*)

fUndamental Answers!

"יגעתי ומצאתי!"

("*I worked on these questions, and I found these answers!*")

1. Insulting any person is a terrible sin, especially when he is a *talmid chacham* who must be treated with great honor! If someone insulted a *talmid chacham*, Beis Din would fine him a minimum of five gold coins.

2. If someone digs a pit on public property and an animal falls into it, he is responsible to pay for damages incurred only if an animal fell into it at night. If the animal fell into the pit during the day, he can claim, "The animal should have looked where it was going!"

3. When does someone gain by losing?

(See Berachos 5a, Kiddushin 24b, Bava Kama 62b)

4. Someone who borrows something from his friend or neighbor is liable for damage that's incurred, even if the item was accidentally damaged. When would a borrower be exempt from paying for accidental damage?

(Bava Metzia 95b)

5. When was ear piercing a *mitzvah*? Why?

(Rashi 21:6)

---

3. There are many examples where people gain by losing: A) The victim of a robbery loses something valuable. However, if the thief is caught, he must pay back double the item's value to the owner. Hence, he gains by losing! B) A Non-Jewish slave goes free if his Jewish owner damages any of his main organs. He, too, gains by losing. For instance, if he loses a finger, he gains his freedom. C) A third scenario deals with suffering. Every person who suffers gains with their discomfort, because the pain and suffering saves one from the punishment of Gehinnom. Even a small amount of suffering in this world deducts a large amount of suffering in the next world.

4. If you borrow something from someone, and that lender is working with you with his object (*ba'alav imo*), you are exempt from paying if that borrowed item was accidentally damaged. Perhaps this is because the lender should have been watching his possession too.

5. The Torah permits the sale of a Jew as a slave in two instances: Bais Din, the court, sells a Jewish thief who has no means to pay back what he stole, and, one can sell himself for money. A Jewish slave would work for six years and go free the seventh year. If after the six years had passed the servant refuses to go free for he loves his master and the accommodations he gave him, the owner would take him to a door, near the *mezuzah*, and pierce his ear. He then continues working until Yovel. The ear is pierced to admonish him that had he been attentive and listened to the Torah, he would not be a slave. If he was sold as a slave for stealing, his ear did not listen to the words of Hashem by Har Sinai, "Do not steal". If he enslaved himself to make money, his ear did not hear that Hashem says, "You are my servants, and not servants to others!" (Vayikra 25:55). Also, the ear piercing served as a warning to others to watch out for a thief. (It is interesting to note that males, who pierce their ears nowadays for immoral purposes, also imply that they are slaves—to their own desires!)

---

6. Is one allowed to sue for trauma that he endured in a car accident, G-d forbid?

(See Bava Kama 84a)

7. Why is one required to pay four or five times the value of what he stole when he steals a cow or sheep and sells or slaughters it afterward, but not when he steals another item?

(See Bava Kama 62b, Taam V'daas quoting Moreh Nevuchim, and Torah Temimah)

8. From which people may we not buy merchandise?

(Bava Kama 10:9)

9. How do you clarify this paradox: The *Mishnah* says: one must take it *slow* when deciding a Torah law, yet the *Gemara* says, one should be *fast* to relate Torah to anyone who inquires about it?

(Mili d'Avos 1:1)

---

6. One can sue for the pain and suffering that he endured in an accident. Although taking legal action is permitted, a lawyer must be careful not to take more money than is truly deserved.

7. The cow and the sheep were the two main resources through which a person earned his livelihood. The cow provided five benefits to its owner: milk, meat, leather, working the field to plant and then afterwards to harvest the crop. The sheep did not work but it provided milk, meat, wool and leather. The Torah punishes a thief four times or five times these animals value for stealing someone's means of support. This alerts a person to keep away from stealing another person's *parnasah* (livelihood).

8. It is forbidden to buy stolen goods from a thief, for the buyer becomes an accomplice in the crime. Our Rabbis also forbid buying wool, milk and kid goats from shepherds, for we suspect they have stolen the merchandise. They also did not permit buying wood or fruits from fruit watchmen, for they suspected them of dishonesty.

9. Hashem wants every single Jew to be well versed in all the areas of Torah so he can answer any question swiftly and sharply. However, one should think twice before answering a halachic question - even if he is well versed in Torah - so that he shouldn't make a careless mistake.

Answers & Facts

10. Why doesn't Beis Din, nowadays, extract the original five standard payments for injuries, namely:
    a) *Nezek* - depreciation;
    b) *Tzaar* - trauma;
    c) *Ripui* - medical bills;
    d) *Sheves* - unemployment;
    and e) *Boshes* - degradation?

(See Shulchan Aruch Choshen Mishpat 420)

11. If a thief stole wood and made a chair with it, must he return that chair, or just the value of the stolen wood?

(Mishnah Bava Kama 9:1, Gemara Succah 31a)

12. A Jewish girl may be sold as a Jewish-maidservant when she is under Bas Mitzvah. Why can't a minor boy be sold as a Jewish-servant?

(Seichel Tov based on Mechilta)

10. Beis Din today does not have the authority that it once had. Therefore, we cannot demand of people to pay the original standard of injury payments. Beis Din nowadays will negotiate and compromise regarding how much the culprit must pay.

11. Ideally, a thief should be required to take apart the chair or the house that he made from the stolen hardware. However, the Rabbis felt that this would discourage thieves from returning the stolen items and doing *teshuva*, so they allowed him to pay the monetary value of the stolen item instead.

12. One of a girl's primary missions in this world is to perform chesed (kind deeds), as she does when she raises a family. A boy's main purpose in this world is to study Torah. A young girl who is sold to help her father's financial struggle is performing an act of chesed to her family, for the extra money would be a great asset to her family due to its precarious financial situation. However, a boy, whose main purpose is to learn Torah, must not be sold as a slave in order to alleviate his family's financial crisis, for when will he get his Torah training? When will he educate himself as a knowledgeable Torah Jew to someday build his own family according to the Torah's guidelines if he doesn't learn at a young age?

13. How much money must one pay if he embarrassed someone by: Slapping? Pulling hair? Twisting an ear? Spitting? Or uncovering a married woman's head?

(Bava Kama 83b; see Rambam Hilchos Chovel U'mazik 3:9)

14. How far must you keep your barbeque grill away from your neighbor's property?

(Mishnah Bava Kama 6:4)

15. Why would someone not want to purchase a Jewish maidservant?

(See Tanna d'Bei Eliyahu Rabbah 23:4)

16. When would a Jewish father need to sell his daughter as an *amah* (Jewish maidservant)?

(See Kiddushin 20a)

---

13. If a person screams in someone's ear, he must pay him a *selah* (a coin used in the time of the Mishnah). If he slaps him, he pays him 200 *zuz*. If he backhandedly slapped him, he gives him 400 *zuz*. If he pulled his ear or his hair, or if he uncovered a woman's hair in the market, he must pay 400 *zuz*. In certain instances it's not enough to say you're sorry after the attack; you must pay a fine to appease the abused victim.

14. The Mishnah mentions different opinions regarding how far you must keep your own fire from your neighbor's property. Some say you must make a clearance of 137 *amos* (205 feet), others say 16 *amos* (24 feet), while some say 50 *amos* (75 feet). The Mishnah concludes by saying that, actually, it depends on how big the fire is. The fire department can tell you the state regulations, too. Note: the first Tanna's opinion of 137 *amos* mirrors the sign on many fire trucks that says to keep 200 feet away.

15. The Torah suggests that the person who purchases the Jewish maidservant should marry the girl, or marry her off to his son. However, since having a second wife would cause ill will among both wives, one would not want to put himself in a situation that would require him to marry another woman by buying a maidservant in the first place.

16. If a person is too stingy to give the Kohanim and the Leviim their rightful share in his crops, Hashem would make him poor, and he would have to sell his daughter as a means of income. Even if it costs money to give these gifts, it is more expensive not to give them!

Answers & Facts

17. In what way is a Jewish servant considered a master?

(Kidushin 22a; see Tosfos there quoting Yerushalmi; Rambam)

18. How is it possible that two adults commit the same crime, with the same intentions, yet one is punished with death, while the other pays money?

(See Shemos 21:15, Teshuvos HaRosh – K'lal 11, and Teshuvos Maharil 51)

19. Why are *we* fortunate that a non-Jewish-slave earns his freedom with the loss of a limb?

(See Berachos 5a)

20. If a young child breaks something, must he pay for it when he grows up after he becomes Bar Mitzvah?

(Mishnah Berurah 343:9, Bach and Taz there, Choshen Mishpat 424:8; see Bi'ur HaGra there)

21. Do women have the *mitzvah* of *Hashavas Aveida* (returning a lost article)?

(See Shita Mekubetzes on Bava Kama 54b; Chinuch)

---

17. The Torah warns a master that he should treat his Jewish servant with more respect and dignity than he treats himself! For example, if the master owns only one pillow, he is required to give it to his servant.

18. If two people bruise the same person, and one is the victim's adult son while the other is a stranger, the son is killed and the stranger must pay for the damage.

19. If a Canaanite slave - who is never supposed to be released – still earns freedom after suffering, certainly a Jewish person who suffered in this world will be free from punishment in the World to Come!

20. After one becomes *bar mitzvah*, he should try to pay for anything he may have previously damaged. Even though he is technically not liable, he should nevertheless do *Lifnim M'shuras Ha'Din* - more than the law requires.

21. Some say that women are exempt from returning lost articles, since it is not proper for a woman to knock on doors to find the owner. Others maintain that she is responsible to return lost items.

22. Does one fulfill the *mitzvah* of *Azov Ta'azov* (helping your fellow man) if he helps someone push his or her car out of the snow?

(See Rambam's Sefer Hamitzvos: Negative Commandment #270)

23. When did a cow cause a non-Jew to convert to Judaism?

(Midrash Aseres Hadibros, Pesikta Rabbasi 14)

24. From where does the *Gemara* learn that one should rather do a favor for an enemy than for a friend?

(See Bava Metzia 32b)

25. If an animal swallowed your cell-phone, how much does its owner have to pay you?

(Mishnah Bava Kama 2:2)

---

22. Just as it is a great *mitzvah* to alleviate a person's aggravation by helping him get his animal up and going again, it is surely a great *mitzvah* to jump start another person's car or push it out of the snow. An organization called Chaverim was founded to help get cars going especially after an upsetting flat tire.

23. A rabbi once sold his cow to a non-Jew, and the cow refused to work on Shabbos. The Torah commands all Jewish owners to let their animals rest on Shabbos, so the cow was used to not working on Shabbos. The non-Jew came to the rabbi to return the cow since he was not getting a full week's work out of it. The rabbi told the non-Jew that he might be able to fix the problem. He whispered into the cow's ear that now he is permitted to work, since he belongs to a non-Jew. The cow then started to work. The non-Jew was so inspired that an animal kept Shabbos. "If an animal can honor Shabbos," he reasoned, "surely the human being, who is superior to the animal kingdom, must surely honor the Maker of the world!" He became a Ger and eventually became a great Rabbi! He was called Rabbi Yochanan ben Torta (Torta means ox in Aramaic).

24. The Gemara tells us that if you have a choice between helping your friend who needs you to help him unload his animal that is collapsing under its heavy burden, and, your enemy who needs your help loading an animal, you must help the enemy first! Even though the friend's animal is in distress and the Torah tells us not to cause undue pain to an animal, the Torah says that it's more important to overcome the Yetzer Hora's (evil inclination) urges, and make peace with an enemy!

25. If an animal consumes something inedible, the owner must pay half its value. Since an animal doesn't normally eat such things, it is considered an unusual manner of damage.

Answers&Facts

Questions & Riddles

26. How many times does the Torah repeat the warning to respect and love a convert and not hurt him in any way?
(Midrash Halachah)

27. Why does a Jewish man who stole and became an *eved* (slave) have to marry a Non-Jewish maidservant if his master wants him to?
(Choreiv-Rabbi Samson Raphael Hirsch zt'l)

28. When should a person imagine himself as a poor man?
(Rashi to 22:24)

29. On which day of Sivan was the Torah given, the sixth or the seventh?
(Yoma 4a)

30. We generally follow the majority in Jewish law. (For example, by *shechitah* where we must cut two pipes in the animal's neck, it is sufficient if one is fully cut and

---

26. Several times the Torah warns us to love and respect a convert. A convert naturally feels uncomfortable in his new surroundings, so the Torah warns us repeatedly to make him feel at home. Many times even Jews feel uncomfortable with their fellow Jews who come from different backgrounds. Sometimes an Ashkenazic Jew feels out of place in the company of Sephardic Jews, and vice versa. We must strive not to be prejudiced, and to make each other feel comfortable. After all, *"Achim Anachnu!"* (We are brothers!) Spare our fellow Jew culture shock!

27. The Jewish slave who stole might have assumed that he did not have to be careful with the *mitzvos bein adam lachaveiro*, between him and his fellow man. Maybe he felt satisfied that he only keeps *mitzvos bein adam lamakom*, between him and Hashem. We therefore humble him by showing him that *kedusha* is also earned by caring for your fellow man. Since he was dishonest, he is on a lower spiritual level, and is given a non-Jewish maidservant to bear children for his owner.

28. When one gives *tzedaka* (charity) or a loan to one in need, he must feel as if he was in that needy situation himself. As the saying goes, "Put yourself in his shoes!"

29. The Rabbis are uncertain whether the Torah was given on the 6th or the 7th of Sivan.

30. When the Torah gives a specific number, such as four corners for *tzitzis*, we do not say that you follow the majority.

---

304 » *TorahShows' Questions & Riddles* ■ *Mishpatim*

most of the second one is cut.) So why don't we follow the majority to okay a *Tallis* even if one corner is *pasul*, or to validate a Mikvah even with just 21 *se'ah* out of the required 40, or 20 lashes to suffice for the 39 *malkus*?

(See Sefer 'Middos V'Shiurei Torah' quoting Chasam Sofer and Rav Chaim Brisker)

31. Why does the Torah say that one who damages another persons eye has to pay "An eye for an eye," if it does not literally mean that? *(Rambam)*

32. Which *mitzvah* does a *G'mach* (Free Loan Society) manager do so often? *(Sefer Hamitzvos #66)*

33. Yehoshua camped by Har Sinai during the forty days the Torah was being given. Why did he stay there all alone for almost six weeks? *(Rashi, Shimush Talmidei Chachamim)*

34. Which non-Jewish-slave deserved *"semicha"* (Rabbinical ordination)? *(Tiferes Yisroel on Berachos 2:6)*

---

31. The Torah is implying to the perpetrator that had Hashem wished He could punish him "measure for measure". If he damages someone's eye he might lose his own eye. The Torah gives him a chance to do *teshuva* by allowing him to pay money. If he does not do a perfect *teshuva*, he might end up losing his own vision.

32. It is a big *mitzvah* to lend poor people money. G'mach's (free loan organizations) often save the day. It is truly praiseworthy to set up such a fund throughout every Jewish community. Jewish bankers should speak to a competent Posek to understand the *heter iska* and its limitations to avoid lending with interest.

33. To the devout student, it is not a wonder why he should try to live close to his Rebbe. However, to a common person, it may sound odd why Yehoshua would stay away from his family and Klal Yisroel for so long, alone by the mountain, waiting for his Rebbe. The truth is that a devoted student cannot part from his Rebbe! He feels that even if he is able to get an extra thirty minutes walking down the mountain with his Rebbi, it is well worth the wait.

34. Tevi, the servant of Rabbi Gamliel, was a true *talmid chacham*. He was even worthy of Semicha. It is no wonder that he merited such greatness, because he always tried to be close to his Rebbe. (The Mishnah in Sukkah (2:1) notes that he wanted to sleep in the Sukkah under a bed just to be close to his teacher and master.)

Answers&Facts

35. Why did Rabbi Eliezer free his non-Jewish-slave when he entered a Shul?

(Berachos 47b)

36. Which *mitzvah* in this week's *parsha* helped a man who died come back to this world?

(Visions of Greatness vol. IV, Shemos 22:21)

37. Why don't we wear Tefillin all day long?

(Pesikta Rabbasi 22)

38. Which aveira does one transgress if he disrespects a Rebbe or a Torah Scholar?

(See Moshav Zekeinim 22:27; sefer Hamitzvos #71)

39. In one place, the Torah says to return your enemy's lost object, while in another place, it says to return your brother's lost object. Why does it switch?

(See Meshech Chochmah)

35. Rabbi Eliezer freed his non-Jewish slave in order to complete a *minyan*. Imagine giving up hundreds and thousands of dollars of potential service just to make a *minyan*!

36. The *mitzvah* of helping a widow by providing for her needs is so great that it can increase someone's lifespan. There is a remarkable story of a person who was virtually dead, but the Beis Din Shel Maalah let him come back to this world since he had done such a great chesed by supporting a widow.

37. The Torah says, "You should not take the Name of Hashem your G-d in vain." Our Rabbis feared that if someone wears his *tefillin* all day he might sin with the Name of Hashem upon him. In order not to risk this, we don't wear *tefillin* all day.

38. If someone disrespects a Torah scholar he transgresses the *mitzvah*: "The prince of your people you should not curse."(22-27)

39. The first time the Torah mentions the *mitzvah* of returning a lost object, it speaks of returning it to your enemy, because this was said when the Torah was given. At that time, all the Jews adhered to the Torah, so the only one who deserved the title, enemy, was someone who went against the Torah. Once the Bnei Yisroel worshipped the Eigel though, who are they to refer to someone who does not keep the Torah as an enemy, when they themselves committed such a terrible act against the Torah!? Thus, after the giving of the Torah we must be more tolerant and truly look at each other as brothers, not as enemies.

40. What is the fine for the owner of a *mu'ad* (warned-bull) that killed someone?

(Tosafos on Bava Kama 27a)

41. From where do we learn that we must make blessings before performing many mitzvos?

(See Mili d'Berachos 35a, Yerushalmi Berachos 10:1, and Torah Temimah; Rashba)

42. A non-Jewish-slave goes free when he gets injured. Which type of injury sets him free?

(Rashi to 21:26)

43. Which *mitzvah* demands that things must be done in the right order?

(Sefer Hamitzvos #72; See Mishnah Horiyos 3:7)

44. Did Moshe Rabbeinu "physically" go up to *Shamayim* (Heaven) to receive the Torah?

(See Michtav M'Eliyahu 3:172; Succah 5a)

---

40. Beis Din decides in each case how much one should pay if his *mu'ad* animal killed a person after they had warned the owner to execute the bull.

41. If we make a blessing on food [Birkas Hamazon], which only nurtures the body, then certainly we should make a blessing when we learn Torah and do *mitzvos*, which nurture the soul! There are some *mitzvos* that we do not make a blessing on, because they are dependent on another person, such as charity or Kibud Av V'em (Honoring your Father and Mother). In such cases, how can we make a *beracha* if the person on the receiving end might not accept it? Nevertheless, we must still realize that we should be grateful for every *mitzvah* that we can do!

42. A non-Jewish slave is set free if his owner caused him to lose a limb or organ that cannot be replaced, such as an eye, a tooth, a finger, a toe, an ear, his nose or his *milah* organ.

43. The Torah requires that a crop owner give his first teruma to a Kohen, then maaser to a Levi and the poor. One must stick to the order that the Torah gives and may not give to the Levi before giving to the Kohen. The Torah teaches us to get our priorities straight. It also reminds us who deserves more credit. The Kohain serves in the Beis Hamikdash, so he goes first. The Levi sings in the Beis Hamikdash so he gets next; everybody comes after them.

44. Hashem gave Moshe the Torah in heaven. There is a question amongst the *Meforshim*, whether it was Moshe's spirit or his actual body that went up to Heaven.

Answers&Facts

45. Why did Moshe need to be on Har Sinai for forty days and forty nights without eating?
(Tanna d'Bei Eliyahu)

46. How was Moshe Rabbeinu's prophecy superior to that of all the other prophets?
(Rambam)

47. If a doctor accidentally killed a patient, is he required to go to an *ir miklat*, a City of Refuge?
(Rashi to 21:14)

48. How many *dafim* (pages) are there in the Shas Bavli (Babylonian Talmud)?
(See ArtScroll's "Great Chassidic Masters," pg. 140)

45. It takes forty days for a fetus to develop as well as for a person to develop a new habit. When Moshe Rabbeinu defied the laws of nature and went up to heaven to learn Torah with Hashem for forty days, he demonstrated that he was absolutely superior to any other person. The fact that he didn't eat while in heaven symbolized that one should not run after physical pleasures if he really wants to achieve spiritual accomplishments!

46. When a prophet heard Hashem, he fell into a comatose deep sleep, because the experience was too overwhelming for him to take standing up. Moshe Rabbeinu, however, was able to stand and converse with Hashem as if he was talking to his best friend.

47. A doctor that accidentally kills a patient is not required to run to a City of Refuge. (We don't want to discourage anyone from entering an idealistic profession.)

48. There are 2,709 *dafim* (double-pages) of Shas. That makes 5,418 *amudim* (pages). The great sage, Rabbi Meir Shapiro h"yd, suggested that devoted men learn a folio (two pages) a day. By sticking to that pace, they will be able to complete Shas every seven and a half years, and celebrate one of life's greatest challenges and accomplishments, and be best prepared for this world and the World-To-Come!

49. Why do Jews follow the *Bas* Kol, the heavenly voice, which said, "The *halachah* is like Beis Hillel", but not the *Bas Kol* that said, "A certain *halachah* was like Rabbi Eliezer"?

(Tosfos on Bava Metzia 59a)

50. How frequently should one go to visit his Rebbe?

(Midrash Halachah, Ritva on Rosh Hashanah 16b)

51. When would someone be exempt from payment for injury, even though he ran into someone and damaged him?

(Mishnah Bava Kama 3:6, Rambam Hilchos Chovel U'mazik 6:9)

52. What must a damager do *after* he pays for the injuries of someone that he has harmed?

(Mishnah Bava Kama 8:7, Rambam Hilchos Chovel U'mazik 5:9)

---

49. Beis Hillel generally had the majority over Beis Shamai, so we apply the rule that we follow the majority, whereas when Rabbi Eliezer argued with the Chachamim, they were the majority, so the *halacha* should really follow their opinion.

50. Some say a Jew should visit his Rebbe everyday to clarify all the Torah questions he has that day. Others say that one should visit on *Chagim* (Holidays). Some point out that visiting on the holiday doesn't apply today because that was only an obligation in the time of the Beis Hamikdash. Nevertheless, it is imperative to have a constant association with a fine Rav. It is a sin to be too bashful and apprehensive to ask *shaylos* and guidance from the Rabbi.

51. One is encouraged to run when it is close to *Bein Hashemashos* (twilight) on Friday evening, lest he desecrate the Shabbos. If such a person accidentally bumped into someone at that time, he is exempt from paying for damages.

52. After one pays for the injuries he caused, he must ask forgiveness as well. The Torah teaches us not to physically or emotionally hurt another Jew!

53. In which three instances would the Sanhedrin (High Court) lock someone up in jail? *(Rashi, Sanhedrin chapter 9)*

54. What must you do to when using a microwave for heating up meat and dairy separately? *(Yalkut Yosef)*

55. When is one exempt from paying for burning up another person's money? *(Mishnah Bava Kama 6:5)*

56. What does the *Mishnah* mean when it says regarding women and children that their contact is bad; isn't that prejudice?

(Mishnah Bava Kama 8:4)

53. If someone kept on transgressing a sin that is punishable by *kareis*, even after getting *malkus*, Beis Din locked him into a tight jail and fed him barley until his stomach burst. This punishment also applies if a person killed someone and there were no valid witnesses who saw the crime. (For example, they saw the murder take place but their testimony is invalid because of technical issues: they were watching from different windows, or they didn't give him the required warning.)

54. It is preferable to have separate microwaves. If a person has only one, he can use that same one if he cleans it thoroughly before using it for meat after dairy, and vice-versa. Some put soap-water in the oven and boil it for a number of minutes before putting in the other type of food. Regardless, you should then double-wrap the food before placing it into the microwave.

55. If someone sets fire to someone's house, he is only responsible to pay for visible items, such as furniture. The Torah exempts him from paying for anything hidden. However, he may be liable in the Heavenly Court.

56. A woman doesn't possess her own money, for her money belongs to her husband (according to the Gemara). A woman therefore can't pay for her own damages. In addition, children aren't mature enough to be held responsible for their actions. Chazal therefore warned that getting into an accident with women or children is very harmful, since if you hurt them you have to pay them, but if they hurt you, they are exempt!

57. Why is a pit-digger or someone who places a stumbling block on the road, exempt from paying if *keilim* (utensils) were damaged by that pit?
(Mishnah Bava Kama 5:6)

58. When are you permitted to kill someone?
(Gemara Sanhedrin 72a, Mishnah Sanhedrin 8:7)

59. How do we know that a father loves his son more than a son loves his father?
(Mishnah Sanhedrin 8:6)

60. How do we see the Torah has pity on everyone's honor — even a thief's?
(Bava Kama 79b)

61. How does Hashem test the rich and the poor?
(Shemos Rabbah 31:2)

---

57. One is only responsible for direct damages incurred; the breaking of utensils in the pit is considered indirect damage, and the courts cannot hold a person liable for such damage. (He will, however, be held liable by *dinei Shamayim*, the Heavenly Court.)

58. You are permitted to kill someone in self-defense. However, if you can save yourself by just injuring the other party, (i.e. by shooting the attacker in the leg) then you are required to do so.

59. If a father was breaking into his son's house through a tunnel in order to steal, the son may not kill his father in self-defense, since we know that a father would not kill his son under any circumstances. On the other hand, if a son was breaking in through a tunnel to steal from his father, the father may kill him in self-defense if he believes that his son would kill him in the process.

60. The Torah's fines are commensurate with the humiliation the thief had to endure while committing the crime. When one steals a sheep and slaughters or sells it, he only pays four times the value, whereas if he does the same with a cow he pays five times more, for there is more shame in hauling sheep than leading a cow.

61. Hashem challenges everybody! The rich person is tested to see if he will open his hand and his wallet to assist the poor. The poor person is tested if he will accept the suffering and react positively to it. Lucky is the person who

62. What underlying message did Hashem give Moshe when He said that He would send an angel to lead the Bnei Yisroel?

(Tanchuma)

passes life's tests! If the wealthy one passes his test and gives charity, he will enjoy prosperity in both worlds. Similarly, if the poor person accepts his fate with a smile, he will be similarly rewarded in Gan Eden. But if the wealthy person is stingy and turns away from the needy, he may lose his money. The world rotates a "wheel of fortune" ; the rich man may not necessarily be rich tomorrow, nor will the poor man today be poor tomorrow. Hashem can switch their positions!

62. When the Bnei Yisroel originally accepted the Torah, Hashem Himself went before them to protect them. After they sinned with the Eigel, Hashem told Moshe that they don't deserve His personal guidance anymore. He would now treat them like the Gentile nations by giving them an angel to look after them. It is incumbent upon us, again, to accept Hashem's *mitzvos* favorably no matter the hardship so that Hashem Himself protect us in this painful *galus*, and bring the ultimate *Geulah Shelaima!*

Dedicated in loving memory of my wife
AVIVA YOCHEVED RUCHAMA BAS SIMA CHAYA A"H
and L'ilui Nishmas my father
ZECHARYA BEN YEDIDYA A"H
Dr. Elliot Ghatan and family

Questions & Riddles

?

1. Why were the *Keruvim* atop the *Aron Kodesh* formed with childrens' faces? *(Sefer Chassidim, Chochmah U'Mussar)*

2. Why did Hashem command the Jews to build Him a Mishkan? *(Shemos Rabbah 33:1)*

FUNdamental Answers!

"יגעתי ומצצאתי!"

("I worked on these questions, and I found these answers!")

1. The golden Aron Kodesh held the Luchos that Hashem gave to Moshe on Har Sinai. The Aron was placed in the holiest place in the world, the Kodesh HaKodashim, to signify that one achieves closeness to Hashem through learning Torah. The Keruvim, two angelic figures, adorned the top of the Aron Kodesh. Their faces resembled those of children, one boy and one girl, representing the inherent purity that children possess. Hashem placed their figures on top of the Aron Kodesh to express His special love for the Torah study of pure children. In fact, Chazal stress that the entire world exists in the merit of *tinokos shel beis rabban*, young Yeshivah students!

2. Hashem loved the Torah so much that He could not part with it when He gave it to the Bnei Yisroel. The Midrash expounds on this concept with a beautiful *mashal*: A king married off his only daughter to a prince who lived in a far away land. The king pleaded with his new son-in-law, "I can't part from my only daughter! Please build a little chamber for me next to your palace so I can visit you." Similarly, Hashem said to the Bnei Yisroel, "I can't part from the Torah which I gave to You. Please make a home for me (the Mishkan) so I can reside near you!"

3. Why was the *Aron Kodesh* missing from the second Beis Hamikdash?

(Yoma 21a, Ben Ish Chai)

4. When will a stream of water flow from the *Kodesh Kodashim* (Holy of Holies)?

(Yechezkel 47:2)

5. Will the final Beis Hamikdash be built by humans?

(Rashi to Rosh Hashanah 30a, Tosafos on Succah 41a, Tanchuma, Shavuos 15a, Rambam, Ritva, Rav Shimshon Pinkus zt"l)

6. Why was Betzalel chosen to build the Mishkan (Tabernacle)? After all, he was just a *Bar Mitzvah* boy at that time!

(Tanchuma on Vayakhel, 4; Shemos Rabbah 40:1 and 48:3: Sanhedrin 69b)

3. The Aron symbolizes Torah study, and the Aron's absence in the Second Beis Hamikdash symbolized a serious decline of Torah wisdom at that time. For example, the Kohanim who served in the Second Beis Hamikdash were not as proficient in Torah knowledge as those who served in the first Beis Hamikdash. Many of the later Kohanim were amei ha'aretz (ignorant), who were imposters and some did not believe in the Torah. This was a great pity, since Kohanim are supposed to be extremely devoted to Hashem and to learn Torah diligently.

4. A stream of water will flow from the Kodesh HaKodoshim to the entire world when Moshiach builds the Third Beis Hamikdash. The water will heal the sick and will make all salty waters sweet. This stream will demonstrate to all that Hashem, whose Shechinah rests in the Kodesh Kodoshim, is the source of all life and blessing.

5. The Rabbis disagree about who will build the Third Beis Hamikdash. Some say that it will be built by humans. Others believe that it is being built in Heaven, and it will descend from Heaven surrounded by fire. Our tradition teaches that we can help build the heavenly Beis Hamikdash! Every time we perform a mitzvah and learn Torah, a brick is added to the Beis Hamikdash. Conversely, whenever we do an aveirah—especially Bitul Torah - a brick is removed, thereby postponing its construction! Rabbi Shimshon Pincus zt"l said that the Beis Hamikdash in Heaven will descend to the one below, just like the soul descends into the body!

6. Betzalel, the Mishkan's chief architect and builder, was Chur's grandson. Chur was murdered as he protested the terrible acts of those who built the Eigel (the Golden Calf). Hashem does not let a good deed go unrewarded; He prom-

7. At first, Nosson HaNavi had authorized Dovid Hamelech to build the first Beis Hamikdash. Why, then, did Hashem tell Nosson to hurry and stop him?

(Rashi to Shmuel II 7:4)

8. In earlier days, Tu B'Av was a joyous day on which people would get married. Why did Chazal make such a holiday immediately after Tisha B'Av, the saddest day of the year?

(Toras Ha'olah expounding Taanis 26b)

9. Why was Moshe's Mishkan buried and hidden away?

(Tanna d'Bei Eliyahu 18:34 and 25:12, Sforno)

---

ised Chur that his grandson will build the Mishkan. Betzalel was also Miriam's great-grandson. Betzalel, Dovid Hamelech and ultimately Mashiach, descended from Miriam in reward for her unwavering fear of Hashem when she helped the Bnei Yisroel give birth in Mitzrayim, in defiance of Pharaoh's orders.

7. One of Dovid Hamelech's outstanding characteristics was that when he came up with a plan to honor Hashem, he immediately got to work at it. In fact, he would swear that he would neither eat nor sleep until he fulfilled the *mitzvah*. Hashem therefore told Nosson to rush immediately and tell Dovid that he will not build the Beis Hamikdash. "Dovid Hamelech doesn't hesitate when he undertakes a project in My honor," Hashem explained to Nosson. "Stop him before he contracts all the builders to build the Beis Hamikdash. I don't want him to lose their respect or incur a financial loss."

8. On Tisha B'Av, we mourn the destruction of the Beis Hamikdash, Hashem's home on this world. Even though Hashem's home no longer exists, Chazal point out that Hashem's *Shechinah* can reside in every Jewish home. People would marry on Tu B'Av, shortly after Tisha B'Av, to express to Hashem that even though He does not have a permanent home on earth, we nevertheless want Him to reside in our homes. When Jews get married, they form new homes in which Hashem can reside!

9. Moshe's Mishkan was much holier than the Beis Hamikdash. The Mishkan was built exclusively by the Bnei Yisroel, whereas the Beis Hamikdash was built by non-Jewish workers as well. In addition, those who donated in a more wholehearted fashion to the Mishkan than those who donated to the Beis Hamikdash. The Beis Hamikdash was therefore eventually destroyed by non-Jews. One's intent for the *mitzvah* makes it more holy! Also, the wood for the Mishkan was from Yaakov Avinu, and in his merit it will be everlasting.

10. The Aron Kodesh consisted of three boxes: two golden boxes and one wooden one. Why was the wooden box placed in between the two golden boxes?

(Ohr Hachaim, Rabbi Yitzchak Schwartz shlit'a, Chizkuni, Torah Sheleimah)

11. Why did the Menorah have seven branches?

(See Menachos 28a; Toras Ha'olah quoting Be'er Heitev in Orach Chaim 1:6)

12. Why is the Kosel Hama'aravi (Western Wall) the only surviving wall from around the Beis Hamikdash?

(Aggadah Atikas Yomin)

13. Why did Moshe tremble when Hashem commanded the Jews to make Him the Mishkan as a "home"?

(Shemos Rabbah 33:1 and 34:3; Pesikta)

---

10. Gold is a precious and beautiful resource. The Torah is priceless and beautiful too, so it is placed in a golden box. However, gold is not a living object. It doesn't grow or bare fruit. A wooden box, which was comprised of living matter, was sandwiched between the golden boxes. This implies that Torah must be learned in a lively manner, with enthusiasm ("*mit a bren*") that encompasses one's entire being!

11. The Menorah represented wisdom, which is symbolized by light. The seven branches of the Menorah correspond to the seven main branches of the Torah: Chumash, Navi, Kesuvim, Mishnah, Gemara, Halachah, and Kabbalah. One must try to excel in all areas of Torah, and the Be'er Heitev wrote that one should give great priority to Mishnah, the center light.

12. The Kosel Hama'aravi was donated by the poorest Jews. This wall was most dear to Hashem for these people donated with a great sense of humbleness, love and sacrifice for the *mitzvah*. Hashem swore that His *Shechinah* (Divine Presence) would never leave that wall! [Interestingly, many enemies have tried repeatedly to destroy it, yet it stands defiantly!]

13. Moshe trembled and asked, "How can Hashem, Who encompasses the entire universe, fit into a home?" Hashem answered, "You do your part to make Me a home, and I will dwell in it!" In Hashem's supernatural love for Am Yisroel He miraculously focuses His *Shechinah* (*kaviyochol*) to be near us!

---

14. How did the *Keruvim* express Hashem's warm relationship with the Jewish People?

(Bava Basra 99a)

15. What did the *Keruvim* do before the Beis Hamikdash was
destroyed?

(Yoma 54a; See Rabbeinu Chananel; Meam Loez)

16. Why was the fire upon the mizbeiyach shaped like a
"lion" during the First Beis Hamikdash, and shaped like a
"dog" during the Second Beis Hamikdash?

(Yoma 21b, Harei Besamim)

17. Which *mitzvah* was performed seven times in history?

(Sefer Haicha Timtzah-Rabbi Mordechai Weintraub shlit'a, Zevachim 118b)

---

14. When the Jews were following Hashem's Will, the Keruvim faced each
other. If, however, they were not following His Will, the Keruvim turned
away from one another. On the Yomim Tovim the Jews saw them hug!

15. When the Bnei Yisroel obeyed Hashem's Torah, the golden Keruvim would
face each other. If they disregarded the Torah or did not get along with each
other, the Keruvim would miraculously turn away from each other. As the Beis
Hamikdash was to be destroyed, the Keruvim were about to turn away from each
other, as a sign that Hashem was upset with His people. Before doing so, they
hugged each other one last time and then turned away. Their actions expressed the
fact that even though Hashem was angry with His children and had to destroy the
Beis Hamikdash, nevertheless, He still loves them! (Rabbeinu Chananel explains that
when the Gemara says that the non-Jews saw the Keruvim hugging each other it
refers to a design on the wall, not the Keruvim on the Aron Kodesh.)

16. The head of a person, which houses the brain, symbolizes the neshamah,
man's spiritual side, while the body symbolizes man's physical side. A lion's
head is the largest part of its body, while the rest of its body is much narrower. A
dog's head, in contrast, is narrow as it is proportioned to its body. During the First
Beis Hamikdash, the Jews were more spiritually focused, as signified by the lion's big
head. During the second Beis Hamikdash, there was a decline in appreciation for
spirituality for the people attended to their physical needs just as much as their spiritual needs; therefore, they were compared to a dog whose size is symmetrical.

17. The *mitzvah* "Make Me a Sanctuary so that I may dwell in your midst..." was
ultimately performed seven times in history, each time the Bnei Yisroel built a
Mishkan or the Beis Hamikdash. The Mishkan was built five times: in the Midbar,

Answers&Facts

פרשת תרומה ■ ושננתם לבניך » 317

18. Why did the Mishkan collapse when the Bnei Yisroel tried to set it up?

(Shemos Rabbah 52:2, Tanchuma on Pekudei 11)

19. Why was the Mishkan only erected in Nissan if it had been completed in Kislev, four months earlier?

(Pesikta Rabbasi 6, Tanchuma on Pekudei 11)

20. How were the Kohanim able to walk on the *Mizbeiyach Hanechoshess* (Copper Altar) without burning their feet from the heat atop the *Mizbeiyach*? In addition, why didn't the fire melt its copper plating over time? After all, metal is a good conductor of heat!

(Rabbeinu Bachya, Tosafos on Chagigah 27a, Tanchuma 11)

Gilgal, Shilo, Nov, and Givon, plus the two Battei Mikdash that stood in Yerushalayim. [Note: When a new shul is built it is also a fulfillment of this *mitzvah* to some degree, since a shul is a *Mikdash Me'at*, a miniature Beis Hamikdash.]

18. The Bnei Yisroel tried repeatedly to erect the Mishkan, but they could not get it to stand! Only Moshe Rabbeinu, with his tall stature and great spiritual and physical strength, was able to set it up properly. This showed the Bnei Yisroel that you cannot build a dwelling for Hashem (or any project for that matter) without the support, assistance and approval of the leading Rabbis.

19. The Bnei Yisroel completed building the Mishkan by the 25th of Kislev. However, the Mishkan was not set up until the month of Nissan, for Hashem told the Bnei Yisroel to wait for the month in which Yitzchak Avinu was born. Yitzchok Avinu, who willingly went to the *akeidah*, is our greatest role model of someone who was willing to sacrifice *himself* for Hashem. Hashem wanted to impress upon the Jewish People that every person should dedicate his life to His service through learning Torah and listening to the word of Hashem, and not feel content by merely sacrificing animals, birds, and flour offerings as *Korbanos*.

20. The holy fire that burned on the *Mizbeiyach* was a special fire that would not harm a human being! In fact, this fire burned continuously on the Mizbeiach for hundreds of years and never melted the *Mizbeiyach's* metal.

---

21. How do we see that it's important to learn with a *chavrusah* ("learning friend")? How do we see its valuable to sponsor Torah programs?

(Sefer Chassidim, Chida)

22. Why were the broken *Luchos* also kept in the Aron Kodesh?

(Tanchuma 7)

23. Why was the "Mishkan" called by that name?

(Shemos Rabbah 35:4)

24. Why wasn't Rav Hoshiya impressed with the extravagant *Batei Ke'nesios* (Synagogues) that Rabbi Chama showed him in Lod?

(Yerushalmi Peah 8:8)

---

21. The *Keruvim* on top of the Aron Kodesh were two angelic figures that faced each other. This symbolized that Torah that was placed inside the Aron Kodesh, should be learned with another person, in a group, or, most importantly, with a Rebbi! Some commentaries say that when we learn from good *sefarim* it is considered as though we learned with a good *chavrusa* (learning partner). The Keruvim also symbolized the Yissachar-Zevulun team (where someone commits himself to support a *talmid chacham*) that makes Torah scholarship attainable. Hashem showed that both partners are equally important!

22. Hashem wants us to accord more honor to Torah scholars than to a Sefer Torah itself! The Gemara in *Makos* (22b) states, "How foolish are the Babylonians who stand up for a Sefer Torah but won't rise for a Talmid Chachom!" When a *Talmid Chachom* ages he might forget what he learned, and people might disrespect him. The broken Luchos were also kept in the Kodesh Kodoshim, in a place where they will be honored, to symbolize that we must honor a *talmid chacham* even though he is now "broken" due to old age or illness.

23. The word Mishkan in Hebrew consists of the same letters as *Mashkon* (collateral). Hashem said the Mishkan and both Battei Mikdash would serve as collateral. If the Bnei Yisroel sin, Hashem would take them away instead of wiping out the Bnei Yisroel. Moshe asked Hashem: "What will serve as collateral once the Mishkan and the Mikdash have been destroyed?" Hashem answered, "I will take one *tzaddik* (i.e. he will die) and I will forgive all their sins." In fact, Chazal say that the death of a *tzaddik* is more painful than the destruction of the Beis Hamikdash!

24. Rabbi Hoshiya was dismayed that community funds were used to build very expensive buildings as houses of worship and study. He felt that they should

Answers&Facts

25. Why was the *Aron Kodesh* measured in halves: 2½ *amos* by 1½ *amos* by 2½ *amos*?

(Me'am Lo'ez, Kaf Hachaim 1:31, K'sav Sofer)

26. How did the *Pirchei Kehunah* (young Kohanim) support themselves with "grapes of gold"?

(Yoma 39b, Mishnah Middos 3:8, Tiferes Yisroel)

27. Which extraordinarily colorful creature existed only until Moshe Rabbeinu's time?

(Shabbos 28b, Koheles Rabbah 1:28, Tanchuma 9, The Family Midrash Says on Shmuel II and Melachim I)

build simple buildings and use the remaining money to support Torah scholars so they will have the means to study Torah day and night and teach the holy Torah to the entire community. This would be far more beautiful to Hashem than some extravagant building that remains empty most of the day and doesn't house teams of Torah scholars who are constantly learning!

25. The Aron Kodesh's half measurements remind us that we should never feel content with our Torah knowledge. We should always feel that we have only attained "half" (actually, a fraction) of what we are capable of knowing. There is still much more Torah to learn no matter how much we already know, for Torah is *"wider than the earth and deeper than the ocean!"* We must therefore go to the Torah scholars to better educate ourselves and attend all types of Torah classes in order to enrich our wisdom and fear of Hashem. Approach rabbonim, ask and apply their instructions. The halves also remind us that we should always be humble, not arrogant.

26. Vines of gold grapes hung atop the entrance to the Beis Hamikdash. These golden vines would miraculously grow as if they were real plants! The *Pirchei Kehunah* (young Kohanim) were allowed to pluck a gold grape off the vine, sell it, and support themselves as a reward for serving in Hashem's Palace!

27. The Sasgona was a unique, multi-colored animal. Its hide, which featured a beautiful array of colors, was used to cover the Mishkan. This creature only existed until the time of Moshe Rabbeinu. It was created exclusively for Hashem's Mishkan and it became extinct thereafter. The name Sasgona is actually a play on words; it means that it rejoices over its colors. Every Jew possesses many hidden talents. Like the colors of the Sasgona, we should all develop these talents and use them for Hashem's honor!

28. Why wasn't Dovid Hamelech allowed to build the Beis Hamikdash?

(Shmuel II chapter 27, Anaf Yosef on Berachos 3a, Yalkut Shemoni)

29. Why did a Kohen pass away after he discovered the secret hiding place of the Aron Kodesh?

(Re'vivan Shekalim 6:2, Yoma 54a)

28. Hashem didn't want David Hamelech to build the Beis Hamikdash for the following reasons:

A. The Beis Hamikdash represents *Shalom*, peace. Since Dovid fought in many battles, it was not appropriate for something that brings peace to the world to be built by someone who fought in battle. Although the wars he fought were *milchamos mitzvah* since he was fighting the enemies of the Jewish people, the Beis Hamikdash needed to be made by someone who represented peace, like Shlomo Hamelech, at a more peaceful era

B. Dovid's Beis Hamikdash would have been built with such holiness that Hashem would never have destroyed it. Hashem knew that it was to the Jewish people's advantage that the Beis Hamikdash could be destroyed. Instead of directly punishing the Jews, Hashem would destroy the Beis Hamikdash.

C. When Dovid killed the Philistine giant Goliath and won many battles, Jewish women threw money and valuables at him. He collected these riches and stored them for use in the Beis Hamikdash. Once, when the Bnei Yisroel were suffering from hunger and famine, and poor people needed additional charity, Dovid refused to give the money that he had allocated for the Beis Hamikdash to them. Hashem did not want the Beis Hamikdash to be built with those funds because *it is more important to give tzedaka (charity) to the poor than to build the Beis Hamikdash!* (Note: Although the Navi (Shemuel II 8:15) does explicitly praise Dovid Hamelech's generosity and philanthropy; Chazal point out that he erred in not using the "Beis Hamikdash Fund" since it should have been used to help the poor instead.)

29. Many years before the destruction of the Beis Hamikdash, King Yoshiyahu hid the Aron Kodesh, so that it wouldn't fall into enemy hands again. A Kohen once found the secret hiding place of the Aron Kodesh. He died before he got a chance to reveal its whereabouts to others, lest the gentile invaders find it and desecrate it. The Aron Kodesh was actually under one of the tiles of the wood storage room in the Beis Hamikdash. Rabban Gamliel and Rav Chananya's respective families would bow when they passed by the wood room of the Beis Hamikdash in reverence for the Torah Hakedoshah inside the Aron Kodesh that was hidden there!

30. On which place was Hashem's *Shechinah* (Divine Presence) centered in the Mishkan?

(Shemos Rabbah 34:1, Gemara Berachos 8a)

31. What miracle occurred with the poles of the Aron Kodesh every Yom Kippur?

(Yoma 54a; See Yerushalmi Yoma 1:4; Menachos 98, Yerushalmi Bava Basra 6:2)

32. When would all the Bnei Yisroel actually see the Aron Kodesh inside the Kodesh Kodoshim?

(Yoma 54a)

33. Why did Hashem create gold?

(Shemos Rabbah 35:1)

---

30. Hashem centered His infinite Presence on the small space of an amah by an amah above the Aron Kodesh. His *Shechinah* is also in the place where Torah law is being studied intensely!

31. The poles of the Aron Kodesh stretched from one wall of the Kodesh Kodoshim to the other. The Kohen Gadol had no room to reach the Aron when he entered the Kodesh Kodoshim on Yom Kippur. It seems a miracle occurred: he walked right through the golden poles! This teaches us that one should never despair, "How can I learn the entire Torah? There's no way I can grasp it all!" Hashem will make a miracle, if necessary, for anyone who wants to reach His Torah! The Chida writes: "I know many people with outstanding abilities that did not develop into *talmidei chachomim*, and many people with limited capabilities who worked hard to learn Torah, and became exceptional Torah scholars!"

32. The *Paroches* (curtain separating the Aron Kodesh from the rest of the Beis Hamikdash) would be lifted during the *Shalosh Regalim* (Pesach, Shavuos and Succos), so the Bnei Yisroel could see the Aron Kodesh in the Kodesh Kodoshim. Can you imagine the *chizuk* (encouragement) the Bnei Yisroel received when they saw the Keruvim facing each other, which demonstrated Hashem's tremendous love for His people!

33. Hashem created gold only because it was going to be used in the Mishkan and Batei Hamikdash!

---

34. From were do we see that Hashem loves to see us work hard?

(Avos d'Rabi Nosson 11)

35. How should we be like the Keruvim?

(Taam V'daas)

36. Which Jews used to fly (even before the Wright brothers invented the airplane in 1903)?

(Yehoshua 3:13, Shemos Rabbah 36:4, Sotah 35a)

37. How can your own body be a Mishkan (dwelling place) for Hashem?

(Chida in Tziporen Shamir 218)

38. Where is the Aron Kodesh today?

(Shoshanim L'Dovid Shekalim 6:1, Maharsha on Yoma 54a)

---

34. The Torah says, "The Bnei Yisroel worked to make the Mishkan." Only *then* did Hashem's Presence dwell with them. We see that Hashem loves when people work! (Chazal say that *Adam l'amal yulad*, Hashem created man to work. This doesn't mean that one should work to the point where he neglects his family and spiritual manners, it means that idleness is dentrimental since it ievitably causes one to come to sin).

35. Just as the golden Keruvim were designed with their wings spread upward and their faces toward each other, a Jew should focus heavenward to honor Hashem by doing *mitzvos*, and, at the same time, respect his fellow man. One is equally obligated to follow the mitzvos between God and man and between man and his fellow man. A person cannot truly be considered a complete *tzaddik* unless he constantly fulfills both types of *mitzvos*!

36. The Kohanim that 'carried' the Aron Kodesh were not actually carrying it; it carried them! This became obvious when they got to the Jordan River: the Aron Kodesh just floated over the water while they held on.

37. The Chida dramatically connects each component of the Mishkan to its correlating organ in the human body, (the range of which is beyond the scope of this book. Check it out & enjoy!) One example is with the Keruvim's wings. They imply that your arms should be like wings hovering over students to teach them the Torah.

38. Some say that the Aron Kodesh is located in a tunnel under the Har Habayis. Others say that the enemy captured it when they destroyed the Beis Hamikdash and it's now hidden at the Vatican in Rome.

Answers&Facts

39. Why did Uzah die instantly when he tried to protect the Aron Kodesh from accidentally falling?

(Shmuel II 6:7, Tanna d'Bei Eliyahu 29, Sotah 35a)

40. Why did the roof of the Mishkan consist of so many beautiful colors?

(Emes L'Yaakov, Rabbi Yitzchak Feitman shlita)

41. Which Mesechta of Shas has been described as a story?

(Tosafos Yom-Tov's introduction to Mesechta Middos)

42. From where did the Bnei Yisroel acquire the jewels for the Mishkan?

(Yoma 75a, Shemos Rabbah 35:8)

43. When did Hashem tell Moshe to build a Mishkan — before the Eigel or afterward?

(Tanchuma 8, Tanna d'Bei Eliyahu 17:12, Taam V'daas; see Bamidbar Rabbah 12:6, The Midrash Says)

39. Dovid Hamelech led the Bnei Yisroel to bring the Aron Kodesh back to Yerushalayim in an elaborate procession accompanied by music, singing and dancing. They mistakenly put the Aron Kodesh on a new wagon drawn by cows, instead of carrying it themselves as befitting such a holy vessel. One cow stumbled, and it appeared as though the Aron would fall. Uzzah grabbed on to the Aron Kodesh to protect it. He was killed immediately. Uzzah committed a Chillul Hashem because he made it appear as if the Torah needs help, when, really, we need the Torah to help us through life!

40. The Bnei Yisroel are comprised of many different types of Jews: Some specialize in *tefillah*, others in learning Gemara, and others in *chessed* (charitable work), etc. This shows that we are a nation of many colors, so to speak. The colorful roof of the Mishkan served to demonstrate to Hashem that His people are beautiful when considering the complete spectrum of the Bnei Yisroel.

41. Mesechta Middos discusses the various areas in the Beis Hamikdash and their functions.

42. Precious jewels descended with the delicious *mann* every morning. The *tzadikim* gathered them for use in the future Mishkan.

43. There is actually a difference of opinion regarding when Hashem commanded Moshe to build the Mishkan. Some say that Hashem invited the Bnei Yisroel to make Him a Mishkan as a reward for joyfully accepting the Torah and saying "Na'aseh v'nishmah". Others believe Hashem gave the *mitzvah* to rectify the

44. Did Klal Yisroel accept money from non-Jews to build the Second Beis Hamikdash?

(Ezra 4:3)

45. Where does Hashem consider the ideal place for His Shechinah (Hashem's Holy Presence) to dwell?

(Alshich, Sh'lah, Baal Haturim, Nefesh Hachaim Shaar 1:4, see Bach Orach Chaim 47)

46. How was it decided where the money that one donated was to be used?

(Taam V'daas, Maharil Diskin, Lekach Tov)

47. Who said *"Vei!"* ("Alas!") when the Mishkan was completed?

(Bamidbar Rabbah 12:7)

48. How long did it take the Bnei Yisroel to make the Mishkan?

(Shemos Rabbah 52:2, Seder Hadoros)

Chillul Hashem that resulted when they made the *Eigel*. These commentaries maintain that the Torah was not written in chronological order; therefore, the Torah states the commandment to build the Mishkan even before the *Eigel*.

44. Only donations from Jews were accepted by Ezra Hasofer for the Beis Hamikdash.

45. Hashem doesn't want His presence to rest only in a building as magnificent as the Beis Hamikdash, a Beis Midrash or a synagogue. Hashem wants His *Shechinah* to reside in us! We all possess the ability to bring the *Shechinah* within ourselves through Torah that we learn and the *mitzvos* we perform. Wow!

46. One's money was used in direct relation to his intent for the *mitzvah*: If someone donated to the Mishkan with a purer, more wholehearted intent, his money would be used for a holier component of the Mishkan.

47. The Bnei Yisroel were allowed to make a *bamah* (a personal altar) to bring a *korban* before the Mishkan was built. The *bechorim* (first-born males) would officiate at the *bamah*. They lost this opportunity once the Mishkan was made, for only the Kohanim now served. The *bechorim* thus cried, "Vei, we lost the privilege to serve Hashem as Kohanim!"

48. It took the Bnei Yisroel three or five months (depending on differing views) to construct the Mishkan. Contrast that with the construction of the Beis Hamikdash, which took angels and artisans seven years.

Answers&Facts

49. How many Aronei Kodesh did the Bnei Yisroel possess?

(See Menachos 28b, Ramban Devarim 10:5, see Sotah 8:1)

50. Which supernatural workers helped build the Beis Hamikdash?

(Shemos Rabbah 52:4, Shir Hashirim Rabbah 1:4)

51. What type of wall will be surrounding the future Beis Hamikdash?

(Zecharyah 2:9, Tanchuma on Ki Sisa 13)

52. What special building did Moshe see in Heaven?

(Pesikta Rabbasi 20:3)

53. Which living people are rewarded as if they died *"Al Kiddush Hashem"* (Sanctifying Hashem's Name)?

(Sefer Chassidim 14 and 40)

---

49. The Bnei Yisroel had two Aron Kodesh: one stayed in the Mishkan, and one went before the Bnei Yisroel during battle. The Aron that went out to war would perform miracles. Two sparks would shoot out of the Aron Kodesh and hit the enemies in the desert! When we learn Torah (which the Aron symbolizes) we afford the best protection for Klal Yisroel from their enemies!

50. Angels and demons assisted in the construction of the Beis Hamikdash!

51. A wall of glowing fire will surround the Third Beis Hamikdash. Aside from it being a beautiful and awesome phenomenon, it would deter those who should not touch it. Oh, may that Kiddush Hashem be in our time, Amen.

52. Hashem opened the seven heavens and Moshe beheld the Beis Hamikdash Shel Maalah! (the spiritual Beis Hamikdash that is in the highest heavens)!

53. Anyone who does a *mitzvah* that entails shame or embarrassment is rewarded as if he died *al Kiddush Hashem*, sanctifying G-d's Name! I think a fundraiser provides a good illustration of this: Every Yeshiva or organization needs fundraisers to raise the necessary funds to pay for the day-to-day expenses and to help the yeshiva grow. That job can sometimes be quite painful. The funds poured in by the Mishkan, but nowadays, due to the struggling economy and poor public appreciation of the Torah, one must really be *Moser Nefesh* to solicit. Although the *meshulachim* (collectors) are often the unsung heroes, they are the ones working behind the scenes that cause great things to happen. How enormous their reward will be for their ongoing sacrifice for the sanctification of Hashem's Name!

---

54. When would sparks of fire shoot out of the Aron Kodesh?

(Bamidbar Rabbah 5:1, Devarim Rabbah 7, see Shmuel I 4:11)

55. Which vessels of the Mishkan did Moshe first visualize in a fiery form?

(Menachos 29a)

56. Why did Hashem order that the Mishkan should be made out of cedar wood?

(Shemos Rabbah 35:2)

57. Who prepared the wood to be used for the Mishkan centuries earlier?

(Rashi, Tanchuma)

58. Why didn't the members of Beis Garmu family want to teach their *Lechem Hapanim* baking techniques to anyone?

(Yoma 38a)

---

54. The Aron Kodesh often emitted sparks of fire to stop snakes, scorpions and other dangerous elements from harming the Jews. Today, when international terrorists wish to harm us, G-d forbid, we must learn more Torah. The Gemara (Sotah 21a) says: "Torah protects and saves!" Torah eradicates physical and spiritual threats that want to harm the Jews!

55. Hashem presented fiery models of the Aron Kodesh, Menorah, and Shulchan to Moshe so that those charged with constructing them could fathom their design properly..

56. Hashem did not want fruit trees to be used in His house. This teaches us not to destroy fruit trees for our own benefit. If Hashem, who created everything in the world for His Honor, did not want the Bnei Yisroel to commit *Baal Tashchis* (unnecessary waste of fruit trees), we certainly shouldn't waste fruit bearing trees either! Since the tall cedar doesn't produce fruit it could be used.

57. Yaakov Avinu saw with Divine prophecy that the Bnei Yisroel would build a Mishkan. He therefore planted cedar trees in Mitzrayim for its future construction. He instructed his children to take the wood along when they would eventually leave Mitzrayim.

58. The members of Beis Garmu family were worried that people might use their Showbread recipe for *avoda zara*. They therefore kept it a family secret.

Answers&Facts

---

59. Which element atoned for a sin committed with that very same element?

(See Shekalim 1:1)

60. Why should we keep studying the architectural design of the Beis Hamikdash even though it doesn't stand today?

(Tanchuma 96:14, Yachin U'Boaz Mesechta Midos, Derech Eretz Zuta)

61. Under which circumstances would the middle light of the Menorah (which burned miraculously) be extinguished?

(Tiferes Yisroel Chagigah 3:8)

62. Why did the Aron Kodesh have gold both outside and inside it?

(Yoma 72b, Bamidbar Rabbah 4:12)

59. The gold upon the Aron Kodesh atoned for the gold that was given for the Eigel, the Golden Calf.

60. When we learn about the Beis Hamikdash, we are credited as if we rebuilt it! Our learning also demonstrates our strong belief and trust that Mashiach will build the third Beis Hamikdash. We study its laws to know where everything will be and how to perform the *avoda*. The plans are written in Yechezkel so we know where everything will be. The Chofetz Chaim placed great emphasis on learning Seder Kodoshim.

61. If a Kohen was an *am ha'aretz* (an unlearned person), and *tamei*, who entered the Beis Hamikdash without prior immersion in the *mikvah*, and touched the golden Menorah, the middle flame that was always lit would be extinguished. This symbolized that open miracles take place only when the Bnei Yisrael are pure!

62. The gold on all sides of the Aron teaches us the proper way of life, to which those who study Torah must adhere. Just as the Aron Kodesh is beautiful within and without, the Torah scholar's inner character must be consistent with his public appearance. One must fear G-d in public and in private.

63.

Why did Hashem command, *"And You shall take for Me donations"*? Wouldn't it be more appropriate to say *"And you shall give for Me..."*?

(Da'as Chachomim quoting Rav Yisroel of Ruzhin)

63.

Hashem is telling us that when you give to charitable causes you are really taking for yourself because you get His blessing back in return! If people would only know what a privilege it is to support Torah causes, they would approach the rabbis before the rabbis solicit them! Surprisingly, it is the fundraiser is the one who gives the donor the chance to enjoy the blessings and reward of supporting his worthy cause.

Dedicated in honor of our parents
BENNY AND SHERYL LEVY
by Elie and Ezra Levy & Family

פרשת תצוה

1. Why isn't Moshe Rabbeinu's name mentioned in Parshas Tetzaveh?

(Torah Mi'Tzion, Rabbeinu Yosef Chaim, Baal Haturim, Kol Eliyahu)

fUndamental Answers!

"יגעתי ומצאתי!"

("I worked on these questions, and I found these answers!")

1. The Bnei Yisroel disappointed Hashem several times while they traveled through the desert. They complained about the *Mann*; Korach rebelled against Moshe's authority; they made the *Eigel* - a Golden Calf, among other things. At such moments, Hashem wanted to destroy them, G-d forbid! Moshe Rabbeinu always helped the Bnei Yisroel with his prayers and defense. After the Eigel, for example, Moshe pleaded to Hashem, "You must either forgive the Bnei Yisroel, or else erase me from Your book [the Torah]." Hashem forgave the Bnei Yisroel. Nevertheless, Moshe's name had to be erased from the Torah because once words are spoken by a *tzaddik*, even if they are conditional, they are fulfilled. Therefore, Moshe's name is not mentioned at all in *Parshas Tetzaveh*. Incidentally, the seventh of *Adar*, which is Moshe Rabbeinu's birthday and yahrtzeit, always falls out the week of *Parshas Tetzaveh*.

2. Why did Alexander the Great merit that the Kohen Gadol - Shimon Hatzaddik - appeared in his dreams, to encourage him about his upcoming battles?

(Mussar HaMishna Yoma 69a)

3. Why isn't the Mizbeiyach HaKetores mentioned with all the other *Klei Hamishkan* (vessels of the Mishkan) that are listed and described previously in Parshas Terumah?

(Ramban, Torah Mi'Tzion, See Rashi parshas Korach)

4. Why were there two *Mizbachos* in the Mishkan and in the Beis Hamikdash?

(Kli Yakar, Taam V'daas quoting Yoma 21a)

---

2. Alexander studied under Aristotle, the famous Greek philosopher. Alexander's ambition was to conquer the world and make it a better place. Since he had noble aspirations, the Kohen Gadol appeared to him in a dream to give him confidence, and encouraged him. This shows that if you truly want to make the world a better place, Hashem will send you great help and teamwork to make it possible!

3. The Torah first details the Bigdei Kehuna and only then completes its discussion of the vessels of the Mishkan by detailing the Golden Mizbeyach. The Golden Mizbeiyach was used for *Ketores* offering. The *Ketores* is a special offering, for Hashem loves *Ketores* more than any other *Korban!* This is proven by the fact that on Yom Kippur, the holiest day of the year, the Kohen Gadol preformed the *Avodah* in the Kodesh Hakodashim, the holiest place on earth, with the *Ketores!* Therefore, it's mentioned separately.

4. The human body has two main decision-makers: the brain and the heart. The two mizbachos (altars) symbolized that just as we offer sacrifices to Hashem on two vessels, we should always sacrifice our minds and hearts desires to Hashem to fulfill His will! It has been said that the best Korban to sacrifice on the *mizbeiyach* of your heart is the Yetzer Hora (evil inclination) itself!

---

5. Which *halacha* (law) about Tefillin do we learn from the Tzitz of the Kohen Gadol?

(Tosafos to Yoma 8a, Rambam Hilchos Tefillin 4:14)

6. What wondrous *segulos* do the *Avnai HaChoshen* (gems upon the Kohen Gadol's breastplate) possess even today?

(Shemos Rabbah 38:8; see Rabbeinu Bachya)

7. What did Moshe Rabbeinu inscribe on the *Urim Ve'tumim?*

(Yoma 73, Erchei Kodesh, Kupas Harochlim, Targum Yonason, Ramban, Mizrachi, Rikanti)

---

5. The Kohen *Godel* must always be aware of the Tzitz, which says Hashem's Name, which is worn on his forehead. He must constantly remember that it is there and must act in an appropriate manner. When we wear Tefillin, which says Hashem's name not once, but 42 times, we must always be careful to act in a superior and respectful manner. Therefore, very young boys don't wear Tefillin, because they might come to joke around and disrespect the name of Hashem, G-d forbid. The Tefillin demand constant seriousness and awesome recognition of Hashem's Presence.

6. Mystical influences are mentioned with each of the twelve *Choshen* gems. If someone is righteous, the stones can be very beneficial to him! *The twelve gems are ruby, emerald, crystal, carbuncle, sapphire, pearl, topaz, turquoise, cow's eye, crystal-lite, onyx, and jasper.* To mention some several of their beneficial *segulos*: the ruby can help a pregnant woman who wears it not to suffer a miscarriage, and her delivery will be easier. The emerald can cool a person from the heat. It even helps people cool down their negative desires. The crystal can make the people wearing it smarter. Whoever wears the carbuncle, his enemies will run away from him. The sapphire helps one to be able to see well. (The *Luchos* were made out of this stone.) It also relieves any swelling or pain a person might have in his body. The pearl is a *segula* that the person who wears it will be more successful in business, and it helps a person to sleep better at night. The turquoise helps a person ride on his horse. The cow's eye can aid a person to be courageous in battle and not be frightened. The crystalline is a *segula* for good stomach digestion. The onyx helps you find favor, grace, and charm before people who look at you, especially before a king. The jasper is a *segula* to clot the blood, and for blood pressure. (I do not know the exact specifications of how these prescriptions work.)

7. Moshe wrote the Name of Hashem on the *Urim V'tumim*. There are different opinions about which one of Hashem's Names was written: the 4-letter Name, the 42-letter Name, or the 72-letter Name. This empowered the gems to light up brightly and deliver responses to those worthy of inquiring of the *Choshen*.

8. How were the bells on the *me'il* similar to the *Tzitzis* on our *Talleisim?*

(Shaarei Aharon 28:35)

9. How many times did the Bnei Yisroel have to light the Menorah of the Mishkan throughout their forty-year journey in the *Midbar?* How often did they light the Menorah of the Beis Hamikdash?

(Tanchuma, Taam V'daas quoting Rav Chaim Brisker)

10. When did Moshe Rabbeinu feel sad, and how did Hashem encourage him?

(Shemos Rabbah 37:4, Taam V'daas)

11. Which Kohanim will not get to serve Hashem in the future Beis Hamikdash?

(Shemos Rabbah 38:3)

---

8. Just as our tzitzis are to make us aware of Hashem and to obey His commandments, the ringing bells on the Kohen Gadol's *me'il* remind everyone that they should follow faithfully in the *Derech Hashem*.

9. The (*Ner Ha'Maaravi* of the) Menorah was lit only once in the Mishkan! During the forty two times they traveled en route to Eretz Yisroel, they placed a pan over the fire. Ordinarily, this would prevent oxygen from reaching the fire and would extinguish it, but miraculously, the *Ner HaMaaravi* of the Menorah stayed lit for 40 years straight! Even in the Beis Hamikdash, Rav Chanina, the assistant to the Kohanim, reported that miracles happened constantly with the Menorah. There were times when the Kohen would light the Menorah on *Rosh Hashana* and it would stay burning all year! Some say that the Kohen would just add oil everyday to fulfill the *Mitzvah* of lighting the Menorah even though it was still brightly lit.

10. When Hashem told Moshe to inaugurate Aharon and his sons to become Kohanim *Gedolim* for the generations to come, Moshe felt down: "How did Aharon my brother merit that *all* his descendants will be holy?" Hashem encouraged Moshe that all the Torah scholars of future generations would be considered his students, and one's students are like his own sons! This appeased Moshe Rabbeinu.

11. Kohanim who are not dedicated to Torah will not be allowed to serve in the Third Beis Hamikdash!

---

12. Why were the *Avneitim* (belts) of the Kohanim so long (32 *amos* = approximately 50 feet)?

(See Shita Mekubetzes to Erchin 15a, see Baal Haturim 28:6)

13. How did Rabbi Yehuda HaNasi honor the Kohanim when he wrote the *Mishnayos*?

(Mili d'Berachos 2a)

14. How long was Moshe the Kohen Gadol? Why didn't Moshe remain the Kohen Gadol?

(Shemos Rabbah 37:1, Ramban)

---

12. The numerical value of the word 'לב' (heart) is 32. The Kohanim had a very long belt tied around the middle portion of their body to remind them that no matter how hard you work to do mitzvos, the main objective is that your heart should be involved in the *mitzvah*! One must do mitzvos wholeheartedly. If someone performs mitzvos superficially, the *mitzvah* loses its value in Hashem's eyes. The Kohanim, the official servants of the King and the role models of Bnei Yisroel, must be very careful that all their *avodah* is performed with their heart. It should be pointed out that adults have 32 teeth because Hashem wants our mouth and our heart to be in sync, especially when we pray! The 32-amah belt also acts as a separation between the upper, more spiritual part of the body, and the lower, more physical half. This divide reminds the Kohanim that they must be more involved in spiritual pursuits than physical pleasure. [It is for that reason *Chassidim* wear a *gartel* when they daven, which is called *avoda shebelev*, the work of the heart.]

13. Rabbi Yehuda HaNasi mentions the Kohanim in the first *Mishnah* in *Shas*. Even though the *Mishnah* is discussing *Kerias Shema* and the *Mishnah's* point isn't specifically related to Kohanim, he nevertheless explained that *the time we say Shema at night is* the same time that Kohanim who became *tamei* and purified themselves in a *mikvah* can eat *teruma*.. [The Halacha is that even if a Kohen purifies himself in the daytime, he must wait until nightfall to eat *teruma*. Rabbi Yehuda HaNasi taught us that the time to say *Shema* in the evening is the same time that those Kohanim may eat *teruma*.] This reminds us that we should always keep Kohanim foremost in our mind by honoring them. Also, just like they are known act quickly in their *avodas Hashem*, so too we should be quick to say *Shema* and do all *mitzvos*.

14. When Moshe was standing at the *s'neh*, the burning bush, Hashem ordered him to go to Mizrayim and free the Bnei Yisroel. Moshe possessed extraordinary humility and refused to go! He insisted that Hashem choose any other Jew, especially his brother Aharon who was superior to him. The dialogue went back and forth for a week. Since Moshe should not have refused Hashem, Hashem refused to give him the title of High Priest in future generations. Some authorities say that Moshe officiated as Kohen Gadol only the first week that the Mishkan stood, while others say that he officiated all 40 years in the desert, but it did not stay with his sons.

Answers&Facts

---

15. From where did they take the fire to light the Menorah?

(Toras Kohanim 24:2, Mishnah Tamid 6:1)

16. When would the *Urim Ve'Tumim* give an unfavorable response? (One such instance was at the episode of the Pilegesh B'Givah, where a civil war broke out between the Bnei Yisroel and *Shevet Binyomin*; at that time, the *Urim Ve'tumim* had seemingly encouraged the terrible and costly battle in which many Jews were killed.)

(See Yerushalmi Yoma 7:3, and see Sefer Shoftim chapter 20)

17. What reward does one get for illuminating *Shuls* and *Batei Midrashim*?

(Torah Sheleimah, Midrash Hagadol)

15. The fire to light the Menorah was brought from the Mizbeiyach Hachitzon, the outer alter. This symbolized that you need *tefillah* to help you achieve success in Torah! The Mizbeiyach represents *Avodah* (which today is Tefillah), and the light of the Menorah represents Torah. It's for this reason that many Bnei Torah will write on the top of their notes 'BS"D', which is really a 'written prayer' for help from Heaven!

16. The *Urim V'tumim's* answer depended on the worthiness of the *Bnei Yisroel* at that time. In the aftermath of the *Pilegesh B'Givah* incident, the *Urim V'tumim* had said '*alu*', to go up. The Bnei Yisroel understood it to mean that they should fight against the tribe of Binyamin, the tribe who perpetrated that atrocity. A civil war ensued in which many Bnei Yisroel were killed.

17. One who lights up the synagogues and study halls will merit descendants who will be kings! We see this from Avial, who merited that Shaul Hamelech, the first king, was his great great grandson. Avial was nicknamed '*Ner*', a candle. He always provided oil for the synagogues throughout Eretz Yisroel. Shaul's lineage was 'Shaul ben Yair ben Kish ben Ner.' Shaul's father was named Yair, which also means light. There is a special correlation between the mitzvos of candle lighting and bearing great descendants. The *Gemara* says that those who are careful with *Nairos* Shabbos will have children who light up the world with their wisdom.

18. Which *mitzvah* mentioned in *Parshas Tetzaveh* did Moshe need to be shown how to do?

(Rashi, Menachos 29a and Tosafos there, Toras Chinuch)

19. Which *aveiros* would the *Bigdei Kehuna* atone for?

(See ArtScroll notes on Zevachim 88b, Tosafos,Vayikra Rabbah 10:6, Midrash Talpiyos)

20. How can an ordinary *Yisroel* become as holy as a member of *Shevet Levi*?

(Rambam Hilchos Shemittah V'yovel)

21. When did the gems on the Choshen glow or dim?

(Midrash Hagadol, Radak on Yehoshua 7:12, Yoma 73b, Ramban, The Midrash Says)

---

18. Moshe needed to see exactly how the Menorah should be prepared. Hashem showed it to him in the form of fire. If Moshe Rabbeinu needed occasional visual aids to grasp Torah, certainly we should try to give our students visual presentations to help explain the Torah more clearly! *(It is to fill this need that we started "TorahShows". It is a series of multi-media audio-visual slide-show presentations that present the beauty of Torah to the Jewish community. In an age of televisions (lo aleinu), our "Torahvisions" is a sweet alternative!!)*

19. The Kohen Gadol's uniform is mentioned next to the *korbanos* to imply that they atone for our sins just as the *korbanos*. The shirt atoned for murder, the pants for immorality, the hat for arrogance, the belt for impure thoughts, the *Choshen* for injustice, the *Eiphod* apron for *Avodah Zarah*, the *Me'il* for *lashon harah*, and the *tzitz* atoned for brazenness.This applies when teshuva is done.

20. Any Jew that devotes his life to constant worship of Hashem through diligent Torah study is considered as if he is a descendent of *shevet* Levi, the elite class of Bnei Yisroel who possess great holiness.

21. If someone in any *shevet* would commit a grave sin, the gem that represented his tribe on the *Choshen* would dim. For instance, when Achan stole from the banned spoils of Yericho, the Bnei Yisroel were able to find the culprit by noticing the dull appearance of the gem of his tribe Yehudah, the carbuncle. The only time that the *Choshen* gems glowed was when the community leaders were allowed to inquire from it. During the Second Beis Hamikdash no one possessed *Ruach Hakodesh* to receive that form of Heavenly communication!

Answers&Facts

22. Why couldn't the Bnei Yisroel inquire from the *Urim V'Tumim* during the Second Beis Hamikdash?

(Yoma 73b, Rambam Hilchos K'lei HaMikdash 6:6)

23. When should you imagine that you are standing inside the *Kodesh Kodoshim*?

(Mishnah Berurah Hilchos Tefillah 94:3)

24. Which non-Jewish kings wore the *Bigdei Kehuna*?

(Megillah 12a)

25. Why didn't the Kohen Gadol put Tzitzis upon his *Me'il* — which was a four cornered garment?

(Davar B'ito)

26. Why didn't the Kohen Gadol wear his golden *Bigdei Kehuna* for certain parts of the day on *Yom Kippur*?

(Yerushalmi Yoma 7, Vayikra Rabbah 21, Rosh Hashanah 26a)

---

22. During the Second Beis Hamikdash, Kohanim *Gedolim* during that time did not possess the necessary *Ruach Hakodesh* to be able to decipher its message. Nevertheless, the Kohen Gadol wore the *Urim V'Tumim* so he would not be missing a garment.

23. When you pray before Hashem and take three steps forward, you are supposed to imagine that you are walking into a new world: that of the Holy of Holies, where you stand before the King of Kings! (If we only knew how holy and powerful prayers really are!)

24. Balshetzar and Achashveirosh wore the *Bigdei Kehuna*. Both were severely punished: Balshetzar himself was killed, and Achashveirosh's wife Vashti was killed.

25. A Kohen Gadol wore a four-cornered garment that did not require *tzitzis*. *Tzitzis* reminds us to serve Hashem by performing the *mitzvos*. The *begadim* of the Kohen Gadol already reminded him to serve Hashem through fulfilling the *mitzvos*.

26. On Yom Kippur, the Kohen Gadol prays to Hashem to forgive the Bnei Yisroel. One of the worst sins that Jewish people ever committed was when many worshipped the *Eigel*, the Golden Calf. We do not want to recall this grave error on Yom Kippur, the annual Day of Atonement, so the Kohen Gadol would not wear his golden clothes when he went into the Kodesh Kodashim. Instead, he dressed humbly with pure white linen.

27. Why were the names of the twelve tribes written on the *Avnei Shoham and* again on the *Avnei Melu'im?*

(*Shemos Rabbah 38:8, Sotah 36a*)

28. Which Jews were allowed to inquire from the *Urim V'Tumim?*

(*Mishnah Yoma 7:5*)

29. We know that the *Kohanim* had a special uniform that was both honorable and beautiful, as befitting the individuals who served Hashem in the Beis Hamikdash. Did *Levi'im* also wear special clothes for their various jobs? In addition, how are *Talmidei Chachomim* instructed to dress?

(*Rambam Hilchos K'lei HaMikdash 10:13; see Rambam Hilchos De'os 5:9*)

---

27. When Hashem would see the names of our righteous forefathers and their sons, the Shevatim. He would recall their good deeds, and remember ours as well. The gems with the inscriptions were placed upon the Kohen Gadol to bring us merit and good will. The names were written again on the Avnei Shoham, which were placed on top of his shoulders, to *remind the Bnei Yisroel* of their great ancestry! When they recognized their great lineage, they would automatically behave in a more refined and dignified manner. We should take great pride in our heritage and behave accordingly too!

28. The following individuals could ask for guidance from the *Urim V'tumim*: 1) the Jewish king 2) the Kohen Gadol 3) the *Av Beis Din* (head of the Jewish court) and 4) a Jew that the Bnei Yisroel needed, such as a war general.

29. Leviim wore a special uniform when they served in the Beis Hamikdash. A *talmid chacham* must dress in a very dignified manner as well. His clothes must be nice and clean, without any stains or spots on them. He should not wear royal clothes made with gold or purple, which will draw undue attention to him. Neither should he wear pauper's clothes, which disgrace the one who wears them. Rather, he should wear normal clothes that enhance the one who is wearing them. His skin should not be visible through the clothes. His clothes should not flow on the ground behind him like a haughty person; they should only reach his ankle. Today, some Roshei Yeshivah wear a special garment called a kapata or frock. In general, every Jew must wear clothing that reflect his status as a Ben Melech (child of the King). They must dress differently and even have different hairstyles than gentiles.

Answers & Facts

Questions & Riddles

30. Why was there a crown on top of the *Mizbeiyach Haketores?*

(Kli Yakar)

31. Why did the Kohen Gadol need to have *new* clothes tailored every year?

(Rambam Hilchos K'lei HaMikdash 8:4, Midrash Talpiyos)

32. Was the Menorah of the Beis Hamikdash lit on Shabbos?

(Midrash Halachah)

33. Which liquid can improve your memory?

(Horiyos 13b, Menachos 85b)

34. How do we know that money donated for community projects should be collected by at least two people?

(Bava Basra 8b; see Rav Ovadyah Mi'Bartenura on Peah 8:7)

30. The crown upon the *Mizbeiyach* signified that those who serve Hashem will merit that the crowns that were given and subsequently taken away at *Har Sinai* would be returned to them in the future!

31. New clothing makes a person very happy. Accordingly, one makes a she-hechiyanu when he wears a new garment for the first time. The Kohen Gadol must be *very happy* in order to serve Hashem. After all, he is a servant of the highest order! It was therefore important that he would always have a fine new uniform. (We find a similar concept about new clothes in regard to the *Yomim Tovim* - that a husband is responsible to purchase new clothing for his wife to help her rejoice on the holidays.)

32. The Menorah needed to be kindled on Shabbos.

33. Olive oil is very good for your memory. (Olives, on the other hand, are bad for the memory.)

34. The *pasuk* uses the plural, "they collected" when speaking about the collection of gold, silver, etc. for use in the Mishkan. The procedure was to collect in pairs to avoid anybody suspecting a collector of pocketing money for himself. In order that there shouldn't be anyone in *"yichud"* (seclusion) with the money, they collected in groups!

35. Which two creatures appeared upon the *Eifod*?

(Midrash Halachah)

36. How did they engrave the square gems of the Choshen Hamishpat?

(Sotah 48b, Kli Yakar Melachim I chapter 5; see Gittin 68a; Zohar Parshas Noach 74a)

37. Hashem Yisborach told Moshe, *"Venikdash b'Chevodi,"* which Rashi explains to mean that the Mishkan would be sanctified through the death of *tzadikim*. Indeed, this actually happened later on the opening day of the Mishkan when Nadav and Avihu died. Why was that the preferred way of sanctifying Hashem's *Shechinah* (Holy Presence)?

(See Torah Temimah 39:43 quoting Zevachim 115b; Ohr Hachaim)

38. Did the Kohanim wear Tefillin?

(Zevachim 19)

39. Which *mitzvah* is precious to Hashem as the two *Korban Tamids*, and we can also do it twice a day?

(Yalkut Shimoni 835)

---

35. The lion and the eagle were embroidered into the *Eiphod*. This surely reminded the Kohen Gadol and all those who beheld him of Yehuda ben Teima's maxim: "Be bold as a leopard, light as an eagle, swift as a dear, and mighty as a lion, to carry out the will of your Father in Heaven!" (*Avos 5-23*)

36. The miraculous *shamir* worm was used to engrave the names of the Avos and the Shevatim onto the precious gems of the *Choshen* and the *Avnei Shoham*.

37. Hashem did not want the Bnei Yisroel to take advantage of the constant atonement offered in the Beis Hamikdash, lest people sin without reservation. Therefore, on the opening day of that wonderful place, *tzaddikim* died. The Bnei Yisroel were shown that life must be taken seriously, for everyone's actions have major consequences. *Be'kerovai Ekadesh*, by those close to Me I was honored!

38. It seems that the Kohanim wore the Tefillin *Shel Rosh* while they performed the *avodah* (Temple Service), but not the *Shel Yad*.

39. When we say Shema morning and evening, it is as dear to Hashem as the Korban Tamid, which was sacrificed in the Beis Hamikdash morning and evening. There are other *"Temidim"* (lit. constants) which should be fulfilled constantly,

Answers&Facts

40. How do we know the time zones that we are required to pray *Shacharis & Minchah?*

(Berachos 26b)

41. Chazal tell us that the Mizbeiyach (and the *Bigdei Kehuna)* served as an atonement for the Bnei Yisroel. How is this hinted at in the word *Mizbeiyach?*

(Midrash Tanchuma on Parshas Tzav 14)

42. What is the only *Korban* that can be brought before the *Korban Tamid?*

(Pesachim 59b)

even nowadays: "*Shivisi Hashem L'Negdi Tamid* – I set Hashem before me, *always*" (*Tehillim* 16-8) to be cognizant of Hashem's presence before us at all times, and "*Tov Lev Mishteh Tamid* – The happy at heart are always at a party," (*Mishlei* 15-15), which means we should always serve Hashem with joy, realizing how lucky we are to be close to Hashem. Others say there is a different *pasuk* which says, "My sins are before me always" (*Tehillim* 51-5). A person should always feel humbled by his sins, for this will encourage him to repent.

40. We learn the times for our daily prayers from the times of the daily *Korbanos*, since our prayers serve in place of the sacrifices! Although our *Avos*, Avrohom, Yitzchak, and Yaakov set up our Shacharis, Mincha, and Maariv prayers, the times that we say these *tefillos* correspond to the time that it was permitted to bring the Tamid in the morning and afternoon. Generally, the morning Tamid was brought between daybreak and the fourth hour of the day, which is the time we must pray Shacharis. The afternoon Tamid was generally brought during the final two and one-half hours of the day. This time period is called *Mincha Ketana* and is the preferred time to pray Mincha. The earliest time the afternoon *Tamid* was ever brought – was one half-hour after midday – when *Erev Pesach* fell out on *Erev Shabbos*. This is therefore the earliest time we can daven *Mincha* daily.

41. The word *Mizbeiyach* is an acronym for the four things it brings *you:* מחילה, זכות, ברכה, חיים? *Forgiveness, Merit, Blessing, and Life*. Look what a person stands to gain when he strengthens his bond with Hashem! No wander they used to sing: "How beautiful are you *mizbeiyach!*"

42. The *Ketores* may be brought before the Korban Tamid.

43. When did the Bnei Yisroel stop bringing the *Korban Tamid?*

(Taanis 26b)

44. Why wouldn't a *Kohen* get the opportunity to offer the *Ketores* twice in his lifetime?

(Mishnah Tamid 5:2, Gemara Yoma 26a)

45. How beneficial is it to recite the *Ketores?*

(Mi'zahav U'mi'paz, Kaf Hachaim)

46. How were the Kohanim able to work in the Beis Hamikdash under the open sky - in the cold winter months - without coats or boots?

(Me'am Lo'ez)

---

43. On the 17th of *Tammuz*, 3828, the Roman oppressors prevented the Bnei Yisroel from bringing any more sheep for the Korban Tamid. There was a terrible earthquake throughout Eretz Yisroel on that ill-fated day. It became a fast day.

44. Whoever would sacrifice the *Ketores* would become wealthy! Naturally, every Kohen wanted to have a chance to possess that *segula* to become rich. Therefore, they would not let any Kohen bring it twice. They wanted to make sure that every Kohen would have a chance at this *segula*. Many people believe today that saying *Parshas HaKetores* from a parchment will bring the reader wealth and prosperity as well!

45. Saying *Parshas HaKetores* daily wards off death, sickness, poverty, and suffering! The one who says it merits great mercy from Heaven, and great success in all his endeavors. How wise it is not to skip saying *Ketores* every morning and afternoon! It's even a *segulah* for bearing children. Some (Sephardic) Jews are careful to have it written on a parchment to add to the reader's *kedusha* as he reads it. Sometimes you might notice it hung up in the synagogue in order to give everybody a chance to read it and merit its blessing.

46. It was a great miracle that the Kohanim were protected from flu and sickness in the cold winter months. This symbolized that those who serve Hashem with sacrifice and devotion merit special protection! I believe that the fiery passion in which they served Hashem, warmed them.

Answers&Facts

47. Why did the Kohen Gadol need bells on his priestly vestments?

(*Gemara Yoma, Me'am Lo'ez*)

48. What can we learn from the quality of the oil used for the Menorah?

(*Lekach Tov, Kol Ram Menachos 86a, Ohr Hachaim*)

49. What did both the *morning Korban Tamid* and the *afternoon Korban Tamid* signify?

(*Torah Mi'Tzion*)

50. What was engraved upon the Choshen's gems besides the names of the Avos and the Shevatim?

(*Yoma 73b, Shemos Rabbah 38:9, Yerushalmi, Rambam Hilchos K'lei HaMikdash 9:7*)

47. The Kohen Gadol's bells would signal any angels that were in the Kodesh Hakodashim to leave as he entered on Yom Kippur. It was his private time with Hashem! When he left, it would signal that they could return. Another purpose of the bells was so that the Bnei Yisroel would know that the Kohen Gadol was alive. If he was not worthy, he would die in the Kodesh Hakodashim, and they would need to pull him out with a rope. [This happened very often in the time of the Second Beis Hamikdash when many Kohanim *Gedolim* weren't worthy of the job.] The bell also served as a reminder to people that the Kohen Gadol is in the vicinity and they should come to him to learn Torah. (Nowadays, schools have a different sort of bell that calls everyone to come learn.)

48. Just like the Menorah's oil must be pure – unclouded and without any foreign substances - when you illuminate your students with Torah knowledge, you must present it clearly and precisely, leaving no room for doubts or uncertainties. The pure oil also teaches us that if a person really wants to enjoy the light of Torah, he must make sure his mind is not infected with negative or corrupt thoughts and influences. Your mind, which houses your Torah knowledge, must be kept pure. Care must be taken to make sure it doesn't become polluted.

49. A person's life can be compared to the morning and night periods. The morning is when things shine bright, and he is filled with energy. A person also experiences the night, which is when things seem dark and gloomy. A person is reminded that he must serve Hashem with equal dedication at all times, whether things are up or down, and whether he is in his youth, the peak of his strength, or in the sunset of his life, when he ages and his strength ebbs away.

50. Some say that the names of the shevatim, *plus* these additional words: "Avrohom, Yitzchak, Yaakov", and "Shivtei K-ah" or "Shivtei Yeshurun" were engraved into the gems of the *Choshen*.

51. **When was the Menorah lit during the day?**

(Ramban)

52. **Why was the Menorah situated on the left of the Shulchan, and not on its right side?**

(Peninim-Rabbi A.L. Scheinbaum shlit'a)

53. **Who was holy, and went into the holy, before the Holy, on behalf of the holy?**

(Shemos Rabbah 38:7)

54. **What else was inside the courtyard of the Mishkan besides the vessels mentioned explicitly in the Torah?**

(Mi'shulchan Gavo'ah quoting the Brisker Rav)

55. **Which people are even greater than Kohanim?**

(Mishnah Horiyos 3:7; see Megillah 21a)

---

51. If the *Ner Ha'Maaravi* was extinguished, the Kohen Gadol would have to relight it during the day, because there must *always* be at least one lit flame on the Menorah.

52. To one who stands outside the Kodesh Hakodashim, it appears that the Menorah is on the left of the Shulchan. However, to one who is more spiritual and views things from the Kodesh Hakodashim's vantage point, the Menorah is on the right! The Menorah represents wisdom while the Shulchan represents wealth. We must never forget which is more important.

53. The holiest person, the Kohen Gadol, had to enter the holiest place, the Kodesh Hakodashim in the Beis Hamikdash, to go before the Holy God, Hashem, to get atonement for the holiest people, the Bnei Yisroel.

54. The Brisker Rav z"tl said that there must have been a *mikvah* in the courtyard of the Mishkan. He bases this on the *pasuk* that says Moshe was commanded to bring Aharon and his sons to the entrance of the Ohel Moed and *then* immerse them in water to purify them. (I never saw it drawn in the illustrations of the Mishkan, but just as the Beis Hamikdash had a Mikvah so did the Mishkan!)

55. A *talmid chacham* should be accorded more honor than a Kohen. He should be given precedence over a Kohen who is not learned. Indeed, sometimes Maran Harav Ovadia Yosef, shlit'a, goes up for the Kohen's *aliyah l'Torah*, even when there are Kohanim present in the room!

Answers&Facts

56. Which popular sets of seforim (holy books) were named after the jewels and gems of the *Choshen?*

(Arba Turim, Ketzos Hachoshen, Avnei Shoham, Avnei Miluim, etc.)

57. How are Jews similar to olive oil?

(Shemos Rabbah 36:1)

58. Why was the *Urim V'Tumim* called that name?

(Yerushalmi Yoma 7)

59. Why didn't the Beis-Avtinas Family want to teach anybody their special formula for making the *Ketores?*

(Yoma 38a)

60. Why were there 72 bells on the Me'il?

(Zevachim 88b, Ramban, Toras Ha'olah, Rabbeinu Bachya)

---

56. The monumental work known as the *Tur* was named after the gems of the *Choshen Mishpat*. Also, the *Ketzos Hachoshen* and the *Avnei Milu'im* were named after these priceless gems on the Kohen Gadol's uniform. The great Gedolim who authored them realized that Torah is filled with gems and jewels. We must realize that every single word of Torah that we learn and acquire is far more valuable than the most magnificent and exquisite diamond!

57. Just as oil rises to the top, the Jewish people will eventually rise over the nations that oppress them! In addition, just as oil can only be extracted after the olive was pressed, so too, a Jew becomes greater after suffering and pressure.

58. *Urim V'Tumim* means to "Illuminate and Complete". The *Urim V'Tumim* solved any questions or puzzles that were presented to it. It enlightened everyone with the right plan of action. A classic example is mentioned in the beginning of Sefer Shoftim, after Yehoshua passed away. The Bnei Yisroel needed to know which Shevet should lead the battle against the wicked and dangerous Cana'anim. The *Urim V'tumim* illuminated Yehuda's gem and the letters that spelled "Yaaleh" which means, "He should go" lit up.

59. The Avtinas Family did not want to teach the secret formula of the *Ketores* and its capability to make the smoke rise straight up like a pillar, lest someone misuse it for pagan purposes.

60. Rabbeinu Bachya calculates that the world was created in 72 daylight hours during the six days of creation. The 72 ringing bells should remind us that the entire world was created for one purpose – *Avodas Hashem!*

---

346 » *TorahShows' Questions & Riddles* ■ *Tetzaveh*

61. Why is it common practice for Bnei Torah to wear black hats?

(Ben Torah V'Yeshivah, Rabbi Avigdor Miller zt'l; see Shir Hashirim 1:5)

62. What were the *Kosnos Ohr,* the special garments that Hashem gave Adam and Chava?

(Otzar Hayedios, Asifas Gershon)

63. What does Hashem love even more than the bringing of *Korbanos?*

(Shemos Rabbah 38:4)

---

61. A hat is a symbol of one's affiliation. A baseball player, police officer, or the guards at Buckingham Palace proudly wear their hats. A black hat represents the class of Bnei Torah, the group of Bnei Yisroel completely dedicated to the study of Torah as transmitted by our *Roshei Yeshiva.* Rabbi Avigdor Miller, *zt"l,* once said, "I am more proud of a boy wearing a black hat than his wearing Tefillin. Although Tefillin is a *mitzvah d'oraysa* and a black hat is only a custom, it is an idealistic expression of commitment to Torah scholarship!"

62. Some say that the *Kosnos Ohr,* the special Heavenly clothing that Hashem gave Adam and Chava, were *Bigdei Kehuna.* Others disagree, because why would Chava wear them? Only men wore these clothing! They explain that the *Kosnos Ohr* were Tefillin. Some extraordinary women wore Tefillin, such as Michal bas Shaul Hamelech, and Rashi's daughters, thus Chava wore them too.

63. Hashem loves when we learn Torah more than when we bring *Korbanos!* Indeed, Hashem told Dovid Hamelech, "I appreciate your words of Tehillim and Torah more than the thousands of *Korbanos* that your son Shlomo will offer in the Beis Hamikdash!"

In loving memory of
AVI MORI RAV AVROHOM ELBAZ z'TL
3 ADAR 1990
by Dr. and Mrs. Larry Kurz and Family

Answers&Facts

פרשת כי תשא

?
1. Why was the *Machatzis Hashekel* (a half-shekel tax) collected in the month of Adar?

(Yerushalmi Shekalim 1, K'sav Sofer)

fUndamental Answers !

"יגעתי ומצאתי!"

(*"I worked on these questions, and I found these answers!"*)

1. Hashem, who knows the future, was aware that one day Haman Harasha would bribe Achashveirosh with 10,000 silver coins for permission to exterminate the Jews. Therefore, Hashem ordered the Jews to first give silver money for *Korbanos* as a *kaparah* (atonement), to protect them from the terrible impact of Haman's money. Consequently, the money was, and will again be, collected in *Adar*, the month that Haman wanted to kill the Jews. Also, *Adar* precedes *Nissan*, the month that marks the New Year for the *Korbanos*. The money that was raised through the *Machatzis Hashekel* was used for the following year's *Korbanos Tzibur* (communal offerings), such as the *Korban Tamid*, and the *Mussaf* that was brought on Shabbos, Yom Tov and Rosh Chodesh. Thus, it was truly communal offerings, for everyone donated money toward the *Korbanos*.

2. Why is every Jewish man required to give a "half" shekel, and not a "whole" shekel? *(Torah Mi'Tzion, Alshich)*

3. Why didn't Moshe Rabbeinu grasp *mitzvah* #105, *Machatzis Hashekel,* until he saw a fiery presentation of it? *(Bamidbar Rabbah 12:3, Tanchuma, Mechilta)*

4. Why were there thirteen collection chests in the Beis Hamikdash? *(Shekalim 6:5)*

5. How do we see that if you give money to charity, you get it right back? *(Baal Haturim)*

2. The half-Shekel symbolizes unity. Hashem wants us to realize that we need each other! No Jew should ever feel he is completely perfect. He must work with other Jews as a team. This can be best compared to two people that want to express their love for each other., sometimes they would share a token that was cut into two halves. We give half a *Shekel* to Hashem's Beis Hamikdash to show our unity and love for one another!

3. Moshe could not understand how such a small amount of tzedaka could atone for one's grave sins. Wouldn't a person need to pay with his life for rebelling against Hashem!? Hashem showed him that since one's money is very dear to a person, he would receive a *kapara* when he gives it away to the needy! This teaches us a lesson: never feel a gift is too small; it's the thought that counts!

4. The thirteen collection chests in the Beis Hamikdash were used for:
1. New *Shekalim,* (the present year's collection);
2. Old *Shekalim,* (from the last year's collection);
3. To purchase burnt offerings consisting of birds;
4. To buy firewood for the Mizbeiyach;
5. To purchase frankincense for the *Ketores* and the Shulchan;
6. To buy gold for decoration and beauty;
7-13. To purchase animals to be offered on the Mizbeiyach when there were no other *Korbanos* being offered (*keitz hamizbeiyach*). These *Korbanos* were brought in order to keep the Mizbeiyach busy with sacrifices. The world exists in the merit of the sacrifices, for they atone for our sins.

5. The Torah implies with the use of the word *"venasenu"* (ונתנו), that the Jewish people should give funds to others, and they will automatically receive funds right back as a reward! This word in Hebrew reads the same way foreword and backward, implying that you never lose by giving charity. On the contrary, it is the surest guarantee not to lose your wealth.

6. Why is there no obligation for women or teenagers to give the annual *Machatzis Hashekel*? After all, don't they need a *Kapara* too?

(*Chizkuni, Seichel Tov*)

7. Why did the *Kiyor* (Laver) originally have only two spouts,and ten more had to be added later?

(*Toras Ha'olah*)

8. Can you enumerate more than 20 instances where we are required to wash our hands? What happens to people who don't?

(*Shulchan Aruch Orach Chaim 4:18, Shoneh Halachos*)

---

6. Women are traditionally supported by their husbands and don't earn a living. The Torah does not demand that a man pay for his wife's *Machatzis Hashekel*, for the women were not involved in the Eigel which the half-*shekel* atoned for. Teenagers, too, don't have to pay, because the Heavenly Court does not usually punish people under the age of 20. However, if they want to ensure themselves a *kapara*, it's a good idea for them to give it as well. It is commendable for a father to give *Machatzis Hashekel* even for his young children, just as many do *Kaporos* before Yom Kippur for each child.

7. Kohanim needed to wash their hands and feet before serving in the Beis Hamikdash. Originally, Kohanim were so excited about their privilege to serve in the Bais Hamikdash that they didn't mind waiting in line by the water fountain. However, their enthusiasm diminished due to the spiritual decline that took place over the years, to the point where they were no longer willing to wait in line. Ben Katin added more spouts to shorten their waiting time.

8. The Jewish people wash their hands very often. This helps fulfill Hashem's commandment that we should be a Holy People. The following is a list of the many times that we are required to wash our hands: upon awakening, leaving the bathroom, leaving the bath-house (after taking a bath or a shower), after touching our shoes, after touching our legs, after scratching our head, after walking in a cemetery or walking along with a funeral procession, after touching the dead, after touching a bug, after touching a part of the body that is usually covered - especially a sweaty part, before praying, before eating bread at a meal, before eating food that was dipped into a liquid (i.e. a wet pickle, a washed fruit, or a cookie dipped in milk), *mayim achronim* (washing after a meal of bread to remove the harmful salt of Sodom that might be on the fingers), after

Answers&Facts

9. Which *aveira* is as severe as all the *aveiros* combined?
(Shemos Rabbah 25:16)

10. Why didn't Aharon Hakohein vehemently protest the Eirev Rav's making of the Eigel?
(Sanhedrin 7a)

11. Which oil has the amazing ability to make a short person tall?
(Tanchuma on Parshas Emor 4, The Midrash Says on Vayikra)

12. Why did Yehoshua forbid his soldiers from taking any spoils at Yericho?
(Midrash Halachah)

touching an idol-worshipper, after touching an animal, after letting blood (such as after donating blood or after a dialysis treatment), after a haircut, and after cutting your nails. One should not take this *mitzvah* lightly. Our Rabbis warn that someone who does not wash his hands when required will suffer from a phobia. If he is a Torah scholar, he will forget his learning, and if he is an unlearned he will become very forgetful.

9. Chillul Shabbos is such a terrible *aveira* that whoever desecrates the Shabbos gets punished as if he committed every *aveira* in the Torah. On the other hand, one who is properly *Shomer* Shabbos is rewarded as if he had performed all the *mitzvos*! (*Bitul Torah* and *Lashon Hara* are also listed as the worst sins.)

10. Aharon saw that the Eirev Rav murdered his nephew Chur when he protested that they were worshiping the Eigel. He was worried that if he protested and was killed too, the Bnei Yisroel would never be forgiven! But if they were only involved with *Avodah Zarah*, at least they could do *teshuva* and be forgiven.

11. The *Shemen HaMishcha* had an amazing power: When it was poured on a short Kohen, it would miraculously make him grow tall!

12. Hashem ordered Yehoshua to conquer Yericho even though it would be done on Shabbos. Therefore, He did not want anyone to derive benefit from work done on Shabbos by taking from the spoils of war. We are not allowed to benefit from *Maasei* Shabbos (work performed on Shabbos). For instance, if one accidentally cooks on Shabbos, no one may eat from the cooked food during that Shabbos.

13. Which beautiful ornaments did the Bnei Yisroel lose
after the Eigel was made?

(Shemos Rabbah 45:4, Tanchuma on Parshas Ki Sisa 26, see Yechezkel 16:12)

14. How could the worshippers of the *Eigel* be so foolish to
proclaim "this cow saved us from Egypt"?

(Shemos Rabbah 42:6, Tehillim 106:20, K'sav Sofer, See Melachim I 12:28)

15. Why were the Bnei Yisroel almost wiped out (Heaven
forbid!) because of the sin with the *Eigel*, if mainly the
Eiruv Rav sinned?

(Shabbos 89b)

16. What wonderful things would have happened had the
Eigel never been made?

(Shemos Rabbah 32:1)

---

13. The glorious crowns that the angels brought to the Bnei Yisroel for saying *na'aseh v'nishma* were taken away after the sin of the Eigel. These crowns are likely to come back when Mashiach comes!

14. Hashem opened all the heavens when He revealed himself at Har Sinai. The Bnei Yisroel were able to see the feet of angles, which resembled the feet of oxen. The Eirev Rav (that included Egyptian magicians who had converted after witnessing Hashem's wonders) thought that maybe cows were divine. They therefore made the Eigel. Also, a plate of gold that was engraved by Moshe with the words *Alei Shor* (arise ox) was thrown into the fire. Moshe had made it in order to bring up the coffin of Yosef (who was compared to the mighty ox) from the Nile, so it possessed spiritual powers to make an ox emerge. Others say that four creatures were featured on Hashem's throne: man, ox, eagle, and lion. Once the man leading them was gone (Moshe) they looked to the next in line on Hashem's throne, the ox, to be their new leader.

15. The Bnei Yisroel were criticized for not standing up and protesting when the Eigel was made. This is a most frightening fact: One who doesn't try to stop an aveira is punished as if he himself had committed it!

16. Had the original Luchos never been broken, no Jew would have ever died, and no non-Jew would ever have been able to harm any Jew! In addition, no one would ever forget any Torah he had learned.

Answers & Facts

Questions&Riddles

17. Why didn't a *Kallah* (bride) need perfume in Yerushalayim in the times of the Beis Hamikdash?
(Yoma 39b)

18. Who was murdered for giving *mussar*?
(See Sanhedrin 7a; Tanchuma, Bamidbar Rabbah 15:21, Shemos Rabbah 41:7, The Midrash Says)

19. What does the Rambam say about one who doesn't wash his hands before praying?
(Rambam Hilchos Tefillah 4:1, Teshuvos HaRashba 191)

20. How may one prove Hashem's unparalleled tolerance and patience for us?
(Shemos Rabbah 41:4, Tanchumah 15, Tomer Devorah)

21. Which other Tzadikim glowed like Moshe Rabbeinu?
(Berachos 5b, Yalkut on Parshas Vayechi, Tanchuma on Parshas Chukas)

---

17. The *Ketores'* delightful scent permeated Yerushalayim to the point that even a bride on her wedding day felt no need to apply any fragrance!

18. Chur rebuked the Bnei Yisroel in a tough manner, so the sinners killed him. It is a rare art and most difficult skill to delicately and effectively rebuke a wrongdoer.

19. One who prays without washing first has fulfilled the *mitzvah* in an inferior fashion!

20. We must realize Hashem's enormous patience and tolerance in that even though people sin He does not punish them immediately. He still provides them with their daily needs. Hashem possesses so much mercy that even when some Jews offered heavenly *Mann* as a sacrifice to the Eigel, Hashem still gave the life nourishing *Mann* and the holy Torah to the Bnei Yisroel!

21. A special radiance emanated from Moshe Rabbeinu. Chazal actually compare Moshe Rabbeinu and Yaakov Avinu to the sun. Rav Yochanan and Rav Masya Ben Charash are two Rabbis mentioned by Chazal who had a glowing aura upon them as well. We can all possess a special radiance to some degree, as Shlomo Hamelech writes: "The wisdom of a person lights up his face (*Koheles 8-1*)."

---

22. **Why shouldn't you feel bad if you learn Torah and forget most of it?**

(Nedarim 38b, Avodah Zarah 19a)

23. **Why does the Torah call Yehoshua a "youngster" when he was actually 56 years old at the time?**

(Ibn Ezra, Ramban)

24. **Why were the people in the city of *Tur-Shimon* massacred?**

(Eichah Rabbah 2:5)

25. **Which Jewish man cannot be counted for a *Minyan*?**

(Yalkut Yosef, Maharsha on Kerisus 6b)

---

22. It is a terrible sin to forget Torah wisdom. However if one tries his best to review and to take notes, and still can't recall all that he learned, he will be reminded of it in the World to Come when everyone will cherish the Torah knowledge that they amassed. There is a famous story about Rabbi Mordechai Gifter z'tl, the previous Telzer Rosh Yeshiva. He needed to take certain medications that deprived him of his extraordinary memory. He felt very bad that he could not remember much of what he had learned in his lifetime. He commented to his doctor, "If I keep forgetting what I learned, what am I going to do in Olam Haba? I need to remember my learning for then?" The doctor, who was a Jew, replied: "The medicine only robs your physical strength. But whatever you learn will be there for you in Olam Haba." Rabbi Gifter cried and said, "*Nichamtani!*" (you comforted me.)

23. Yehoshua was energetic like a youth—even in his older years. He didn't slow down as is common with elderly people.

24. In the city Tur-Shimon, they used to play ball on Shabbos, which no doubt diminished the spirit of the day. Playing ball on Shabbos desecrates the holiness of Shabbos. (I don't know whether there was an *eiruv* or not.) Chazal also blame them for their *Bitul Torah!*

25. Someone who desecrates Shabbos in public may not be counted for a minyan.

Answers&Facts

26. Why did David Hamelech count the Jews without a token? Didn't he know that one must count the Bnei Yisroel only with a token?

(See Tanchuma 1; Yoma 28b)

27. Why did they blow the *Shofar* on Fridays in earlier times?

(Tanchuma on Parshas Mattos 2)

28. Which Mitzvah did the gentiles try imitating in the year 4805?

(See Beitzah 16b)

29. Why must we wash our hands three times when we wake up in the morning?

(Mishnah Berurah 4:1)

26. Rabbi Yaakov Elman, *shlita,* in his wonderful translation of Navi, titled *The Living Nach* (Pg. 372) lists nine opinions why Dovid forgot to count the Jews with the prescribed method of the *Machatzis Hashekel.* Hashem was angry with the Bnei Yisroel because:

A. Uriyah was "murdered", and the Bnei Yisroel did not protest it;
B. The Bnei Yisroel didn't demand that the Beis Hamikdash should be built;
C. The rebellion of Avsholom and Sheva ben Bichri;
D. They gave into the demands of the cruel Givonim to kill Shaul's sons;
E. Shaul's sons weren't properly buried;
F. Dovid was counting on big numbers for his military strength;
G. Secret sins that were being committed by Jews.

27. There was a custom in Jewish communities to sound the *shofar* as an alarm to signal the people to stop their work on Fridays and get ready for Shabbos. It was sounded again to remind them that it was time to light the candles. Some close-knit religious neighborhoods (in Eretz Yisroel, Boro Park, Flatbush and others) still sound sirens to alarm the people not to be late for Shabbos, G-d-forbid.

28. Some non-Jews decided to make Sunday their day of rest and to go to their temple. However, it is the sacred day of Shabbos Kodesh that testifies to Hashem's greatness and brings His Divine blessings!

29. There is a form of *tumah* (impurity) that rests upon a person's hands when he sleeps. It can only be removed by washing *Negel Vasser* when we wash our hands three times in an alternating manner.

30. Which *Rasha* made *two* Eigels (Golden Calves)?

(Eichah Rabbah 1:23)

31. When won't a person forget the Torah he has learned?

(She'al Avicha)

32. When were women more G-d-fearing than men?

(Pirkei d'Rabi Eliezer)

33. Which days did Moshe go up to Heaven and come down when he received the second Luchos?

(Tosfos)

34. How often should we review the many *Halachos* of Shabbos?

(Pele Yo'etz, Zichru Toras Moshe, Mishnah Berurah)

---

30. Yeravam ben Navat, the King of the Ten Shavatim, made two Eigels to lead his followers astray. He was afraid that if his people go to Yerushalyaim to serve Hashem in the Bais Hamikdash and see Rechavam, the King of Yehudah, they would want him to be their king. Now that they had their own place to serve- the Eigels that he set up, they didn't have go to the Beis Hamikdash where they would see Rechavam. Such is the destructive nature of jealousy; it can even lead a person to serve *Avodah Zarah*, chas v"shalom. It's poison to ones character..

31. If you learn Torah solely for Hashem's sake, (*lishma*) and not for your own honor you will merit many great things (See *Avos* 6-1). You will also retain all that you learned.

32. When the Bnei Yisroel made the Eigel, the women did not want to give their jewelry for Avodah Zarah. The men forcibly removed it from them.

33. After the Bnei Yisroel sinned with the Eigel, Moshe begged Hashem to for-give them. He went back up Har Sinai on a Monday to receive the second Luchos and returned on a Thursday. Since those days were associated with teshuva and Matan Torah, they are considered special days to ask for forgiveness and mercy. We therefore add *V'Hu Rachum* to the *Tachanun* prayers on Monday and Thursday.

34. One should frequently study and review the laws of Shabbos. Both men and women should try to complete the general laws and details of *Hilchos* Shabbos at least once a year! Many venerable *Rabbonim* agree that one who constantly studies the laws of Shabbos will always learn new laws that he/she never knew before!

Answers&Facts

---

35. When would one need to keep most of the *Halachos* of Shabbos every day?

(Shabbos 69)

36. Who merited having a son who became a Torah authority particularly because he closed his business early every *Erev* Shabbos?

(Kol Haneshamah)

37. Why was *chelbenah* used in the *Ketores* if it had a bad odor?

(Rabbeinu Bachya)

38. How is the *T'nach* compared to a bride?

(Taam V'daas, Shemos Rabbah 41:6)

39. How can concentrating on Hashem's 13-Word-Name save you from sin?

(Kaf Hachaim Hilchos Tefillin 38)

35. If someone is marooned on an island or in the desert and has lost track of days, he must keep Shabbos every day, just in case that day is indeed Shabbos. He is only permitted to perform a *melacha* that's necessary for his survival.

36. It has been related that the *Rema's* father merited to have and raise one of the greatest *halacha* masters of all time due to his own Torah learning (even on *Purim* when Torah study is usually minimized) and because he closed his shop early on *Erev* Shabbos!

37. The ketores teaches us that we should include sinners in our company (at a *fast* or a Minyan), with the hope that they be inspired from everyone's positive attributes and do teshuva! *If only everone would be mekarev someone!*

38. Brides would adorn themselves with 24 ornaments. It has been said that the *Tanach* consists of 24 holy books for us to adorn our *souls!* Also, just as a bride wants her groom's constant attention and affection, the Torah wants ours too! The Midrash comments that just as a *Chassan* enjoys hearing his *Kallah's* voice, we should enjoy hearing the voice of the Torah! We must strive to teach and learn Torah in an exciting and enjoyable fashion.

39. One of the most challenging mitzvos is to constantly guard our thoughts. This is most difficult, since, by nature, the mind wanders. One must exert himself to maintain pure thoughts especially while wearing *Tefillin*. By concentrating on Hashem's 13-Word-Name which shows His eternal compassion & His absolute

40.
When did the letters of the Torah soar into the air?

(Pesachim 87, Shemos Rabbah 46:1)

41.
Why did Moshe Rabbeinu smash the *Luchos*?

(Shabbos 87a, Toras Chinuch quoting Rav Dovid Goldwasser shlita)

42.
Who prayed so intensely that his body became feverish?

(Berachos 32a)

43.
Did Hashem ever forgive Klal Yisroel for the sin of the *Eigel*?

(Sanhedrin 102a; see Bava Kama 55a)

44.
What did Shlomo Hamelech mean when he said: "One out of a thousand men I found, but I didn't find any women?"

(Rabbeinu Bachya, Koheles 7:28)

---

mercy, one will find it easier to keep purer thoughts. The 13-Word-Name is: "ה' ה' אל רחום וחנון ארך אפים ורב חסד ואמת נוצר חסד לאלפים נושא עון ופשע וחטאה ונקה" which can be translated as follows: *"Hashem, Hashem [Master of All Always] the Almighty G-d, Merciful, Compassionate, Slow to Anger [even towards the wicked], Abundantly Kind, Truthful, Keeper of Kindness for Thousands [of Generations], Forgiver of Sin, Negligence and Misdeed, and Purifier!"* This Name serves as a *segula* to help a person keep his mind free of impure thoughts.

40. When the Bnei Yisroel were involved with the sin of the Eigel, the letters of the Torah floated back up to Heaven. The Luchos became too heavy to bear for they were devoid of the Torah's letters, and fell from Moshe's grasp!

41. Moshe's cracking of the Luchos implied that the generation needed a different approach to *Avodas Hashem*, for they had not succeeded in ascending to the appropriate spiritual level they were expected to attain.

42. Moshe prayed so intently for the Bnei Yisroel – a total of 960 hours – that he became *sick*. We really owe our existence to Moshe for saving us again and again!

43. Hashem did not entirely forgive the Bnei Yisroel for the Eigel. All the subsequent hardships that have been endured throughout history - persecutions, expulsions, pogroms and holocaust - are partly as retribution for worshiping the Eigel. *Rachmana lesheizvan.*

44. 3,000 men were involved in the Eigel. There were about 3,000,000 people at *Matan Torah*. So King Solomon said he found 1 from 1,000 men involved in that Avodah Zarah – but none were women!

---

45. Why did Moshe wear a hooded mask?
(Kli Yakar)

46. What happened to the Atlantic Ocean when the Luchos were smashed?
(Zohar vol. 2:113b)

47. What is the difference between: *chochmah* (wisdom), *binah* (understanding), and *da'as* (knowledge)?
(Rashi, Shemos Rabbah 48:4)

48. Why don't some people tell how many children and grandchildren they have?
(See Taanis 8b; Bava Metzia 84b, Bava Basra 118a)

49. Why is Yom Kippur a most happy day?
(Taanis 26b)

---

45. The *Shechinah* shone so brightly from Moshe's face that he tried to cover it with a mask. This proves his unparalleled humility!

46. The Atlantic Ocean rose to flood the world as a punishment for the *Chillul Hashem* the Eigel caused. When Moshe realized what was happening, he immediately crushed the Eigel, ground it into powder, and punished all the perpetrators.

47. Simply speaking, *chochma* is what you learned from others, *tevunah* is what you figured out using your own intellect, and *da'as* is *Ruach HaKodesh*. Others explain that *chochma* refers to the knowledge of Torah, *binah* to the understanding of *halacha*, and *da'as* is the wisdom of the *Gemara*.

48. People with large families don't want to get any *ayin hara*, evil eye (from others' jealousy), so they often won't relate how many children they actually have. Chazal even said that it is a good omen if one's first child is a daughter, for no one will give the mother an *ayin hara* by asking, "How many sons did this woman bear?"

49. Yom Kippur is a very happy day, because that's when Moshe brought us the gift of the Torah the final time! Also, we rejoice because Hashem forgives our sins and shortcomings this day each year by welcoming us to do teshuva. Anyone who looks at Yom Kippur as a difficult and exhausting day is missing the essence of the day.

---

50. What suffered from *Ayin Hara* in Parshas Ki Sisa?

(Tanchuma)

51. What is the correlation between *Machatzis Hashekel* and Yosef Hatzaddik?

(Bereishis Rabbah 80:18, Tanchuma 10)

52. Why wasn't Moshe the one to make the vessels of the Mishkan?

(Shemos Rabbah 40:2)

53. Why were there two *Luchos*?

(Shemos Rabbah 41:6)

54. Why were the *Luchos* made from stone, and not from metal?

(Shemos Rabbah 41:6)

55. What *Bas Kol* (Heavenly voice) emanates from Har Sinai everyday?

(Avos 6:2, Shemos Rabbah 41:7)

---

50. The sacred Luchos were broken since they were given amid much fanfare, and susceptible to *ayin hara*. Staying 'low key' is often better in the long run.

51. Yosef was sold as a slave for the price of a *Machatzis Hashekel*. We give that price *annually* to atone for our ancestors' *sibling rivalry*.

52. Moshe was the king of Klal Yisroel! Hashem told him that the king does not work himself. He delegates tasks to others. Betzalel was told to build the Mishkan instead.

53. The two Luchos *should* remind us of the two worlds: *Olam Hazeh* and *Olam Habah*. It also symbolizes the two types of mitzvos, *Bain Adam La'Makom* - between Hashem and us, and *Bain Adam Lechaveiro* -between our fellow men and us.

54. Hashem wants our mouths to always speak Torah, like the millstone that continuously grinds wheat for flour.

55. A wailing cry emanates daily from Har Sinai saying, "*Oy* (Woe) to the people that shame the Torah [by ignoring its study and its practice]; they are dishonored before Hashem!"

Answers&Facts

---

56. Who saved all of us with his powerful prayers? Why did he mention Mitzrayim?

(Shemos Rabbah 43:2)

57. What did Moshe Rabbeinu snatch?

(Shemos Rabbah 43:2)

58. How did Moshe survive without eating, drinking, or sleeping for 120 days?

(Shemos Rabbah 47:7)

59. Why was the *Torah Sheba'al Peh* (Oral Law) not written down like the *Torah She'biksav* (Written Law)?

(Shemos Rabbah 47:1)

---

56. Moshe saved Klal Yisroel time after time through his eloquent and passionate prayers. He mentioned their enslavement in Mitzrayim to defend the Bnei Yisroel's involvement in the Eigel. He pleaded: "They lived for so long under the rule of the Egyptians, who were notorious idolaters. Is it their fault when they lived so long under such negative influences?"

57. Moshe held onto two *tefachim* of the Luchos, Hashem held on to two *tefachim* of the Luchos while two *tefachim* remained in the middle. Hashem was going to hold back the gift of the Torah when they worshiped the Eigel. Moshe *grabbed it from Hashem*, so to speak. This act demonstrates that if you want to master Torah, you have to grab the opportunity to learn it. As it says in *Pirkei Avos* (4:12): "If you want to neglect the study of Torah, you will find many excuses to neglect it."

58. When a king is counting his fortunes and treasures, he doesn't want to interrupt his good time to eat or sleep. Similarly, Moshe did not want to take a break from his enjoyment of learning Torah! Hashem miraculously sustained him. Hashem said, "Because you suffered to acquire the Torah I will give it to you." As our sages say (*Berachos* 5b), Torah is acquired through the painstaking effort of pursuing it.

59. Hashem knew that the other nations would take the Torah and translate it as their Bible. He left the notes of the Torah, the *Torah Sheba'al Peh*, to be handed down generation to generation exclusively through our Jewish leaders. Only those who know the Oral Torah will be able to authentically claim that the Torah is theirs!

---

60. What did the *Satan* do to trick some of the Bnei Yisroel into worshipping the *Eigel?*

(Shabbos 89a)

61. Which famous people in history said, *"Mi La'Hashem Eilay"* ("Whoever is for G-d, come with me")?

(Sefer HaChashmona'im, Shemos 32:26)

62. When did *Hakadosh Baruch Hu* wrap Himself in a *tallis* [so to speak]?

(Rosh Hashanah 17b, The Midrash Says)

---

60. The Satan first created an illusion that Moshe was dead and was transported in heaven in a coffin. In the state of panic that ensued, the Eirev Rav built the golden Eigel. The Satan went into the Eigel's mouth to appear as if it was talking to fool them into assuming it was alive and powerful.

61. Moshe Rabbeinu announced, "Whoever is with Hashem come with me, in order to avenge the sinners of the Eigel". All of Shevet Levi followed him. Centuries later, a descendant from Shevet Levi, Yehuda Hamakabi, reiterated that same cry to rally fighters to revenge the tyranny of the wicked *Yevanim* during the story of Chanukah.

62. When Moshe asked Hashem to forgive the sins of the Bnei Yisroel, Hashem benevolently demonstrated how the Jewish people could always arouse His mercy. Hashem wrapped Himself in a Tallis (as it were) and He showed Moshe how to pray for mercy by mentioning Hashem's 13-Word-Name, which describes His Divine mercy and compassion for humanity. Sephardim and Chasidim have the custom to say this awesome Name of Hashem every day that *Tachanun* is said.

פרשת ויקהל

1. How do we see that each and every Jew is more precious to Hashem than the Beis Hamikdash?

   (Chasam Sofer; see Bamidbar Rabbah 8:19)

2. Shlomo Hamelech used the supernatural Shamir worm to cut the stones for the Beis Hamikdash. What did Betzalel use to cut the stones for the *Avnei Shoham* and the *Choshen Mishpat?*

   (Sotah 48b, Kli Yakar Melachim I chapter 5)

FUNdamental Answers!

"יגעתי ומצאתי!"

("I worked on these questions, and I found these answers!")

1. If a Jew's life is in danger from a fire G-d forbid, on Shabbos, we are allowed to extinguish the fire to rescue him. However, if (theoretically) the Beis Hamikdash was on fire on Shabbos, you would not be allowed to put out the fire! This shows that every Jew, regardless of his religious status, is more precious to Hashem than His Beis Hamikdash!

2. Betzalel used the phenomenal shamir worm to engrave the names of the Shevatim on the stones of the *Choshen* and *Avnei Shoham*. The shamir was able to split a rock as it crawled on it! It was again used in the days of Shlomo Hamelech when he built the Beis Hamikdash.

3. How did Rav Huna merit extraordinary wealth by honoring Shabbos?

(Megillah 26b)

4. Why were ladies' mirrors used for the *Kiyor* (fountain)?

(Bamidbar Rabbah 9:12, Shach, Rikanti, Darash Moshe, Me'am Lo'ez)

3. Rav Huna's mother, who was poor, sold her spare hair-covering to buy wine *L'kavod* Shabbos. Rav Huna himself gave his belt as collateral when he borrowed money to buy wine for Kiddush on Shabbos. When Rav Huna went to the synagogue on Shabbos, Rav saw him wearing a rope around his waist instead of a belt. "Why are you wearing a cheap rope?" Rav asked him. "Today is Shabbos, and you should wear your finest clothing on this holy day!" Rabbi Huna answered that he had to give away his regular belt in order to purchase wine in honor of Shabbos. Rav blessed him that he should merit great wealth for honoring Shabbos; eventually, Rav Huna became a very wealthy man. Hashem saw his self-sacrifice to honor the Shabbos, and He rewarded him accordingly. The Gemara even says that the reason why Jews in many countries were wealthy was because they honored the Shabbos.

4. The mirrors symbolize the purity and *tznius* (modesty) of Jewish women:

A) The Jewish women endured great sacrifice to have children when the Bnei Yisroel were enslaved in Mitzrayim. Many men felt it was futile to have children since Pharaoh decreed to kill all the newborn boys. Nevertheless, the women knew it was their role to nurture Hashem's chosen nation by having children and raising them to be G-d fearing Jews. These righteous women used mirrors to make themselves more endearing to their husbands. Hashem considered this an act of holiness. Therefore, the mirrors of these holy women were used for the kiyor, which was used to wash the hands and feet of the Kohanim to add holiness to their Avoda in the Mishkan.

B) If a woman was accused of being a Sotah, she was brought next to that same *kiyor* in humiliation. The *kiyor* reminded her that she chose not to act like her ancestors in Mitzrayim who remained holy and pure even though they were surrounded by the immoral Egyptian society that was rampant at the time.

C) Many times a woman would bring a sacrifice for *kapara*. It is proper for a Kohen not to stare directly at the woman offering the Korban, out of modesty, so he would instead glance instead at the mirrors of the *kiyor*, which reflected the person who brought the sacrifice.

5. From where do we learn that we must distance ourselves from bad friends and negative influences?

(Me'am Lo'ez on Vayakhel quoting the Zohar)

6. What does the *pasuk* in *Shir HaShirim* (1:5) mean when it says, *"I am black and I am beautiful"*?

(Shemos Rabbah 49:2)

7. When did the Bnei Yisroel try to find favor before Hashem by using something that they had previously used for a sin?

(Shemos Rabbah 40:1, Tanchuma Beshalach 24)

---

5. Moshe Rabbeinu saw the devastating effects the Eirev Rav's weak faith in Hashem had on the Bnei Yisroel. They made the Eigel, causing death to the Bnei Yisroel, for, had the Bnei Yisroel not sinned with the Eigel, no Jew would have ever died. Moshe Rabbeinu assembled everybody on the first Shabbos after Hashem forgave them for the Eigel, because he wanted to underscore the importance of gathering into groups to learn with the Rav. By doing so, they would spend their time with good people, rather than associating with evil people. He taught them how to spend Shabbos, so Shabbos can protect them and can help bring the *Geulah Shelaima* to Klal Yisroel when they properly observe it.

6. Many nations of the world have called the Jews "dirty and ugly" in their anti-Semitic propaganda, but we know that Hashem says we are beautiful! Also, non-Jews claimed that Hashem abandoned the Jewish People during the sin of the Eigel, and now, their reputation is ruined and "black". Therefore, Hashem commanded them to make a Mishkan so that He would dwell among them, proving to the world that they are still beautiful before Hashem! In addition, during the year, people are "black" from sins, but when Yom Kippur comes and they repent, they are clean and beautiful again!

7. The Bnei Yisroel donated earrings for the Mishkan. It was very fitting that they now donated them for a holy cause because many of them had previously sinned with earrings when they donated them to make the Eigel. One achieves complete *teshuva* and *tikun* (repentance and repair) when he performs a *mitzvah* in the same area in which he sinned.

Answers&Facts

8. Why did Moshe tell the Bnei Yisroel to stop donating toward the Mishkan's construction? Wouldn't they always need a cash flow for maintenance?

(See Darash Moshe; Toras Ha'olah)

9. How does the 100 *berachos* that we are required to recite daily correlate with the 100 posts that supported the Mishkan?

(Seichel Tov, Chiddushei Harim, Baal Haturim)

10. How does our keeping Shabbos benefit the rest of the week?

(Pesikta Rabasi 23:9, Mechilta Beshalach 5, Aruch Hashulchan 242:2, Chofetz Chaim, Shabbos 118)

---

8. The Gemara Beitza (36b) says that it is a *mitzvah* to give money to the Beis Hamikdash even when there is no real need. However, Moshe did not keep accepting donations from the Bnei Yisroel. He wanted to teach them that you do not have to give all your money to the Beis Hamikdash to honor Hashem; you can honor Hashem even by using your money for your personal needs! How is that so? If a person eats to be healthy and strong to serve Hashem, or if a person buys a bed that is more comfortable so that he can rest better and learn Torah with more energy the next day, it is considered as honoring Hashem. One does not have to think that the only way to serve Hashem is by giving money to the synagogue or doing a *mitzvah*. We serve Hashem when we use our resources to improve our avodas Hashem so we can better serve Him.

9. Just as the posts on the bottom of the Mishkan were rather small, yet they held up the Mishkan, similarly, the *berachos* and Amens we say seem small and insignificant, yet they can serve as a great merit for *kapara* and long life. The Gemara tells us that the Bnei Yisroel were spared from terrible tragedies when Dovid Hamelech instituted the *halacha* that we must make 100 Berachos a day. When a person answers "Amen" with great concentration, even if he deserved a terrible punishment, his Amen can atone for his sins! Just as people who offered sacrifices in the Mishkan received forgiveness from Hashem, Amen too can achieve a personal atonement. Amen is *b'gematria* (numerical value) 91, which is the numerical value of Hashem's two Names Y-K-V-K (=26) and A-do-noy (=65) combined (26+65=91). Therefore, when one says Amen, he declares his *Emunah* (faith) in Hashem as the only G-d. The Gemara (Sanhedrin 111a) adds that Amen stands for *Al Melech Neaman* (Hashem is the fair King). Also it is good to think when you say Amen that it stands for *Ani Moser Nefesh*! (I am willing to serve Hashem with sacrifice!)

10. Hashem blessed Shabbos that it be a day that generates blessing. We proclaim in *Lecha Dodi* every Friday night, "Let us go greet the Shabbos for it is the source of all blessings!" It has been noted that the *mitzvah* of Shabbos is mentioned in seven different *parshios* of the Torah, and reiterated a total of twelve times. This

---

11. What does the *pasuk* mean when it says, "There were 'enough' and 'extra' materials donated for the Mishkan"?

(Ohr Hachaim, Rabbeinu Bachya)

12. Which three *mitzvos* are the greatest signs of our close relationship with Hashem?

(Shabbos 61a)

13. In previous generations, how early did many Jews welcome in the Shabbos?

(See Aruch Hashulchan 242:5)

14. Why do Jews get a *neshama yeseira* (extra soul) for Shabbos?

(Iturei Torah)

---

symbolizes the fact that the more effort you put into keeping Shabbos properly, the more you will prosper during seven days of the week and the twelve months of the year. One who keeps the laws of Shabbos—by abstaining from work and basking in the day which testifies that Hashem created and controls the whole world—will be blessed that the entire work-week will be more successful. Many times, when people would come to the Chofetz Chaim for a blessing, he would tell them, "If you honor Shabbos more, you will experience more blessing in your life!"

11. The Beis Hamikdash of this world corresponds to the Beis Hamikdash in Heaven. The Torah tells us that enough was donated as a merit for the Beis Hamikdash in the upper world and extra for the Mishkan in this world! In addition, Hashem made a miracle, that the extra donations fit into the Mishkan's construction even though they really weren't needed.

12. The Torah calls Shabbos, Bris Milah, and Tefillin an "*Os*", a special symbol of the strong, irrevocable bond that exists between Hashem and the Bnei Yisroel.

13. Many Jewish communities used to start Shabbos as early as possible (which is Plag Hamincha - 75 minutes [*zemaniyos*] before sunset). They would pray, welcome the Shabbos, eat the meal, and still have time to take a walk as the sun was just setting! They so appreciated this special day of blessing - knowing that it is a *mitzvah* equal to all other *mitzvos* - that they were eager to begin the Shabbos as early as possible. Unfortunately, in today's hectic world many people rush into Shabbos at the last minute. Life would be much better if people would bring in Shabbos earlier and end it later. Some people are anxious a whole Shabbos for Shabbos to end already. That is a shortsighted thought, for it does not allow them to maximize the blessings of this special day!

14. The purpose of the 'Extra Soul' on Shabbos is to increase one's perception of Torah, and one's ability to consider the ways of Hashem in a more encompassing manner. It also allows us to rest easier, become happier, and eat and drink with more satisfaction to rejuvenate ourselves for another week of energized Torah study and *mitzvos* observance.

Answers&Facts

---

15. Why is the word *Nessiim* (Presidents) spelled without the letter *'yud'*?

(Rabbeinu Bachya, Kli Yakar)

16. Who was one of the youngest teachers in history?

(Ohr Hachaim, Shach)

17. Where is it hinted in the Torah not to get angry, especially on Shabbos?

(Torah Mi'Tzion quoting the Zohar, Ben Ish Chai)

18. Why do mourners say *Kaddish* on Shabbos? Aren't the wicked spared from *Gehinnom* on Shabbos anyway?

(Torah Mi'Tzion quoting the Arizal)

19. How long before sundown on Friday afternoon must we usher in the Shabbos?

(Shulchan Aruch 261:2, Igeros Moshe Orach Chaim volume 2 siman 6)

---

15. While the entire Bnei Yisroel rushed to donate for the Mishkan, the Nesi'im took their time. They said, "Let the Bnei Yisroel donate whatever they can, and we will contribute whatever they didn't donate". Since they did not express enough eagerness to participate, the Torah took out the letter Yud from their name, which represents Hashem's Name. This symbolizes that they did not act the way a president should act. They should have acted as role models for everyone else by taking the initiative to get involved and donate.

16. Betzalel was merely thirteen years old (a *bar mitzvah* bachur), yet he taught and ordered everyone how to design and construct the Beis Hamikdash.

17. The Torah says, "Do not kindle a fire in all your homes on the Sabbath Day." This refers not only to the typical fire that we are not permitted to light on Shabbos, but also to the 'fire of anger' and a 'hot temper'. One must be extra careful not to burn the fire of anger within himself, which Heaven forbid, harms the soul. The Gemara (Pesachim 113b) says that Hashem has a special love for people who always control their anger.

18. Kaddish doesn't only save one's deceased relatives from *Gehinnom*, it also has the *segula* to raise them to higher levels in Gan Eden! A mourner could therefore say Kaddish even after the first year, even though we know one's punishment in Gehinnom decreases after that year. One who says Kaddish gives a chance to his deceased relative(s) to enjoy greater levels of pleasure from Hashem's Divine Presence in Gan Eden.

19. Approximately five minutes before sundown on Friday, a Jewish person must refrain from any work and accept the Shabbos upon himself. Some people think they can work the entire eighteen minutes after candle lighting until sunset, but this is

---

20.
Why does the first Mishnah in Mesechta Shabbos deal with the prohibition of carrying? *(Rambam, Tosafos Shabbos 2a)*

21.
Of all the 39 types of forbidden work on Shabbos, why does the Torah only mention these four explicitly: kindling a fire, planting, harvesting, and carrying? *(Me'am Lo'ez)*

22.
Why does the Mishnah forbid women to wear jewelry in a public place on Shabbos? *(Mishna Shabbos 6:1, Shulchan Aruch Orach Chaim 303:18)*

---

not so; they must transform part of the weekday into Shabbos. This is called "Tosefos Shabbos", adding to the Shabbos, and the minimum amount of time one should add is about five minutes. There is another practical reason why one shouldn't work after candle lighting. Someone might inadvertently work past sunset since the clock he is looking at might be slow, which can unfortunately result in one desecrating Shabbos and making Chillul Hashem. What blessing can result from work that is done close to Shabbos?! The Rabbis tell us that work done after midday Friday will not bring any lasting benefit, and one should consider this even amidst the struggle to make a living.

20. The Mishnah enumerates the 39 categories of work forbidden on Shabbos; carrying is the last one mentioned on that list. Yet Mesechta Shabbos speaks first about this *melacha* of carrying before mentioning all the other *melachos*! This is because many people think there is nothing wrong with carrying. They don't feel that it is work. Hagaon HaRav Yisroel Belsky, *shlita*, pointed out an amazing fact: "The Gemara spends more pages discussing the *aveira* of carrying on Shabbos than on any other *aveira* in the entire Torah!" Being one of the 39 forbidden categories, carrying is such a serious sin that one who is guilty of carrying is stoned to death, the worst capital punishment Beis Din can administer. Ironically, it has been said that the most common *melacha* of the 39 *melachos* that people used to bring Korbanos for was accidentally carrying on Shabbos! Therefore, a person must really go to great lengths to double and triple-check his pockets before he goes outside the home to avoid committing this serious *aveira*. Women have fewer pockets in their clothing than men do, and will therefore not inadvertently carry as often as men might do.

21. One might think that since part of honoring Shabbos is to eat delicious food, certain actions that are necessary for cooking food should be permitted. We are therefore told, "No! All food preparations that involve work should be done before Shabbos." That is the only way can we properly observe the Shabbos.

22. It was common practice for women to take off their jewelry to show their friends. Chazal therefore restricted women from wearing jewelry outside in the *Reshus Harabim* lest they inadvertently walk 4 *amos* (approx. 6 ft) in the *Reshus Harabim* while showing their friend their jewelry and commit the severe *aveira* of carrying on Shabbos. In the home, however, it is proper to wear jewelry to honor

Answers&Facts

---

23. When is it fitting to light two candles, besides *Erev* Shabbos and *Yom-Tov*?

(Minhag Yisroel Torah 419, Yosef Ometz 683, Moreh B'etzbah 179)

24. When should or shouldn't a Rabbi make an *Eiruv* for his city?

(Teshuvos HaRosh 21, Shulchan Aruch Orach Chaim 366, Mishna Berurah, Chasam Sofer)

25. Why did the *Rabbanan* decree that many items are *'Muktza'* (not movable) on Shabbos?

(See Mishna Berurah 308 quoting Rambam and Raavad)

Shabbos. Nowadays, women are lenient and wear jewelry outside in the *Reshus Harabim* on Shabbos because: a) Many women would not listen to this Rabbinical restriction even if they were told explicitly not to wear jewelry. b) There is an abundance of jewelry today, especially costume jewelry; therefore, it is not as common as earlier times to take off a piece to show a friend. c) We do not really have a bona fide *Reshus Harabim* as in the olden days. Nevertheless, it should be noted that there still are some families that do not wear jewelry in the *Reshus Harabim* on Shabbos, in order to prevent any possibility of inadvertently desecrating the Shabbos.

23. Many Jews have a beautiful custom to light two candles on the table Motzaei Shabbos in honor of the *Melave Malka*. It sets the tone for an enlightened week ahead. Some also light two candles on Rosh Chodesh.

24. It is very praiseworthy for a Rabbi to make an Eruv in his city to prevent people from carrying on Shabbos. Baltimore, Cleveland and Monsey are examples of the major Jewish cities that have kosher Eruvin. However, Sephardic Jews have a problem using an Eruv that was designed for Ashkenazic Jews, since the Rambam does not allow the Eruv-poles to be more than ten *amos* (approx. 15 feet) apart from each other, which is usually the case. Sephardim generally follow the Rambam's opinion, who himself was a Sephardi. There are many Rabbonim who do not want an Eruv in their cities, lest the ignorant start carrying and using sporting equipment and the like, which would take away from the holiness of Shabbos.

25. There are four main reasons why the Rabbis enacted the prohibitions of Muktza: a) To prevent one from doing a forbidden *melacha*. (e.g. If he touches a hammer he may come to build with it.) b) One should not spend the day doing things that are devoid of the spirit of Shabbos. (e.g. he might start playing with a rock collection, or organizing the garage.) c) There are some people who are retired and don't work anyway, so Shabbos for them would not be a different day than any other day. By instituting the prohibition of Muktza, Chazal reasoned that the restrictions

26. Can one walk his dog by its leash on Shabbos?
(Mishnah Shabbos 5:1, see Maran in Hilchos Shabbos 305:15)

27. How many candles should a woman light in honor of Shabbos?
(HaShabbos V'hilchoseha 5:6)

28. Who dedicated himself to build the Mishkan more than anyone else?
(Shemos Rabbah 50:5)

29. Should a poor person borrow money in order to purchase Shabbos delicacies?
(Tur Hilchos Shabbos 242)

---

will enhance one's manner of rest as appropriate for the day. d) The Rabbonon said certain things are Muktza as a precautionary measure to make sure people would not carry anything into the *Reshus Harabim*. By making people aware not to touch certain things, they will be less likely to carry on Shabbos.

26. Some permitted walking a leashed animal, such as a dog or a pony, on Shabbos, on three conditions: a) The leash does not stick out of the owner's hand more than a *tefach* (3-4 inches), b) The leash must not hang down within one *tefach* of the floor. c) He must be ahead of the animal, not behind it. Many Poskim forbid walking the dog by the leash, since it might lead to Chillul Shabbos. If one owns a dog, he should check out with his Rav the procedure to follow when it needs to go out.

27. A woman should light two candles in honor of Shabbos: One representing her, and one representing her husband. In addition, one corresponds to the *mitzvah* of "Zachor" – remembering to honor Shabbos, and one corresponds to "Shamor" - to abstain from any work on Shabbos. Some women have the custom to light seven candles, and some women have the custom to light a candle for each child. Other women light an extra candle for good *mazal* (luck)!

28. Betzalel didn't make every component of the Mishkan, yet he is given all the credit, since he dedicated himself to build the Mishkan more than anyone else! Also, Betzalel cared more about making Hashem's Mishkan more than anyone else did; therefore, the Torah writes that "Betzalel who made it..." although many Jews participated in building the Mishkan.

29. A poor person should borrow money to purchase a special dish or treat for Shabbos. Hashem says, "Borrow on My account [for my Shabbos] and I will repay you!" Other Poskim say it is better for a person not to borrow, because it is not nice to bother people. Everyone agrees, however, that at least something special must be added to the Shabbos menu.

Answers&Facts

30. What did one righteous Jew do to merit that Hashem rewarded him with a valuable caper-bush that grew on his property to support him?

(Gemara Shabbos)

31. In what *zechus* has Bnei Brak always been spared from serious bomb attacks by the Arab terrorists ימח שמם?

(Chazon Ish)

32. How can you prove that most people need to sharpen their knowledge of the laws of Shabbos?

(Shabbos 118, Pesikta Rabbasi 23:9)

33. Which *Gadol* keeps a *Ta'anis Dibbur* (Fast from Talking) every Shabbos? Why?

(Mishmeres Chaim, Kol Haloshon)

---

30. The Talmud tells us the story of a righteous Jew who noticed a crack in his wall while walking in his yard on Shabbos. "I will repair it after Shabbos," he said to himself. He then realized that it was disrespectful for the Shabbos to plan work that will be done during the week, so he swore never to fix that breach in that wall as a reminder to keep Shabbos holy. He didn't have to fix the hole anyway. Hashem rewarded him that a caper-bush, a most valuable tree, grew in that hole and protected the yard. He became very wealthy from that tree's valuable produce. Again, we see that honoring Shabbos brings wealth.

31. The Chazon Ish frequently quoted Chazal that says, "When we guard the Shabbos the *mitzvah* of Shabbos guards us!" As we know, whenever we do a *mitzvah* we create an angel that protects us. Bnei Brak has by far the highest percentage of a city population that is Shomer Torah & Shabbos in the world, for everybody in the city keeps Shabbos, so they have less to fear of dangerous terror attacks!

32. The Gemara says: "Whoever keeps the Shabbos scrupulously can make a wish and it will come true!" How many people do you know that can actually make their wishes come true? This must mean that people are not as knowledgeable in the laws of Shabbos as they should be.

33. The famous Rosh Yeshiva and Posek Hador, Hagaon HaRav Chaim Pinchos Scheinberg, *shlita*, is very careful not to utter any words on Shabbos other than words of Torah and Tefillah. This *minhag* is based upon the fact that when Rabbi Shimon Bar Yochai's mother was speaking a lot on Shabbos, her son asked, "Mommy, isn't it Shabbos today?" This implies that one should spend the Shabbos involved in spiritual pursuits, and not on mundane matters. After all, we find by the other *Os*, the Tefillin, that we may not act carefree when wearing it. We must behave in a more sincere and respectful manner.

34. Why are women commanded to build the Beis Hamikdash? After all, isn't it a time-related *mitzvah*, since it may not be built on Shabbos or at night? Women are normally exempt from performing such *mitzvos*!

(See Rambam Hilchos Beis Habechirah and commentaries)

35. Why shouldn't you let children sit on a table?

(See Chagigah 27a, Menachos 97a)

36. Why may we not make a seven branch *Menorah*?

(Binyan Beis Hakeneses)

---

34. There is a tradition that the Third Beis Hamikdash will be built miraculously in Shamayim through our good deeds and then descend to this world. Perhaps women will help to build the third Beis Hamikdash, because their good deeds will help build the Beis Hamikdash. Therefore, every Jew should do mitzvos so that our *mitzvos* will form the stones necessary to complete the building and then it will appear! The sefer Arvei Nachal writes that big *tzaddikim* create big bricks and smaller *tzaddikim* smaller bricks, but *reshaim* take off bricks by their sinning. Hagaon Harav Matisyahu Solomon, *shlita*, said that the bigger stones of the Kosel Hama'aravi represent the *tzaddikim* of the earlier generations merits and the smaller stones represent the later generations deeds. All that's missing in the Beis Hamikdash is one more pebble (*mitzvah*) to complete it. Who knows whose perfect *mitzvah* will be the one to end Galus and bring the Geulah?!

35. When the Bais Hamikdash stood, the Mizbeiyach brought *kapara* to the Jewish people when they sacrificed Korbanos. Hashem in His kindness gives us a chance to get *kapara* from our table today as well—if we invite poor people to our table, and we say Divrei Torah at the table. It then becomes like the sanctified Mizbeiyach. Therefore, it's very important not to embarrass the table by sitting on it, for it's like a Mizbeiyach.

36. You are not allowed to reproduce the shape of the Menorah that was in the Beis Hamikdash. Therefore, you are not allowed to make a three dimensional seven-branch Menorah. You are allowed to make an eight branch or a five branch Menorah. The Torah says "this Menorah is seven branches," implying that it is only allowed to be made for the Beis Hamikdash and nowhere else. This signified that authentic Torah law (which is signified by the Menorah) came out of the Rabbis of the Beis Hamikdash. They sat in the Lishkas Hagazis, the chamber of the hewn stone. They were the final and most authoritative Halachic body in the world. If a Rabbi in a different country wanted to decide a questionable Torah law, he was reminded that there is only one seven-branched Menorah, which is in the Beis Hamikdash, and he should go there for a final *p'sak*! (Some authorities say that this is why Chanukah is celebrated eight days rather than seven, so we shouldn't have to make a seven branch Menorah.)

Answers&Facts

37. Name the three loves you should have in your life?

(Be'ar Moshe, Baal Shem Tov 37:9)

38. How was the Mishkan greater than the Beis Hamikdash?

(Tanna d'Bei Eliyahu 25:13)

39. How were the 39 types of work - that are forbidden on Shabbos - necessary when making the Mishkan?

(Meleches HaMishkan)

40. For how many years did the Mishkans and the *Batei Hamikdash* stand?

(Zevachim 118b)

---

37. One should love Hashem, the Torah, and Hashem's people—the Bnei Yisroel!

38. The Mishkan was made solely by devout Jews, whereas the Beis Hamikdash was made by devout Jews along with non-Jews. Shlomo Hamelech commissioned Chiram the King of Tzur to send over thousands of artisans to help design this magnificent edifice. Since non-Jews were involved, they were eventually allowed to destroy it. The Mishkan that was made completely by Jews was never touched by non-Jews. Today the Mishkan is hidden under a tunnel near Har Habayis. In the future, Hashem will reveal it, along with the third Beis Hamikdash, and rest His *Shechinah* in it once-and-for-all!

39. The first eleven Melachos of Shabbos were performed when they made dyes to color the materials for the Mishkan. The next eleven were done to make the curtains. The next two were to make nets to catch the chilazon. The next seven were to make leather hides for the covering. The following two were to number the beams that they should be placed in the right places. The next three were for building and repairs (the actual construction). The next two were to make coals and to melt the metals and boil the dyes. The last two were to transport the beams upon the wagons to the next location.

40. Moshe made the Mishkan in the desert and it was used for thirty-nine years. When the Bnei Yisroel entered Eretz Yisroel they erected the Mishkan in Gilgul which lasted 14 years. They then moved to Shiloh where they set up a more permanent structure which stood for 369 years. When Eli HaKohen died, Shiloh was destroyed. They then erected it in Nov where it stood for 57 years. When Shmuel Hanavi died they went to Givon where the Mishkan stayed another 57 years. Shlomo Hamelech built the Beis Hamikdash in Yerushalayim, which stood 410 years. Ezra Hasofer built the second Beis Hamikdash which lasted 420 years. Altogether, the Mikdash of Hashem was here on Earth for 1366 years.

41. What lesson can we derive from the prohibition not to remove the poles from the Aron Kodesh? *(Oznayim L'Torah)*

42. What common problem exists with the refrigerator light bulb on Shabbos? *(Chashmal B'halacha)*

43. When was a Yisroel allowed to eat the *Lechem Hapanim*? *(Shmuel I chapter 21, Menachos 95b, Rashi)*

44. Is one permitted to play with building-blocks, such as lego, on Shabbos? *(Ohr L'Tzion, Muktzeh: A Practical Guide by Rabbi Simcha Bunim Cohen shlit'a -ArtScroll)*

---

41. The poles on the sides of the Aron Kodesh that were used to transport it from place to place were never to be removed. This symbolizes that Torah institutions need people to support them: just as the support of the Aron Kodesh was never to be removed, similarly, the supporters of Torah in the community should never remove themselves from helping these worthy organizations. Incidentally, the Aron Kodesh lifted those who carried it. Accordingly, the bearers of Torah organizations will be elevated to greater spiritual heights in the merit of their dedicated support.

42. All too often, people who have a light in the refrigerator forget to unscrew the bulb before Shabbos. This can result in Chillul Shabbos. (It is probably best to take it out altogether, or purchase those Shabbos safety latches.)

43. Dovid Hamelech had to flee from his father-in-law, Shaul Hamelech. It was one of the most turbulent times in Navi, for there were political affairs between two great tzadikim. In his flight for survival, Dovid was almost starving to death, and he went to the city of Nov, a city full of Kohanim. He begged Evyasor the Kohen Gadol to please give him something to eat. To save David's life, he gave him from the actual Lechem Hapanim.

44. It is not considered a real act of building to play with lego on Shabbos, since work that is forbidden on Shabbos is only something that is going to last. There are many Poskim that permit playing with lego for children under Bar Mitzvah. However, some Rabbis say that this would only be permitted for girls, not for boys, because boys have a *mitzvah* to learn Torah day and night, and we must instill in our children from a young age that life is more than just fun and games. If anything, youth programs should be developed in every synagogue to attract children to come learn Torah in a fun environment, and then they won't have the need to entertain themselves with other games. PIRCHEI AGUDAS YISROEL is famous for their special fun and fascinating Shabbos afternoon groups and inspiring extra-curricular programs.

45. How did Dama ben Nasina get a gem for the *Choshen Mishpat?*

(See Kiddushin 31a)

46. What do Shabbos and the Beis Hamikdash have in common?

(Rav Shimshon Pincus zt'l)

47. How happy should we be every [Erev] Shabbos?

(Tur Orach Chaim 262:2)

48. Why are hospitals often big, whereas *Shuls* are often small?

(Rav Mendel Kaplan zt'l)

49. Why shouldn't a Rebbi teach new Torah topics to his students on Shabbos?

(Maran Hilchos Melmadim)

50. Why was Ohaliav selected to work with Betzalel to build the Mishkan?

(Shemos Rabbah 40:4)

45. Dama ben Nasina was a jeweler who had the original stone that was inscribed with the name of Binyamim. It was reward for his honoring parents.

46. It has been said that "Shabbos is the Beis Hamikdash of time!" Just as the Beis Hamikdash is a holy place where one can connect with Hashem, Shabbos is a holy time where one could better connect with Hashem.

47. We must be exuberant when Shabbos approaches, just as we would wait excitedly for a royal person to visit us, or if we just found a great treasure!

48. One sage once commented that maybe hospitals are so large because Shuls are so small! He was implying that if people prayed better there would be much less of a need for emergency services! In fact, Chizkiya the Jewish king hid the Sefer Refua (Book of Remedies) so that people would turn their hearts to Hashem in prayer and repentance and recover that way!

49. A teacher of Torah should review with his students on Shabbos and not burden them to learn new material on Shabbos. [Authors note: One should try to learn new Torah for himself as this will cause an aliya to his anscestors, as the Zohar says, it adorns them with crowns in Gan Eden after Shabbos!]

50. Hashem doesn't want any Jew to have an inferiority complex, so He wanted someone from a minor Shevet to work along with someone from a major Shevet. This teaches us to have great self-esteem. Anybody can make it!

51. Why did Moshe Rabbeinu erect and dismantle the Mishkan over and over again for seven days, even on Shabbos?

(Shabbos 87b, Sechel Tov)

52. Why is it best to light the Shabbos candles even earlier than the required time of 18 minutes before sunset?

(Aruch Hashulchan)

53. Why did Moshe want to make the *Aron Kodesh* first whereas Betzalel wanted to make the Mishkan first?

(Taam V'daas)

54. Why does the Torah teach us Hilchos Shabbos (in the beginning of Parshas Vayakhel) right after it mentions that Moshe Rabbeinu's face radiated with a special glow (mentioned at the end of Parshas Ki Sisa)?

(Baal Haturim)

---

51. Moshe was alluding to something very important when he put up the Mishkan and took it down over and over again the first week. He was reminding us not to get discouraged if we try to elevate ourselves through our good deeds and we fall spiritually from time to time. As Shlomo Hamelech writes, "Seven times a *tzaddik* may fall, yet he gets up again!" (Mishlei 24:16)

52. On Erev Pesach, we stop eating Chometz several hours before Pesach so we won't come to eat Chometz on Pesach, an act punishable with kareis. Similarly, one should stop working before Shabbos as early as possible, at least 18 minutes before sunset to avoid a sin that is punishable with *kareis*, G-d forbid.

53. The question whether to make the Aron Kodesh first or the Mishkan first, was dependent on how holy the Jewish people were. Originally, before the sin of the Eigel, Moshe felt the Aron Kodesh could reside among the Jews, and the Aron Kodesh could therefore be made before the Mishkan. Once they sinned though, Betzalel felt that they were not holy enough to have the Aron Kodesh directly with them, and it needed the Mishkan to be made first in order to house it.

54. Chazal tell us that a person's face has a special radiance on Shabbos. Right after the Torah says that Moshe Rabbeinu's face glowed from *kedusha*, the Torah teaches us how to make our faces glow somewhat as well.

55. Who was commanded to light a fire even on Shabbos?
(*Mechilta*)

56. Why is it important to study *Mishnayos Middos?*
(*Rabbeinu Bachya, Tanchuma Parshas Tzav, Avos d'Rav Nosson 4, Metzudas Dovid Yechezkel 43:11*)

57. Why does the Torah list the donated items in descending order of their value—gold, silver, copper, wool, linen, goat's hair, and only afterwards it mentions the precious gems?
(*Ohr Hachaim*)

58. Which *shevet* merited that the *Shechinah* rested in its territory at Shiloh, Nov, Givon, and Yerushalayim?
(*Zevachim 118b, Yerushalmi Megillah 1:12*)

59. Why did the *Lishkas Hagazis* (Temple Courtroom of Justice) have to hold over 150 people?
(*Sanhedrin 4:4*)

55. The Avodah of the Beis Hamikdash is done on Shabbos even when it entails lighting a fire.

56. It is very important to study the design of the Beis Hamikdash as illustrated and explained throughout Mesechta Middos. This shows Hashem our interest and anticipation to once again serve Him in the Beis Hamikdash, and have His *Shechinah* rest with us. Our Rabbis say that one who studies the structure of the Beis Hamikdash is as if he rebuilt the Beis Hamikdash! Also, soon it's going to be rebuilt and you're going to want to know where everything is to be found.

57. Since the Nessi'im did not rush to donate to the Beis Hamikdash and they only donated at the end, the priceless gems that they ended up donating did not have the importance before Hashem as the other items that Am Yisroel rushed to deliver. We see from here that our enthusiasm counts to Hashem to some degree even more than our actual fulfillment of the *mitzvah.*

58. Shevet Binyomin merited that the Mishkanos and the Beis Hamikdash were on his property. This was because he wasn't involved in the *sinas chinam* (unjustifiable hatred) that caused the sale of Yosef. Also, he never bowed down to Eisav.

59. The Sanhedrin (Jewish Supreme Court) was seated in a semi circle so the judges could all see each other. The Chief Dayanim sat on 71 seats. Before them were three rows of Torah scholars; each row held 23 seats. Then there were seats for the three scribes who recorded all court cases. In addition, there was room for the people coming to court and their witnesses.

60. Why didn't Shlomo Hamelech drink wine for seven years?"

(Vayikra Rabbah 12:5)

61. How could the Jews have forgotten to keep Yom Kippur during the year that they dedicated the second Beis Hamikdash?

(Tanchuma 2:17)

62. Which famous European *Yeshiva* had a large model of the Beis Hamikdash in a room to help those dedicated to master *Seder Kodshim?*

(Yeshivas Chachmei Lublin)

---

60. While the construction of the Beis Hamikdash was going on, Shlomo Hamelech did not drink any wine. This expressed his determination to get the work done and not relax.

61. The year that the Beis Hamikdash was dedicated was such a joyous time that the Bnei Yisroel celebrated ecstatically. The seven days before Sukos, which included Yom Kippur, were declared days of joy and festivity. The Jews became frightened that maybe they were guilty of not fasting on Yom Kippur. A *Bas Kol* (Heavenly Voice) rang out and promised all of them great reward in Olam Haba [and Olam Hazeh] because their intentions were for Heaven!

62. In the Yeshiva of the great sage Rabbi Meir Shapiro H"yd there was a large model of the Beis Hamikdash to help facilitate the understanding of the service inside the Beis Hamikdash. Many educators and artists have labored to create models of the Beis Hamikdash and their work should be cherished and promoted!

Answers&Facts

פרשת פקודי

1. How did the treasurers handling all of the donations brought to the Beis Hamikdash avoid suspicion of theft?

(Shemos Rabbah 51:2; see Shekalim 3:2)

fUndamental Answers!

"יגעתי ומצאתי!"

("I worked on these questions, and I found these answers!")

1. The treasurers and agents who took the donations for the Beis Hamikdash were not allowed to touch the money while wearing a hemmed garment, shoes, sandals, socks, *Tefillin*, or an amulet. This was a precaution so people would not suspect them of pocketing any money. If that agent would become poor, people would thus say, "He's being punished because he stole from the treasury chamber." If he became rich, people might say, "It's because he stole from the treasury chamber." The treasurers also had to make an accounting at the end of each day of how much money was donated that day, how much money was spent, and exactly how the money was used. The agents had to replace any missing money from their own pockets. We see from here that even though tzedakah collectors are honest and trustworthy, it is imperative that they give a clear accounting to other reputable community members so that no one should suspect them of foul play. *Chazal* say that a person must always show integrity before people in the same manner that he shows integrity before Hashem.

2. How will the third Beis Hamikdash be more similar to the Mishkan than to the first two Batei Hamikdash?

(Seforno 40:31)

3. What *beracha* did Moshe give the Bnei Yisroel after they completed the Mishkan?

(Yalkut Shimoni based on Seder Olam)

4. Which five things were unfortunately missing from the second Beis Hamikdash?

(Yoma 21b)

5. Why did Moshe Rabbeinu have to wear a seamless robe when counting the donations for the Mishkan?

(Yerushalmi Shekalim 3:2; see Bach on Yoreh De'ah 257 quoting Tur and Rama)

2. Just as the Mishkan had a Divine cloud above it during the day and a **Divine fire above it** during the night to honor Bnei Yisroel, the final Beis Hamikdash will also have a **wall of fire** surrounding the Am Hashem, giving it great glory and reverence throughout the world!

3. Moshe blessed the Bnei Yisroel that Hashem's pleasantness should dwell upon their handiwork. Hashem had *already* promised that His Divine Presence would be with them, but Moshe blessed them anyway. He was worried that the sin of the *Eigel* would prevent Hashem from dwelling amongst the Bnei Yisroel. We can learn from here that the leader of the generation should always **bless those who are active in community projects**, so they will be more eager to help in the future. Some say Moshe blessed the Bnei Yisroel in **quality** - that each person should be as great as one thousand people. He also blessed them that no enemy should damage their precious work. That is why the Mishkan was buried safely in a tunnel near the Beis Hamikdash when it was no longer needed. (Incidentally, the Mishkan was even holier than the Beis Hamikdash, since only Jewish artisans built the Mishkan.)

4. The second Beis Hamikdash did not have:

a) The *Aron Kodesh* with its *Kapores* (golden covering upon the *Aron*) and *Keruvim*,

b) The special lion-shaped *fire* that was burning on top of the *Mizbeiyach*,

c) The *Shechinah* (Close Presence of Hashem),

d) *Ruach HaKodesh*, and

e) The *Urim V'tumim*, through which the people used to make urgent inquires.

5. Moshe Rabbeinu wore a seamless garment when he handled the money and the valuables that were donated to the Mishkan to avoid suspicion of theft!

6. Why did Shlomo Hamelech add ten *Menoros* and ten *Shulchanos* in the Beis Hamikdash?

(*Melachim I 7:49, Menachos 29a, 96a; Asifas Gershon quoting Derashos of Ibn Sho'iv*)

7. If funds were short, which *keilim* (vessels) of the *Beis Hamikdash* were able to be made of lead or other metals?

(*Toras Ha'olah based on Rambam Hilchos Beis Habechira 1:19*)

8. What did the Mishkan prove to the Bnei Yisroel and the world?

(*Tanchuma*)

This shows that even if you are a great leader, you should not assume that people will judge you favorably. You must do whatever you can to avoid arousing their suspicions. Even Moshe Rabbeinu who never took one thing from the community, such as funds for himself, or even a donkey to ride, had instigators commenting behind his back that he was pocketing money. Moshe Rabbeinu's honesty was proven to all when only he was able to erect the heavy Mishkan, for they understood that Hashem gave him the superhuman strength to do so because he was scrupulously honest.

6. Shlomo Hamelech added ten Menoras and ten Shulchans to correspond to the **ten** different times the *Shechinah* was brought to Earth: Through Adam, Avrohom, Yitzchak, Yaakov and Moshe, and when the *Shechinah* rested in the Mishkan in the desert, and subsequently in Gilgal, Shiloh, Nov, and Givon.

7. Officially, the Menorah, Shulchan, Mizbeiyach HaKetores, and all the other smaller vessels such as shovels, pans, spoons and bowls, had to be made from metal, preferably gold. If new ones were needed and there wasn't enough money to buy new golden vessels, the Bnei Yisroel were allowed to use lead vessels temporarily, until they were able to replace them with gold. However, the Aron Kodesh always had to be made out of gold, for *Kavod HaTorah*. The Ponevizher Rav *zt"l* was *moser nefesh* to place a golden *Aron Kodesh* in the Ponevezh Yeshiva in Bnei Brak, even going through the painstaking effort to transport it from its former country to Israel. Its majestic aura creates a great *Kiddush Hashem*, as befitting a world-leading Torah institution!

8. The Mishkan proved to the world that Hashem forgave the Jews even though many of them sinned with the *Eigel*, and that He still loves His children – the Bnei Yisroel! That is why it is called, "The Mishkan of Testimony."

Answers & Facts

---

9. Why was Ohaliav (of *Shevet Dan*) chosen to work with Betzalel (of *Shevet Yehuda*) to build the Mishkan?

(Shemos Rabbah 40:4, Melachim I 7:14)

10. Why did the *Kohen Gadol's* shirt need to be reinforced on its neck?

(Midrash Talpiyos)

11. Why did the *me'il* (apron) have pomegranate shapes dangling from it?

(Seichel Tov)

12. Why don't all Jews wear a head-plate that says *Kodesh LaShem as they wear Tefillin?*

(Tochachos Mussar)

9. Both Betzalel and Ohaliav spearheaded the building of the Mishkan to prove that any person, whether he is from a very prestigious family (like that of the royal family of Shevet *Yehudah*) or from an ordinary family (like that of Shevet *Dan*), can rise to great accomplishments if he wants to and tries! Similarly, Shlomo Hamelech from shevet Yehuda and a man named Chiram from shevet Naftali were very active in constructing the first Beis Hamikdash. Hashem does not want anyone in Klal Yisroel to look condescendingly at another Jew. He therefore wanted someone from the largest, most prestigious shevet working side-by-side with someone from a smaller, seemingly less-important shevet. Everybody is equal before Hashem! In addition, we see that Hashem empowers people to do for the community, especially when He knows that their ancestors were devoted to that particular *mitzvah* too!

10. When the Kohen Gadol would enter the *Kodesh Kodoshim*, the *Satan*, with his tremendous desire to harm people, would grab on to his clothing. The shirt was reinforced around its neck so that it should not tear. The Kohen Gadol was also required to wash his hands after coming out of the Kodesh Kodoshim, in case the Satan actually touched him.

11. The Kohen Gadol wore pomegranate shapes in order to defend Klal Yisroel. The pomegranate looks like an ordinary fruit, yet it has so many seeds; approximately 613! This symbolizes that even simple Jews do many *mitzvos!*

12. Most people do not live on the high moral standard where everything they do is a Kevod Shamayim. It would therefore not be proper to wear a tiara that states "Holy to God", if people might sin even while they're wearing it.

13. How long did it take for Moshe to collect all the materials that were needed to build the Mishkan?

(Shemos Rabbah 51:2)

14. Which *pasuk* is appropriate to say before doing a *mitzvah*?

(Yesod V'shoresh Ha'avodah - Tehillim 90)

15. Why was oil used to anoint the Mishkan and its vessels?

(Sanhedrin 16b, Toras Ha'olah)

16. Why didn't all the *Goyim* convert when they heard of the miraculous fire-pillar, clouds-of-glory, and *Mann* that accompanied the Bnei Yisroel for the forty years in the desert?

(Lev Eliyahu)

17. What did Hashem answer Moshe Rabbeinu when he asked, "How is it possible for me to erect the heavy Mishkan?"

(Rashi, Tanchuma)

---

13. It took just two days to collect all the valuable materials and money necessary to build the Mishkan. Imagine how many Torah projects would thrive if Yeshivos and worthy organizations were able to raise money so quickly!

14. It's good to say: *"Vehi noam…"* (*Tehillim* 90-17), which means: "May Hashem's pleasantness be upon us, and may He establish the work of our hands" before performing a *mitzvah*. Hashem loves our prayers so much that He wants them to accompany our performance of the *mitzvos*. (For example, the *Lesheim Yichud* prayer many say before Sefiras Haomer ends with this *posuk*.)

15. Oil has the unique ability to float above all liquids, as if it is superior to them. This reminds the Jews that the Kohanim, the kings, and those objects used in the Mishkan are not just ordinary people or vessels; they are holy. We must treat them in a more respectful manner.

16. It is possible that the non-Jews thought the phenomenal miracles in the desert came about through magic.

17. Hashem told Moshe to make it appear as if he was laboring to put up the Mishkan when it really went up by itself. This is a great message for life! Sometimes we wonder, "How can we make a great contribution to Klal Yisroel?" Hashem says, "You just go through the motions, and I will do the work to make it happen!"

Answers & Facts

18. Where did the beautiful gems that adorned the uniform of the *Kohen Gadol* come from?

(Baal Haturim)

19. How did the Jews know that Moshe Rabbeinu's income and expense report for the Mishkan was absolutely accurate?

(Ohr hachaim)

20. Where did Rabbi Yehuda HaLevi make a Mishkan for Hashem?

(Kuzari)

21. Why aren't any of the *Bigdei Kehuna* found anywhere today?

(Toras Ha'olah)

22. How did Yosef Hatzaddik overcome his *Yetzer Hara* by thinking about the *Avnei Shoham*?

(Sotah 36b, Meshech Chochmah)

---

18. When the Mann fell from heaven, gems and precious stones fell along with it. The *tzaddikim* gathered them for use in the Mishkan, and to honor their wives with gifts.

19. When the Bnei Yisroel's collective teamwork could not budge the heavy Mishkan, they had to call Moshe to help them. When Moshe's hands touched the material, it all went into place by miracle. They then admitted that his hands must have been absolutely clean (from any theft) to have such a miracle occur through them.

20. Rabbi Yehuda Halevi said that he made a Mishkan for Hashem's *Shechinah* in his heart! The best place to make Hashem's Presence rest is in ourselves. We can do this through the Torah we learn and the *mitzvos* we do with *kedusha*.

21. The *Bigdei Kehuna* were buried after their use, as is befitting holy items, lest they become desecrated. In addition, the belts of the Kohanim contained *shatnez* (a wool and linen combination). They did not want these belts to be found, lest someone wear it and commit the *aveira* of wearing *shatnez*. This is why the frayed belts of the Kohanim were used as wicks for the Menorah on *Succos* during the *Simchas Beis Hasho'aivah*.

22. When Yosef Hatzaddik was put to the ultimate test of temptation with Potiphar's wife, he envisioned his father standing before him saying: "All

Questions & Riddles

23. What will happen to one who does not go out to *daven* in *Shul?*
(Pele Yo'etz quoting Zohar, Gemara Berachos 8a)

24. Where is it better to pray: In a *Beis Hak'nesses* filled with Jews, or in a *Beis Midrash* that has a much smaller crowd?
(Gemara Berachos 8a, Aruch Hashulchan 90:13)

25. Why did the Beis Hamikdash, which Shlomo Hamelech built, appear to have been constructed by itself?
(Shemos Rabbah 52:4, Shir Hashirim Rabbah 1:4; see Gittin 68b)

26. When did Hashem's *Shechinah* return to Earth?
(Pesikta d'Rav Kahana 1:2; see Levush Techeiles 112, The Midrash Says)

---

my sons will be mentioned in the future Beis Hamikdash through the Avnei Shoham. Do you want your name to be left out, as it says, 'The names of the wicked are blotted out'?!" A chill went up Yosef's spine, which helped him compose himself and demonstrate total self-control.

23. One who does not want to leave his comfortable home to pray with a Minyan in the Beis Kenesses, will eventually have to leave his home anyway by going into exile! (Perhaps he will have to travel for business instead of earning his livelihood locally.)

24. It is greater to pray in a place of Torah study (like a Beis Hamidrash) than to pray in a Shul, because Hashem's *Shechinah* dwells today in a place where people study His laws. Surprisingly, even the Kohanim of the Beis Hamikdash opted to pray in the Lishkas Hagazis where Sanhedrin sat and ruled on Torah laws instead of praying in the Beis Hamikdash itself!

25. Hashem sent many angels and spirits to help the construction of the magnificent Beis Hamikdash. Even demons were used in its construction! (Now you can understand how such enormous stones could be lifted into position years before cranes and pulleys were invented.)

26. Different generations were guilty of driving Hashem's *Shechinah* away from residing on Earth due to the terrible *aveiros* they had committed. The *Shechinah* left this world when the Bnei Yisroel made the Eigel. When the Mishkan was erected, Hashem forgave them and brought His *Shechinah* back to Earth. Similarly, the *Shechinah* left the world during the Churban Beis Hamikdash, and returned when the second Beis Hamikdash was rebuilt.

Answers&Facts

27. Where was the Mishkan hidden?

(Sotah 9a, and see Tanna D'Bei Eliyahu 25)

28. Were the Bnei Yisroel allowed to sacrifice on a *bamah* (private altar) while they lived in the Midbar?

(Zevachim 117a)

29. What do the crowns of the *Aron Kodesh*, the *Shulchan*, and the *Mizbeiyach* symbolize?

(Yoma 72b)

30. What did the hooks of the Mishkan's roof resemble?

(Shabbos 98b)

31. Who planted the cedar trees that were used in the construction of the Mishkan?

(Yerushalmi Pesachim 4:1, Tanchuma 9, Rashi parshas Terumah)

---

27. The Mishkan that Moshe made was hidden in a special tunnel near the Makom Hamikdash! (Did you ever stop to consider that when you were praying at the Kosel Hama'aravi?) Hashem loved the Mishkan that was made with such pure hearts so much that He said He would restore it and rest His *Shechinah* in it in the future.

28. The Bnei Yisroel were not allowed to sacrifice Korbanos on a private alter in the desert.

29. The crown upon the Mizbeiyach alludes to the Kohanim. The crown upon the Shulchan alludes to the Jewish Kings. And the crown upon the Aron Kodesh refers to any individual who wants to study the Torah and merit the Keser Torah!

30. The silver hooks that were visible on the ceiling of the Mishkan resembled the sparkling stars in the sky. This symbolized that our actions have direct influence on the entire world at large!

31. Avrohom Avinu planted cedar trees to be used for the building of the Mishkan. Yaakov Avinu saw with Ruach Hakodesh that the Mishkan was going to be built in the desert, so he took those cedars with him to Mitzrayim and replanted them there. He then ordered that his descendants cut them down and take them out when they leave Mitzrayim.

---

32. What material was the *Mizbeiyach* of Shiloh made from?

(Zevachim 61b)

33. Why was a rose garden planted west of the Beis Hamikdash?

(Midos 1:3, Shiltei Gibburim)

34. Why was a replica of *Shushan Habira* engraved above the eastern gate of the Beis Hamikdash?

(Midos 1:3, Rav Ovadya M'Bartenura, Rambam, Tiferes Yisroel)

35. Why was the *Mizbeiyach* in the Beis Hamikdash enlarged to be 32 *amos* by 32 *amos*?

(Midos 3:1, Seichel Tov)

---

32. Some say the *Mizbeiyach* of Shiloh consisted of hollowed copper filled with stones.

33. The *Shechinah* resided west of the Beis Hamikdash, so they planted roses there to express their love and affection for Hashem.

34. The second Beis Hamikdash was allowed to be rebuilt after the Purim story occurred. To show their profound appreciation for King Koresh of Shushan (Achashveirosh's son from Esther Hamalka) who had authorized the project, the capital city of Shushan was engraved over the main gate that was used to enter the Beis Hamikdash. This also demonstrated that the Bnei Yisroel were patriotic towards their host ruler of that time, so they wouldn't be suspected of revolting. This clearly shows us that we should show respect for our host country. It is a statement of goodwill when a *Yeshiva* or a *Shul* here in America displays the American flag in appreciation of the *Medina Shel Chesed* (kind and benevolent country) we live in!

35. The *Mizbeiyach* was a prefect square: 32 *amos* high by 32 *amos* wide. This was to remind the Bnei Yisroel that the main objective is to perform the *Avodas Hashem* with your heart, whose Hebrew word, "*Lev*", equals 32. Chazal say, *Rachamana liba baei*, "The All-Merciful [Hashem] wants our heart!" It has been also pointed out that we have 32 teeth. Also Hashem is hinting to us that he wants the prayers that are said with our mouths to emanate from the heart. It's for this same reason that the *avneit* (belt) was 32 *amos* long.

Answers&Facts

36. Must you tear your clothes when you see the *Har Habayis* nowadays?

(Shulchan Aruch Orach Chaim 561, Igeros Moshe volume 3 Yoreh Dei'ah 52:4)

37. Is it permissible to pray in a synagogue where the *Aron Kodesh* is not situated on the eastern wall?

(Otzar Hayediyos quoting Rav Chaim Brisker zt'l, See Chofetz Chaim in Machane Yisroel)

38. Why weren't steps made for the *Mizbeiyach* instead of its ramp?

(Rashi Parshas Yisro, Sforno)

39. Why were golden grapevines suspended at the entrance of the *Heichal* of the Beis Hamkidash?

(Midos 3:8, Rambam, Tiferes Yisroel, Yoma 39b)

---

36. You must tear your clothes in grief when you visit the Kosel for the first time in 30 days. Some people try to avoid tearing *keriya* and go after midday Friday when one is not required to tear *keriya*, or switch their garments with someone else. It is not proper to evade this important *halacha* since Chazal guarantee, "Whoever mourns over the destruction of the Beis Hamikdash will merit to celebrate its rebuilding!"

37. Quite a few Shuls are built without the *Aron Kodesh* accurately facing *Yerushalayim*. Some say it is preferable not to pray in such a *Shul*, because we are supposed to direct our hearts and our prayers towards Yerushalayim.

38. Some say that steps would cause the Kohen to spread out his legs as he hurriedly climbed the steps to perform the *avoda* in the Beis Hamikdash. That would be immodest, for his body may be exposed; therefore, a ramp was used instead. The ramp also reminded the Kohanim to take humble steps. This teaches us that we should not delude ourselves in thinking that we can quickly jump up the ladder of spirituality.

39. Grapevines need to be suspended on posts when they grow or else they would fall to the ground. Similarly, the Bnei Yisrael need to be supported by our Rabbis in all their efforts. It also implied that those who support Torah causes are very close to Hashem. It also demonstrated that Hashem wishes to bless us as symbolized by a grapevine, which produces rich products.

40. What occurred after *Beis Din* examined a *Kohen* and declared him to be officially fit to serve?

(Midos 5:4, Seichel Tov)

41. Why did Shlomo Hamelech delay making the Beis Hamikdash until three years after he became king?

(The Family Midrash Says on Melachim I)

42. What year was Beis Hamikdash built?

(Melachim I 6:38)

43. Why did Shlomo Hamelech design two more gigantic *Keruvim* to stand on the sides of the *Aron Kodesh*?

(The Family Midrash Says on Melachim I)

44. Which two descendants of *Shevet Yehuda* and *Shevet Naftoli* built the first Beis Hamikdash?

(Shemos Rabbah 40:4, Melachim I 7:14)

---

40. When a Kohen was found by the Sanhedrin to be fit to serve in the Bais Hamikdash, he would celebrate with a great feast. This is one of the reasons a 13 year-old boy has a big feast to celebrate his Bar Mitzvah, when he becomes a full-fledged member of the Bnei Yisroel!

41. Shlomo Hamelech wanted to first establish the Kingdom of Yisroel before putting all his energies into building the Beis Hamikdash. However, he was criticized for this; the Beis Hamikdash is so important for the Bnei Yisroel's *Avodas Hashem*, that he should not have tarried at all.

42. The first Beis Hamikdash was completed in the year **2936** (nearly 3,000 years ago). That was 488 years after *Yetzias Mitzrayim*.

43. Shlomo Hamelech made two large golden *Keruvim* to stand in the Kodesh HaKodoshim on the sides of the *Aron Kodesh*. Those tall figures were not facing each other but were rather facing the entrance and exit of the Beis Hamikdash, to remind the Bnei Yisroel that the *Shechina* was ready to leave quickly if they were to sin!

44. Shlomo Hamelech from Shevet *Yehuda* and Chiram from Shevet *Naftali* were the main supervisors who oversaw the building of the first Beis Hamikdash.

Answers&Facts

Questions&Riddles

45. Why did Shlomo Hamelech employ gentiles to help construct the Beis Hamkidash, if at the construction of the Mishkan it was only Jews who built it?

(Tanna D'bei Eliyahu 18, Emes V'Emunah)

46. Why was the Mishkan much smaller than the Beis Hamikdash? And why was it made from wood and not from stone?

(Abarbenel)

47. Why were many guards stationed outside the Beis Hamikdash?

(Midos 1:1)

48. Where were lions, oxen, and eagles engraved in the Beis Hamikdash?

(The Family Midrash Says on Melachim I)

45. Shlomo welcomed non-Jews to help construct the Beis Hamikdash. He tried to establish goodwill with the neighboring nations with the hope that there would be peace in the world. However, since these non-Jewish workers' intentions were not pure (for they probably just worked to earn the money) the Beis Hamikdash did not last forever! **Success is determined by the intentions the workers put into a project!**

46. The Mishkan had to be carried by the *Leviim* as it was transported through the desert. To ease their burden, Hashem did not command it to be too big, nor was it made of heavy stone; rather, it was made of lighter wood.

47. Hashem's house does not need guards, as Hashem controls the entire universe. The purpose of the guards stationed around the Mishkan was strictly to honor Hashem, as it is befitting for any king to have honor guards, such as those that stand in front of Buckingham Palace in London.

48. Designs of lions, oxen and eagles were engraved on the *Kiyor* wagon. The following four images were engraved on Hashem's *Kisei Hakavod*: man, represented by the perfect person - Yaakov Avinu; a lion, the king of the beasts; an ox, the king of domesticated animals (Yechezkel Hanavi asked that it be switched so it should not remind of the sin of the Golden Calf. It then became the image of a child.); and the eagle, the king of the birds. When one keeps himself pure, as symbolized by washing from the *Kiyor*, one merits to become a *merkava* (chariot) for the *Shechinah*!

49.
Where did the *Kohanim* on duty rest at night?

(Midos 1:8)

50.
When was Chanah's *tefillah* for a son granted?

(Ben Yehoyada Berachos 31)

51.
Why is the *Kodesh Kodoshim* called the *D'vir* and the *Kodesh* called the *Heichal*?

(Abarbenel, The Family Midrash Says on Melachim I quoting Rav Shimon Schwab zt'l)

52.
Why did Hilny Hamalka donate a type of *Menorah* to the Beis Hamikdash?

(Yoma 3:10)

---

49. There was a special warm room called the *Beis Hamokeid* where the Kohanim on duty could rest through the night. They couldn't just leave the Bais Hamikdash and sleep at home; they had to be 100% devoted to their *Avodas Hashem*. It's very easy for one to get distracted from his important task when he leaves the Beis Hamikdash. For this reason, Chanah left her young son Shmuel to live in the Mishkan so he would grow up to be completely faithful to Hashem! Therefore, parents should not object to sending away their sons to sleep-away *Yeshivos*, because this undisturbed learning can be most beneficial for them!

50. Chanah prayed to Hashem in a most passionate and dramatic manner. However, her fervent *tefillah* bore fruit only when she prayed in the presence of Eli, the Kohen Gadol. We learn from here that it is important to pray near righteous people, so our tefillos will be answered in their merit.

51. Hashem's holy voice appeared to emanate from the *Aron Kodesh*. It was from there that He communicated with Moshe Rabbeinu. The *Kodesh HaKodoshim* was therefore called "*D'vir*" whose root word means 'speaking'. Also, the word *Heichal* is derived from the word "capable." This reminds us to pray towards the Beis Hamikdash, to Hashem who is All Capable!

52. Queen Hilny donated a rather amazing Menorah to the Beis Hamikdash. It was situated in a place where it would reflect the sun's rays and cast them throughout Yerushalayim. In the morning it would signal the people that it was time to recite the Shema.

Answers&Facts

---

53. Why did Shlomo Hamelech design a *mikvah* supported by twelve golden oxen? Wasn't he scared that it would recall the sin with the Golden Calf?

(See Rosh Hashana 26a)

54. How did the two golden crowns in the *Heichal* honor Chailem, Tovia, Yedaya, and Chein ben Tzefanya?

(Midos 3:8, Zecharaya 6)

55. If the *Beis Hamikdash* was finished in *Cheshvan*, why did Shlomo Hamelech wait eleven months, until *Tishrei*, to celebrate its dedication?

(Abarbenel, Rosh Hashana 10b, The Family Midrash Says on Melachim I)

56. How did Hashem demonstrate to Moshe the construction of the Mishkan?

(Pesikta Zutrasi)

53. The twelve oxen symbolized the twelve *Shevatim*. Shlomo did not fear that it would remind Hashem of the sin of the Golden Calf, since here the cows were used to hold up the Mikvah that the Kohanim would use to serve Hashem. The only time we are concerned not to use an item that is a *mekatreg* (prosecuter) is when it were to be used as is, in the *Kodesh Kodoshim*. For example, a horn of a cow was disqualified by the Rabbis because the *shofar* calls out to Hashem in the *Kodesh HaKodoshim*. Also the golden vestments of the Kohen Gadol were not allowed to be there either.

54. The four individuals who donated the two golden crowns for the *Yachin* and *Boaz* pillars were honored by having their name engraved on them.

55. Shlomo Hamelech needed the extra eleven months to finish the interior of the Beis Hamikdash and to invite and gather all the people to the *Chanukas Hamikdash*. Also, Shlomo wanted to celebrate the *Shechinah* resting with the Bnei Yisroel in the Beis Hamikdash in Tishrei, the month in which the Avos were born, since they were the ones who brought the *Shechinah* to Earth, and hopefully, it would last in their great merit (Although Yitzchok was born in Nissan, he was "reborn" by the *Akeida* which happened in Tishrei).

56. Hashem demonstrated to Moshe how to make the Mishkan by showing each part of it in fire. This symbolized that Hashem wants us to serve Him with a fiery passion!

57. Why were the two tall pillars by the entrance to the *Heichal* called *Yachin* and *Boaz*?

(Metzudos Melachim I 1:7, Abarbenel, The Family Midrash Says on Melachim I)

58. What were the 38 *Ta'im* (chambers) in the *Beis Hamikdash* used for?

(Midos 4:3)

59. Why did Shmuel and Dovid Hamelech divide the *Kohanim* into 24 shifts?

(Rashi Taanis 4:2)

60. Why was the *Ulam* of the *Beis Hamikdash* shaped like a lion?

(Midos 4:6, Yeshaya 29, Harei Besamim)

---

57. The name Yachin implied that we want Hashem to establish the Beis Hamikdash as our eternal home. Boaz implied that the Jewish people would merit strength and endurance through the many *korbanos* that they sacrificed in the Beis Hamikdash. Others learn that the two pillars corresponded to the two types of *mitzvos* in the Torah: *asei* and *lo s'asei* (The Do's and the Don't's). With our actions we establish Hashem's honor in this world (*mitzvos asei*), and we need strength to overcome our evil urge to sin (*mitzvos lo sasei*). Thus Yachin, meaning establish, and Boaz, meaning strength, were fitting names for these pillars. The two crowns upon the gigantic pillars also reminded Am Yisroel of the two crowns they received when they said, *"Naaseh V'nishma"* (We will keep the Torah, and we will listen to our Rabbis). It was in the merit of saying these two words that Hashem told Moshe to make a Mishkan for Him to dwell with the Bnei Yisroel!

58. The *Ta'im* were storage rooms for the Kohanim's equipment that was needed to keep the Beis Hamikdash operating smoothly.

59. Shmuel and Dovid wanted the Kohanim to have the opportunity to serve Hashem in the Beis Hamikdash for at least two weeks a year. By dividing the Kohanim into 24 groups, they would all get to serve at least two weeks a year - one week in the summer and one week in the winter.

60. A lion is a symbol of strength! The first *siman* in Shulchan Aruch states that we are commanded to strengthen ourselves like a lion in the service of the King of Kings, Hashem Yisborach. The ulam of the Beis Hamikdash was designed like a lion, to remind us to arouse ourselves in our Avodas Hashem like a lion. The lion is wide at the head and narrow at the rear. This serves as a reminder how we should prioritize our life: our main organ, our brain in the head, should be filled with a large amount of Torah knowledge. The narrow rear, represents our physical part, symbolizing that it should play a less significant role in our lives!

Answers&Facts

Questions & Riddles

61. Why do we pray everyday for the rebuilding of Yerushalayim?

(See Yeshaya 51, Hoshea 3:5, Megilah 29a, Sukah 41a, Yirmiya 30)

62. What did the 70 lights of Shlomo Hamelech's additional ten *Menorahs* signify?

(Rabbeinu Ephraim Vayakhel)

63. Why is the *Beis Hamikdash* sometimes referred to as a *Succah*?

(Tanchuma on Emor 22)

61. Yerushalayim is not only the capital of our homeland, Eretz Yisroel, it is the focal point of our *avodas Hashem* as well. It was the home for the *Sanhedrin*, the seat of the Torah Authorities, and it was there that Hashem's Honor was manifested on planet Earth in the Beis Hamikdash. May it be rebuilt speedily in our times so it will once again serve as the nerve center for our *avodas Hashem*, and be the heart of the universe, from which will flow lifes blessings.

62. The seventy lights of the added Menorahs (each of the ten Menorahs had seven lights) symbolized that the seventy non-Jewish nations were gaining knowledge and blessing through the Jews.

63. Just as the *Sukkos* sheltered the Bnei Yisroel in the desert, the Beis Hamikdash similarly shields the Bnei Yisroel. May we merit experiencing this impregnable security system with the rebuilding of the Beis Hamikdash in our time, Amen.

**Children enjoying Rabbi Maimon Elbaz's
amazing TorahShows.**

*Now you, too, can enthrall and entertain, young and old with this
collection of inspiring and passionate Divrei Torah.*

DATE DUE

DEMCO, INC. 38-3012

Five Towns/Far Rockaway
Judaica Library
25 Central Ave.
Lawrence, NY 11559